Itinerant Curriculum Theory

Bloomsbury Critical Education
Series Editor: Peter Mayo

Books in this series explore the relationship between education and power in society and offer insights into ways of confronting inequalities and social exclusions in different learning settings and in society at large. The series will comprise books wherein authors contend forthrightly with the inextricability of power/knowledge relations.

Advisory Board:

Antonia Darder (Loyola Maramount University, USA), Samira Dlimi (École Normale Supérieure, Rabat, Morocco), Luiz Armando Gandin (Federal University of Rio Grande do Sul, Mexico), Jose Ramon Flecha Garcia (University of Barcelona, Spain), Ravi Kumar (South Asian University, India), Antonia Kupfer (University of Dresden, Germany), Peter McLaren (Chapman University, USA), Maria Mendel (University of Gdansk, Poland), Maria NIkolakaki (University of Peloponnese, Greece) and Juha Suoranta (University of Tampere, Finland)

Also available in the series:

Course Syllabi in Faculties of Education: Bodies of Knowledge and their Discontents, International and Comparative Perspectives, edited by André Elias Mazawi and Michelle Stack

Critical Education in International Perspective, Peter Mayo and Paolo Vittoria

Critical Human Rights, Citizenship, and Democracy Education: Entanglements and Regenerations, edited by Michalinos Zembylas and André Keet

Ecopedagogy: Critical Environmental Teaching for Planetary Justice and Global Sustainable Development, Greg William Misiaszek

Education, Individualization and Neoliberalism: Youth in Southern Europe, Valerie Visanich

Hopeful Pedagogies in Higher Education, edited by Mike Seal

Pedagogy, Politics and Philosophy of Peace: Interrogating Peace and Peacemaking, edited by Carmel Borg and Michael Grech

Feminism, Adult Education and Creative Possibility: Imaginative Responses, edited by Darlene E. Clover, Kathy Sanford and Kerry Harman

Forthcoming in the series:

Nurturing 'Difficult Conversations' in Education, edited by Katarzyna Fleming and Fufy Demissie

Decolonizing Indigenous Education in the US, Samuel B. Torres

Itinerant Curriculum Theory

A Declaration of Epistemological Independence

Edited by
João M. Paraskeva

BLOOMSBURY ACADEMIC
LONDON • NEW YORK • OXFORD • NEW DELHI • SYDNEY

BLOOMSBURY ACADEMIC
Bloomsbury Publishing Plc, 50 Bedford Square, London, WC1B 3DP, UK
Bloomsbury Publishing Inc, 1359 Broadway, New York, NY 10018, USA
Bloomsbury Publishing Ireland, 29 Earlsfort Terrace, Dublin 2, D02 AY28, Ireland

BLOOMSBURY, BLOOMSBURY ACADEMIC and the Diana logo are trademarks of Bloomsbury Publishing Plc

First published in Great Britain 2024
Paperback edition first published in 2026

Copyright © João M. Paraskeva, 2024

João M. Paraskeva has asserted his right under the Copyright, Designs and Patents Act, 1988, to be identified as Editor of this work.

For legal purposes the Acknowledgements on p.xviii constitute an extension of this copyright page.

Series design by Catherine Wood
Cover image © Studiojumpee/Shutterstock

All rights reserved. No part of this publication may be: i) reproduced or transmitted in any form, electronic or mechanical, including photocopying, recording or by means of any information storage or retrieval system without prior permission in writing from the publishers; or ii) used or reproduced in any way for the training, development or operation of artificial intelligence (AI) technologies, including generative AI technologies. The rights holders expressly reserve this publication from the text and data mining exception as per Article 4(3) of the Digital Single Market Directive (EU) 2019/790.

Bloomsbury Publishing Plc does not have any control over, or responsibility for, any third-party websites referred to or in this book. All internet addresses given in this book were correct at the time of going to press. The author and publisher regret any inconvenience caused if addresses have changed or sites have ceased to exist, but can accept no responsibility for any such changes.

A catalogue record for this book is available from the British Library.

Library of Congress Control Number: 2024933915.

ISBN: HB: 978-1-3502-9298-7
PB: 978-1-3502-9302-1
ePDF: 978-1-3502-9299-4
eBook: 978-1-3502-9300-7

Series: Bloomsbury Critical Education

Typeset by Deanta Global Publishing Services, Chennai, India

For product safety related questions contact productsafety@bloomsbury.com.

To find out more about our authors and books visit www.bloomsbury.com and sign up for our newsletters.

Contents

List of Table	vii
Contributors	viii
Series Editor's Foreword	xv
Acknowledgements	xviii

1. On the Importance of Paraskeva's Itinerant Curriculum Theory
   William H. Schubert — 1
2. Against Epistemic Suicide! Itinerant Curriculum Theory: A Declaration of Epistemological Independence *João M. Paraskeva* — 11
3. Decolonial-Hispanophone Curriculum: A Preliminary Sketch and Invitation to a South-South Dialogue *James C. Jupp, Micaela González Delgado, Freyca Calderón Berumen and Caroline Hesse* — 37
4. Decolonizing the English Curriculum in Argentina by Itinerating the Curriculum Landscape with Minds, Bodies and Emotions *Graciela Baum* — 55
5. Returning to the Cultural Foundations of China's Curriculum Reform: ICT and Confucian 'Wind' Education *Weili Zhao* — 69
6. The Itinerant Curriculum Theory in the Chilean Context of Curriculum Control and Standardization: Toward a Constituent – Itinerant – Curriculum *José Félix Angulo Rasco* — 81
7. Itinerant Curriculum Theory in the Turkish Context *Fatma Mizikaci* — 97
8. Leaving the United States in Fear and Tears: Young Chun Kim's Lonely but Brave Scholarship as a Critical Text of Decolonizing Curriculum Studies *Jung-Hoon Jung* — 115
9. A Possible Utopia for Cognitive Justice: Towards an Itinerant Curriculum Theory as a *Deterritorialized* Critical Pedagogy *Rosa Vázquez Recio* — 129
10. ICT and Curriculum as Everyday Creation: A Doable Possibility of the Emancipation of Curriculum Theory *Inês Barbosa Oliveira* — 143
11. Decolonizing International Relations Theory: Towards an Itinerant Curriculum Theory to challenge the Endless (Hi)story of Coloniality *Mekia Nedjar* — 161
12. Moving the Abyssal Lines: Contemporary Disputes within Brazilian Curriculum Field *Maria Luiza Süssekind* — 179

13 Itinerant Curriculum Theory and Decolonization: Alternate Planes of Projection for the Global South, Africa, South Africa and Beyond *Shervani K. Pillay* 189

14 Decolonizing Thai-Centric Curriculum Is Yet Enough?: Transgressing Beyond 'Currere' to Itinerant Curriculum Theory *Omsin Jatuporn* 203

15 Curriculum in the Viral Age: Itinerant Curriculum Theory as a Just Path *Todd Alan Price* 221

16 Itinerant Curriculum Theory: Contributions to the Study of 'Education *in* Rights' in the Context of the Brazilian Public Defender's Office *Arion Godoy and Maria Cecilia L. Leite* 241

Index 257

Table

1.1　Young Chun Kim's Representative Empirical Studies on Korean Education　120

Contributors

Todd Alan Price is a member of the Professors of Curriculum Society and President of the American Association for the Advancement of Curriculum Studies. As Director of Curriculum, Advocacy, and Policy at the National College of Education, National Louis University, Dr Price advises doctoral students, supporting their dissertation completion. He teaches curriculum theory: contemporary issues and practices, critical policy analysis and social justice perspectives on the history and philosophy of American education. Thirty years in higher education, Dr Price is a tenured professor and has served on behalf of the profession and faculty rights in the Illinois Council of the American Association for University Professors. He also serves as a board member of the Illinois Association of Colleges for Teacher Education, where he advocates on behalf of teacher education. His research involves teacher preparation, civic education and the importance of itinerant curriculum theories in the US and international education curriculum studies. Recent publications include 'Challenging Curricular Hegemony Through International Perspectives', *The Curriculum Journal*; 'Blended and Video Conferencing Modalities for the Teaching and Learning Doctoral Candidate', *The Journal of Limitless Education and Research*; and '*After Currere*: The meaning of education in North American curriculum studies', *European Journal of Curriculum Studies*.

José Félix Angulo Rasco, Doctor in Philosophy and Educational Sciences since 1988 and Professor of Education at the University of Cádiz, has participated as a temporary and associated researcher in the School of Pedagogy of the Pontificia Universidad Católica de Valparaíso, Chile. He has directed various research projects funded by the European Union, the Ministry of Education of Spain, and ANID of Chile. He has published articles and books on evaluation, curriculum, qualitative methodology, and curriculum policy. He is a member of the UNESCO Chair in Democracy, Global Citizenship, and Transformative Education (DCMÉT) at Pontificia Universidad Católica de Valparaíso, Chile.

Graciela Baum is an English Language and Literature Professor at the Faculty of Humanities and Educational Sciences at La Plata University, Argentina. She is Head of the Special Didactics and Teaching Practices (II) Chair and Introduction to the English Language Chair. She is an education specialist and has published in the field of decoloniality and situated English language pedagogy; the English Curriculum in Argentina and Decoloniality; teaching English as a language *other* (*lengua otra*); and design of ad hoc decolonial didactic material. She is a researcher, currently directing a project on historicizing and problematizing English study programmes at La Plata University from the perspective of decoloniality.

Freyca Calderón Berumen works as Assistant Professor in Elementary and Early Childhood Education at Penn State, Altoona, United States. She completed her PhD in curriculum studies at Texas Christian University. Her scholarly interests are around critical multicultural/multilingual education and critical pedagogy as an avenue to address social equity and justice and as tools to a decolonizing praxis in education. As a Latina woman in the United States, she seeks to explore possibilities for community building for marginalized and undertheorized groups and contribute to the teacher education field by linking theoretical perspectives with everyday experiences and developing culturally relevant and decolonizing understandings. Her work privileges theoretical intersectionality and qualitative methods. She has conducted research and taught courses centred on social justice, critical methodologies and decolonial perspectives seeking ways to transcend traditional educational paradigms through transformative and culturally responsive pedagogies.

Micaela González Delgado is Professor in the Area of Pedagogical Intervention on the Faculty of Graduate Studies at La Universidad Nacional Autónoma de México (UNAM), Acatlán. She is finishing her master's degree in the area of construction of pedagogical knowledges in the Faculty of Philosophy and Letters at the UNAM. She has worked in the following charges and positions: Instructor in the Department of Teacher Education and Professional Development in the UNAM, Acatlán, at both the graduate and undergraduate levels. She is researcher on the Social Causes of Violence: Territorial Diagnostic Research for the Graduate Studies Unit at the UNAM, Actalán. She is also a researcher and assessor of the Interdisciplinary Communal Social Services in the Program of Rural Development and Environmental Conservation and a researcher of Indigenous Education (preschool, primary and secondary) in Alto Mezquital, Hidalgo, with *Hñähñu* communities. Her teaching charges and praxis include coordinating undergraduate field experiences in the National Historical Museum of the Viceroyalty, the Modern Art Museum, the CENCROPAM, the Cultural Center of SHYCP and the Support and Solidarity Center for Girls.

Arion Godoy has a doctoral degree in education from the Federal University of Pelotas, Brazil, and a research internship at the Center for Social Studies at the University of Coimbra, Portugal. He is Director of Education at the 'Fundação Escola Superior da Defensoria Pública do Estado do Rio Grande do Sul (FESDEP)' and a member of the 'Laboratory Images of Justice' at Federal University of Pelotas. He is a public defender. He graduated in law from the State University of Ponta Grossa – with a specialization in urban law from the Pontifical Catholic University of Minas Gerais. Godoy has a master's in law from the University of Caxias do Sul. Godoy and Public Defender Domingos Barroso da Costa crafted the project 'Defensoria das Famílias', which focuses on developing instruments related to education rights and mechanisms of extrajudicial conflict resolution. The project was awarded an honourable mention in 2016 by the National Council of Justice within the scope of the project 'Conciliar é Legal', sponsored and endorsed by the aforementioned Council. Godoy has published several articles and books. He served at the Court of Justice of Paraná, the Public Defender's Office of Paraná and the Federal Public Ministry.

Caroline Hesse is a (dual language) bilingual education teacher who has taught for nineteen years in various bilingual and monolingual K–21 settings, from high school and middle school to college and elementary levels. She holds a BS from Beloit College and an MA, each from Viterbo University and the Universidad de Salamanca. She holds a doctorate in curriculum and instruction from the University of Texas Rio Grande Valley, USA, where her dissertation and her work overall focused on bilingual education and critical consciousness. She is currently a dual language bilingual education (DLBE) teacher in a Spanish-English DLBE charter elementary school in Madison, Wisconsin, United States. Her research interests lie at the intersections of curriculum, multilingualism, identity, DLBE and social justice. She has published and presented on topics such as Hispanic serving institutions, DLBE, critical consciousness and professional development.

Omsin Jatuporn is Assistant Professor in the Department of Educational Foundations and Development, Faculty of Education at Chiang Mai University, Thailand. Before joining higher education, Jatuporn taught English, Thai and social studies at primary and secondary schools in his regional hometown in the central province of Thailand for eight years. Currently, he is a committee member of the Master's and Doctoral Programs in Multicultural Education and Development Education. He is also a committee member of the Research Center for Multiculturalism and Education Policy at Chiang Mai University. His research interests include critical curriculum studies, justice-oriented teacher education, itinerant curriculum theory and sociocultural foundations of education.

Jung-Hoon Jung has a PhD in Curriculum Studies from the University of British Columbia, Canada. He is a research professor at the BK21 Education for Social Responsibility Research Program in the Department of Education, Pusan National University, Busan, South Korea. He is also the associate editor of the Asian Qualitative Inquiry Journal and the programme director of the Asian Qualitative Inquiry Association. Jung-Hoon Jung has published research articles in internationally recognized journals and two books in English on shadow education and the education and learning culture of South Korea and Northeast Asia. He is committed to curriculum theorization and research on educational culture and educational experience through qualitative research methods. His research mainly focuses on the reconceptualization of curriculum studies from international and post-oriental perspectives. He has been studying the lives of teachers and educational phenomena using qualitative research methodologies. His representative works include *The Concept of Care in Curriculum Studies* (2016), *Shadow Education as Worldwide Curriculum Studies* (Macmillan), *Theorizing Shadow Education and Academic Success in East Asia* (Routledge), *Curriculum Studies and Instruction Research Methodology* (2020), *Posthuman Learning Culture and Internet-Based Private Tutoring in South Korea: Implications for Online Instruction in Public Schooling* (2022), *South Korean Education and Learning Excellence as a Hallyu* (2023) and *Curriculum Theorizing as Post-Colonial Text: Post-Orientalism and Young Chun Kim's Life's Work in South Korea*.

James Jupp is Professor and Chair in the Department of Teaching and Learning, at the University of Texas Rio Grande Valley, United States. He taught in rural and inner-city Title I settings for eighteen years before accepting a position working with teachers, administrators and researchers at the university level. A public school teacher in rural poor and inner-city Title I schools, his first line of research focuses on critical whiteness studies' (CWS's) relevance to education. Additionally, drawing on his experiences living and studying in Spanish-language traditions in Mexico and Texas, his second line of research develops transnational-yet-local perspectives in education with an emphasis on decolonial-Hispanophone curriculum with special emphasis on informing education in the Rio Grande Valley, Aztlán, Gran México. Overall, he has published more than thirty scholarly articles in various venues. His third book, *Itinerant Curriculum Theory: Decolonial Praxes, Theories, and Histories* (2023) explores the impact of Paraskeva's ICT worldwide.

Maria Cecilia Lorea Leite has a law degree from the Federal University of Pelotas, an honors in literature from the Catholic University of Pelotas, a master's in education from the Pontifical Catholic University of Rio Grande do Sul and a PhD in education from the Federal University of Rio Grande do Sul, Brazil. She also has a postdoctorate at Université Paris 8. She is an associate professor at the Federal University of Pelotas. She is vice president of the Southern Regional of the Brazilian Society of Comparative Education and a member of the National Association of Postgraduate Studies and Research in Education-ANPEd. She was also part of the Judicial Images Network of the UK Arts and Humanities Research Council. Lorea Leite published thirty-nine articles in indexed specialized journals, thirty-one book chapters and edited four books. She supervised several master's and doctoral students. She currently supervises six doctoral students. She participated in nine research projects, having coordinated five of them. Her research focuses on the itinerant curriculum theory, democratic management, legal education, legal pedagogy, images of justice, higher education and universities.

Fatma Mizikaci is Professor of Curriculum and Instruction at the Faculty of Educational Sciences at Ankara University, Turkey. She received her PhD from Middle East Technical University in 2001, and since then, she has worked at different higher education institutions. She was a visiting scholar at UNESCO-CEPES during 2004 and 2005. She worked on EU and UNESCO projects for sixteen years and published books on Eastern European and Central Asian education systems and policies. During 2015 and 2016, she was a visiting scholar for the Turkish Research Institution at Chapman University to work on a project entitled Critical Discourse Analysis of California University Systems with Peter McLaren. Her recent publications include *Curriculum, Teachers Technology: A Turkish Context* (2022, co-editor), *Critical Pedagogy and the Covid-19 Pandemic: Keeping Communities Together in the Times of Crisis* (2022, chief editor), *A Language of Freedom and Teacher's Authority: Case Comparisons from Turkey and the United States* (2019, chief editor) and *Higher Education in Turkey* (2006–20). Her other published works include journal articles and books on curriculum, curriculum policy, privatization, accreditation and curriculum discourse studies and higher education systems and policies in Turkey, Central Asia,

Europe and the United States; Mizikaci has been teaching courses such as Curriculum and Instruction, Controversial Issues in Curriculum, Ideology and Philosophy in Curriculum, Qualitative Research in Curriculum and Controversial Issues in Higher Education, Turkish Education System, and Curriculum Issues at the undergraduate and graduate levels at Ankara University. She is currently the chair of the Curriculum and Instruction Division at the Faculty of Educational Sciences.

Mekia Nedjar is Assistant Professor of International Relations at the Department of Political Science and International Relations, Oran 2 University-Algeria. She received her PhD from Autonoma University-Madrid. Her main research interests range from knowledge production, modes of thinking in security studies, international relations in/about MENA and Global South to the intersection of EU construction and colonialism. She has published (in English, Arabic and Spanish) on IR, systemic fragility and the problem of securitization in/about MENA. Nedjar's research explores the importance of the itinerant – curriculum – theory to unpack Eurocentric ways framing international relations.

Inês Barbosa Oliveira is Adjunct Professor of the Postgraduate Program in Education (PPGE) at UNESA. She previously held the following positions: Full Professor at the State University of Rio de Janeiro (UERJ), President of the Brazilian Curriculum Association (ABdC – 2015–19), Coordinator (2021–3) of GE Cotidianos of ANPEd and Member of the Fiscal Council of the same entity (2015/19). She did her PhD in Sciences Et Théories de L'éducation at the Université de Sciences Humaines de Strasbourg (1993), and she completed her postdoctorate at the Center for Social Studies of the University of Coimbra (2002). She works in the area of education, in the field of curriculum studies and also in the area of everyday school life as practical policy. All of her work is advanced from the perspective of education as fundamental to human rights, dignity and sustainability. From this perspective, she focuses on issues of social emancipation and the role of education in this process, along with notions of cognitive justice and horizontal citizenship. Having developed the notion of curriculum as everyday life, she has books and articles on her research topics published in Brazil and abroad. She is included in the Index of the 10,000 most influential researchers in Latin America and one of the 100 most cited in education research.

João M. Paraskeva is a Mozambican-born public intellectual, pedagogue and critical social theorist. He is also a former literacy, middle grades and high school teacher in Southern Africa. He is a Full Professor of Educational Leadership and Policy Studies at the University of Strathclyde, Glasgow, UK. He was the founding Chair of the Department of Educational Leadership and Graduate Program Director of the Doctoral Program in Educational Leadership and Policy Studies at the University of Massachusetts Dartmouth. Paraskeva championed the post-abyssal turn in the field and the struggle against the epistemicides, advocating an itinerant curriculum approach as the future for the field's theory that needs to embrace the world's epistemological difference and diversity. Through his work, the field is flooded with a new semantic – 'epistemicides', 'reversive epistemicides', 'critical curriculum river', 'generation of utopia', 'curriculum involution', 'curriculum imparity', 'curriculum mechanotics', 'curriculum occidentosis', 'curriculum exfoliation', 'curriculum isonomia', 'curriculum ecology', 'momentism', 'curriculum disquiet', 'theorycide', 'curriculum imparity', 'non-aligned theory', 'indigeneoustude' and 'sepoys of coloniality', among others. He is an awarded intellectual and his work has been translated into nations such as South Korea, China, Finland, Greece, Spain, Argentina, Chile, Mexico, Brazil, Angola and Portugal. His publications include *Conflicts in Curriculum Theory* (1st edition 2011) (updated paper back edition 2014) & (2nd edition 2022); *Curriculum Epistemicides*; *Towards a Just Curriculum Theory*; *Curriculum and the Generation of Utopia*; *The Curriculum: A New Critical Comprehensive Reader*; *Curriculum: Whose Internationalization?*; and *Critical Perspectives in the Denial of Caste in the Educational Debate*.

Shervani K. Pillay is Associate Professor at Nelson Mandela University in South Africa. She works in the Department of Post-Graduate Studies in the Faculty of Education. Her focus is higher education within the African and South African contexts. Her areas of research interest include curriculum development and design, decolonization, social and cognitive justice, itinerant curriculum theory, chaos complexity theory and the idea of the university.

Rosa Vázquez Recio is a teacher at the University of Cádiz, Spain, and she is a member of the teaching staff of the Department of Pedagogy. She has held administrative positions in two degree programmes: Coordinator of the Master's in Educational Research for Teaching Professional Development from 2015 to 2019 and Coordinator of the Doctoral Program in Educational Research and Practice from 2019 to the present. She earned both degrees at the University of Cádiz and presently teaches in master's and doctoral degree programmes. Her main research focuses on educational policy for equity and social justice from an intersectional perspective in rural and urban settings. Within this perspective, her areas of study revolve around school management, gender equity, school dropouts, initial teacher training and curriculum. She has published over thirty academic articles in various journals, books and book chapters in prestigious publishing houses, including Peter Lang. She is an Ibero-American Network of Universities member committed to human rights education and inclusive citizenship (Equality and Gender Commission).

William H. Schubert, a former public school teacher, is Professor Emeritus and University Scholar at the University of Illinois Chicago (UIC), United States, where he was Chair of Curriculum & Instruction, Director of Graduate Studies and Coordinator of the PhD Programme in Curriculum Studies. At UIC, he received university-wide awards for teaching and mentoring. His scholarship focuses on curriculum theory, development and practice throughout society and culture, including institutionalized schooling. His publications include over 20 books and 300 articles and chapters, recently including the three-volume online *Oxford Encyclopedia of Curriculum Studies* with Ming Fang He. Schubert has served as President of the Society of Professors of Education, the Society for the Study of Curriculum History and the John Dewey Society. He is an elected member of Professors of Curriculum, an elected fellow of the

International Academy of Education and a 2004 recipient of the Lifetime Achievement Award in Curriculum Studies from the American Educational Research Association. His papers and books are archived in the William H. Schubert Curriculum Studies Collection in the Zach S. Henderson Library at Georgia Southern University. Moreover, he has consulted widely throughout the United States and in many other countries, such as China, Mexico, Korea, Germany and Canada.

Maria Luíza Süssekind is a faculty member at Universidade Federal do Estado do Rio de Janeiro (UNIRIO), Brazil. She is also a mother of two who writes from the South. As a Brazilian public intellectual and social activist, she works primarily with social and cognitive justice subjects within curriculum, educational policies for difference and the marks of colonialism as epistemicides and patriarchalism within public schools. Currently, Süssekind acts as Vice President of the Southwest region at ANPEd (Brazilian Association for Postgraduate and Research in Education). After teaching history at basic schools for twelve years, she held a Magister Scientia degree at UFRRJ (Rural Federal University of Rio de Janeiro). She earned a doctorate in education degree at UERJ (State University of Rio de Janeiro). She completed postdoctoral studies with William F. Pinar at UBC in Canada. Süssekind is a leading voice in curriculum theory and has several important articles, book chapters and books published in Portuguese and English.

Weili Zhao, PhD, obtained in 2015 from the University of Wisconsin-Madison, is Professor of Curriculum Studies at Hangzhou Normal University, China. She received the 2019 Early Career Outstanding Research Award granted by AERA and worked as an assistant professor at the Chinese University of Hong Kong. With intellectual training in both discourse analysis and curriculum studies, she has been historicizing discourses, languages and translingual practices (translation) as both a colonial and decolonial gesture in transnational curriculum knowledge transfer and (re)production against the modernity-coloniality problematic. Zhao has published a monograph with Routledge, edited two books for Springer and Routledge and guest edited two SSCI journal special issues, twenty-plus journal articles and about twenty book chapters. She is also on an international editorial team for doing a Routledge book series on Post-qualitative, New Materialist, and Critical Posthumanist Research.

Series Editor's Foreword

This new book series was introduced against an international background that comprised and continues to comprise situations that are disturbing and intriguing. The onset of Covid-19 has thrown into sharp relief arguably the major casualty of this pandemic, an unprepared, failed state. We have been left with a state shorn of the facilities and provisions one would expect of a purportedly 'democratic' entity that dances not only to the tune of capital accumulation but also to that reflecting the concerns of all people under its jurisdiction. The latter is certainly not the case as, with regard to the provision of social safeguards, the state has, in many places, almost been rendered threadbare by its accommodation of nefarious neoliberal policies which leaves everything outside the demands of capital to the market and voluntary organisations. While wealth is concentrated, as a result, in the hands of a few, there are those who are left to struggle for survival in a Darwinian contest that rewards the 'winners' and renders others disposable. Questionable wealth is concentrated in the hands of a few, who take advantage of their network of spin-doctors and 'fake news' soothsayers, to play the victim with regard to the pandemic. They and the many policymakers who accommodate them deflect their responsibility onto ordinary citizens and further justify curtailing the state's social spending, to the detriment of the many, 'the multitudes,' as referred to by Michael Hart and Toni Negri.

The series was launched at a time when the 'social contract', ideally one which transcends the capitalist framework (as Henry Giroux astutely remarks), is continuously being shredded as several people are removed from the index of human concerns. Many are led to live in a precarious state. Contract work has become the norm, a situation that renders one's life less secure. There is also criticism targeted at the very nature of production and consumption with their effects on people and their relationship to other social beings and the rest of the planet, hence 'questionable wealth'.

They are also difficult times because the initial enthusiasm for the popular quest for democracy in various parts of the world has been tempered by eventual realism based on the fact that strategically entrenched forces are not removed simply by overthrowing a dictator. Far from ushering in a 'spring,' the uprisings in certain countries have left political vacuums – fertile terrain for religiously motivated terrorism that presents a real global security threat. This threat, though having to be controlled in many ways, not least tackling the relevant social issues at their root, presents many with a carte blanche to trample on hard-earned democratic freedoms and rights. The situation is said to further spread the 'culture of militarization' that engulfs youth, about which much has been written in critical education. Terrorist attacks or aborted coups allow scope for analyses on these grounds, including analyses that draw out the implications for education.

The security issue, part of the 'global war on terror', is availed of by those who seek curtailment of human beings' right to asylum seeking and who render impoverished migrants as scapegoats for the host country's economic ills. The issue of migration would be an important contemporary theme in the large domain of critical education. This phenomenon and that of Covid-19, as with any other pretext, are availed of by powers acting exclusively in the interest of capital. This leads to a further siege mentality marked by increasing otherising, scapegoating, surveillance and incarceration. Security extends beyond the culture of fear generated through terrorism to include health issues such as the pandemic, the latter said to be spread by those who, in reality, are the least equipped to work and live safely in their homes, including rejected asylum seekers and other migrants denied citizenship, those who live in restricted and overcrowded spaces or . . . who do not have a home – period. They face a stark choice: exposure or starvation. Barbarism, in Rosa Luxemburg's sense of the term, is a key feature of this choice and the society in which many live.

The series was introduced at a time when an attempt was made for politics to be rescued from the exclusive clutches of politicians and bankers. A more grassroots kind of politics has been constantly played out in globalized public arenas such as the squares and streets of Athens, Madrid, Istanbul (Gezi Park), Cairo, Tunis and New York City. A groundswell of dissent, indignation and tenacity was manifest and projected throughout all corners of the globe, albeit, as just indicated, not always leading to developments hoped for by those involved. Yet hope springs eternal. Some of these manifestations have provided pockets for alternative social action to the mainstream, including educational action. Authors writing on critical education have found, in these pockets, seeds for a truly and genuinely democratic pedagogy that will hopefully be explored and developed, theoretically and empirically, in this series.

It is in these contexts, and partly as a response to the challenges they pose, that this new series on Critical Education was conceived and brought into being. Education, though not to be attributed powers it does not have (it cannot change things on its own), surely has a role to play in this scenario; from exposing and redressing class politics to confronting the cultures of militarization, consumerism, individualism, and ethnic supremacy. The call among critical educators is for a pedagogy of social solidarity that emphasizes the collective and communal in addition to the ecologically sustainable.

Critical educators have for years been exploring, advocating, and organizing ways of seeing, learning, and living that constitute alternatives to the mainstream. They have been striving to make their contribution to changing the situation for the better, governed by a vision or visions of systems that are socially more just. The ranks of the oppressed are swelling. Hopefully, it is the concerns of these people that are foremost in the minds and hearts of those committed to a social-justice-oriented critical education. I would be the first to admit that even a professed commitment to a critical education can degenerate into another form of radical chic or academic sterility. We need to be ever so vigilant towards not only others but also ourselves, coming to terms with our own contradictions, therefore seeking, in Paulo Freire's words, to become less incoherent.

This series offers a platform for genuinely socially committed critical educators to express their ideas in a systematic manner. It seeks to offer signposts for an alternative approach to education and cultural work, constantly bearing in mind the United Nations Sustainable Development Goals that, albeit difficult to realize, serve as important points of reference when critiquing current policies in different sectors, including education. The series' focus on critical education, comprising the movement known as critical pedagogy, is intended to contribute to maintaining the steady flow of ideas that can inspire and allow for an education that eschews the 'taken for granted.'

In this particular volume, João M. Paraskeva assembles a team of writers on different nuanced aspects of curriculum studies. The curriculum has always been a terrain of struggle among different viewpoints often reflecting a 'total conception of ideology' in the sense once strongly put forward by Chilean sociologist, Jorge Larrain, in his classic *The Concept of Ideology*. These viewpoints, when systematic, reflect a specific *weltanschaung* or comprehensive world view, in plain English. It is an ever shifting terrain, a moving struggle as people change contexts throughout unstable lives, either through free choice or more likely through the force of necessity. The curriculum, in a world of liquidity and flux, involving risk, is, also in this regard, an itinerant curriculum characterised by contextually contingent selections from the different cultures of society. Who makes the selection and from which location within the power structure? What is ignored, overlooked, consciously or unconsciously, jarring with the specific 'imagined community' being projected? How are these choices affirmed or resisted? Which countercultural productions occur in different curricular contexts? Is the resistance passive, characterised by disengagement, or active in disruptive, political ways? These are some of the curricular contestations highlighted, among many other issues, in this precious volume.

Peter Mayo
Series Editor,
UNESCO Chair in Global Adult Education,
University of Malta,
Msida, Malta

Acknowledgements

As I have always said, a book is a collective process involving many people. And each book has its history that evolves through debates, exchanges of views, conflicts, advances and setbacks. I am very grateful to all of them. Even though I run the risk of forgetting to mention some of them, I dare to leave on record, alphabetically, my profound thanks to peers such as Anthony Brown, Antonia Darder, Angela Valenzuela, Boaventura de Sousa Santos, Bernadette Baker, Cameron McCarthy, Cathryn Teasley, Clyde Barrow, David Hursh, Dwayne Huebner, James Jupp, Jurjo Torres Santomé, Manuel Silva, Maria Alfredo Moreira, Maria Luiza Süssekind, Inês Oliveira, Nelson Maldonado-Torres, Paget Henry, Peter McLaren, Peter Mayo, Ramon Grosfoguel, Richard Quantz, Tero Autio, Thomas Pedroni, Thomas Popkewitz and William Schubert, with whom I have learned tremendously. A special word of profound gratitude to the contributors of this volume – Arion Godoy, Caroline Hesse, Fatma Mezikaci, Freyca Calderón Berumen, Graciela Baum, Inês Barbosa Oliveira, James Jupp, José Félix Angulo Rasco, Jung-Hoon Jung, Maria Cecilia L. Leite, Maria Luíza Süssekind, Mekia Nedjar, Micaela González Delgado, Omsin Jatuporn, Rosa Vázquez, Recio, Shervani Pillay, Todd Price, Weili Zhao and William Schubert – for their commitment to ICT and exploring its endless epistemological rivers.

In my work, I never forget how much I have learned with 'my' students. Here, in Scotland is no different. I have learned in many ways with my students from China, Ghana, India, Kenya, Saudi Arabia, Qatar, Kuwait, and Scotland, which helped refine my understanding of education and curriculum matters. I appreciate Mark Richardson and Elissa Burns at Bloomsbury for their care and patience in manuscript production. Many thanks to Peter Mayo for his constant encouragement to have this volume in his series. My endless indebtedness to my dear wife Isabel and my daughter Camila for walking with me, knowing so well, as Matsuo Bashō argues, that 'every day is a journey, and the journey itself is home'. Also, I thank my siblings Pandelis and Jorge, whose lives are vivid examples of the outcome of what was once a promised revolution. Last but not least, to my beloved parents and best friends, who sadly did not live enough to see so many of our conversations reflected in this book.

1

On the Importance of Paraskeva's Itinerant Curriculum Theory

William H. Schubert

Anyone who is interested in curriculum studies should see this book as a harbinger of what curriculum studies should be. João M. Paraskeva has accomplished much to move curriculum studies into an expanded posture in educational inquiry thus far in his career, and this book continues that work. Let me explain what I mean. As I reflect on Paraskeva's elaboration of Itinerant Curriculum Theory (ICT), I also reflect on my fifty years of experience in the curriculum field. I began master's study in 1966 at Indiana University and learned about the existence of a curriculum field, although I was primarily interested in philosophy of education at the time. As a public school teacher from 1967 to 1975, I grew to appreciate curriculum theory so much that I took a sabbatical leave to do a PhD in it at the University of Illinois at Urbana-Champaign (1973–5), under the remarkable guidance of J. Harlan Shores. After that excellent experience, I worked through the professorial ranks at the University of Illinois at Chicago (UIC), from which I retired as a professor emeritus in 2011. So, I entered the curriculum field towards the end of the days when curricularists saw themselves as facilitators of the ideals of democratically derived nationalistic purposes in schools. Many curriculum professors at that time saw themselves as technical guides to implementation in schools and sometimes as Socratic questioners to help educational and governmental leaders clarify democratically derived ideas in policy and practice.

Sadly, curriculum scholars began to realize that the *raison d'être* for studying curriculum was largely an unwarranted myth, no matter how much curriculum scholars tried to and advance John Dewey's (1916) vision of participatory democracy. During the period of my life in which I was a graduate student and teacher, I was also a participant-observer in civil rights and peace movements of the 1960s and early 1970s. Therein, I began a lifelong questioning of the domination of the corporate state in the United States and other so-called *first-world* nations as they continued construction of a new World Empire. Of course, I still harboured within myself the Deweyan ideals of participatory democracy. Nonetheless, as a student and teacher who realized that the best way to become educated and advance these ideals was to be as much of a deschooled, unschooled, self-educator as possible, that is, by de-institutionalizing myself from the corporate state. I became committed to developing curricula of my own education within the course of living and shared it with my students implicitly and explicitly. I realized that public education, in which I participated as a teacher, graduate student and professor, often was not representative of the public it purported to represent; rather, at best, it perpetuated values and priorities that benefited upper socio-economic and cultural echelons – which we in movements to change society opposed, calling them *The Establishment*, which C. Wright Mills (1956) labelled *the power elite*.

While working to make a living within institutional frameworks, I knew that I had to pursue self-education to gain a basis from which to overcome at least some of the influence of the power elite. As a beginning professor I often sought out others with whom to share such self-education. Through family, friends and colleagues at UIC, I was fortunate to find kindred spirits who pursued similar quests to learn, grow and share with students. Through curriculum conferences (e.g. Bergamo, Curriculum & Pedagogy, AATC, AERA, AAACS, IAACS, Professors of Curriculum) I met an expanding coterie of professors from other institutions who shared ideas that challenged the largely male, white, Western curriculum field. Together, we supported continuous creation of curriculum that was embodied in lived experience and critically challenged the field, opening it to more diverse possibilities. Whenever I tried to contribute to the history of the curriculum field (e.g. Schubert and Lopez Schubert, 1980; Willis et al., 1993; Marshall, Sears and Schubert, 2000; Schubert et al., 2002; Marshall et al., 2007; Schubert, He and Schultz, 2015; He, Schultz and Schubert, 2015; Schubert, 1986/1997; 2010a; 2017; 2022), I struggled with co-authors and with myself about whether the field should be portrayed as the largely white, male, Western field it has been or whether it should be portrayed in the way we thought it should be, which would be through critical lenses that included more diversities of authors and works that addressed basic curriculum questions. Within the so-called American (i.e. US) curriculum field, which too often has appeared to think it founded curriculum thought, we wrestled with inclusion of cultural groups that traditionally have been neglected. We thought that such inclusion would be best if brought about by curriculum scholars who had experience with and/or were members of estranged cultural groups. As years passed, we included more diversity – epistemologically, socio-economically, culturally, politically, racially and more. We built on the work of many scholars and colleagues in the field and central ideas of the expanding field summarized early on by a key mentor, Paul Klohr (1980): organic view of nature; individuals as creators of knowledge and culture; experiential bases of method; emphasis on preconscious experience; new sources of curriculum literature; emphasis on liberty and higher levels of consciousness; means and ends that include diversity and pluralism; political and social reproduction; and new language forms, all of which I built upon in *Curriculum: Perspective, Paradigm, and Possibility* (Schubert, 1986: 176–80).

Before publishing this book on ICT, Paraskeva built a stairway of books and articles that led to his advocacy of ICT. I urge readers to read these works because readers should realize that Paraskeva's expansion of curriculum studies to be inclusive of ideas and practices from the Global South is an expansion of his earlier work. For instance, his first edition of *Conflicts in Curriculum Theory* (Paraskeva, 2011) interprets work begun in the late 1960s and early 1970s to perceive what would become curriculum studies as a field that studied the multiple forces that shape human lives, not only by relegating curriculum studies to the institutionalization of education in schools. This is not to say that schools, and especially insightful and caring teachers, cannot work in the cracks (Schultz, 2017) of corporate state dominance to hone their imaginations, bases for critique and experience of praxis. Paraskeva also has continued to show in novel ways that curriculum scholars built upon previously neglected sources from cultures that challenged imperial propaganda.

Five years after his first edition, *Conflicts in Curriculum Theory*, Paraskeva (2016b) asked a profound question in an edited volume: *Curriculum: Whose Internationalization?* For me, this invoked memories of Frantz Fanon's (1963) interrogation of how *the wretched of the earth* were made wretched by empires that profited from their pain of enslavement/servitude. This, of course, reminded me of Michael Apple's (1979) raising of similar questions in curriculum about whose knowledge and who benefits from responses to the lexicon of questions about what is worthwhile in curriculum discourse (Schubert, 1986; 2009a). Paraskeva understands that the rhizomatic origins (Deleuze and Guattari, 1987) of the wretchedness of so many inhabitants of Planet Earth are derived from and experienced in today's versions of colonialism and imperialism of the Global South and much of Asia, as Edward Said (1993) so brilliantly showed. This wretchedness is perpetuated by linguicide and culturicide, accompanying ecological destruction, and, as Paraskeva (2016a) argued in one of his major and awarded books – *Curriculum Epistemicide* – their curricular partner, *epistemicide*, that is, the rampant extermination of knowledge.

Epistemicide (Paraskeva, 2011; Santos, 2014) is especially virulent in indigenous and aboriginal realms thrust into economic despair by imperial quests for profit (Nussbaum, 2010; Chomsky, 1999) in the Global South if impoverished inhabitants do not contribute obediently to the neoliberal curriculum of myriad dimensions of public pedagogy (Giroux, 2010; Sandlin, Schultz and Burdick, 2010). The extinction of knowledges makes the dominant and dominating white canon more dominant and dominating. Paraskeva (2017) has clarified this as an ethical stance that seeks justice (2017) and builds a novel conceptualization of utopia that may never be attained (Paraskeva, 2021), work that takes me back to my own work on utopia through the imagination of John Dewey (Dewey, 1933; Schubert, 2009b).

As I reflect on the trajectory of Paraskeva's work, I envision a range of scholars and intellectual orientations that have pushed the curriculum field in broadened directions. He makes me think about where the field is and should be going and what has been left out of its history. Each chapter represents a dimension of continuous expansion of curriculum studies as a basis for improving education in a world that has long been dominated by one imperialistic realm or another. The curriculum field largely was initiated as an academic area to facilitate effective and efficient translation of national purposes into curriculum for schools and related institutions. Its history includes periods of questioning whether democratic practices and policies actually have represented public interests (i.e. genuine interests of the public), such as during the social reconstructionist movement in the United States from the late 1920s (John Dewey, Harold Rugg, George S. Counts and Theodore Brameld) and later during the civil rights and anti-war movements and cultural revolutions entwined with them from the late 1950s through the early 1970s. Curriculum scholars and those who influenced them (e.g. Maxine Greene, Dwayne Huebner and James B. Macdonald, Paulo Freire, Ivan Illich, Esther Zaret, Bernice Wolfson and Louise Berman) brought a much broader idea of curriculum as whatever influences individual and social thought and action, along with a critical mistrust of institutions that purported to be democratic. Many called for greater justice to be accorded to less served social classes and racial/ethnic/cultural groups. This evolution of the curriculum field brought a diversity of forms of inquiry and focused attention on needs of those who were left out. Reflection on this history brings to memory Joel Spring's (1972) call for understanding that this educational policy and practice is markedly shaped by the *corporate state*. I see the corporate state as embodying a multifaceted education through myriad cultural spheres (including schooling) that convey public pedagogies of neoliberal values as is criticized in the corpus of Henry Giroux's work (Giroux, 2015) that espouses a profit-over-people (Chomsky, 1999; Nussbaum, 2010) outlook that has opposed social justice by perpetuating what Michael Apple (1993) aptly called *official knowledge*. Just over two decades after introducing the term *corporate state* Spring (1994) called on scholars to attend to insights of those who had been left out in America: Native Americans, African Americans, Mexican Americans, Puerto Ricans and Asian Americans.

It is a big step, indeed, to move from providing for those left out to accepting their insights and practices as worthwhile to know and experience. For instance, my first doctoral dissertation advisee William Watkins (1993) called for a new conceptualization of African American curriculum orientations and for the tapping of radical Black protest thought (Watkins, 2005; 2015), while work by Cameron McCarthy (1990) illustrated the need for African American insights to be heard for educational understandings, for example, in the work of James Baldwin and Ralph Ellison, and postcolonial perspectives (Dimitriadis and McCarthy, 2001). By the mid-1990s in curriculum studies, the extraordinary work of Pinar, Reynolds, Slattery and Taubman (1995) provided a new kind of synoptic text that reinterpreted the history of the field orchestrated by discourses or texts of curriculum study: political, racial, gender, phenomenological, post-structuralist and postmodern, autobiographical/biographical, aesthetic, theological, institutionalized (curriculum development, teachers and students) and international. It was intriguing to many that curriculum study had been founded to provide for schooling (the institutional), and ten of eleven categories of text that emerged in a mere two decades pertained to the broader notion of curriculum as a human endeavour that was more akin to cultural studies or outside curriculum (Schubert, 1981, 2010c) or public pedagogy (Sandlin, Schultz and Burdick, 2010). Much of the emergent literature showed what Henry Giroux predicted, namely that public pedagogy revealed the massive curricular or educational impact of neoliberalism and the need for its critique throughout multiple spheres of social and political life. Further countering the message or massage long given to burgeoning curriculum scholars of the United States, the United Kingdom and other empires before them, that curriculum studies is an idea unique to the White, Western, mostly male traditions needs to be countered, along with manifest destiny and the traditional notions of the canon, as Paraskeva and Steinberg (2016) vividly showed. By the second decade of the twenty-first century, I valued the work of Wayne Au, Anthony Brown and Delores Calderon who expanded curriculum studies by exploring multicultural roots (Brown and Au, 2014; Au, Brown and Calderon, 2016) that could and should be tapped for insight and understanding. Likewise, I found helpful perspectives advanced by Ruben Gaztambide-Fernandez's (2015) call for unsettlement through the *Browning* of curriculum. Ming Fang He, Brian Schultz and I also tried to be inclusive by including a range of diverse perspectives (He, Schultz and Schubert, 2015) in a reference guide for those who wanted to become more aware of curriculum studies. The need to be inclusive was also shown by the two-volume history that Marla Morris offered as an attempt to present key concepts of curriculum studies that have emerged since the aforementioned publication of (Pinar et al. 1995); she treats categories of work that include historical, political, multicultural, gender, literary, aesthetic, spiritual, cosmopolitan, ecological, cultural, postcolonial and psychoanalytic (Morris, 2016a; 2016b). Morris also developed a set of autobiographical or personal intellectual history articles by curriculum scholars for the *Encyclopedia of Innovation in Education* (Peters and Heraud, 2021). Most recently Ming Fang He and I edited the online and hardbound (three-volume) *Oxford Encyclopedia of Curriculum Studies* (Schubert and He, 2022), which has imagined overlapping and interpenetrating categories of literature that include: contextual and cultural aspects of curriculum; critiques of domination and oppression in curriculum; dimensions of curriculum; expanded subject matters in curriculum; literary and artistic foundations of curriculum; paradigms and forms of inquiry in curriculum studies; participants/actors in curriculum; school-oriented curriculum; and world (global to local) diversity of curriculum in and out of school (Schubert and He, 2022: xv–xxx).

Emerging from all of this, I see Paraskeva's ICT as a peripatetic travelling spirit that circulates through the world, accumulating an understanding of ways that human beings in diverse settings (e.g. cultural, national and community) compose themselves and others. I see this as a world version of Mary Catherine Bateson's (1989) *composing a life* that she has envisioned for individuals. The implication seems clear that it is not one composition for all – rather for individuals – and the same would be the case for the world, regarding ICT. As this ICT metaphoric spirit moves and grows, it shares with groups encountered, influencing them; similarly, each group visited augments the robustness of ICT. Like empires of the past, today's so-called *first-world* nations (especially the United States and its nationalist and corporate allies) continue to propagate traditions of imperialism that have long conquered, colonized, dominated, enslaved or exterminated those who are not considered among the first-world eminence. Clearly, education from corporate-state schools (Spring, 1972) bespeaks propagandization. ICT accumulates alternative visions and practices, such have been anticipated by scholars attuned to worldwide perspectives (e.g. Prakash and Estava, 1998; Hansen, 2007; Garrison, Hickman and Ikeda, 2014; Gallegos, 2017; Scott, 2012).

Paraskeva's critique of epistemicide, thusly, is a call for ICT as a force that gains strength as it weaves through the world and cultivates a repertoire of possibilities that offers solidarity with particular needs in diverse places, especially in the Global South and in oppressed dimensions of the deficiently labelled *first world* (i.e. less recognized spheres of the Global South, embedded in what could be called the Global South within the Global North, West and East). Moreover, as solidarity coalesces among the scattered *Global Souths*, its power will hopefully flourish to overcome oppressions faced. Paraskeva characterizes ICT and sets the stage for its flourishment, by declaring commitment to epistemological liberation. Paraskeva's chapter is not only noteworthy conceptually, it is also exemplary in its citation of authors from the Global South, who are rarely cited in curriculum books in the US/UK legacy, which has long defined itself as 'the curriculum field'. In subsequent chapters, the authors illustrate possibilities for ICT in different cultures/countries, too seldom included in curriculum discourse, such as Argentina, Thailand, Argel, China, South Africa, Mexico, Chile, South Korea, Spain, Native America, Brazil, Hong Kong, as well as several African countries and Arab Middle Eastern regions, and more.

I conclude by saying that since I discovered and became committed to the value of learning through study and reflection as a student, teacher and professor, I continue to pursue the never-ending array of curriculum questions: What is worth knowing, needing, experiencing, doing, being, becoming, overcoming, contributing, sharing, wondering, imagining and improving (Schubert, 2009a)? While curriculum studies still can pertain to schooling, it can enhance participation in any aspects of life. I look forward to more ICT stories and critical interpretations from more nations, cultures, realms of experience, places of suffering and spaces of overcoming. That is why in my early days as a professor I was enthused to learn that others in the burgeoning curriculum field from the 1970s through the 1990s saw curriculum work as central to any subject or topic. Therefore, I encourage awareness of possibilities and praxes of persons in the many school and non-school realms wherein curriculum studies provides valuable perspectives. Particularly, I urge readers to ponder the remainder of this book carefully and imagine the possibilities of ICT for contributions to justice and education throughout the world.

References

Apple, M. W. (1979), *Ideology and Curriculum*, New York: Routledge.
Apple, M. W. (1993), *Official Knowledge: Democratic Education in a Conservative Age*, New York: Routledge.
Au, W., A. L. Brown and D. Calderon (2016), *Reclaiming the Multicultural Roots of the U.S. Curriculum: Communities of Color and Official Knowledge in Education*, New York: Teachers College Press.
Bateson, M. C. (1989), *Composing a Life*, New York: Penguin (Plume).
Brown, A. L. and W. Au (2014), 'Race, Memory, and Master Narratives: A Critical Essay on U. S. Curriculum History', *Curriculum Inquiry*, 44 (3): 358–89.
Chomsky, N. (1999), *Profit over People: Neoliberalism and Global Order*, New York: Seven Stories Press.
Deleuze, G., and Guattari, F. (1987), *A Thousand Plateaus: Capitalism and Schizophrenia*, Minneapolis: University of Minnesota Press.
Dewey, J. (1916), *Democracy and Education*, New York: Macmillan.
Dewey, J. (1933), 'Dewey Outlines Utopian Schools', *New York Times*, April 23, 7.
Dimitriadis, G. and C. McCarthy (2001), *Reading and Teaching the Postcolonial: From Baldwin to Basquiat and Beyond*, New York: Teachers College Press.

Fanon, F. (1963), *The Wretched of the Earth*, New York: Grove Press.
Gallegos, B. (2017), *Postcolonial Indigenous Performances: Coyote Musings on Genízaros, Hybridity, Education, and Slavery*, Boston: Sense.
Garrison, J., L. Hickman and D. Ikeda (2014), *Living as Learning: John Dewey in the 21st Century*, Cambridge: Dialogue Path Press.
Gaztambide-Fernandez, R. (2015), 'Browning the Curriculum: A Project of Unsettlement', in M. F. He, B. D. Schultz and W. H. Schubert (eds), *Guide to Curriculum in Education*, 416–23, Thousand Oaks: Sage Publications.
Giroux, H. A. (2010), 'Neoliberalism as Public Pedagogy', in J. A. Sandlin, B. D. Schultz and J. Burdick (eds), *Handbook of Public Pedagogy: Education and Learning beyond Schooling*, 486–99, New York: Routledge.
Giroux, H. A. (2015), *Dangerous Thinking in the Age of the New Authoritarianism*. New York: Routledge Publishers.
Hansen, D. T., ed. (2007), *Ethical Visions of Education: Philosophies in Practice*, New York: Teachers College Press in association with the Boston Research Center for the 21st Century.
He, M. F., B. D. Schultz and W. H. Schubert, eds (2015), *Guide to Curriculum in Education*, Thousand Oaks: Sage Publications.
Klohr, P. R. (1980), 'The Curriculum Field – Gritty and Ragged?', *Curriculum Perspectives*, 1 (1): 1–7.
Marshall, J. D., J. T. Sears, L. Allen, P. Roberts and W. H. Schubert (2007), *Turning Points in Curriculum: A Contemporary Curriculum Memoir*, 2nd edn, Columbus: Prentice Hall.
Marshall, J. D., J. T. Sears and W. H. Schubert (2000), *Turning Points in Curriculum: A Contemporary Curriculum Memoir*, Columbus: Prentice Hall.
McCarthy, C. (1990), *Race and Curriculum: Social Inequality and Theories and Politics of Difference*, Bristol: Falmer.
Mills, C. W. (1956), *The Power Elite*, London: Oxford University Press.
Morris, M. (2016a), *Curriculum Studies Guidebooks. Volume 1, Concepts and Theoretical Frameworks*, New York: Peter Lang.
Morris, M. (2016b), *Curriculum Studies Guidebooks. Volume 2, Concepts and Theoretical Frameworks*, New York: Peter Lang.
Nussbaum, M. (2010), *Not for Profit: Why Democracy Needs the Humanities*, Princeton and Oxford: Princeton University Press.
Paraskeva, J. M. (2011), *Conflicts in Curriculum Theory*, New York: Palgrave Macmillan.
Paraskeva, J. M. (2016a), *Curriculum Epistemicide: Towards an Itinerant Curriculum Theory*, New York: Routledge.
Paraskeva, J. M., ed. (2016b), *Curriculum: Whose Internationalization?* New York: Peter Lang.
Paraskeva, J. M. (2017), *Towards a Just Curriculum Theory*, New York: Routledge.
Paraskeva, J. M. (2021), *The Generation of Utopia: Decolonizing Critical Curriculum Theory*, New York: Routledge.
Paraskeva, J. M. and S. R. Steinberg, eds (2016), *Curriculum: Decanonizing the Field*, New York: Peter Lang.
Peters, M. A. and R. Heraud, eds (2021), (& M. Morris's selections on Curriculum Theory), *Encyclopedia of Innovation in Education*, New York: Springer.
Pinar, W. F., W. M. Reynolds, P. Slattery and P. M. Taubman (1995), *Understanding Curriculum*, New York: Peter Lang.
Prakash, M. S. and G. Esteva (1998), *Escaping Education: Living as Learning within Grassroots Cultures*, New York: Peter Lang.

Said, E. (1993), *Culture and Imperialism*, New York: Knopf.
Sandlin, J. A., B. D. Schultz and J. Burdick, eds (2010), *Handbook of Public Pedagogy: Education and Learning beyond Schooling*, New York: Routledge.
Santos, B. (2014), *Epistemologies of the South: Justice against Epistemicide*, Boulder: Paradigm.
Schubert, W. H. (1981), 'Knowledge about Out-of-School Curriculum', *Educational Forum*, 45 (2): 185–98.
Schubert, W. H. (1986/1997), *Curriculum: Perspective, Paradigm, and Possibility*, New York: Macmillan.
Schubert, W. H. (2009a), 'What's Worthwhile: From Knowing and Experiencing to Being and Becoming', *Journal of Curriculum and Pedagogy*, 6 (2): 21–39.
Schubert, W. H. (2009b), *Love, Justice, and Education: John Dewey and the Utopians*, Charlotte: Information Age Publishing.
Schubert, W. H. (2010a), 'Curriculum Studies, Definitions and Dimensions Of', in C. Kridel (ed.), *Encyclopedia of Curriculum Studies*, 229–37, Thousand Oaks: Sage.
Schubert, W. H. (2010b), 'Journeys of Expansion and Synopsis: Tensions in Books that Shaped Curriculum Inquiry, 1968-Present', *Curriculum Inquiry*, 40 (1): 17–94.
Schubert, W. H. (2010c), 'Outside Curricula and Public Pedagogy', in J. A. Sandlin, B. D. Schultz and J. Burdick (eds), *Handbook of Public Pedagogy: Education and Learning beyond Schooling*, 10–19, New York: Routledge.
Schubert, W. H. (2017), 'Growing Curriculum Studies: Contributions of João M. Paraskeva', *Journal of the American Association for the Advancement of Curriculum Studies*, 12, no. 1 (Summer): 1–21.
Schubert, W. H. (In Press, 2022). 'Introduction: A Chronology of Curriculum Questions', in W. H. Schubert and M. F. He (eds) [I. Nunez, P. Roberts, S. Ross and B. Schultz (Assoc. eds)], *Encyclopedia of Curriculum Studies*, xli–lxix, Oxford: Oxford University Press.
Schubert, W. H. and M. F. He, eds [I. Nunez, P. Roberts, S. Ross and B. Schultz (Associate eds)] (2022), *The Oxford International Encyclopedia of Curriculum Studies*, Oxford and New York: Oxford University Press (3 Volumes). On-line version began in 2021, and continues to be augmented.
Schubert, W. H. and A. L. Lopez Schubert (1980), *Curriculum Books: The First Eighty Years*, Lanham: University Press of America.
Schubert, W. H., M. F. He and B. D. Schultz (2015), 'Prelude', in M. F. He, B. D. Schultz and W. H. Schubert (eds), *Guide to Curriculum in Education*, xxiii–xxix, Thousand Oaks: Sage.
Schubert, W. H., A. L. Lopez Schubert, T. P. Thomas and W. M. Carroll (2002), *Curriculum Books: The First Hundred Years*, New York: Peter Lang.
Schultz, B. D. (2017), *Teaching in the Cracks: Openings and Opportunities for Student-centered, Action-focused Curriculum*, New York: Teachers College Press.
Scott, J. C. (2012), *Decoding Subaltern Politics, Ideology, Disguise, and Resistance in Agrarian Politics*, New York: Routledge.
Spring, J. (1972), *Education and the Rise of the Corporate State*, Boston: Beacon.
Spring, J. (1994), *Deculturalization and the Struggle for Equality: A Brief History of the Education of Dominated Cultures in the United States*, New York: McGraw-Hill.
Watkins, W. H. (1993), 'Black Curriculum Orientations: A Preliminary Inquiry', *Harvard Educational Review*, 63 (3): 321–38.
Watkins, W. H., ed. (2005), *Black Protest thought and Education*, New York: Peter Lang.

Watkins, W. H. (2015), 'The Neglected Historical Milieu', in M. F. He, B. D. Schultz and W. H. Schubert (eds), *Guide to Curriculum in Education*, 303–10, Thousand Oaks: Sage Publications.

Willis, G. H., W. H. Schubert, R. Bullough, C. Kridel and J. Holton, eds (1993), *The American Curriculum: A Documentary History*, Westport: Greenwood Press.

2

Against Epistemic Suicide!

Itinerant Curriculum Theory: A Declaration of Epistemological Independence

João M. Paraskeva

Theory potentially destabilizes social life.
(Eagleton, 1990, 27)

Our field faces a *theorycide*. There is no way to hide it. Let me highlight two intricate intertwined issues among the multiple reasons for such a condition. The first relates to what I call – drawing from José Gil (2009) – 'curriculum involution' (Paraskeva, 2020a; 2020b). That is, the battles between hegemonic and counter-hegemonic traditions, and within each tradition, created a theoretical vacuum; neither the advocates of the regulatory curriculum nor the heralds of the emancipatory curriculum managed to claim a complete victory. We face a theoretical vacuity, an 'odd impasse' through which the curriculum epistemicide and reversive epistemicide continue perpetuating (Paraskeva, 2016; 2018; 2021a; 2021b; 2022a; 2022b; 2022c). We are sinking into a void defined by a paradox: neither the old social order remains safe nor the new social order emerges. The inability to fully establish 'their human being and social matrix' is the malaise affecting dominant and counter-dominant platforms. Paradoxically, these battles would become much more a symptom 'of the current state of the field than a strategic response to it', as Eagleton (1990, 35) put it.

The second – and connected to the former – is related to the fact that the modern Western Eurocentric epistemological platform that serves as a matrix for counter-hegemonic Eurocentric models is irreversibly exhausted. Modernity dominant and counter-dominant plateaus 'within the curriculum field shown themselves to be inadequate in explaining some of the most urgent problems we are facing' (Alba, 1999, 482). As Terry Eagleton (1990, 53) argues, the modernist matrix 'cannot help positing itself as independent of any conditions of material production, and so insidiously perpetuates false consciousness'. To complexify Eagleton's argument I would stress that such matrix do not exactly fall into a false consciousness but rather into a parcial consciousness.

As I have had the opportunity to examine in greater depth in other spaces (Paraskeva, 2022a; 2022b; 2022c; 2023b) a brief foray into the most varied critical, anti-colonial and decolonial literature (within and beyond the field of the curriculum) (Anyon 1997; Apple, 1979; Giroux, 1981; McLaren, 1994; Kliebard, 1995; Schubert et al, 1980; 1986; 2017; Pinar, et al, 1995; Baker, 2009; Ellsworth, 1989; Paraskeva, 2011; Huebner & Paraskeva, 2022; Watkins, 2003; Mignolo, 2018 ; Galeano, 1997; Quijano, 2000) allows us to understand the complex dynamics inherent to these two issues.

Counter-hegemonic traditions have always shown an incapability – in many cases epistemological haughtiness – to realize that the Eurocentric epistemological matrix could not respond to the challenges and needs proclaimed by the vast diversity and difference of the world's epistemological perspectives. Such traditions never dared to go beyond their modern Western Eurocentric epistemological comfort zone and reach out to non-modern, non-Western, non-Eurocentric epistemological perspectives to grasp the world's complex needs and challenges. Appallingly – like the dominant traditions – they were also epistemicidal, paving the way for the consolidation of an abyssal reason (Santos, 2014). By ignoring the limitations of its reason, counter-hegemonic traditions also ignored that not all post-critical epistemological rivers have an emancipatory river bed and that there is not only one alternative emancipatory matrix (Eagleton, 1990, 76; 2015).

To rely on Gil's (2009) framework out of such a '[epistemological] civil war' – as Thomas Docherty (1996, 59) would put it – no '[real] tragedy' erupted, as such a war was stripped of its tragic dimension. Instead, a '[curriculum] involution occurred' (Gil, 2009, 28; Paraskeva, 2020a; 2020b), which points to a 'regression'. No transformation occurred. Improvement was synonymous with regression. The dominant and counter-dominant reason became 'predatory reason' (Eagleton, 1990, 66). The incapacity to overcome such 'involution' (Paraskeva, 2020a; 2020b), such theoretical 'regression' triggers a *theorycide* momentum – clear evidence of the curriculum's *capitis diminutiu*, which prompts its *hypertrophia theoricae*. The *theorycide* is not necessarily an absence of theory – or a perpetual theoretical killing – but a coup d'état, an attack on the space and time of theory, a theoretical mope. The field is at its knees – exhibiting an impressive theoretical agony – before a 'non-theory theory' temple. The *theorycide* saturates the field and unfolds its 'inner [theoretical] irreconcilability' (Eagleton, 1990, 55), choking the field with anaemic responses to a world that haunts us with difficult questions (Santos, 2008).

Dwayne Huebner's gutturals rang the alarm bells during the 1970s. Angry with the field, he proclaims his 'enough is enough' momentum. The field was generally predictably arrogant, ignoring what I called the 'Huebner question' (Paraskeva, 2022b). Very few within our field's hemispheres took the danger that Huebner proclaimed seriously. A few decades later, William Pinar goes against the grain and 'forces' the need to place 'theory' at the centre of what he had called a 'complicated conversation'. Unfortunately, his intentions/concerns met the same fate as Huebner's. Such *theorycide* is the accurate epistemological color of what I have framed as the 'Huebner syndrome' (Paraskeva, 2022b). Unfortunately such 'complicated conversation' fell into an uncontrolled epistemicidal spiral. Even those who would feel most uncomfortable with this statement admit that, at the very least, the production and theoretical debate in the field is not at the level that the field once exhibited. This malady is not an isolated case; it pervades the humanities. Theory 'is not what it used to be [four or five decades ago]' (Elliot and Attridge, 2011; Wolf, 2011).

Over the past decades, I – and others – have tried to help look for 'solutions' to this theoretical shipwreck we find ourselves in, ways to provoke an irreversible short circuit in this 'non-theory theory' delusional stage, to reverse such *theorycide*, to look for a kind of non-derivative defibrillator that theoretically revives the field through and towards an alternative and just 'theory-state'. I have repeatedly argue that the way we have been producing our critical and post-critical theories needs to die. There is really no future without death (Saramago, 2008). This is not a call for the death of the critical, but for the death of how we have been thinking and doing curriculum theory, research and development. I have been advocating that it is important to work from *nuestros locales* (Jupp, 2023) in a just global solution, one that must represent not just a radical co-presence of different and diverse epistemological traditions but precisely a radical co-habitus (Paraskeva, 2023b) of such diverse and differences. In itinerant curriculum theory (ICT) terms, radical co-habitus is a full-blast isonomy (Karatani, 2017), a totalitarian absence of epistemological rulers and rule, thus helping to decentre Eurocentric modernity from within. ICT is also a curriculum isonomia metamorphoses (Paraskeva, 2021a).

Such 'theorycity' – a just way to unblock such involution (Paraskeva, 2020a; 2020b) – implies deterritorializing curriculum theory, which involves a commitment to fight for a different non-divisive research platform, one that pushes research to a 'level of instability, not stability, generating concepts also, in itself, unstable' (O'Brien and Penna, 1999, 106). In doing so, a deterritorialized curriculum theory increasingly becomes an itinerant theory, a theory of non-spaces (Auge, 2003). In essence, one needs to assume a rhizomatous approach that sees reality beyond dichotomies, beyond beginnings and endings (Gough, 2000) – an approach that breeds from the multiplicity of immanent platforms and, from its 'centreless' and 'peripheryless' position, defies the myth of clean knowledge territories (Deleuze and Guattari, 1987; Eco, 1984). Such an itinerant position should be seen as subversively transgressive. The 'purpose of curriculum theory[ists] is to travel, to go beyond the limits, to move, and stay in a kind of permanent exile' (Said, 2005, 41). A theory of non-places and non-times is, in essence, a theory of all places and all times. The curriculum theorist is a constant migrant (Jin, 2008), a 'permanent nomad of his own all multifaceted consciousness' (Pessoa, 2014, 113), who experiences a series of (epistemological) events (Khalfa, 1999). The itinerant theorist is a 'real dinamogenus' (Gil, 2010, 13). Such migrant being and thinking situates the itinerant theorist; 'it beckons us to recognize that how we perceive and experience the world (individually or communally), how we identify problems and name solutions, and how we locate ourselves in the world are all inseparable to the struggle for cognitive justice' (Darder, 2016, xi), thus helping to short circuit the functionalist trap that is sinking Western Eurocentric dominant and the counter-dominant platforms (Süsskind, 2017; Oliveira, 2017; Moreira, 2017).

In arguing for an ICT, I am claiming an atypical epistemological approach that will be able to deconstruct the images of thought, thus rethinking the utopia through re-utopianizing thinking fuelling the emergence of radical collective and individual subjectivities (see Banhabib, 1986); ICT is a metamorphosis, exhibiting 'a double purpose though; (a) to reinvent maps of social emancipation and (b) subjectivities with the capacity and desire for using them; that is no paradigmatic transformation would be possible without the paradigmatic transformation of subjectivity' (Santos, 1995, 482). In doing so, ICT brings back to the fore social imagination (Berardi, 2012) but within an endless pluriversal horizon and matrix.

Such an approach will unfold naturally into voluntary and involuntary creations (Merelau-Ponty, 1973). Furthermore, the curriculum worker and creator need to be seen as 'an *auctor*, which is *qui auget*, or the person who augments, increases, or perfects the act (in fact), since every creation is always a co-creation, just as every author is a co-author' (Agamben, 2005, 76). To create, the theorist 'needs a foothold' (Pessoa, 2014, 214), and the strength of such foothold comes from his/her 'extraordinary exteriority' (Gil, 2010, 14), that is, the 'interior and exterior constitute a space of implosion' (Gil, 2010, 15). The core of ICT is that it ferociously challenges any attempt at a bunker theory practice or a bunker praxis. In examining the complex conundrum of the Portuguese identity, the great Mozambican-born philosopher José Gil (2009) argues that identity matters are not detached from the cruelty of an 'only one-dimensional way' (p. 38). That is, the cult of 'the one best theory-practice' 'is intimately connected with all the commonsensical commonsense lack of evidence of so-called credible alternatives, that "cocoons" the subject in invisible and visible bunkers' (Gil, 2009, 38). In a way, to upgrade Gil's (2009) arguments, a palpable 'selficide' is systematically produced by blocking 'truth' from itself and from the very own self, a self that can only exist 'in inner violence'. I argue that our field does not have a lack of identity; quite the opposite, it has a healthy excess of identity (Gil, 2009).

ICT is not a bunker theory (Gil, 2009); it works under a radically new pluralistic conceptual grammar (Jupp, 2017, 4) 'emphasizing (a) the coloniality of power, knowledge, and being; (b) epistemicides, linguicide, abyssality, and the ecology of knowledge; and, (c) poststructuralist hermeneutic itinerancy'; such pluriversal grammar allows to think 'a prudent knowledge for a decent life' (Santos, 2007a, 47), defending the epistemological as political. In this context, ICT respects epistemological diversity. While being an 'occupying epistemology' (Santos, 2018, 2), its aim is not 'to overcome the hierarchical dichotomy between North and South but rather to overcome such normative dualism' (Santos, 2018, 7). Thus, the claim of a just theory sees the collective struggle for knowledge as a struggle that must go far beyond the Western epistemological platform. ICT is a clear appeal against the precariousness of any ossified and fixed theoretical position (Paraskeva, 2018; 2019). ICT walks towards knowledge emancipation, thus opening up the canon of knowledge regulation; it is not a grand narrative of a great theory as 'knowledge-emancipation does not aspire to a great theory, it aspires to a theory of translation that serves as an epistemological support for emancipatory practices' (Santos, 1999, 206); it is a 'non-derivative theory of translation' (Paraskeva and Huebner, 2023, 16); it reacts against the 'structural violence triggered by the epistemicidal nature of our curriculum, as well as the traps, silences, and omission within the critical and post-critical impulses' (Recio, chapter 9), unfolding a different liberatory praxis that is a non-abyssal.

It is not a 'grand' theory; it is only a theory – perpetually itinerant – of greater knowledge, fully aware that such greater knowledge, as Tse (2017) argues, is reachable only through a 'full consciousness that everything is continually transformed inside and outside our mind' (p. 66). Itinerancy, thus, is not real; it is 'the real(ity)'. ICT is 'an epistemic minga, a collective farming for the collective good' (Santos, 2018, 146). In this sense, ICT does not just face the outside (Gil, 2010, 16) as it is indeed the outside – but not an outsider – yet steams discrete 'sensationism' – the opposite of sensationalism – 'the only reality is the sensation of consciousness' (Gil, 2010, 65); it is a theory that situates curriculum theory as in motion, not a staid theory, but *viral theorizing* or action; it disarms the absolutism of the neoliberal viral model, it is prudent not to romanticize the epistemological platforms of the Global South, and 'Incredibly flexible, nimble, and able to pivot' a radical co-habitus of different differences within and between the Global South and the Global North (Price, chapter 15). ICT is a rearguard counter sense theoretical. approach that materializes the death of the Eurocentric postmodern epistemological subject that refuses to recognize the legitimacy of epistemological perspectives beyond the Eurocentric matrix. ICT thus is not the 'death of man' – as epitomized by Foucault (1973) but the 'death of the Prosperous subject and its cognitive empire.

ICT is a wordily theoretical approach; it is the theory of *palavrar*. It is an attempt to build a theory '*que palavre e não que diga*' (Pessoa, 2014, 226). In this sense, the itinerant theorist is constantly mining the meaning (Williams, 2013), knowing fully well that what is around is somewhat more crucial than the dust, noise and grain provoked by the mining. Thus, an ICT is inherently 'an exfoliation' (Gil, 1998, 127) metamorphosis, 'a sill of infinite mournings' (Couto, 2008, 105), an anti- and post- 'mechanotic' (Al-i-Ahmad, 1984, 31) momentum that will seek to create 'a powder, gentle, maneuverable, and capable of blowing up men without killing them, a powder that, in vicious service, will generate a life, and from the exploded men will be born the infinite men that are inside him' (Couto, 2008, 68). In such context, ICT is a 'pluriversal polyphony, a polylectal rather than ideolectal conception of cultural and political imagination' (Santos, 2018, 12), so crucial in an era paced by the death of imagination. I argue for a 'new form of political affirmation grounded in a global pluriversal *epistemological* visions and interests to be favored and courses of action to be followed that are sustained in people's history' (Pokwewitz, 1978, 28). As Jupp (Chapter 3) argues, ICT refers to non-derivative 'elaborated praxis of critical theory by students, teachers, or activist educators in diverse contexts of the distinct geo-regions of the world'. ICT epitomizes the legitimacy of Caliban reason (Henry, 2000).

The educational and curriculum theorist must be understood as an epistemological pariah challenged by an inexact yet rigorous theoretical path (Deleuze, 1990). It is a 'frontier and baroque' theory in a perpetual 'transitionality' state (Santos, 1995). In this sense, an itinerant theorist is immersed in a metamorphosis 'so perpetually incomplete that even dreams dislike because they have defects' (Pessoa, 2014, 126); so perpetually deep that it hurts the imagination (Gil, 2010, 86), it hurts the 'physical brain' (Pessoa, 2014, 234). ICT is the perfect utopia because it is conscious of the imperfection of what is perfect, conscious of the perfection of the imperfection. Hence, being perfect contradicts being complete, yet the theorist is thirsty for being complete leaving him/

her in a perennial state of useless pain. ICT reflects a subject that when 'he/she thinks sees him/herself in the process' (Pessoa, 2014, 73) and fully 'understands that if one knew the truth one would see it' (Pessoa, 2014, 96). ICT 'captures, vampirizes, and calls on the subject to complete it' (Gil, 2010, 29). Such an itinerant theory(ist) provokes (and exists amid) a set of crises and produces laudable silences. The theory(ist) is a volcanic chain, showing a constant lack of equilibrium, and thus is always a stranger in his/her language. The itinerant theory(ist) is profoundly sentient of the multiplicities of lines, spaces and dynamic becomings (Deleuze, 1990). ICT therefore echoes Huebner's (1966; 1959) challenges of a radically different 'semantology', thirsty seeking for a new language. ICT – and the struggle against the curriculum epistemicide – Schubert (2017, 12) argues, 'enacts the call for new languages for curriculum studies' (p. 12). ICT implies 'cross-epistemic and diverse transcultural entanglements paving the way for a praxis of trans-habits' (Ghosh, 2016, 12). Such trans-habits are itinerant, thus 'staying not "crossed" rather "acrossed" diffractively bringing diverse and different contingents together' (Ghosh, 2016, 12).

ICT does try to say something to the field. It presents new terrains and theoretical situations. ICT participates in the complicated conversation (Pinar, 2000; Trueit, 2000) – that cannot bend under the yoke of Western academicism – challenging Western curriculum epistemicides and alerting us to the need to respect and incorporate non-Western epistemes. Pinar (2013) acknowledged the influential 'synopticality' of ICT:

> There are other discourses influential now, sustainability perhaps primary among them. Arts-based research is hardly peripheral. . . . One sign is the synoptic text composed by João M. Paraskeva. Hybridity is the order of the day. Pertinent to the discussion is that even Paraskeva's determination to contain in one 'critical river' multiple currents of understanding curriculum politically floods its banks; he endorses an 'itinerant curriculum theory' that asserts a 'deliberate disrespect of the canon' (Paraskeva, 2011, 184). In Paraskeva's proclamation, this 'river' has gone 'south' (Paraskeva, 2011, 186). That South is Latin America, where we can avoid 'any kind of Eurocentrism' (Paraskeva, 2011, 186) while not 'romanticizing indigenous knowledge' (Paraskeva, 2011, 187). Addressing issues [such as hegemony, ideology, power, social emancipation, class, race, and gender] implies a new thinking, a new theory . . . an itinerant curriculum theory. (Pinar, 2013, 64)

ICT, as new influential discourse, as Pinar (2013) put it, is highly relevant, Zhao (2019) argues, as it opens up the eugenic colonial sociabilities (Santos, 2018) built on 'language, knowledge, culture and educational' cleansing of the South (p. 27). ICT short circuits the logic and the monumentality of dominant curriculum reason, as Mbembe (2017) would put it. In this sense, ICT is *corazonar*, that is, to warm up reason, a reason that has been *corazonada*, and, thus, it 'cannot be planned as it occurs out of joined struggles, building bridges between emotions' affections on the one hand, and knowledge/reasons, on the other' (Santos, 2018, 101). It goes without saying how 'spirituality is towing in *corazonar*, converting it into a non-Western-centric form of insurgent energy against oppression and unjust suffering' (Santos, 2018, 100; also see Paraskeva, 2023a; 2023b). Such *corazonar* collides, as Baum (Chapter 4) teaches us, with English as a non-native language that produces, reproduces and legitimizes the 'self/other logic based on subordinate inclusion'. She frames English as a language other – the language of the Damned, as Fanon (1967) would put it – in the quest to contribute to the emergence of a delinking space (Amin, 1990) where English is no longer the language of 'knowledge/power'.

Corazonar implies a non-derivative theoretical course defined by a cutting-edge, *Malangatanian* and *Pollockian* set of processes, not because it is abstract but because it is oppressive in its freedom. Hence, ICT is a theory of 'disquiet' (Pessoa, 2014), challenging the 'disquiet paralysis' (Gil, 2009, 20), yet knowing full well that it is through disquiet that subjectivities emerge (Gil, 2009). It is not a solo act, however; it is a populated solitude. This itinerant theoretical path claims a multifaceted curriculum compromise and 'runs away' from any unfortunate 'canonology'. ICT, as Darder (2016) unpacks, claims for a political praxis that 'must be both epistemologically fierce and deeply anchored in the sensibilities of our subalternity – the only place from which we can truly rid ourselves of the heavy yoke of Western sanctioned tyranny, which has wrought bitter histories of impoverishment, colonization, enslavement, and genocide' (p. x). *Corazonar* is transformative as it questions the 'current complicated conversation' in the field, the conventional situated notion of *currere*. While both are crucial, the former needs to delink from eugenic harbours and move towards a non-abyssal and just conversation; the latter, 'for deconstruction, reconstruction, and decolonization is not enough, and this must be situated in the present moment to move from *currere* toward ICT as implicated in Deleuze's notion of politics of desire which emphasize an individual's desire to make something happen not only for his or her own's sake but also for the transformation of the society' (Jatuporn, Chapter 14). ICT is non-derivativelly anti-dialectical, and in such such sense complexifies postmodern Foucaultian (Foucault, 1982) and Deleuzian (Deleuze, 1985) impulses. It is a theory that erupts out of the ashes of difference and diversity within and beyond Eurocentric and non-Eurocentric epistemes. As a deterritorializing commitment, ICT detotalizes the field, that is the field enjoys an unbreakable authority, the authority of epistemological freedom.

Such an ICT is an anthem against the indignity of speaking for the other (Walsh, 2012; Deleuze, 1990). ICT, as Mizikaci (Chapter 7) argues, denounces and rejects any 'talk that talks for people in the name of people', an egregious mistake produced by some progressive counties, thus unleashing a monumental claim that progressive education would be the solution to fight dogmatism and regressive praxis. ICT, as she documents, is a struggle against the epistemicide as well as reversive epistemicide – in which the dismantling of indigenous languages represents one of its symptoms. Conventional dominant and counter-dominant movements speak for the other and do so in the language of coloniality. As Jupp (Chapter 3) documents, ICT responds to the 'indigenous intellectual production', to the 'decolonial-Hispanophone curriculum values and conditions of indigenous intellectual production, both historical and present-day'. ICT thus challenges the sociology of absences as the only way to grasp 'silences, needs, and unpronounceable aspirations questions' (Santos, 1999, 206); it challenges 'how can silence be spoken without it necessarily speaking the hegemonic language that intends to make it speak?' (Santos, 1999, 206); it is the curriculum praxis of the sociology emergences, as Santos (2018) would put it – an itinerant theory 'of the sociology of absences and emergences'; the former 'would be geared to show the measure of the epistemicide caused by northern epistemologies, while the latter would be oriented to amplify the meaning of the latent and potentially liberating sociabilities' (Santos, 2018, 276), paving the way for a just pedagogy, one that fosters southern epistemologies. In such a sense, ICT is not an *ortonimus* theory. Quite the opposite (Gil, 2010), it is a 'hetero-theory'. The theorist multiplies her/himself to feel her/his own individual and collective subject (Gil, 2010); to be sincere, the itinerant theorist contradicts himself every minute (Gil, 2010) as reality is massively contradictory. ICT is neither a 'diminished theory' (Pessoa, 2010, 230) nor presents an over-the-top view related to any other epistemological formation.

The itinerary theory(ist) is more than an eclectic approach; as I have argued, it is a constellation, a profoundly (in)discipline, yet does not correlate with any disciplinary grid that ossifies modern Western Eurocentric epistemological platforms. It 'reacts against the vegetal academy of silence' (Pessoa, 2014, 270). ICT confronts and throws the subject to a permanent, unstable question, 'What is to think?' ICT is a metamorphosis of the endless multifarious epistemological 'alphabet[s] of thought' (Gil, 2009, 25). In this sense, ICT 'reads differently because it is written and spoken in a different way' (Gil, 2010, 20); ICT pushes one 'to think differently, but also to learn differently and to better understand what it means to learn, and what does it mean to think' (Gil, 2009, 35). It is epistemologically radically different; it is a new epistemological logic, so crucial to deterritorialize and delink from the traditional fundamentally Eurocentric dominant and counter-dominant logic but above all to reignite – in a radical way – the utopia for a just world (see Eagleton, 2015). ICT implies discontinuity. As Pillay (Chapter 13) argues, ICT challenges how 'curriculum neutralizes its ideological and dehumanizing intentions of othering'.

Moreover, ICT pushes one to think in the light of the future as well as to question how can 'we' actually claim to know the things that 'we' claim to know if 'we' are not ready specifically to think the unthinkable but to go beyond the unthinkable and to struggle with its infinitude. ICtheorists 'abandoned what we think we know' (Fukuoka, 2022, p. 36). In this context, ICT challenges not just presentism (Pinar, 2004) and momentism (Paraskeva, 2011) but also 'contemporarysm' (Paraskeva, 2011; 2016; 2021a; 2021b; 2022a; 2022b; 2022c). In Gil's (2018, 404) terms, 'never has a time been so contemporary as to appear to embody much more than the contemporary time'. One is no longer 'contemporary of' but simply 'contemporary'. In essence, everything has become contemporary. The yoke of the present-now – in which our field is sinking – is viral, a new barbarism that wipes out ethics of memory regarding a past that was always a future for a given generation at a specific point. Each 'now' is a 'now' of an absent past or future. Each 'present-now' is a 'present-now' of a 'particular now'. Devoided from a future reality – diluted within a 'shrinking present' (Rosa, 2015) – societal transformational impulses have been triggered by having the past as a reference, and, commonsensically, one thinks about change in terms of 're-covering, re-building, re-habilitate' (Williams, 2013, 281). The human being produced by the democratic Cartesian matrix 'leaves and exists for the pure present' (Badiou, 2011, 13), a present that is the only one possible, that is, 'the present of Europe' (Mignolo,

2018, 110). Modernity's present time, Mignolo (2018) advances, 'was understood to be the only present, the present of Europe' (p. 110). As we are contemporaries of everything – past and future – 'everything is present, we are only "contemporaries" because everything is contemporary and present' (Gil, 2018, 405). This dangerous cult of 'the contemporary' completely dilutes any utopian hypothesis – however remote it may be – within common sense. One ceases to be 'contemporaries of' – which puts one in existence and experience without historical parallel. The context of contemporaneity is contemporaneity itself.

ICT, I reiterate, is to be (or not to be) radically unthinkable. However, it is a theory of another humanity. It is about this world, though. It is people's theory. ICT is not only a metamorphosis between what is thought and non-thought and unthought but is also fundamentally about the temerity of the colonization of the non-/un-/thought within the thought. ICT speaks volumes to Eagleton's claims that 'theory destabilizes social life' (Eagleton, 1990, 27); it attempts to understand how big is infinite, the infinite of thought and action. If one challenges infinity, 'then it is chaos because one is in chaos'; that means that the question or questions (whatever they are) are inaccurately deterritorialized and fundamentally sedentary. ICT 'thinks the movement of infinity' (Gil, 2009, 97) or the (im)possibility of 'finiteness' of the infinity. ICT implies an understanding of chaos as domestic, as public and as a *punctum* within the pure luxury of immanence. In such a multitude of turfs, ICT needs to be understood as *poesis*. It plays in the plane of immanence. Since immanence is 'a life', ICT is 'a life'; ICT 'uses what it is not like it is', as Tse (2017) would put it (p. 67). A life paced by a *poesis* or a revolution? 'Yes, please' in a complete *Žižekian* way. ICT is, above all, the language for/of doing (Deleuze, 1995). ICT is a *poesis* that itinerantly throws the subject against the infinite of representation to grasp the 'omnitude' of the real(ity) and the rational(ity), thus mastering the transcendent (see Paraskeva, 2023a). Being more *poesis* than just theory (and not because it is less theory), its itinerant position *epitomizes* a transcendent 'nomadography', which is not transcendental. To be more precise, ICT, as Tse (2017) would put it, 'awakens what will never end and is housed in it' (p. 104). To rely on Deleuze and Guattari (1987), 'It is not death that breaks [the itinerant theorist] but seeing, experiencing, overthinking life. Signs, events, life, and vitalism are profoundly linked. Its organisms that die, not life' (p. 143). As Deleuze and Guattari (1987) felicitously unveil, such inquiry implies an itinerant theorist that is not just a war machine that judiciously collides with ossified truths and fossilized realities. However, its itinerant existence is only possible in a permanent theatre of war. Needless to say, ICT is not a cavalier way to grasp history. In this sense, it refuses to 'walk backward towards the future' (Williams, 2013, 281). Nor is it just a pale reaction against how history has been *quasi-suffocated* by hegemonic and particular counter-hegemonic conventional traditions. Although a geophilosophical concept/praxis, it goes beyond an aesthetic wrangle between sedentary theoretical hegemonic, particular counter-hegemonic platforms and nomad(ic) approaches, free from walls, dams and institutional regression. ICT implies a beyond-nomadic inquiry, one that the foci occupy the truly total itinerant capacity of 'space(less)ness', a permanent smooth itinerant position, a perpetual search that wholeheartedly aims at saturation yet the saturation of non-saturation. The 'nomadography' of such theory is framed in the non-stop itinerant posture in which creators of *poesis* seemed to be part of the history of thought but escape from it either in a specific aspect or altogether. ICT challenges the irrelevance of modern Western Eurocentric disciplinary knowledge as is. ICT attempts to turn curriculum theory against itself as well. It is a philosophy of liberation, which is sentient of the pitfalls of the internationalization dynamics within the curriculum field. The itinerant posture provides a powerful space in which to engage in a global conversation that is attentive to the 'globalisms' (Santos, 2008); profoundly aware of the multiplicities of public spheres and subaltern counter-publics (Fraser, 1997); genuinely attentive to the production of localities (Hardt and Negri, 2000) and militant particularism (Harvey, 1998) and to the (de)construction of new, insurgent cosmopolitanism (Santos, 2008; Popkewitz, 2007); conscious of the wrangle between the globalized few and the localized rest (Bauman, 1998); and yet profoundly alert to the dangerous hegemony of the English language. Such conversation needs to occur in languages other than English (Darder, 1991; Wa Thiongo, 2012).

ICT challenges modern Western Eurocentric abyssal thinking that fosters 'epistemic oppression, and epistemic injustice, and legitimizes the persistent epistemic exclusion that hinders the other contribution to knowledge production' (Nedjar, chapter 11). It challenges one of the fundamental characteristics of abyssal thinking: the impossibility of co-habitus of the 'two sides of the abyssal line'. Such a theoretical approach is an 'itinerantology' that addresses *las heridas abiertas* (Anzaldua, 2007) of the coloniality of power. Such 'itinerantology' is fully aware *que las heridas abiertas* cannot be addressed by ignoring 'how compressed specific dialectical positions of Marxism are – or specific dialectical positions of specific Marxisms – thus obliterating fair and inclusive analysis' (Paraskeva & Süssekind, 2018, 71). ICT is a form of decolonial thinking that 'recognizes an ecological coexistence of varying epistemological forms of knowledge worldwide, paying attention to knowledge and epistemologies largely marginalized and discredited in the current world order' (Zhao, 2019, 27).

ICT is not merely an invocation or evocation (Schubert, 2017, 10). ICT touches the 'real' nerve (Dabashi, 2015) by challenging dominant and specific counter-dominant traditions within the modernity Western Eurocentric epistemological matrix (Appadurai, 1996), as part of the epistemicide. However, as a future for the field, ICT alerts the need to walk away from all forms of romanticism regarding the non-modern, non-Western, non-Eurocentric epistemes. ICT is not a nationalistic theoretical platform. ICT fights any form of indigenoustude (Paraskeva, 2011); it is about decolonizing native narratives by 'considering the relationship of language to power and also to empowerment' (Mallon, 2012, 3). In so doing, it reacts against epistemological blindness, as it opens the veins of a complex beast, dissects its strokes and counter-strokes (Janson and Paraskeva, 2016), denounces and announces the involution phase of the field as well as its *occidentotic* fungus (Paraskeva, 2020a; 2020b) and offers just ways out of it, through a just 'pluriversal' epistemological reading and doing of the 'wor(l)d'. ICT reacts against 'the violent power of the identical that becomes invisible', as Han (2018, 10; see also Paraskeva, 2020b) would put it; it reacts against the fading of otherness in an era in which 'the negativity of the other gives place to the positivity of the identical' (Han, 2018, 10). In ICT terms, the identical is pornographic, that is, '[in] pornography, all bodies resemble each other, they break down into identical body parts. Stripped of all language, the body is reduced to the sexual that knows no other difference than sexual' (Han, 2018, 15). ICT calls against an 'ontic deficit' that permeates society (Han, 2018, 13). Its pluriverse nature smashes the obscene link 'between the identical and the identical' (Han, 2018, 16; Benhabib, 1986; Diop, 1987). ICT, Pillay (Chapter 13) argues, 'provides a fuzzification of the rigidity of colonial logic as it is enabled through the curriculum and its many iterations. Its fuzzy logic disarms the modernist logic of binary exclusions and certainty and enables a new way of being in the world- with- *others* -who- are -human -like- me.'

ICT moves towards a blend between experiences and expectations, an alternative logic of utopianism that redirects towards a 'possibility to wait with hope' (Santos, 1999, 213), thus making the new utopia – a decolonial one, utopian otherwise – the 'desperate realism of a waiting that allows itself to fight for the content of waiting, not in general but in the exact place and time in which it is' (Santos, 1999, 213). Thus, hope, in ICT terms, 'does not lie in a general principle which provides for a general future. It resides instead in the possibility of creating fields of social experimentation where it is possible to resist the evidence of inevitability locally, successfully promoting alternatives that seem utopian at all times and places except those in which they occurred' (Santos, 1999, 213). Hence, ICT reignites the utopia, since 'the existence does not exhaust the possibilities of existence and therefore there are alternatives susceptible of surpassing what is critical in what exists' (Santos, 1999, 198; Dussel, 1995) – yet a different utopian logic though not because 'the utopian pragmatism disappeared, but because it is not what it used to be' (Gil, 2009, 18), nor that it cannot be. An alternative frame towards alternative utopias cannot be framed – and subjugated – within a matrix that will never allow such utopia's materialization. ICT is not a reinvention or a rehabilitation of past utopianist(s) logic(s), although such constitutes some of its pillars. In Darder's (2016) terms, ICT 'is meant to guide us in transforming our labor into a living praxis of global cognitive justice' (p. xiii). ICT is an epistemological weapon of non-derivative consciencism. (Cabral, 1969; Nkrumah, 1964).

ICT implies one to 'detheorize reality as the only way to reinvent it' (Santos, 1995, 513). It is an epistemological declaration of liberation and independence (Paraskeva, 2019; 2023a; 2023b). It is, thus, the 'pluriversal' rubber stamp of the death of the logic through which modern Western Eurocentric platforms imposed a mono-episteme. As Saramagho (2008) teaches us, 'there is no future wothout death'. ICT ushers in the death of the derivative logic as we have been producing our theoretical artillery – eugenically inflamed.

ICT is not a drone theory; it does not speak for the other. ICT, I re-emphasize, is chaos and its rhythms chaos that 'inaugurates the appearance of things not because it engenders them, but because it withdraws' (Gil, 2018, 376). ICT thus offers a way out of the involution volt, out of *occidentosis* (Paraskeva, 2020a; 2020b). In Jupp's (2017) terms, ICT is a call to 'preserve and advance the historically specific and localized knowledges and languages that underlie cognition – and through cognition cultural practices and social relations– represent the fundamental struggle for social justice' (p. 5). ICT dissects chaos as normalcy that 'presides over the order of the world; as what it establishes because it withdraws – and in withdrawing, allows the emergence of thinkable things because they are discernible, differentiated' (Gil, 2018, 376). Chaos, and ICT in this sense, 'ends with the unthinkable' (Gil, 2018, 376). Therefore, ICT is emancipatory, inaugurating a 'paradigmatic transition from a reactionary (n)eugenic cosmic capacity towards a "chaosmic" capacity, one that imposed "alternative" forms of sociability rather than one form of sociability' (Santos, 1995, x). Chaos is 'apolar', a consequence and a beginning, and so is the curriculum. In this context, ICT challenges the cultural politics of denial, which produces a radical absence, the absence of humanity, the modern subhumanity (Santos, 2015, 30). Such a new theoretical task understands that modern humanity is not conceivable without a modern subhumanity (Santos, 2014) and that denying a part of humanity is sacrificial in that it is the condition for the other part of humanity, which considers itself universal. ICT, thus, aims precisely to a 'general epistemology of the impossibility of a general epistemology'.(Santos, 2014) Such radical co-habitus – the begin-anew (Darder, 2016) – pushes one towards a post-abyssal momentum, a post-abyssal epistemology, which spans an ecology of knowledge (Santos, 2007b, 40). Consequently, there is 'a call for the democratization of knowledge that is a commitment to an emancipatory, non-relativistic, cosmopolitan ecology of knowledge, bringing together and staging dialogues and alliances between diverse forms of knowledge, cultures, and "cosmopologies" in response to different forms of oppression that enact the coloniality of knowledge and power' (Santos, 2007a, xiv). ICT respects three fundamental pillars: '(1) learning that the South exists, (2) learning to go to the South, and (3) learning from and with the South (Santos, 2015, 40). In order to learn from the South, we must first let the South speak up for what best identifies the South as the fact that has been silenced' (Santos, 1995, 510).

Post-abyssal thinking implies a radical break with modern Western ways of thinking and acting. Post-abyssality 'is always "coknowledge" emerging from the process of knowing-with rather than knowing-about' (Santos, 2018, 147). While an overt challenge against the colonialism of the English language (Darder, 1991), as well as a call to arms against all other forms of linguistic colonialism perpetrated by other modern Western languages (Paraskeva, 2011; 2016), ICT is also an alert against what Ahmad (2008) coined as Third World nationalisms and modern Western internationalization and internationalisms. Such a radical break does not mean slurring specific modern Western impulses. The ecology of knowledge needs to be seen as a 'destabilizing collective or individual subjectivity endowed with a special capacity, energy, and will to act with *clinamen* experimenting with eccentric or marginal forms of sociability or subjectivity inside and outside Western modernity, those forms that have refused to be defined according to abyssal criteria' (Santos, 2007b, 41). ICT is a destabilizing epistemology that aims to defamiliarize the canonic tradition of monocultures of knowledge (Santos, 2014). What is crucial within the ecology of knowledge is what Santos (2007b) calls 'action-with-*clinamen*' (p. 40), which 'does not refuse the past; on the contrary, it assumes and redeems the past by the way it swerves from it' (p. 41). In claiming a commitment to the radical co-habitus, ICT is fully engaged in such ecology of knowledge, and the challenge of an itinerant curriculum theorist is to 'unpuzzle' the nexus of physical–metaphysical. Eagleton (1990, 45) argues that co-habitus implies a just 'constellation' of a diverse plethora of onto-epistemological rivers. Drawing on Adorno's negative dialectics reason, Eagleton (1990, 45) advocates 'constellation as a [political] commitment to avoid an oppressive totality'. Co-habitus is a sine qua non condition of an itinerant 'theory-state'; it reflects a just itinerant genealogy of theories;

it is not a mere subtraction or addition of an infinite onto-epistemological multitude of the Global North and South but a commitment to a just co-habitus of constellations that open the veins of conventional hegemonic and counter-hegemonic 'disciplinary norms and consequently of their context' (Wolf, 2011, 35). ICT is thus to 'theorize [non-derivativelly] about theory' (Eagleton, 1990, 24).

We are bodies, not institutions, although a schizophrenic system institutionalizes us. Our task is to unmask why we do not teach this and how we can teach this. This 'this' is not just physical; it is also metaphysical (Paraskeva, 2023a). In that sense, ICT is an ethical take. I argue that ICT pushes above and beyond post-abyssality towards a non-abyssal punctum since it challenges the modern Western cult of abyssal thinking and attempts to dilute such fictional vacuum between the lines. ICT is not just an act of resistance but of re-existence (Walsh and Mignolo, 2018) at the metaphysical level. ICT is undeniable, I reiterate, an epistemological declaration of liberation, freedom and independence (Paraskeva, 2019; 2023b); ICT is a non-aligned theory or the non-aligned epistemological matrix of the itinerant intellectual. It is a 'liberated zone' (Santos, 2018, 31). In this sense, ICT is a dis/positional thinking concerned 'for viewing educational phenomena from alternative perspectives that are not method driven, but instead derived from insights of a disposition that seeks to disentangle scholarship from its traditional dependence on formalities' (Reynolds and Webber, 2016, 5–6).

The struggle against modern Western abyssal thinking is not just a policy matter. It is also above and beyond that. It is an existential and spiritual question so eloquently advocated by Huebner (1966; 1959) and Macdonald (1966a; 1966b) last century. As I keep arguing, Huebner was indeed the *avant la lettre* intellectual, advocating, among other crucial issues, for the urgent need for a new language to dissect educational phenomena. In Huebner's (1966; 1959) terms, such 'abyssality' is trapped within a dangerous eugenic despotic anthropocentric semiology. In one of his more brilliant works (1966), he insisted that curriculum language is immersed in two tyrannical myths: 'One is that of learning – the other that of purpose, almost magical elements the curriculum worker is afraid to ignore, let alone question' (p. 10). He argues that 'learning is merely a postulated concept, not a reality, and objectives are not always needed for educational planning' (p. 10). For Huebner, the major problem in the world of education, 'which has been short-circuited by behavioral objectives, sciences, and learning theory, was the fact that we were not dealing with the autobiography, we were not dealing with life and inspiration' (Huebner, 2002, Tape 1). The language of education is full of 'dangerous and non-recognized [and unchallenged] myths' (Huebner, 1966, 9), which makes it impossible to question whether the 'technologists maybe were going in the wrong direction' (Huebner, 2002, Tape 1). This becomes much more complex and alarming in a society that is facing the fact that 'the problem is no longer one of explaining change, but of explaining nonchange' (Huebner, 1967, 174) and that a human being, by his transcendent condition, 'has the capacity to transcend what he is to become, something that he is not' (p. 174). Furthermore,

> For centuries the poet has sung of his near infinitudes; the theologian has preached of his depravity and hinted at his participation in the divine; the philosopher has struggled to encompass him in his systems, only to have him repeatedly escape; the novelist and dramatist have captured his fleeting moments of pain and purity in

> never-to-be-forgotten aesthetic forms; and the [man] engaged in the curriculum has the temerity to reduce this being to a single term – learner. (Huebner, 1966, 10)

However, as I argued before, the struggle against the Western Cartesian model cannot signify substituting the Cartesian model for another one. Also, the task is to refrain from dominating such a model or to rap with a more Eurocentric humanistic impulse. The task is to pronounce its last words and to prepare its remains for a respectful funeral. The task is not to change the language and concepts, although that is crucial. The task is to terminate a particular hegemonic geography of knowledge, which promotes epistemological euthanasia.

ICT's non-abyssality is 'informed by its epistemological rupture from the coloniality of power and disaffiliation with hegemonic dogma, a process that liberates our field of consciousness, opening the way for resurgences of subaltern perspectives, new expressions of solidarity, and the powerful regeneration of that political force necessary for transforming the social and material conditions of our present existence – not only in the mind but also in the flesh' (Darder, 2016, xiv). ICT is a 'deliberate disrespect of the canon, a struggle against epistemological orthodoxy' (p. xxv), and it attempts 'to bring scientific knowledge face-to-face with nonscientific, explicitly local knowledges, knowledges grounded in the experience of the leaders and activists of the social movements studied by social scientists' (p. xxv). This is the very core of its nutritive faculty, to use Agamben's (1999) Aristotelic approach. An ICT is an exercise of 'citizenship and solidarity' (p. xxv) and, above all, an act of social and cognitive justice. As Žižek (2006) would put it, it is the best way to understand 'how reality can explode in and change the real'. ICT challenges modernity's deceptive dream (Harding, 2008). It is a possible – and clearly fair – way out of the madness (in many ways lethal) of modernity.

I am not claiming a way out that will please everybody. In fact, 'a coherent theory is an imposed theory which falsely mythologizes a pseudo-scientific process that has no more to do with real science than astrology does' (Quantz, 2011, 23). ICT is, however, a consequence of the perpetual lack of a dominant praxis of 'perfect just teaching and learning', as Tse (2017) would say (p. 284). An itinerant theoretical approach dares to violate the methodological canon. It attempts to go beyond some interesting (counter-)dominant clashes to overcome dead ends and screaming silences. Yet, it is an epistemological struggle within the insurgent cosmopolitanism platforms (Sousa Santos, 2008) inside and beyond the dominant Western cartography (Paraskeva 2021a). ICT is to delink towards a polycentric world, as Amin (1990) would put it. There is no question, Darder (2016) sternly claims, that the post-abyssal terrain of itinerant curriculum constitutes a complex and challenging political project, yet one that offers us political solace, philosophical inspiration and pedagogical nourishment on a long and arduous journey. ICT is against the theoretical imparity (Paraskeva, 2023b). It implies

> navigating dialectically the often-murky realm of dominant/subordinate relations of power. Yet, it is precisely by consistently traversing the turbulence of this dialectical tension that we become politically primed to ruthlessly critique

oppression in ways that prevent us from inadvertently collapsing back into oppressive binary contradictions, from which we must constantly struggle to emerge *anew*. And further, it is only through such sustained labor and unwavering commitment to denounce the epistemological totalitarianism of our times that we can garner together the moral indignation and political will to announce new ways of knowing, loving, and being – beyond the abyssal divide of recalcitrant racisms and neoliberal devastation. (Darder, 2016, xiv–xv)

ICT is a pedagogical path that relates to a just educational praxis. A just theory for a just praxis (Stenhouse, 1981). ICT is 'itself a praxis' (Reckwitz, 2023, p. 11), that understands that 'there is no such uncertainty as sure thing' (Burns,1994). In this regard, an itinerant theoretical path is without floodgates because the best sentinels always have no floodgates (Couto, 2008). In so doing, the ICT honours a legacy of accomplishments and frustrations, understanding that delinking will always be to make theory a just theory. To delink and decolonize while honouring the legacy of the radical critical path and taking it to a different level is also a decolonial attempt 'to do critical theory' (Kellner, 1989, 2). Respecting the legacy of such a generation of the utopia (Paraskeva, 2021a; 2022d), such decolonial attempt needs cannot ignore the rich legacy of such a group of phenomenal utopists and needs to keep swimming through a radical critical river while reaching out and recognizing endless tributaries and other rivers and tributaries beyond the river bed of such modern Western Eurocentric river and, in doing so, produce a new logic towards a new needed utopia. ICT is a just way 'to problematize and rethink consciousness ruthlessly or to *begin anew*, by way of our subaltern engagements of Marx's unfinished political-economic project, to deepen and expand its emancipatory vision, namely, the liberation of our humanity – but only now through the complexity of multi-centered epistemological lenses able to withstand the ever-changing character our cultural formations and political manifestations' (Darder, 2016, xiii). ICT is a 'heretopian' theory (Santos, 2018). It is people's theory.

Let me pause for a moment here to clarify a crucial point. We must refrain from romanticizing the ICT. It is not a theory that explains everything. Its itinerant genesis only allows for a fair and non-derivative way of thinking and being in a world that is impossible without the 'recognition' (Fraser, 2003) and respect of multiple and infinite epistemological perspectives. IC*theorists* do not take refuge in ignorance, for example, in not speaking languages other than English – the 'Esperanto' of modernity and coloniality. ICT and its theorists meet with these other epistemological manifestations, aware that no epistemological and linguistic supremacy exists on any discursive platform. ICT is quite sentient that 'theorymometers' – and in education and curriculum, they are innumerable – cannot be drawn by ignoring the vitality and cognitive matrix within the epistemologies beyond the Global North.

Naturally, like any other theoretical approach, ICT faces endless obstacles and egregious challenges in a field that 'is not always magnanimous to the opening of new paths' (Huebner, 2001),[1] especially if these paths are suggested by marginalized voices from a certain elite-dominant and counter-dominant – that control the 'circuits of cultural production'. Richard Johnson's (1983) criticism unfortunately – and regrettably so ignored – also fits like a glove to given (counter-)dominant elites that, unable to think beyond the Eurocentric logic that underlies its divisive Prosperous reason (Henry, 2000), try everything not only to control such circuits of cultural production but also to determine the 'legitimate' and 'illegitimate' circuits, producing the latter as 'non-existent'. In Galicia, a famous saying goes, 'It is pointless to put doors to the sea.' It looks like the field is not – at all – interested in a 'complicated conversation' – at least in the initial spirit as proclaimed by Pinar. It is interested in 'complicate the conversation' within the limits barbedwired by particular Eurocentric epistemological territories. Such 'complicated conversation' – as flagged before, itself epistemicidal (Huebner, 2022) – becomes just 'another' form of power and control. One of the symptoms – and there are countless – which is by no means clandestine of the epistemicidal nerve that saturates this already ill-fated – kinda bourgeois – 'complicated conversation' is the alarming absence of caste as a segregating enzyme in debates on the curriculum as a public good. As I had the opportunity to examine in great detail in another context (Paraskeva, 2023b, p. 19) caste – which precedes the Empire (Ambedkar, 2016; Teltumbde, 2010) – is one of the most obnoxious absences within our field's solar system. Such absence, epithomizes what Jal (2023) calls 'freudian hysterical blindness.' ICT challenges the chamber fo horrors (Ambedkar, 2018) produced by untouchability; it paves the way for an intercultural inter/intra-political theory of translation (Santos, 2018; Paraskeva, 2022c), pioneering in the field a non-derivative Critical Caste Curriculum Theory (CCCT), at the frontline in the struggle against the epistemicidal nature of our field. ICT is a call against curriculum epistemicide and reversive epistemicide, unpacking the functionalist nature of both hegemonic and counter-hegemonic, Eurocentric curriculum traditions that continue to mistakenly confuse caste with class and race. CCCT is 'Dalit Chetna', obsessed with touching (Gajarawala, 2012, pp. 68–69), bringing messier material to the table (Elam, 2021, p. 611) and putting Dalit reason at the core of the anti-caste struggle through education and curriculum

The itinerant theorist, given his commitment to the radical co-presence of different epistemological perspectives, as Santos (2014) teaches us, does not 'hide' in dogmas or in 'complicated conversations' that are nothing more than a hysterical orgy of a musty 'rococo' language that not even those in love with baroque dare to subscribe to anymore – conversations that have only been limited to producing 'everything that exists beyond the North American curriculum registry as' non-existent. Its 'deterritorialized'/'itinerant' engagement paves the way for a healthy thirst against constructed silences, against the dangerous cult of the identical (Han, 2018) selflessly defined by some tribal magistracies in the field that grant themselves the right to determine 'what exists and does not exist', what 'is acceptable and unacceptable'. Doubting – or denying – the despotism of such Eugenic logic is, to say the least, grotesque, aberrant, so aberrant that it sinks into the meshes of epistemological blindness that it constructs. It is this egregious blindness (Santos, 2018) that offsets the imbalances of the Cartesian reason and that provides the possibility of making its existence compatible with the abnormality. We 'all' have to admit that it is not normal, among other things, to argue that there is a legacy of decolonization in the US field, giving examples from . . . Canada!!! Even though one cannot deny the existence of some historical and cultural proximities between these neighboring countries, it is undeniable that they exude clear differences – and that is why this trend is not very cautious. In fact, it aggravates the field's lack of alibi for some of its sociological absences and silences. It epitomizes how deep it is the epistemicidal nature of the so-called 'complicated conversation.' (Paraskeva & Huebner, 2023). Why is it so difficult for those who dominate the curriculum field to deny where and who introduces the notion of 'curriculum epistemicide'? Is it so difficult to obliterate the positive aspects of ICT? Very telling, of how 'they grab' Canada – to give an example of a decolonial legacy in the US field – but not in Mexico. The eugenics of the abnormality of Cartesian reason thus reaches its supreme point. The reason of unreason. A eugenics without eugenics. The decolonization of the field remains a mirage. The IC*theorist* understands that before the dominant and counter-dominant Eurocentric reason, the 'heart would stop if it could think' (Pessoa, 2010). The ICT is, above all, a 'co-habitus' of different ways of reading the world trying to destroy the Eurocentric logic that combines inequality, poverty, injustice, immigration, pandemics, environmental disasters, a logic that is calling into question the existence of the planet. What the itinerant theorist does not do – and will never do – is continue to subsidize processes and procedures on the river bed of a eugenic reason, which does nothing more than encourage haemorrhages of 'irresoluble clashes of incompatibility' (Thomson, 1972).

As we examined previously, Santos (2014) crafted this logic as 'abyssal', a logic that, when challenged, reacts violently using all the mechanisms to ostracize and censor. hooks (1996, 76), for example, was one of the heroines who did not hide in euphemisms when she unmasked both the 'right' and the 'left' in their struggle for social justice. Darder, Mayo and Paraskeva (2017) also torpedoed many reactionary impulses within the counter-hegemonic republic. Eagleton (2003) and Žižek (2009) were corrosive on the daydreams of a Eurocentric counter-hegemonic platform that has little else to offer and is limited to being a blocking force. The examples, though scarce, give us hope. Since it emerged in the field, the ICT has clearly moved with the hegemonic and counter-hegemonic tectonic plates, advocating a deterritorialization and a different non-derivative path, which naturally produces and is produced in different semantics. ICT is to think about the 'theory-in-itself' in a different way. ICT cannot be thought, worked on and criticized – because it must be criticized – in and by the old word. I repeat one should not romanticize. ICT is just an alternative path that forces deterritorialization and responds to the infinite diversity and differences of the world. ICT is an approach that moves curriculum theory beyond conventional counter-hegemonic traditions. Snaza (2014, 171) argues:

> As curriculum theory moves toward ways of thinking that diverge from dominant Reconceptualist work – for example in affect theory (Springgay and Freedman, 2012), critiques of Western epistemologies and their imperialist tendencies (Paraskeva, 2011; Tuck and Yang, 2014), and posthumanism (Snaza, 2010; Snaza and Weaver, 2014; Weaver, 2010) – the problem becomes, more than ever, one of figuring out how we can learn to think and act together in ways that might disrupt the neoimperialist and biopolitical control that has emerged with globalized capitalism. (Snaza, 2014, 171)

The volume that the reader has in his/her hands speaks volumes about the importance of the itinerant theory in different parts of the world. IC*theorists* from different 'nuestros locales' unpack the strengths and challenges facing those committed to a non-derivative curriculum theory and development, the transformative impact of praxis that reflects a translation theory, a radical co-habitus of both sides of the line (Santos, 2014). Contributors of the volume unfold different theoretical latitudes triggered by a deterritorialized nature of ICT and provide examples of ICT in the classroom. They recognize the need for just recognizing the epistemologies from 'nuestros locales' challenging any derivative manichaeist approach. Contributors of this volume epitomize ICT as a declaration of epistemological independence.

In Chapter 3, 'Decolonial-Hispanophone Curriculum: A Preliminary Sketch and an Invitation', James Jupp and colleagues draft a decolonial-Hispanophone curriculum as a Spanish-language, anti-racist, curricular-pedagogical resource that emphasizes indigenous, brown and black geo-regional traditions of Latin America. Drawing on the ICT Jupp and his peers unpack the decolonial thought manifested in historically specific and contextualized ways as an oppositional *cyclical counter-current* inside the historical arc of coloniality. The chapter ends advocating for a commitment to an itinerant, 'Sul-sul'-decolonial-cosmopolite *palavrar*.

Graciela Baum, in Chapter 4, 'Decolonizing the English Curriculum in Argentina by Itinerating the Curricular Landscape with Minds, Bodies and Emotions', excavates non-derivative approaches to decolonize the English curriculum in Argentina. Working on an itinerant curriculum theoretical platform (ICT), Baum insightfully challenges how dominant and counter-dominant curriculum forms reflect 'euro-usa-centric' *dictums* and argues how ICT provides the path to delink from the 'logic of coloniality and the rhetoric of modernity', disclosing the endless potential of 'border voices, *saberes*, feelings, and bodies'. In Chapter 5, 'Returning to the Cultural Foundations of China's Curriculum Reform: ICT and Confucian "Wind" Education,' Weili Zhao's diegesis unpacks the importance of the ICT and its interplay with some 'itinerant' critical axles within Confucianism. Zhao's curriculum's *caminãr* shows the impact of ICT with her research metamorphoses on 'explicating the cultural foundations of China's curriculum thinking and practice'.

José Félix Angulo Rasco, in Chapter 6, 'The Itinerant Curriculum Theory in the Chilean Context of Curriculum Control and Standardization: Toward a Constituent – Itinerant – Curriculum', examines the importance of the ICT to challenge the neoliberal curriculum and pedagogies in Chile. Rasco dissects how ICT brings together different and diverse non-abyssal perspectives to smash a curriculum platform driven by accountability, standards and tests, perspectives that place at the core of the educational and curriculum debates non-derivative pedagogical theory and praxis towards a more just society. In Chapter 7, 'Itinerant Curriculum Theory in the Turkish Context', Fatma Mizikaci unfolds her social-historical position within an ancestry legacy that help shaped her experiences within the dichotomies of the thoughts and knowledges of the West and the East, the North and the South, the religious and the secular. She draws on the ICT to examine what she identifies as the essence of ICT, which is an itinerant path to recognize the geopolitical and historically distinct differences and the role of our field in responding to such different differences. Mizikaci examines how ICT challenges dominant and counter-dominant conventional canons and responds to the needs and challenges faced by historical resistance social movements such as Gezi – that emerged as a democratic demand 'for freedom of speech, for recognition of cultural, gender, life diversity, for social justice'.

Jung-Hoon Jung in Chapter 8, 'Leaving the United States in Fear and Tears: Young Chun Kim's Lonely but Brave Scholarship as a Critical Text of Decolonizing Curriculum

Studies', examines the importance of the ICT in the Korean field and how it responds to the non-derivative struggle led by one of the most prominent South Korean pedagogues Young Chun Kim. In doing so, Jung explores the different metamorphoses experienced by Kim's intellectual *jouissance* in his struggle for a just education, curriculum and pedagogy in South Korea. Kim's struggle epitomizes sublimely not only an act of intellectual – transcendent and immanent – honesty but also the vitality of ICT as a praxis of epistemological independence, placing autochthonous epistemologies as the master key debunking the Eurocentric canon.

In Chapter 9, 'A Possible Utopia for Cognitive Justice: Towards an Itinerant Curriculum Theory as a *Deterritorialized* Critical Pedagogy', Rosa Recio explores how in times of injustice, inequality and inequity, it is necessary to mobilize and create resistance; dissidence and resilience are needed. Recio argues that the task is to delink and deterritorialize critical curriculum theory towards an itinerant path that opens the door for social and cognitive pedagogical praxis.

Inês Barbosa de Oliveira, in Chapter 10, 'ICT and Curriculum as Everyday Creation: A Doable Possibility of the Emancipation of Curriculum Theory', explores the ICT as an approach that opens a door for the theoretical-political dialogue in our field, recognizing and valuing everyday school life as a space of curriculum creation. Drawing on ICT, Oliveira examines the possibilities created by such an itinerant path towards the curriculum as Everyday Creation. Oliveira thus establishes a non-derivative dialogue between ICT and curriculum as everyday practice – a dialogue that has been taking place over the past few years, and its results are already being felt in the most recent production in Brazil.

Mekia Nedjar, in Chapter 11, 'Decolonizing International Relations Theory: Towards an Itinerant Curriculum Theory to Challenge the Endless (Hi)story of Coloniality', unfolds the potential of the ICT within and beyond our field in Argelia and in the Arab world. In doing so, she examines how the reading of the Arab Middle East in international relations is patterned by hegemonic international relations mainstreams framed by Eurocentric epistemologies and the role of educational and curriculum apparatuses in such a framework. Drawing on anti-decolonial and decolonial itinerant educational and curriculum theory, the chapter unpacks how the Arab Middle East curriculum and its concomitant syllabi are derivative of the orthodox canon of thought with an unconventional authority. The chapter also argues how decolonial approaches grounded on a critical itinerant commitment should be viewed as a just road map to diversity and emancipation of the region.

In Chapter 12, 'Moving the Abyssal Lines: Contemporary Disputes within Brazilian Curriculum Field', Maria Luiza Süssekind introduces an epistemological overview of the centred Euro-American abyssal thinking and its trends in Brazilian curriculum field, particularly considering that theoretical disputes label the field's DNA. Crafting from ICT as a way to overcome the abyss of subalternity, she concludes that southern and decolonized theories are displacing the theoretical lines of 'abyssality' towards everyday life practices, which reinforce the understanding of teachers and students as knowledge creators weaving nets from scientific, experiential and other knowledges.

In the 'Itinerant Curriculum Theory and Decolonization: Alternate Planes of Projection for the Global South, Africa, South Africa and Beyond,' Shervani K. Pillay explores how the calls for substantive change and transformation in higher education institutions are eminent. The chapter examines how South Africa is no exception to such calls, given its history of colonialism, which installed a single epistemological hegemony. Such a violation not only effaced rich epistemologies but, in so doing, also erased the ontological status of Black South Africans. Many attempts have been made to address this effacement, but many of these initiatives are fraught with challenges. The source of these challenges can be located in attempts that aim to facilitate change within the same exclusionary frameworks. As a radical theory, the aim of ICT is to provide a plane of projection that forces rejection of such irrevocable slippages. ICT thus provides an impetus for social and cognitive justice and, in so doing, compels us to reimagine and recreate a myriad of possibilities.

Omsin Jatuporn, in Chapter 14, 'Decolonizing Thai-Centric Curriculum Is Yet enough? Transgressing beyond "Currere" to Itinerant Curriculum Theory', unpacks the dominant educational and curriculum conventional discourses in Thailand, which are still under the virus of 'despotic epistemology' implicated in various forms of positivist-functionalist approach and technical-instrumental rationality. Drawing on Paraskeva's itinerant approach, the chapter opens with the emergence of a Thai curriculum river, articulating hegemonic epistemicide in curriculum studies and teacher education and arguing that *currere* for decolonization is not enough. The struggle towards ICT and praxis from the present moment is radically essential.

Todd Price, in Chapter 15, 'Curriculum in the Viral Age: Itinerant Curriculum Theory as a Just Path', dissects how through social media and the explosion of digitally enhanced neural connections, *virality* is the primary condition of our existence in this *viral era*. Virality is always everywhere, omnipresent. The chapter speculates what these biological and technological conditions of virality mean for life and what they portend for education and curriculum. In doing so it advances the role of ICT in addressing the challenges triggered by such virality. The chapter leaves the reader with observations, questions and considerations for further inquiry, again with the assertion that *virality is curriculum*.

Finally, in 'Itinerant Curriculum Theory: Contributions to the Study of "Education *in* Rights" in the Context of the Brazilian Public Defender's Office', Arion Godoy and Maria Cecilia Leite examine Paraskeva's ICT, in context of 'education *in* rights' advocated by the Brazilian Public Defender's Office. The chapter aims to explore the curriculum itinerancy traits designed and developed within the scope of the Public Defender's Office. It is a qualitative approach to critically examine ICT as a social and cognitive justice praxis. In doing so, the chapter scrutinizes dialogical possibilities between ICT and 'education *in* rights' and underlines the importance of place and local in the detriment of supposedly universalizing formulas. Finally, the chapter highlights ICT as a decolonial turn crucial for just curriculum democratic process as a fundamental human rights issue.

Note

1 Personal correspondence (e-mail).

References

Agamben, G. (1999), *Potentialities*, Stanford: Stanfors University Press.
Agamben, G. (2005), *The State of Exception*, Chicago: Chicago University Press.
Ahmad, A. (2008), *In Theory: Classes, Nations, Literatures*, London: Verso.
Alba, A. (1999), 'Curriculum and Society. Rethinking the Link', *International Review of Education*, 45 (5/6): 479–90.
Al-L-Ahmad, J. (1984), *Occidentosis. A Plague from the West*, Iran: Mizten Press.
Ambedkar, B. (2018), *The Annihilation of Caste*, Triplicane: MJ Publishers/ Moven Books.
Amin, S. (1990), *Delinking: Towards a Polycentric World*, London: Zedbooks.
Anyon, J. (1997), *Ghetto Schooling: A Political Economy of Urban Education*, New York: Teachers College Press.
Anzaldua, G. (2007), *Borderlands. La Frontera. The New Mestiza*, San Francisco: Aunt Lute Books.
Appadurai, A. (1996), *Modernity at Large*, Minneapolis: University of Minnesota Press.
Apple, M. (1979), *Ideology and Curriculum*, New York: Routledge.
Auge, M. (1994, 2003), *Não-Lugares: introdução a uma antropologia da supermodernidade*, Campinas: Papirus Editora.
Badiou, A. (2011), 'The Democratic Emblem', In A. Ellen (ed.), *Democracy in What State?*, 6–15, New York: Columbia University Press.
Baker, B. (2009), *New Curriculum History*, Rotterdam: Sense Publishers.
Bauman, Z. (1998), *Globalization. The Human Consequences*, London: Blackwell Publishers.
Benhabib, S. (1986), *Critique, Norm, and Utopia: A Study of the Foundations of Critical Theory*, New York: Columbia University Press.
Berardi, 'F. Bifo (2012), *The Uprising. On Poetry and Finance*, Los Angeles: SemiotextI.
Burns, R. (1994), *The Collected Poems of Robert Burns*. New York: Wordsworth Editions.
Cabral, A. (1969), 'The Weapon of Theory', in A. Cabral, (ed.), *Revolution in Guine Bissau*, 90–111, New York: Monthly Review.
Couto, M. (2008), *Terra Sonâmbula*, Lisboa: Leya.
Dabashi, H. (2015), *Can Non-Europeans Think?* London: Zed Books.
Darder, A. (1991), *Culture and the Power in the Classroom*, Boulder: Paradigm.
Darder, A. (2016), 'Ruthlessness and the Forging of Liberatory Epistemologies: An Arduous Journey', in J. Paraskeva, *Curriculum Epistemicides*, ix–xvi, New York: Routledge.
Darder, A., P. Mayo and J. M. Paraskeva (2017), 'The Internationalization of Critical Pedagogy: An Introduction', in A. Darder, P. Mayo and J. M. Paraskeva (eds), *International Critical Pedagogy Reader*, 1–14, New York: Routledge.
Deleuze, G. (1990), *Pourparlers*, Paris: Les Editions de Minuit.
Deleuze, G. (1995), *The Logic of Sense*, New York: Columbia University Press.
Deleuze, G. and F. Guattari (1987), *A Thousand Plateaus. Capitalism and Schizophrenia*, Minneapolis: The University of Minnesota Press.
Dewey, J. (1933), 'Dewey Outlines Utopian Schools', *New York Times*, April 23, 7.
Diop, C. (1987), *Precolonial Black Africa*, Chicago: Lawrence Hill Books.
Docherty, Th. (1996), *After Theory*, Edinburgh: Edinburgh University Press.
Dussel, E. (1995), *Philosophy of Liberation*, Eugene: Wipf & Stock.
Eagleton, T. (1990), *The Significance of Theory*, Oxford: Backwell.
Eagleton, T. (2003), *After Theory*, New York: Basic Books.

Eagleton, T. (2015), *Hope without Optimism*, New Haven: Yale University Press.
Eco, U. (1984), *Proscript to the Name of the Rose*, New York: Harcourt, Brace and Jovanovich.
Elam, J. D. (2021), 'Conscience and Conscious in the Global South: B.R. Ambedkar, Kwame Nkrumah, and Anticolonial Sociology', *Comparative Literature Studies*, 58 (3): 604–22.
Elliot, J. and D. Attridge (2011), 'Introduction; Theory Nine Lives', in J. Elliott and D. Attridge (eds), *Theory after Theory*, 1–33, New York: Routledge.
Ellsworth, E. (1989), 'Why Doesn't This Feel Empowering? Working through the Repressive Myths of Critical Pedagogy', *Harvard Educational Review*, 59 (3): 297–324.
Fanon, F. (1967), *Black Skins, White Masks*, New York: Grove Press.
Foucault, M. (1973), *The Order of Things*, New York: Vintage Books.
Foucault, M. (1982), 'The Subject and Power', *Critical Inquiry*, 8 (4): 777–95.
Fraser, N. (1997), *Justice Interrupts. Critical Reflections on the "Postcolonialist" Condition*, New York: Routledge.
Fraser, N. (2003), 'Social Justice in the Age of Identity Politics: Redistribution, Recognition, and Participation', in N. Fraser and A. Honneth (eds), *Redistribution or Recognition? A Political Exchange*, 7–109, London: Verso.
Fukouka, M. (2022), *The Dragonfly will be the Messiah*, New York: Penguin Books.
Gajarawala, T. J. (2012), *Untouchable Fictions: Literary Realism and the Crisis of Caste*, New York: Fordham University Press.
Galeano, E. (1997), *Open Veins of Latin America. Five Centuries of Pillage of a Continent*, New York: Monthly Review Press.
Ghosh, R. (2016), 'Introduction. Thinking across Continents', in R. Ghosh and J. Miller (eds), *Thinking Literature Across Continents*, 1–8, Durham: Duke University Press.
Gil, J. (1998), *Metamorphoses of the Body*, Minneapolis: University of Minnesota Press.
Gil, J. (2009), *Em Busca da Identidade. O Desnorte* [*In Search of Identity. The Bewilderment*], Lisboa: Relógio D'Água.
Gil, J. (2010), *O Devir-Eu de Fernando Pessoa*, Lisboa: Relógio D'Água.
Gil, J. (2018), *Caos e Ritmo*, Lisboa: Relógio D'Água.
Giroux, H. (1981), *Ideology, Culture and the Process of Schooling*, Temple. University of Philadelphia Press.
Giroux, H. (2015), *Dangerous Thinking in the Age of the New Authoritarianism*, Abingdon: Routledge Publishers
Gough, N. (2000), 'Locating Curriculum Studies in the Global Village', *Journal of Curriculum Studies*, 32 (2): 329–42.
Han, B. C. (2018), *A Expulsão do Outro*, Lisboa: Relógio D'Água.
Harding, S. (2008), *Sciences from Bellow: Feminisms, Postcolonialities, and Modernities*, Durham: Duke University Press.
Hardt, M. and T. Negri (2000), *Empire*, Cambridge, MA: Harvard University Press.
Harvey, D. (1998), 'What's Green and Makes the Environment Go Round?', in F. Jameson and M. Miyoshi (eds), *The Cultures of Globalization. Post-Contemporary Interventions*, 327–55, Durham: Duke University Press.
Henry, P. (2000), *The Caliban Reason*, New York: Routledge.
hooks, b. (1996), *Class Matters*, New York: Routledge.
Huebner, D. (1959), *From Classroom Action to Educational Outcomes. An Exploration in Educational Theory*, Madison: University of Wisconsin.
Huebner, D. (1966), 'Curricular Language and Classroom Meanings', in J. Macdonald and R. Leeper (eds), *Language and Meaning*, 8–26, Washington: ASCD.

Huebner, D. (1967), 'Curriculum as Concern of Man's Temporality', *Theory into Practice*, 6 (4): 172–9.
Huebner, D. (1976), 'The Moribund Curriculum Field: It's Wake and Our Work', *Curriculum Inquiry*, 6 (2): 153–67.
Huebner, D. (2001), Personal e-mail correspondence Dwayne E. Huebner and João M. Paraskeva.
Huebner, D. (2002), Tape # 1, recorded at 3718 Seminary Rd, Alexandria, VA 22304. Washington, USA.
Huebner, D. (2022), 'A Foreword. Theory not as a Schema for "Acting," but for "Looking"', in J. M. Paraskeva, *Conflicts in Curriculum Theory. Challenging Hegemonic Epistemologies*, 2nd edn, 2–7, New York: Palgrave.
Huebner, D. and J. M. Paraskeva (2022), 'A Curriculum Afterword: The Dialogue', in J. M. Paraskeva (ed.), *The Curriculum: A New Comprehensive Reader*, 529–58, New York: Peter Lang.
Jal, M. (2023), 'Epistemological Untouchability The Deafening Silence of Indian Academics'. In J. M. Paraskeva (ed.), *Critical Perspectives on the Denial of Caste in Educational Debate. Towards a Non-derivative Curriculum Reason*, 257–328. New York: Routledge.
Jin, H. (2008), *The Writer as Migrant*, Chicago: The University of Chicago Press
Johnson, R. (1983), *What Is Cultural Studies Anyway?* Centre for Contemporary Cultural Studies, University of Birmingham, No 74 (Mimeographed).
Jupp, J. (2017), 'Decolonizing and De-Canonizing Curriculum Studies', *Journal for the American Association for the Advancement of Curriculum Studies*, 12 (1): 1–22, 1–25.
Jupp, J. (2023), *Itinerant Curriculum Theory. Decolonial Praxis, Theories, and Histories*, New York: Peter Lang.
Karatani, K. (2017), *Isonomia. Origins of Philosophy*, Durham: Duke University Press.
Kellner, D. (1989), *Critical Theory, Marxism and Modernity*, Baltimore: The John Hopkins University Press.
Khalfa, J. (1999), 'Introduction', in J. Khalfa (ed.), *An Introduction to the Philosophy of Gillen Deleuze*, 1–6, London: Continuum.
Kliebard, H. (1995), *The Struggle For the American Curriculum*, New York: Routledge.
Macdonald, J. (1966a), 'Language, Meaning, and Motivation: An Introduction', in J. Macdonald and R. Leeper (eds), *Language and Meaning*, 1–7, Washington: ASCD.
Macdonald, J. (1966b), 'The Person in the Curriculum', in H. Robinson (ed.), *Precedents and Promise in the Curriculum Field*, 38–52, New York: Teachers College, Columbia University.
Mallon, F. (2012), 'The Promise and Dilemma of Subaltern Studies: Perspectives from Latin American History', *American Historical Review*, 99: 1491–515.
Mbembe, A. (2017), *The Critique of the Black Reason*, Durham: Duke University Press.
McLaren, P (1994), *Life in Schools: An Introduction to Critical Pedagogy in the Foundations of Education*, 191. New York: Longman.
Merlau-Ponty, M. (1973), *The Prose of the World*, Evanston: Northwestern University Press.
Mignolo, W. (2018), 'The Invention of the Human and the Three Pillars of the Coloniality Matrix of Power', in C. Walsh and W. Mignolo, *On Decoloniality. Concepts, Analytics, Praxis*, 153–76, Durham: Duke University Press.
Moreira, M. A. (2017), 'And the Linguistic Minorities Suffer What They Must?: A Review of Conflicts In Curriculum Theory Through the Lenses of Language Teacher Education?' *Journal for the American Association for the Advancement of Curriculum Studies*, 12 (1): 1–17.
Nkrumah, K. (1964), *Consciencism*, New York: Monthly Review Press.

O'Brien, M. and S. Penna (1999), *Theorizing Welfare*, London: Sage.
Oliveira, Ines B. (2017), 'Itinerant Curriculum Theory against the Epistemicide. A Dialogue between the Thinking of Santos and Paraskeva', *Journal for the American Association for the Advancement of Curriculum Studies*, 12 (1): 1–22.
Paraskeva, J. M. (2011), *Conflicts in Curriculum Theory. Challenging Hegemonic Epistemologies*, 1st edn, New York: Palgrave.
Paraskeva, J. M. (2016), *Curriculum Epistemicides* [Preface by Antonia Darder], New York: Routledge.
Paraskeva, J. M. (2018), *Towards a Just Curriculum Theory. The Epistemicide*, New York: Routledge.
Paraskeva, J. M. (2019), '¿Qué sucede con la teoría crítica (urriculum)? La necesidad de sobrellevar la rabia neoliberal sin evitarla', Rosa V. Recio (Comp.), *Reconocimiento y Bien Comun en Educacion*, 191–230, Madrid: Morata.
Paraskeva, J. M. (2020a), 'What Happens to (Curriculum) Critical Theory? The Need To Go Above and Beyond Neoliberal Rage Without Avoiding It', in Tero Autio, Liisa Hakala and Tiina Kujala (eds), *Ajan merkkejä ja siirtymiä opetussuunnitelmatutkimuksessa*, 1–20, Tampere: University of Tampere Press.
Paraskeva, J. M. (2020b), *Justice Against the Epistemicide: Challenging the Putrid Silenced Schizophrenic Frenzy of the Identical*. Preface '교육과정 인식론적 학살 - 탈식민주의와 교육과정 연구' (Korean translation of Curriculum Epistemicides. Seoul: Academic Press.
Paraskeva, J. M. (2021a), *Curriculum and the Generation of Utopia* [Preface by Antonia Darder], New York: Routledge.
Paraskeva, J. M. (2021b), 'Did Covid-19 Exist Before the Scientists? Towards Curriculum Theory Now!' *Educational Philosophy and Theory*, 54 (2): 158–69.
Paraskeva, J. M. (2022a), *Conflicts in Curriculum Theory. Challenging Hegemonic Epistemologies* [Preface by Dwayne Huebner], 2nd edn, New York: Palgrave.
Paraskeva, J. M. (2022b), 'The Original Sin. A Critique of the Curriculum Reason: Towards a 'non-Derivative Critical Curriculum Reason', in J. M. Paraskeva (ed.), *The Curriculum: A New Comprehensive Reader*, 1–62, New York: Peter Lang.
Paraskeva, J. M. (2022c), 'Itinerant Curriculum Theory: The "Heterotopian" Logic. Challenging Curriculum Involution and Occidentosis', in W. Zhao, T. Popkewitz and T. Autio (eds), *Epistemic Colonialism and the Transfer of Curriculum Knowledge across Borders Applying a Historical Lens to Contest Unilateral Logics*, 45–66, New York: Routledge.
Paraskeva, J. M. (2022d), 'The Generation of the Utopia: Itinerant Curriculum Theory towards a "Futurable Future"', *Discourses. Studies in the Cultural Politics of Education*, 43 (4): 347–66.
Paraskeva, J. M. (2023a), 'On Curriculum and Spirituality: Itinerant Curriculum Theory and the Struggle for Non-Derivative Curricutum "Langue" and "Parole"', In R. Venturini (ed.), Curriculum, *Spirituality and Human Rights*, 2–57, Boston: Brill.
Paraskeva, J. M. (2023b), *Critical Perspectives on the Denial of Caste in Educational Debate: Towards a Non-derivative Curriculum Reason*, New York: Routledge.
Paraskeva, J. M. and D. E. Huebner (2023), 'Dialectical Materialism. An Alternative Way of Thinking and Doing Education', *Journal of Curriculum Studies*, 55 (3): 270–89.
Paraskeva, J. M. and M. L. Sussekind (2018), 'Contra a Cegueira Epistemológica nos Rumos da Teoria Curricular Itinerante', *Educação e Cultura Contemporânea*, 15: 54–85.
Pessoa, F. (2010), *Textos Filosóficos*, vol. II, Lisboa: Nova Ática.
Pessoa, F. (2014), *Livro do Desassossego*, Lisboa: Assirio & Alvim.

Pinar, W. (2000), 'Introduction: Toward the Internationalization of Curriculum Studies', in D. Trueit, W. Doll Jr, H. Wang and W. Pinar (eds), *The Internationalization of Curriculum Studies*, 1–13, New York: Peter Lang.
Pinar, W. (2004), *What Is Curriculum Theory?* Mahwah: Lawrence Erlbaum Associates Publishers.
Pinar, W. (2013), *Curriculum Studies in the United States: Present Circumstances, Intellectual Histories*, New York: Palgrave Macmillan.
Pinar, W. et al. (1995), *Understanding Curriculum*, New York: Peter Lang.
Pokewewitz, T. (1978), 'Educational Research: Values and Visions of a Social Order', *Theory and Research in Social Education*, 4 (4): 20–39.
Popkewitz, T. (2007), *Cosmopolitanism and the Age of School Reform. Science, Education, and Making Society, by Making the Child*, New York: Taylor and Francis.
Quantz, R. (2011), *Rituals and Students Identity in Education: Ritual Critique for a New Pedagogy*, New York: Palgrave.
Quijano, A. (1991), 'Colonialidad y Modernidad/Racionalidad', *Perú Indígena*, 29 (1): 11–21.
Quijano, A. (2000), 'Coloniality of Power, Eurocentrism and Latin America', *Neplanta, Views From the South*, 1 (3): 533–80.
Reckwitz, A. (2023), 'Doing Theory', In A. Reckwitz and H. Rosa (eds.), *Late Modernity in Crisis*, 11–26. London: Polity.
Reynolds, W. and J. Webber (2016), 'Introduction: Curriculum Dis/positions', in W. Reynold and J. Webber (eds), *Expanding Curriculum Theory. Dis/positions and Lines of Flight*, 1–11, New York: Routledge.
Rosa, H. (2015), *Social Acceleration. A New Theory of Modernity*. New York: Columbia University Press.
Said, E. (2005), 'Reconsiderando a Teoria Itinerante', in M. Sanches (org), *Deslocalizar a Europa. Antroplogia, Arte, Literatura e História na Pós-Colonialidade*, 25–42, Lisboa: Cotovia.
Santos, B. S. (1995), *Towards a New Common Sense. Law, Science, and Politics in the Paradigmatic Transition*, New York: Routledge.
Santos, B. S. (1999), 'Porque é tão difícil onstruer uma teoria crítica?' *Revista Crítica de Ciencias Sociais*, 54 (Junho): 197–215.
Santos, B. S. (2007a), *Another Knowledge is Possible*, London: Verso.
Santos, B. S. (2007b), 'Beyond Abyssal Thinking. From Global Lines to Ecologies of Knowledges', *Review*, XXX (1): 45–89.
Santos, B. S. (2008), 'A universidade no seculo XXI. Para uma reforma democratica e emancipatoria da universidade', in B. Sousa Santos and N. de Almeida Filho (eds), *A universidade no seculo XXI. Para uma universidade nova*, 13–106, Coimbra: Centro de Estudos Sociais.
Santos, B. S. (2014), *Epistemologies of the South: Justice against Epistemicide*, Boulder: Paradigm.
Santos, B. S. (2015), *If God Were a Human Rights Activist: Human Rights and the Challenge of Political Theologies. Is Humanity Enough?* Stanford: Stanford University Press.
Santos, B. S. (2018), *The End of the Cognitive Empire*, Durham: Duke University Press.
Saramago, J. (2008), *Death at Intervals*, London: Vintage Books.
Schubert, W. (1986), *Curriculum. Perspective, Paradigm and Possibility*, New York: MacMillan Publishing Company.
Schubert, W. (2017), 'Growing Curriculum Studies: Contributions of João M. Paraskeva', *Journal for the American Association for the Advancement of Curriculum Studies*, 12 (1): 1–22, 1–21.

Schubert, W., A. Lopez Schubert, Th. Thomas and W. Caroll (1980), *Curriculum Books; The First Eighty Years*, Lanham: University Press of America.
Snaza, N. (2010), 'Thirteen Theses on the Question of State in Curriculum Studies', in E. Malewski (ed.), *Curriculum Studies Handbook – The Next Moment*, 43–56, New York: Routledge.
Snaza, N. (2014), 'The Death of Curriculum Studies and Its Ghosts', *Journal of Curriculum and Pedagogy*, 11 (2): 154–73.
Snaza, N. and J. Weaver (2014), *Posthumanism and Educational Research*, New York: Routledge.
Springgay, S. and D. Freedman (2012), *Mothering a Bodied Curriculum: Emplacement, Desire, Affect*, Toronto: University of Toronto Press.
Stenhouse, L. (1981), 'What Counts as Research?', *British Journal of Educational Studies*, 29 (2): 103–14.
Süssekind, M. L. (2017), 'Against Epistemological Fascism. A Reading of Paraskeva's Itinerant Curriculum Theory', *Journal for the American Association for the Advancement of Curriculum Studies*, 12 (1): 1–18.
Teltumbde, A. (2010), *The Persistence of Caste. The Khairlanji Murders and India's Hidden Apartheid*, New York: Zed Books.
Thomson, Ph. (1972), *The Grotesque*, London: Methuen.
Tse, C. (2017), *Chuang Tse*, Lisboa: Relogio D'Agua.
Tuck, E. and K. W. Yang (2014), *Youth Resistance Research and Theories of Change*, New York: Routledge.
Walsh, C. (2012), '"Other" Knowledges, "Other" Critiques Reflections on the Politics and Practices of Philosophy and Decoloniality in the Other America. Transmo-dernity', *Journal of Peripheral Cultural Production of the Luso-Hispanic World*, 1 (3): 11–27.
Walsh, C. and W. Mignolo (2018), 'Introduction', in C. Walsh and W. Mignolo, *On Decoloniality. Concepts, Analytics, Praxis*, 1–12, Durham: Duke University Press.
Wa Thiongo, N. (2012), *Globalectics: Theory and Politics of Knowing*, New York: Columbia University Press.
Watkins, W. (2001), *The White Architects of Black Education*, New York: Teachers College Press.
Weaver, J. (2010), *Educating the Posthuman: Biosciences, Fiction, and Curriculum Studies*, Rotterdam, The Netherlands: Sense.
Williams, R. (2013), *Long Revolution*, London: Verso.
Wolf, C. (2011), 'Theory as a Research Programme – The Very Idea', in J. Elliott and D. Attridge (eds), *Theory After Theory*, 34–48, New York: Routledge.
Zhao, W. (2019), *China's Education, Curriculum Knowledge and Cultural Inscriptions. Dancing with the Wind*, New York: Routledge.
Žižek, S. (2006), *Bem-Vindo ao Deserto do Real*, Lisboa: Relógio D'Água.
Žižek, S. (2009), 'How to Begin from the Beginning', *New Left Review*, 57: 43–55.

3

Decolonial-Hispanophone Curriculum

A Preliminary Sketch and Invitation to a South-South Dialogue

James C. Jupp, Micaela González Delgado, Freyca Calderón Berumen and Caroline Hesse

In this chapter, we present a preliminary sketch of decolonial-Hispanophone curriculum and extend the invitation for a South-South dialogue between students, teachers or activist-educators of the geo-regions denominated 'the Americas'. In our sketch, our focus is on better historicizing work that is termed decolonial in order to situate it within historical-social movements that had material consequences rather than analytical frameworks monolithically termed 'decolonial'. By historicizing, we hope to save decolonial work from decolonial abstraction and academicism and reintroduce it to historical-material praxeology.

Decolonial-Hispanophone curriculum, as definition, refers to Spanish-language, anti-racist, curricular-pedagogical resources that emphasize indigenous, brown and Black geo-regional traditions of Latin America. To better historicize decolonial Latin American work, we provide a genealogical sketch of decolonial-Hispanophone curriculum from the sixteenth century through the beginning of the twentieth century. With the sketch, we demonstrate that decolonial thought is manifested in historically specific and material ways as an oppositional *cyclical counter-current* of alternatives, many times extinguished but also brought forward. Working through the sketch, we articulate three historicized concepts. We finish our chapter with an invitation to a South-South decolonial-cosmopolite dialogue.

With the intention of creating emergent transnational communities and social movements, our chapter responds to three questions: How do we historically frame curricular-pedagogical work in the Americas? Which intellectual and historical resources might inform our educational work within present-day coloniality? And, which historicized concepts emerge from the intellectual resources that can inform our South-South decolonial dialogue? In our chapter, we avoid presentisms and historical near-sightedness of decolonial 'frameworks' or 'analytics' and instead provide historical resources that permanently and historically transformed a broader historical panorama.

How do we historically frame curricular-pedagogical work in the Americas?

To start, we emphasize a few basics in decolonial thought. We begin with two historical concepts related to the Americas: historical colonies and present-day coloniality. *The historical colonies* were the model of historical-geographic domination from the sixteenth century until the beginning of the twentieth century. The historical colonies were based on occupation and bureaucratic administration of the conquered via military means. As 'first world system', the historical colonies emphasized economic relations of exploitation that culminated in the historical period called industrialization. By definition, the historical colonies were founded on military and spiritual conquests that formed the first, supremacist, occidentalist, criollx and European world system.

Tied historically to Europe and subsequently to US imperialism, the historical colonies imposed racist cosmovisions to justify the sacking of natural resources and the extraction of working-class surplus value. Differing from European social organization that established social class privileges, in the Americas domination emphasized racialization, especially in relation to enslaved, exploited or, as referred to today, 'cheap' labour. Of course, racialization was tied to other nexuses that included gender, sexuality, culture and language, and these ties accommodated Europeans, criollxs and Anglo-Saxons at the top as the directive and salary-earning class while assigning indigenous, mestizx and Black peoples as a changeable, itinerant and domestic service class. In this way, the nineteenth-century, Malthusian, political body assumed Europeans and Anglo-Saxons as always 'heading up' leadership and, at the same time, racialized subjects were assumed to be the directed social 'appendages'.

Undoubtedly, racial links to exploited labour adapted differently across geo-regions in historically specific ways. In Latin America, these racial links are particular to each nation and differ between indigenous genocide, racial-cultural mestizaje and the promotion of the transatlantic slave trade in the creation of 'modern' nations. Within differing national trajectories, racial nexuses with labour created an ongoing and persistent inequality that has a strong and undeniable presence in the present. For that reason, any historical-social analysis that diminishes race fails to comprehend racialized reality and its continuity. Because it recognizes these links, our sketch of decolonial-Hispanophone curriculum emphasizes and advances intellectual work that recognizes the historical colonies as fundamental bases for the critical reading of reality.

Coloniality represents the continuation of the historical colonies via processes of epistemological enunciation in the present moment. As 'second world system', coloniality continues colonial relations in the present in the production of disciplinary knowledges related to the financial, administrative, political and military knowing and doing. Inseparable from the production of knowledges, coloniality advances a programme of official educational-cultural knowledge production through the matrix of power (e.g. Grosfoguel, 2011). This programme of official educational-cultural knowledge production provides one key dimension of present-day coloniality. Through the matrix of power, coloniality organizes its changing, complicated, geopolitical hegemony. In the ascendance of this global hegemony, coloniality extends 'the first world system' towards 'the second' in non-linear but persistent form.

In this extension, coloniality advances the historical colonies, not through the means of direct invasion, occupation and administration but rather through varied strategies that include economic incentives, 'favourable' trade agreements, educational-curricular 'reforms', pastoral guides like 'free' markets and, simultaneously, violent official and extra-official military invasions for 'anti-democratic' countries. As part of this supremacy, coloniality also presents itself as 'first world' inside the 'third' as a spectacle of 'progress' while this progress serves to destabilize regional economies and degrade world environmental conditions. Following historical white, Anglo-Saxon, Eurocentric supremacy, coloniality presents the 'third world' inside the 'first' as a social problem. All the while, these 'problems' are results of necessary labour migration that is caused by the same destabilized economies.

More recently and with the political astuteness of Donald Trump, coloniality advances a US internal politics and foreign policy that is openly anti-immigrant, racist and fascist to maintain a status quo of racialized, systemic, international, economic white privilege and advantage while labelling immigrants as 'criminals', 'drug dealers', 'rapists' and 'murderers'. What is dangerous about present-day coloniality is that it has created an irrational, mythomaniac, xenophobic, racist and eugenic 'common sense'.

Inseparable from the matrix of power, coloniality advances a programme of educational-cultural reproduction. Differing from historical colonies, coloniality does not occupy or administrate faraway territories but rather predominantly works via educands-students through a programme of reproduction or 'reproductive curriculum' directed towards the production of conformist, accepting, consumer identities that comply with capitalist inevitability. This curriculum is manifest via various strategies including educative centres, competencies or standards, museums with official messages and other means that extend the supremacist, occidentalist, criollx and Anglo-Saxon cosmovisions. Here we note a clear example of coloniality and the reproductive curriculum in the standardized testing and its proliferation from the United States and the Global North towards Latin America.

Within these strategies, the reproductive curriculum eliminates or devalues mestiza, brown and Black traditions and languages. As an 'educational' process, reproductive curriculum imposes modes of modern, new, accepted ways of thinking with stamps of approval from university centres of the Global North metropoles. Moreover, reproductive curriculum sends another selection of 'quaint' yet 'outdated' knowledges to occidentalist museums as representations of a folkloric past heritage. Through the means of reproductive curriculum, coloniality reproduces an abyssal line between the 'inevitabilities' of supremacist, occidentalist, criollx and Anglo-Saxon traditions and mestizx, brown, indigenous and Black traditions that, through the abyssal line, are made non-existent (Paraskeva, 2011; 2016; Santos, 2007).

Additionally, before the same reproductive curriculum, there are different patterns of resistance and re-existent identities. Nonetheless, the great majority of these patterns reflect the same ahistorical, nihilistic and opportunistic directions inherent in hegemonic consumer capitalism. Notable and implicit in reproductive curriculum, coloniality operates through binaries of 'civilization/barbarism', 'savage/modern', 'backwards/advanced', 'underdeveloped/developed' and 'tradition/progress'. As the most general way of managing this binary, coloniality uses the duality of 'problem/ solution' in order to characterize '*un*-modern' historical conditions it understands as barbarism, primitive, backwards, underdeveloped or traditional. In this recent characterization, coloniality understands any and all disagreements with the matrix of power as a 'problem' that needs to be solved or, better said, eradicated.

Implicitly, the critical use of the term 'coloniality' emphasizes a *de*-linking with this supremacist cosmovision outlined earlier. This delinking refers to various strategies of resistance and re-existence, but it also takes place under the historical conditions enunciated by the matrix of power. Because it takes place within these conditions, delinking does not represent an autonomous and individualized autonomy as framed by the false freedom of consumer capitalism. Rather, delinking represents the search for structural, laboural, geo-regional, ecological and historical alternatives. These alternatives emphasize social justice, racial conscientization, localized knowledges, sustainable economies and the reorganization of historical regional knowledge production. Our main work here focuses on representing often ignored historical resources that are not precisely termed 'decolonial' nor part of 'decolonial analytics' but, nonetheless, participated in historical material conditions advancing survivance and historical material social movements called anti-colonial or anti-imperialist.

Which intellectual and historical resources might inform our curricular-pedagogical work?

Decolonial-Hispanophone curriculum values, studies, conditions and, above all, *historicizes* mestizx, brown, indigenous and Black Spanish language traditions particular to Latin America. Far from desiring to control the transmission of knowledges, we provide the following paragraphs as a heuristic-bibliographic outline of resources and possible directions that might advance a South-South cosmopolitan dialogue.

Such a dialogue supposes more profound, elaborated and contextualized research towards a decolonial archive adaptable for particular engagements and local activisms. Each region needs its own resources and decolonial histories, but also, we emphasize transnational-shared intellectual resources that can create social movements of the same scale as the monstrosity of neoliberal (now fascist) capitalism. Knowing that we work within existing historical curricular-pedagogical traditions, we understand our work here as continuation and critique of intellectual work that came before us. To begin the dialogue, we offer the following subsections: Indigenous intellectual production, brown and mestizx humanisms of the sixteenth century, re-significations of the Baroque period and the continued fight from dependence towards independence.

Indigenous intellectual production

Decolonial-Hispanophone curriculum values and conditions indigenous intellectual production, both historical and present-day. Integral to decolonial-Hispanophone curriculum, we repudiate the multitude of times that the Spanish or Europeans destroyed indigenous codices and other indigenous expressions (e.g. Díaz del Castillo, 1632/1992; De Landa, 1566/1978), and we recognize the instances in which indigenous intellectuals hid their codices (e.g. Recinos, 1947/1995), translated them for resistance and conservation (e.g. De Alva Ixtlilxochitl, 1608/1891; Poma, 1615/2013; Tezozómoc, 1598/1994) or *re*-produced them in present-day memory for future generations (Bonfil Batalla, 1988/2019; Menchú y Burgos, 1985; Posas, 1952/2012). We recognize existing collective indigenous intellectual production (e.g. Recinos, 1947/1995; De Alva Ixtlilxóchitl, 1608/1891; Poma, 1615/2013; Tezozómoc, 1598/1994), re-readings and contemporary oral histories from the indigenous archives (e.g. Caso, 1953/2014; Duverger, 2007; Garibay, 1954/2007; León-Portilla, 1961/1995) and present-day contributions (e.g. Marcos, 2001) as key to South-South cosmopolite dialogue.

We emphasize indigenous intellectual production, not to give it a better chamber in the occidentalist anthropology museum but rather to emphasize it in contemporary, present-day, critical readings (Bonfil Batalla, 1988/2019). Simply stated, we understand its study as inseparable from historical self-knowledge and self-determination. Our purpose in reading the indigenous archives is not celebrationist or folkloric like many of the national-consensual historians of the twentieth century, but rather, we approach these archives with the intention of informing our historical-contemporary understandings with understandings of indigenous resistance and presence in both the past and present. In approaching the indigenous archive in this way, we repudiate the US historical common-sense position that 'real Indians' no longer exist. Rather, we understand the example of indigenous proletarian resistance as a dialectic archive that requires an understanding of the past in the present and the present of the past (Bonfil Batalla, 1988/2019; Marcos, 2001; Martínez, 1976/91).

Brown and mestizx humanisms of the sixteenth century

Tied to our understanding of indigenous intellectual production, we value, but also simultaneously condition, brown and mestizx humanisms of the sixteenth century (e.g. De las Casas, 1552/2011; De la Vega, 1590/1967; De Ercilla y Zúniga, 1569/1997; Motolinía, 1866/2001; Sahagún, 1578/2006) that pushed, not for the extermination of indigenous peoples but rather for their continued survivance. These distinct historical, racial, economic, social conditions necessarily must be recognized apart from Anglophone United Statesian intellectual production that often ignores its own hegemonic positional proliferation that is very often understood as monolithic by the US scholars. Besides pushing for humanization, brown and mestizx humanisms narrated clear instances of indigenous resistance and pride before unjust forces of the historical colonies. Overall, brown and mestizx humanisms of the sixteenth century represented a nascent, problematic, incomplete, actual and still potent process that might be called transmodern (e.g. Coronil, 1998; Dussel, 2005).

This mestizaje continues to be important in the present moment because it opens an exterior space of interculturality between occidental and indigenous cultures. Always needing to confront the historical paternalism of the Catholic cosmovision, nonetheless, brown and mestizx humanisms with their social-educative experiments created distinct, Mendelian, syncretic, intercultural, transcultural and specific historical conditions of Latin America that are very distinct from historical Anglophone conditions often exported to the world un-reflectively by the US scholars. Some social experiments of brown and mestizx humanisms contrasted with the genocide, extermination, apartheid and exclusion of Spencerian white supremacy of the United States. We theorize the historical problematics of historical mestizaje in the final section of this chapter.

The College of Santa Cruz de Tlatelolco is emblematic of the brown and mestizx humanism of the sixteenth century. The College represented the utopic aspirations, limits, contradictions and sudden closure of social experiments deemed heretical and indigenizing by the Catholic Church and Phillip II's authoritarianism at the end of the sixteenth century (Duverger, 1987/1996; Ricard, 1933/1974). Founded by Franciscans in 1536, the original purpose of the College was to provide a trilingual education in Nahuatl, Spanish and Latin to cement a New Hispanic-Christian utopia based on an indigenous priesthood. With all the dangers and contradictions of the utopianism of Thomas More, the Franciscans and Bernardino de Sahagún underscored the teaching of language, culture and history in Nahuatl-Spanish interlinguistic and intercultural production. With this group of intellectuals that included Nahuatl trilingual students Antonio Valeriano, Alonso Vegerano Martín Jacobita, and other collaborators, Sahagún (1578/2006) produced his monumental work *General History of New Spain* and many other documents.

The collaborative work of the group attempted to render the Nahuatl cosmovision of the world in an interlinguistic and intercultural way that gave rise to a body of Nahuatl-Spanish double translation work that has not since been equalled in ambition or result. What the College represented for our reading of decolonial-Hispanophone curriculum is a model of radical interculturality inside which languages and knowledges are respected as educational-identitarian resources of the past towards a better future. Moreover, this intellectual production also supports the findings of Mica, second author of this chapter, who works in Hñähñu communities today. Through this work, we emphasize the importance of recovering ancestral traditions that can be leveraged towards alternative *re*-creations of the world.

With this link to present-day relevance, we emphasize that brown and mestizx humanisms represented by the College of Santa Cruz de Tlatelolco ended up suddenly terminated by the anti-indigenous politics of the reign of Phillip II that started in 1571. Because of this reactionary politics, Sahagún's manuscripts and many other documents remained buried in the archives of Madrid or the Vatican because of their heretical content. It was Joaquín Icazbalceta (1866) who rescued these documents and published them in his *Collection of Documents for the Study of Mexican History* and, therefore, promoted the radical mestizx ideologies of the Mexican Revolution, the Chicano Movement in the Southwest United States and other uprisings and decolonial movements in Latin America. In the end, brown and mestizx humanism, tied to social-educational experiments, presented future alternative avenues that were extinguished in the sixteenth and seventeenth centuries because of the oppression of the Spanish Crown and the Catholic Church.

Resignifications of the Baroque period

In continuation, we also recognize curricular-pedagogical resources of the Baroque period in Latin America. Overall, we repudiate the reinstatement of anti-indigenous and anti-mestizx politics, the Catholic Inquisition and the oppressive Counter-Reform. Importantly, we recognize the burlesque, historical and social violence and cruelty of this period that had material consequences in indigenous and mestizx communities (LaFaye, 2002; Phelan, 1970; Picón Salas, 1944/1994).

Following Mariano Picón Salas (1944/94), we emphasize the intellectual ineptitude of the Baroque period and the disconnection between the colonial leadership and the indigenous and mestizx masses. Regarding this ineptitude, the Baroque Period officially abolished the interlinguistic and intercultural impulses of brown and mestizx humanisms of the previous period outlined earlier. Again, with educator Picón Salas (1944/94), we emphasize:

> The general tone of the culture [of the Baroque Period] that the metropoles imposed was that of the complex of transplant. There was the privilege of an erudite elite that lacked any understanding of the indigenous and mestizx masses. Official intellectual work of the period had an exclusive and cryptic character. (p. 131)

Nonetheless, confronting this official epistemicide (Paraskeva, 2011; 2016), the Baroque period offered patterns of historical-social resignification that are not yet concluded but are important for future decolonial projects, especially regarding the reterritorialization of the United States by indigenous and mestizx populations.

Among several examples of Baroque resignification, we note two instances that exemplify decolonial-Hispanophone curriculum: (1) the Baroque cathedrals of Latin America and (2) the indigenous uprisings of the nineteenth century. Part of indigenous-mestizx sensibilities, Baroque Latin American architecture provides an instance of social-historical resignification of hegemonic symbols that became relevant to subsequent mass liberation movements. In Latin American terrains, Baroque architecture transformed itself into a Latin American ultra-Baroque style with strong aesthetic influence from indigenous ornamentation.

Specifically, in ultra-Baroque architecture, the indigenous and mestizx crafters, masons and sculptors elaborated churches, monasteries, sanctuaries and shrines for an entire continent. Paradoxically, while Catholic authorities tried to proliferate orthodoxy, indigenous and mestizx aesthetics and sensibilities were codified in stone, for the future, displaying different unofficial resignifications. With contradictions similar to the sanctification of the Virgen of Guadalupe/Tonantzintla in the sixteenth century, ultra-Baroque cathedrals not only integrated indigenous traditions and content but also, at the same time, indigenized and resignified the religious, Spanish and criollx structures by leaving an indigenous imprint on icons, symbols and aesthetics from the hands of the workers who made them.

Several examples of the Baroque architecture are the Sacred Cathedral of Mexico, the College of Jesuits in Tepotzotlán, the Cathedral of Santa Maria de Tonantzintla and the Cathedral of San Francisco de Acatepéc, among others. Here, we emphasize the importance of taking ownership, reinterpreting and giving other meanings to official hegemonic messages as symbol of resistance and re-existence before colonial extermination and epistemicide. These notions of resistance and re-existence exemplified in the Latin American, ultra-Baroque style are key to decolonial praxis in the present. These are key notions in the present moment because decolonial praxis does not represent a return to an idealized pre-Columbian past but rather a popular resignification of historical knowledges and practices in the present (Bonfil Batalla, 1988/2019). Resignification, exemplified in the ultra-Baroque cathedrals, represents a social, psychic, historical process of retaking official symbols that is a type of border thinking (Anzaldúa, 2015; Mignolo, 2008).

Apart from the architecture of the period but more radical, the indigenous uprisings of the Latin American Baroque period also help us understand the processes of indigenous resignification. The uprisings of Jacinto Canék (1761), Túpac Amaru II (1780–2), Juan Santos Atau Huallpa (1742–55) and Ambrosio Pisco (1781) provide examples of social-historical resignification of previously deprecated indigenous symbols of the colonial period. Jacinto Canék, manifesting the continued autonomy of the Itzá-Maya in Yucatán, organized an army of 500 Indians, declared himself king of the Itzá-Maya and tried to restore Mayan reign to the Yucatán. Túpac Amaru II, fighting against economic suffering in the Andes mountains, executed Spanish officials, organized an army of between 40,000 and 60,000 and took over the south of Perú for several years. Juan Santos Atau Huallpa, looking for a return to Incan reign and cosmovision, rejected his Christian education, threw out Spanish and mestizx collaborators with the Spanish Crown and took over the Tarma and Jauja regions, which remained autonomous regions until his death. Ambrosio Pisco, farmer and successful businessman in territories close to what is today called Bogotá, Columbia, directed indigenous independent troops and negotiated for control of indigenous mining rights in the region. Against the interpretation of indigenous inferiority, indigenous uprisings provide a permanent, symbolic, undeniable and important turn of consciousness that emphasized indigenous presence and protagonism.

This turn of consciousness is manifest in the autonomy of indigenous communities, the rejection of Spanish and European leadership and a recirculation of indigenous cosmovisions. Far from repudiating, denigrating or omitting the past, the uprisings presented a massive indigenous front organized by the representatives of the ancient Mayan and Incan lineages. These lineages recognized, integrated and actualized the indigenous struggle of their time. Similar to the Haitian Revolution of the nineteenth century on the Island of Santo Domingo, those uprisings were identified with much seriousness and fear in the governmental and metropolitan centres as possible permanent rebellions of the indigenous, mestizx and Black popular masses against the criollx and European centres of power in the capitals.

This turn of consciousness informs present-day indigenous sovereignty movements and also movements of autonomy exemplified by sanctuary cities in the United States that have defied the federal government in housing thousands of refugees from the Global South. The vision of the indigenous uprisings provides us with an historical framing of the necessary delinking that is part of decolonial praxis.

The continued fight from dependence towards independence

With the independence period, decolonial-Hispanophone curriculum understands the historical dialectic arc of mestizx ascendance and vindication as always incomplete that requires continued intellectual work and projects for the future. We understand that Latin American independence movements had in their very foundations the social, historical and economic contradiction of a governmental, Europeanized, Spanish, criollx and white minority. As much before as in the present day, this contradiction of a governmental minority has degraded the Latin American social contract and made political promises of the elite into a cruel joke. Because of these past and present-day contradictions, we understand that the fight for independence is urgent, as much then as it is now.

Historically, this minority lived on the backs of mestizx and indigenous masses with special reference to mestizx illegitimacy-bastardy (Molina Enríquez, 1906; Fuentes, 1962/1992; Paz, 1950/1987; Picón Salas, 1944/1994). Within these decolonial-Hispanophone resources, we recognize the revolutionaries' intellectual production as always partial, problematic and contradictory as they advanced the cause of independence from colonial dependence. At the same time, we repudiate the occidentalist, Spanish, criollxs, royalists and other traitors to the people who worked to block the historical mestizx identities of independence and instead wished for a return to Europeanized and criollx social structures and thinking that protected their privileges.

Key in the case of Latin America, we recognize that the assumed 'Independence Period of Latin America' was not a brief period of a single revolutionary war like the case of the United States in North America but rather an historical-social process with relevance to present-day coloniality. Latin American independence from dependence is still coming and it has lasted two centuries of revolts, uprisings and counter-revolutions. While Latin American countries became 'independent', the spectre of Yankee and European imperialism continued with the new faces of coloniality. Between the particular and contradictory instances that we can represent inside decolonial-Hispanophone curriculum, we very briefly emphasize the intellectual production of Simón Bolívar, Jose Martí, Manuel González Prada and Andrés Molina Enríquez as exemplary of decolonial-Hispanophone curriculum.

Anticipated in the curriculum offered by his teacher Simón Rodríguez and the action of other revolutionaries, Bolívar (1815/1997) understood the historical process of governance as distinct from European or Anglo-Saxon models when he emphasized 'the difficulty of prophesizing the natural type of government that should be adopted' (p. 92). Demonstrating similar thinking, Martí (1891/1972) emphasized an independent Latin American politics that warned against the imperialist 'giant who measured seven leagues in his boots' (p. 17), and he also underscored that 'good government in the Americas is not made by the one who knows how to govern in Germany or France, but rather, one who understands what elements make up his own country' (p. 19). Resonant with present-day indigenous circumstances, González Prada (1895/1997) recognized the historical conditions of the proletarian, diverse, racialized indigenous populations in writing 'one shouldn't preach humility and resignation to the indigenous, but rather pride and rebellion' (p. 166).

These four thinkers referenced in this section are representatives of decolonial-Hispanophone curriculum because they advanced the same turn of consciousness that begins to emphasize the importance of a Latin American cosmovision, both regional and transnational. Before this oppressed, historical and material reality, these four thinkers begin to elaborate a social-political vision that served as primary resources for critical Marxian intellectuals of the twentieth century such as José Carlos Mariátegui (1928/2007), Domitila Barrios de Chungara and Viezzer (1978) and Subcomandante Marcos (2001) of our time.

If we understand the Mexican Revolution as a second war for independence, the mestizx-indigenous thinking of Andres Molina Enríquez is emblematic of the four thinkers. Molina Enríquez provided a trajectory that recognized the Revolution as the material expression of the mestizx, brown, indigenous and Black masses. Studied notably by Agustín Basave Benítez, the thinking of Molina Enríquez is fundamental to the Mexican Revolution. Student in the Scientific and Literary Institute of Toluca founded by Ignacio Ramírez ('el Nigromante') in 1846, Molina Enríquez advanced critical and redistributive liberalism that founded the mestizx-indigenous turn of consciousness in both rural and metropolitan areas and that resulted in indigenous land redistributions of Mexican ejidos, always partial and imperfect.

Molinista intellectual production served to advance the need for the Mexican Revolution as the incomplete historical social justice trajectory that later brought about Agrarian Reform and Cardenista unionism after the Revolution. After having served in numerous governmental positions in post-Revolutionary administrations, the same Molina Enríquez woke up thirty years later to declare that the Revolution he helped create had failed. Molina Enríquez makes direct reference to Spanish-criollx coloniality and white supremacy that impeded the Revolution for which he had fought. Molina Enríquez (1938) emphasized:

> The Revolution has not arrived at its end, because the Indians and Indian-mestizos... have not yet made certain their freedom from the apparent 'superiority' and the perverse political action of the Spanish, of the criollos, and the criollos-mestizos. (p. 77)

Molina notes the cul-de-sacs and labyrinths in the liberation of the oppressed that are amply studied by anti- and decolonial intellectuals such as Freire (1970/98) and Fanon (1952/67). These intellectuals focus on defending the mind of the oppressed from the oppressor, and, also, they understand that the best weapon of the oppressor is the minds of the oppressed working with complicity on their own oppression.

Key to the mestizx-indigenous thinking of Molina Enríquez is to follow mestizaje's critical-historical direction and deny the doctrinal-hegemonic version that now is co-opted in official nationalistic histories. Specifically, it is necessary that we follow the social justice, critical, transformative and redistributive directions of historical mestizaje within specific terrains (e.g. Anzaldúa, 2015; Coronil, 1998; Rivera Cusicanqui, 2012) to reorganize transnational mass movements. Following these Molinista trajectories also supported by Bolívar, Martí, González Prada and other critical intellectuals, the archive of decolonial-Hispanophone curriculum from the independence period remains relevant to the South-South cosmopolite dialogue. This independent thought remains relevant because it is here that we find historicized, critical decolonial, transformative and redistributive understandings on a massive, transnational, revolutionary scale rather than reduced to ineffective academic squabbles. To visibilize transnational revolutionary movements, we emphasize the final subsection on communality/pluriversality, later in the chapter.

Which concepts emerge from the preliminary sketch?

In this section, we present three historicized concepts that emerged from the preliminary sketch. These three concepts reflect and, at the same time, should inform the use of and further research on the intellectual content from the preliminary sketch. These three concepts are: (1) the historicity of decolonial thought, (2) mestizx conceptualization and (3) communality/pluriversality. For each concept, we provide an example of curricular-pedagogical practice from Jim or Mica.

The historicity of decolonial thought

The historicity of decolonial thought is the first historicized concept that should found our non-derived, decolonial, South-South, cosmopolite dialogue. Importantly, our sketch requires us to recognize that decolonial-Hispanophone thought has a long and critical trajectory based on Latin American questions.

Far from being a new and abstract paradigm from the social sciences of the Global North, decolonial-Hispanophone curriculum emerges from a long tradition of decolonial thought in Latin America. Belonging to these traditions, decolonial-Hispanophone curriculum represents a series of historicized, situated and contextualized practices in specific geo-regions of Latin America that are tied to historical moments and movements. *Not* pertaining to another 'innovation' imported from cultural studies, critical legal studies or the reconceptualization of curriculum from the Global North, decolonial-Hispanophone curriculum moves us away from the so-called 'theoretical frames' of dominant social science production of US universities.

In order to better theorize its historicity, we advance decolonial-Hispanophone curriculum *not* as another critical counter-narrative. Although we identify counter-narratives as useful ideological resources, nonetheless, we recognize that these reflect and reproduce hegemonic narratives, especially hegemonic notions of linear time. Instead of proposing more counter-narratives, we understand decolonial-Hispanophone curriculum in ways similar to indigenous calendars for which the Aztec-Nahuatl calendar is emblematic. Rather than assuming progressive linear time, the Aztec-Nahuatl calendar assumes cyclical and dynamic wheels-within-wheels that can interrupt, change, destroy or renew epochs. In the present day, dominant and hegemonic notions of progress and historical development have to be destroyed. Contrasting with those, we need concepts of cycles, rupture, generation and renovation to begin the shared work of social-historical reconstruction.

Within this historical trajectory, decolonial-Hispanophone curriculum has presented other alternatives that have been taken advantage of (or lost) in the fight for historical, social, economic and political self-determination across geo-regions. We emphasize that the most important aspect of decolonial-Hispanophone curriculum, what we understand to be historical cycles or 'Aztec suns', is that decolonial radicalism does not present itself as a doctrine or set of knowledges passed down from Anglo-Saxon, French or German authorities, but rather, that decolonial thinking and work emerges from particular Latin American geo-regions.

Specifically, Subcomandante Marcos (2001) informs our project because he locates our contexts within the historical reality of Latin America, within indigenous and mestizx thinking and inside an historical cycle that continues:

> But it occurs to me now that the most important aspect of dreaming in Reality is knowing what is coming to an end, what is continuing, and overall what was started since the violence of the Conquest . . . 180 years after the appearance of Bolívar and Manuelita Sáenz, 85 years after the prophecy of the Flores Magón brothers, 80 years after Emiliano Zapata, 30 years after the dream of Che, dreaming of the revelation of all true an honest Americans. . . . The great oppressor powers have not found the weapon that destroys dreams. (p. 108)

The truth is that systems of domination and exploitation have not attained the ability to annihilate the enzyme of utopia from human cognition. Dreams were never the property of a determined supremacist, occidentalist, criollx or Anglo-Saxon genealogy.

In research conducted by Jim and his colleagues, the historicity of decolonial thought is present in his graduate teaching on curriculum leadership. Jim works in a state university in the border region of the south-west of the United States, Aztlán. Instead of giving the standard course 'Social Foundations of Curriculum', Jim has developed the course 'Cultural and Linguistic Sustainability in Transnational Contexts'. From engagement in this course, curriculum leaders study natural and social history of their region omitted in public schools and universities. Among other readings, curriculum leaders study texts by regional intellectuals including Hinojosa (1977), Paredes (1976) and Anzaldúa (2015). Through these regional curriculum leaders, Jim and his colleagues influence a geo-regional understanding of curriculum, and additionally, this group is collaborating with a local museum in order to finance the translation of historical regional documents dedicated to teachers' critical scholarship.

Mestizx conceptualization

Mestizx conceptualization is the second historicized concept that should found our non-derived, decolonial, South-South, cosmopolite dialogue. Decolonial-Hispanophone curriculum begins with the recognition that historical mestizaje is basic and fundamental to Latin American contributions to the world archive. By and large ignored or looked down on in Europe and the United States, historical mestizaje is key and principal to decolonial-Hispanophone curriculum's historicized, South-South dialogue. Simply stated, mestizaje provides primary materials of the Latin American archive, and we insist that the Latin American archive cannot simply be denied or wished away with Global North social science fads. Far from being a 'new' critical or post-critical discourse, historical mestizaje is fundamental to Latin American intellectual traditions.

Nonetheless, decolonial-Hispanophone curriculum does not begin with the celebrationist habits typical of Latin American intellectuals of previous epochs, but rather, we begin with an understanding that historical mestizaje is problematic. Emergent in the mestizaje archive, we take up the idea of mestizx conceptualization as a rejection of hegemonic-doctrinal, state-co-opted mestizaje. In this rejection and emphasis on located terrains, mestizx conceptualization seeks a restoration of historical mestizaje's Molinista, social justice, critical, transformative and redistributive capacities (Anzaldúa, 2015; Coroníl, 1998; Molina Enríquez, 1938; Rivera Cusicanqui, 2012).

Differing from hegemonic-doctrinal mestizaje, mestizx conceptualization does not refer to the transmission of an historical doctrine. In contrast, mestizx conceptualization provides for located, open-ended, hybridized, generative, curricular-pedagogical interactions that are not tied to European or Anglo-Saxon orthodoxies. This heterogenous discord with orthodoxies even extends to emergent orthodoxies within decolonial thinking in the social sciences. For this reason, mestizx conceptualization implies the use of shared linguistic-conceptual yet hybridized capacities to read and modify neoliberal, individualist reality in subversive, interpellative and collective ways. This reading implies making coloniality visible, studying its forms of production and reproduction and, in this way, also conceptualizing and verbalizing subversive alternatives. Through educative institutions, these verbalized and conceptualized alternatives allow for a geo-regional yet simultaneous transnational message of hope.

If we recognize that reality is made of words and concepts, mestizx conceptualization recognizes the force of subverting, appropriating, resignifying and influencing historical directions through transcultural, negotiated, historicized, unfinished and mestizx means. Therefore, it is necessary to work through new words, concepts, ideas; it is necessary to create a new language for teacher education and education writ large, a language that helps us think differently, in alternative ways, and, when necessary, speak through our silence. For this work, we need to advance mestizx conceptualization in the reading of multiple texts and historical realities, as we hoped to perform in our preliminary sketch of decolonial-Hispanophone curriculum.

This is not easy work if we understand that decolonial-Hispanophone curriculum takes place within the language and institutions that are historically colonial and supremacist. Nonetheless, with Freire (1970/98; 1992/2002) and other sources of independent decolonial thinking (e.g. Anzaldúa, 2015; Martí, 1891/1972; Neruda, 1950/85; Paz, 1950/87, Picón Salas, 1944/94; Rivera Cusicanqui, 2012), we understand that mestizx conceptualization represents not a small-scale or small-minded movement of academics so that a few have 'good careers', but rather, we understand mestizx conceptualization as a *social-psychic-linguistic-historical-esthetic-conceptual-and-territorialized* intervention that modifies reality. This intervention has to provoke a decolonial conscientization for the educator-educand.

Freire (1992/2002) provides us with the foundations of mestizx conceptualization that we elaborate in decolonial-Hispanophone curriculum:

> Therefore, teaching and learning represent moments inside great historical processes – those of knowing, thinking, and recognizing. The educands recognize themselves as such by coming to know objects and discovering that they themselves are capable of signifying, and at the same time identifying themselves as signified. This is the way that educands makes themselves signifiers in the process. (pp. 125–6)

Following the thinking of Freire, we come to the work of conscientization as a complex process, which today can emerge not only through 'literacy' as Freire taught us. Rather, this process requires a creative-and-open, decolonial, geo-regional, but, simultaneous, global readings of historical reality. Through decolonial means, we can begin to understand this historical process of conscientization through the term *mestizx conceptualization*, and in this way, we both *de*-universalize Freire's humanisms and also link him to racialized, decolonial, Latin American epistemologies.

In the research conducted by Jim and his colleagues, mestiza conceptualization is present in his graduate teaching. Again, working with curriculum leaders from the region, Jim provides critical, feminist, post-structuralist and decolonial texts to his students. In the process of dialogue, they also study the notion of historical mestizaje in various texts (Alonzo, 2020) with a particular focus on Anzaldúa (2015). In dialogues, Chicana feminist students achieve the ability to reflect critically, not only about regional oppression of class and race, but they also question the patriarchal reality of their lives as daughters and teachers. In these reflections, they share the goal of bringing this critical perspective to their teaching in public schools. Several of these students develop critical research as part of their studies, and these studies impact public schools and their students.

Communality/pluriversality

Communality/pluriversality is the third historicized concept that should found our non-derived, decolonial, South-South, cosmopolite dialogue. In speaking of communality/pluriversality, we retake geo-regional forms of communal organization that have been erased from curricular-pedagogical dialogue by the so-called 'global competencies'.

For those of us who have lived close to and participated in curricular-pedagogical communal learning, we can notice the need to link the commons (related to inheritance, the use and conservation of natural resources), the cultural (related to tradition, language, values and cosmovisions) and local economics (related to the political-educative project, collective learning). In linking the commons, the cultural and the economic, we find these elements necessary to recover the communal force that can provide particular empowerment, sources of memory and identity. In this way, communality/pluriversality represents a return to active social-historical resignification. This resignification allows us to take control of daily sense-making and reconnect with geo-regional memory.

In addition to the communal and geo-regional, communality/pluriversality emphasizes the analysis of the matrix of coloniality (Grosfoguel, 2011; Mignolo, 2008; 2009). Taking the matrix into account, communality/pluriversality cannot only advance via notions of isolated, geo-regional delinking as it appears in some philosophical or anthropological studies. In contrast, communality/pluriversality functions through a dialectic that works with local geo-regional resources (the common, the cultural and the economic) *and* links to transnational communities across the Americas.

Overall, communality/pluriversality forms a network that can combat and resist neoliberal and global forces (Marcos, 2001; Mignolo, 2008; Santos, 2007). In order to understand the limits of twentieth- century state socialism, communality/pluriversality advances a common regional network of understanding but at the same time represents:

> The collective aspiration of oppressed groups to organize their resistance and consolidate their political coalitions to the same scale as those leveraged by the victimizing oppressors. Of course, this scale is global, anti-hegemonic and global. (Santos, 2007, 10)

Having these aspirations, communality/pluriversality provides a dialectic that recognizes the geo-regional resources mentioned earlier but, simultaneously, forges connections with transcultural resistant currents in order to be integrated into a decolonial movement. Santos (2007) described communality/pluriversality as insurgent cosmopolitanism (Jupp, Calderon Berumen and McDonald, 2018; Paraskeva, 2011; 2016). This insurgent cosmopolitanism advances a local resistant network but, at the same time, an anti-hegemonic global one.

In research conducted by Mica and her colleagues, communality/pluriversality is present in her work with Hñähñu communities in Mexico. In community workshops, adult Hñähñu students along with their children elaborate on the reconstruction of collective social-historical, geographic, political and economic knowledges. In this way, cultural continuation is provided through vital social y educational space within communities. Through the means of language, this is possible given the circumstances and mechanisms of orality that provide meaning and signification in their community.

The invitation to a South-South dialogue

We finish our chapter with an invitation to a South-South, decolonial, non-derived and cosmopolite dialogue. In summarizing our sketch, in the first section we argued that the problem of curricular-pedagogical work must be situated within the arc of the historical colonies and present-day coloniality. Planting our work this way, we emphasized the need for a re-evaluation of historical resources that we leverage to conceptualize the work we do as educators-activists. Following this notion of re-evaluation, in the second section we provided a preliminary sketch of intellectual resources that we called decolonial-Hispanophone curriculum.

We provided our sketch, *not* to indicate that the resources we signalled are the only valuable *great books*. To the contrary, we provided the preliminary sketch to emphasize the need for a Latin American historical horizon based on indigenous, mestizx, brown and Black resources to found and suggest future, more specific research, destined to local-particular and transnationally informed projects. After the sketch, in the penultimate section, we presented three historicized concepts that reflect and simultaneously inform the dialogue we would propose: the historicity of decolonial thought, mestizx conceptualization and communality/pluriversality. In the trajectory of the chapter, we emphasized that decolonial-Hispanophone curriculum provides a geo-regional and transnational dialectic to resist global capitalism.

To conclude our work here, we consider the historical reality that presently stalks us. It is necessary to identify that ignoring present-day racialized coloniality is an act of intellectual bad faith, similar to blocking out the sun to light a candle. We present the rest of the chapter, including our sketch and the three historicized concepts, with an expressed subjunctive and dialogical tone, knowing that we do not have all the necessary answers; therefore, at the end of our chapter, we avoid offering the typical conclusions or the ever-present 'implications' of the Anglophone research report. In contrast, we finish our chapter by identifying a start, a start of a subjunctive dialogue, a South-South and cosmopolite dialogue, one which emphasizes geo-regional and decolonial intellectual resources to better inform our praxis with educands, teachers and teacher educators or educator-activists.

References

Alonzo, A. (2020, Junio), 'La historia del Valle de Rio Bravo', Invited presentation for EDCI 8338 given 6 July 2020.

Anzaldúa, G. (2015), *Light in the Darkness/Luz en lo oscuro*, Durham: Duke University Press.

Barrios de Chúngara, D. and M. Viezzer (1978), *Let Me Speak! Testimony of a Woman in the Bolivian Mines*, trans. V. Ortiz, New York: Monthly Review Press.

Basave Benítez, A. (2002), *México Mestizo: Análisis del nacionalismo mexicano en torno a la mestizofilia de Andrés Molina Enríquez*, 2nd edn, Ciudad de México, México: Fondo de Cultura Económica. (Obra original publicada 1992)

Bolívar, S. (1997), 'Carta de Jamaica', in G. M. Varona-Lacey (ed.), *Introducción a la literatura hispanoamericana: De la Conquista al siglo XX*, 87–100, New York: National Textbook Company. (Obra original publicada 1815)

Bonfil Batalla, G. (2019), *México profundo*, Ciudad de México, México: Fondo de Cultura Económica. (Obra original publicada 1988)

Caso, A. (2014), *El pueblo del sol*, Ciudad de México, México: Fondo de Cultura Económica. (Obra original publicada 1953)

Coronil, F. (1998), 'Más allá del occidentalismo: Hacia categorías geohistóricas no-imperialistas', in E. Mendieta's (ed.), *Teorías sin disciplina: Latinoamericanismo, poscolonialidad, y globalización en debate*, 121–96, Ciudad de México, México: Editorial Porrúa.

De Alva Ixtlilxóchitl, F. (1891), *Obras históricas de Don Fernando de Alva Ixtlilxóchitl* (Notas por Alfredo Chavero), Ciudad de México, México: Oficina de Fomento (Obra original escrita 1608)

De Ercilla y Zúniga, A. (1997), 'Selección de *la Aruacana*', in G. M. Varona-Lacey (ed.), *Introducción a la literatura Hispano-Americana: De la conquista al siglo XX*, 42–9, Lincolnwood: National Textbook Company. (Obra original publicada 1569)

De Landa, D. (1978), *Yucatan before and after the Conquest*, trans. W. Gates, London: Dover. (Obra original publicada 1566)

De la Vega, G. (1967), *Comentarios reales*, Buenos Aires, Argentina: Colección Austral. (Obra original publicada 1590)

De las Casas, B. (2011), *Brevísima relación de la destrucción de las Indias*, Madrid, España: Editorial Catedra (Obra original publicada 1552)

Díaz del Castillo, B. (1992), *Historia verdadera de la conquista de la Nueva España*, 15th edn, México, Distrito Federal: Editorial Porrúa, S.A. (Obra original publicada 1632)

Dussel, E. (2005), '13. Transmodernidad e interculturalidad (interpretación desde la filosofía de la liberación)'. http://www.afyl.org/transmodernidadeinterculturalidad.pdf. (Levantado enero 2013)

Duverger, C. (1996), *La conversión de los indios de Nueva España*, Ciudad de México, México: Fondo de Cultura Económica. (Obra original publicada 1987)

Duverger, C. (2007), *El primer mestizaje: La clave para entender el pasado Mesoamericano*. UNAM.

Fanon, F. (1967), *Black Skin, White Masks*, New York: Grove Press. (Original work published 1952)

Freire, P. (1998), *Pedagogía del oprimido*, Ciudad de México, México: Siglo Veintiuno Editores. (Obra original publicada 1970)

Freire, P. (2002), *Pedagogy of Hope*, New York: Continuum. (Original work published 1992)

Fuentes, C. (1992), *La muerte de Artemio Cruz*, Ciudad de México, México: Fondo de Cultura Económica. (Obra original publicada in 1962)

Garibay, A. M. (2007), *Historia de la literatura Náuhatl*, Ciudad de México, México: Editorial Porrúa. (Original work published 1954)

González Prada, M. (1997), 'La educación del indio', in G. M. Varona-Lacey (ed.), *Introducción a la literatura Hispano-Americana: De la conquista al siglo XX*, 162–7, Lincolnwood: National Textbook Company.

Grosfoguel, R. (2011), 'Decolonizing Postcolonial Studies and Paradigms of Political Economy', *Transmodernity*, 1: 1–32.

Hinojosa, R. (1977), *Generaciones y semblanzas*, Berkeley: Editorial Quinto Sol.

Icazbalceta, J. (1866), *Colección de documentos para la historia mexicana, Tomos uno y dos*, México: Antigua Librería, Portal de Augustinos No. 3.

Jupp, J. C., F. Calderon Berumen and K. McDonald (2018), 'Advancing Testimonio Traditions in Educational Research: A Synoptic Rendering', *Journal of Latinos and Education*, 17: 18–37.

Lafaye, J. (2002), 'El indio: problema espiritual', in *Quetzalcoatl y Guadalupe: La formación de la consciencia nacional*, 71–95, Ciudad de México, México: Fondo de Cultura Económica. (Obra original publicada 1972)

León Portilla, M. (1995), *Los antiguos mexicanos*, Ciudad de México, México: Fondo de Cultura Económica. (Obra original publicada 1961)

Marcos, S. (2001), *Nuestra arma es nuestra palabra: Escritos selectos*, New York: Siete Cuentos Editorial.

Mariátegui, J. C. (2007), *Siete ensayos de interpretación de la realidad peruana*, Ediciones Era. (Obra original publicada 1928)
Martí, J. (1972), 'Nuestra América', in *Antología José Martí*, Madrid, España: Biblioteca General Salvat. (Obra original publicada 1891)
Martínez, E. (1991), *500 Years of Chicano History/500 años del pueblo Chicano*, Albuquerque: SWOP.
Menchú, R. and E. Burgos (1985), *Me Llamo Rigoberta Menchú y así me nació la consciencia*, Ciudad de México, México: Siglo Vientiuno Editores.
Mignolo, W. (2008), 'Hermeneútica de la democracia', *Tabla Rasa*, 9: 39–60.
Mignolo, W. (2009), 'Epistemic Disobedience, Independent thought, and Decolonial Freedom', *Theory, Culture, and Society*, 26: 159–81.
Molina Enríquez, A. (1906), *La reforma y Juárez*, Ciudad de México, México: Tipografía de la viuda de Francisco Díaz de León.
Molina Enríquez, A. (1909), *Los grandes problemas nacionales*, Ciudad de México, México: Imprenta de A. Carranza e Hijos.
Molina Enríquez, A. (1938), *La reforma agraria*. Ciudad de México, México: Imprenta de A. Carranza e Hijos.
Motolinía, T. de (2001), *Historia de los indios de la Nueva España*, Mexico: Porrúa. (Obra original publicada 1866)
Neruda, P. (1997), 'Canto General', in R. Alberti (ed.), *Pablo Neruda: Antología poética*, 4a edn, Madrid: Espasa Calpe, S.A. (Work originally published 1950)
Paraskeva, J. M. (2011), *Conflicts in Curriculum Theory: Challenging Hegemonic Epistemologies*, New York: Palgrave.
Paraskeva, J. M. (2016), *Curriculum Epistemicide: Toward an Itinerant Curriculum Theory*, New York: Routledge.
Paredes, A. (1976), *Cancionero tejano-mexicano*, Champaign-Urbana: University of Illinois.
Paz, O. (1987), *El laberinto de la soledad*, Ciudad de México, México: Fondo de Cultura Económica. (Obra original publicada 1950)
Phelan, J. L. (1970), *The Millennial Kingdom of the Franciscans in the New World*, Berkley: University of California Press.
Picón Salas, M. (1994), *De le Conquista a la Independencia*, Ciudad de México, México: Fondo de Cultura Económica. (Obra original publicada 1944)
Poma, F. G. (2013), *Nueva crónica y buen gobierno*, trans. J. L. Urioste, Ciudad de México, México: Siglo XXI Editores. (Obra original publicada 1615)
Posas, R. (2012), *Juan Perez Jolote: Biografía de un Tzotzil*, Ciudad de México, México: Fondo de Cultura Económica. (Obra original publicada 1952)
Recinos, A., trans. (1995), *Popul Vuh: Las antiguas historias del Quiché*, Ciudad de México, México: Fondo de Cultura Económica.
Ricard, R. (1974), *The Spiritual Conquest of Mexico*, Berkley, CA: University of California Press. (Obra original publicada 1933).
Rivera Cusicanqui, S. (2012), 'Reflections on the Discourses and Practices of Decolonization', *The South Atlantic Quarterly*, 11: 95–109.
Sahagún, B. (2006), *Historia general de las cosas de nueva España*, Ciudad de México, México: Editorial Porrúa (Obra original publicada 1578; obra recirculada 1866)
Santos, B. de S. (2007), 'Human Rights as an Emancipatory Script? Cultural and Political Conditions', in B. De Sousa Santos (ed.), *Another Knowledge is Possible: Beyond Northern Epistemologies*, 3–40, London: Verso.
Tezozómoc, H. A. (1994), *Crónicas mexicanas*, Cuidad de México, México: Universidad Nacional Autónoma de México.

4

Decolonizing the English Curriculum in Argentina by Itinerating the Curriculum Landscape with Minds, Bodies and Emotions

Graciela Baum

In this chapter, I argue for the possibility and historical opportunity to decolonize the English curriculum in (the educational system in) Argentina. My claim is that it is high time the geo-corpo-political (Mignolo y Tlostanova, 2006; Mignolo, 2006 and 2009) conditions for settling said curriculum are in the hands of those whose aim is to decolonize both the contents and the terms that have historically operated, superimposing a modern/colonial racialized, gendered, elitist order. These Euro-US-centric *dictums* have permeated our field and forged copy-paste, obedient, anglicized and depoliticized identities.

Taking up itinerant curriculum theory (ICT) (Paraskeva, 2016; 2017; 2019; 2021; 2022), I claim that a nomadic turn to the fixed point into which tradition – both critical and conservative – has fettered us can become the *ligne de fuite* (Deleuze and Guattari [1980] 1987) away from all monocultures (Santos, 2006a) and towards multiplicity and pluriversality. Thus, a pedagogizing, critically intercultural (Walsh, 2009; 2017) curriculum that enables students and educators alike to see into the colonial pattern of power (Quijano, 1992; 2000) will disclose the potential of border voices, senses, *saberes*, feelings and bodies. Therefore, it will allow us to delink (Mignolo, 2007; 2013; 2015) from the logic of coloniality and the rhetoric of modernity, firmly setting a situatedly itinerant, popular and anti-meritocratic stance in line with the conception of English as a language other (*inglés lengua otra*) (Baum, 2021).

To this end, and in line with my situated approach, I first touch upon the double-sided phenomenon modernity/coloniality, dwelling swiftly on how this is perceived and received and addressing the 'decolonial method'; second, I briefly look into the role of English in the global scenario simultaneously revisiting and historicizing the colonial impact of Spanish in Abya Yala with regards to native peoples and immigrants and how this relates to English language teaching (ELT). In the third place, I overview the main points and some legislative cornerstones that underlie the Argentinian educational system to then move into a quick outline of the foreign language teaching sphere. Finally, I inspect ELT and language other in the local context.

A few opening lines on a somewhat biographical note

Reading into ICT in the light of the decolonial perspective, I have found the possibility of an encounter in and beyond both – an encounter of multiple voices, embodied differently, differently languaged and even dysphonic, dysmorphic in a very sensory and gnoseological[1] way. This would radically challenge our modern domesticated sense of likeability and consumability: our regimes of beauty and rightness. Along with such a turn, I can hypothesize an increased level of social discomfort and an emerging torrent of questions about the presence of alien, outsider (non-modern) elements invading our common sense and stability. There lies the key for ICT and decolonial education to start problematizing the known, the established, the instituted as valid, true, universal. *The colonial*.

Therefore, this encounter – I argue – is also a powerful alliance from, in and towards the Global South, since looking back to 1492 to trace imperialism/colonialism (and present-day coloniality) should urge us into the understanding of the simultaneous macro-destitution perpetrated in the constitution of the abyssal line of modernity (Santos, 2018), of the colonial difference in absolute currency to this day.

Hence, my research interest – decolonizing the English curriculum – is more than academic. It is *sentipensante* (Fals Borda, 1979) and has probably been with me since before my graduate studies; it outsizes, leaks and exceeds disciplinary boxes and theoretical boundaries. As such, it has travelled diverse and multiple roads where I have come across insightful perspectives which have nurtured my vision and amplified its scope.

Even though I am rooted in the decolonial perspective and feed on its inspiring genealogy of Latin American thinkers – where I have been intending to anchor my work – I am indebted to a long list of ordinary people and teamers apart from authoresses, authors, colleagues and thousands of students in whose company and conversation I have grown as a living being, understanding how much I stand in equality to all other living beings, human and non-human.

ICT has been one of those tenderly revealing lines of thought whose tenets bear such wisdom and handiness that – after reading thoroughly into it – I found I had been applying some of them intuitively in my classes. The journey into ICT has been enriching and, at times, soothing of all the injustice and pain caused by the deadly hegemonic and homogenizing inertia and anglophile bandwagonism that co-opts curricular views in the field of ELT. I was happily impacted by the amount of intellectual energy and political commitment around ICT, its vitality and dynamism; also, I contacted João M. Paraskeva – its 'father' – who in utter friendliness and solidarity invited me into this collective, horizontal, deterritorialized chapter. To him, I am profoundly grateful.

Decolonizing the English curriculum

As regards the English curriculum which rules ELT in my country and region, the collaboration I have been intending to make is a situated one – decolonial in nature and in dialogue with ICT, smoothly growing into a mixed, interpenetrating theory-practice non-divide where knowledge, being, feeling and living flow in the direction of liberation from oppressive, Euro-US-centric, canonical, suppressive forces. So, when it comes to decolonizing the English curriculum in Argentina, and I dare say Latin America, we cannot but resort to the so-called '*sui generis* decolonial method' to approach concepts involved in the design of English curricula. It – in the words of its creators – consists of the following three stages:

> 1. Showing its genealogy in Western modernity, which allows us to transform the universal pretence of validity of Western concepts and turn them into historically situated concepts; 2. Showing its coloniality, that is the way in which they have worked to erase, silence, denigrate other forms of understanding and relating to the world; and 3. Building upon this terrain the decolonial option as a non-normative space open to the pluriversality of alternatives. These are, in my opinion, the three steps of what we can call a decolonial method. (Mignolo et al., 2015, 130)[2]

These three phases accurately describe, account for and guide our comprehension of the flows (Mignolo, 2019) in the coloniality of power (Quijano, 1992; 2000): from (1) the constitution of Western modernity and its hegemonic coalescence with universal history, (2) simultaneously destitutive of all beforeness to (3) the reconstitution of an option that is an alternative epistemology to modern alternative epistemologies. On a regular basis, I see this understanding happen in my classroom: (1) dismantles the Western universal narrative and allows for the '*Aha*'-insight which is iconically voiced for internal sense sinking, concept rebuilding and awareness raising; (2) reveals the trick, the '*Oh*'-mind-blowing-helplessness of realizing how much of a double-sided, reciprocally constitutive phenomenon modernity/coloniality is and the impossibility to opt out; and (3) introduces the border seminal space that gets configured, the 'Phew-Ahh'-breather that conjures feelings, sensations and words of hope, re-existance and communality. It is (3) that can shelter our reaching out to heal the colonial wounds open ever since colonial epistemes – and scholastic/literacy trends feeding on them – formatted an imaginary into the existence of difference as inequality, that is, as superiority/inferiority. The superiority of those superior beings from superior regions (later countries) who spoke superior languages and who bore and produced superior knowledge.

Briefly surfing history back to the conquest, we can track and trace the role of the Spanish and Portuguese empires/languages (companions by necessity) in their 'civilizing' messianic mission in Abya Yala.[3] Modern languages have taken up said superiority as an inherent condition and deployed an active role in their utter greed for domination, usurpation and erasure. Appropriation and colonization through proper names (proper nouns) is but an example clearly portrayed in the denaming and renaming of Abya Yala into América. Modern languages (Spanish, Portuguese, English, French, German and Italian) have acted to the service of imperialism/colonialism: continental, overseas, transatlantic, global – you name it. The latter pertains to coloniality, that is, the impossibility of the postcolonial, of the outsideness of capitalism. This world order has enabled the ubiquitous pregnancy of 'the language of languages', a kind of superlanguage able to signify the hyper-heterogeneous subjectivities. At odds with any kind of justice.

English has overthrown all other modern colonial languages to eventually become *the* so-called global, international language (euphemism for less politically correct formula). Under these conditions, we argue that the teaching and learning of the English language to non-English-speaking people has come to (been made to) embody and enact a symbolic capital that articulates with colonial complicities.

Let us see into the matter. Globally, English is the language of power because it rules meaning-making; it governs scientific knowledge production in terms of its communication; it defines central and/or peripheral participation in business and finance, in scientific communities of practice and their legitimizing canon/standard. Therefore, English is the language of money: money talks English. For these reasons, it is the first (if not only) non-native language officially taught in formal compulsory education and by large the most chosen at university courses in Argentina, reproducing the self/other logic which is based on subordinate inclusion (Andreotti, 2011). It is locally required in its highest proficiency levels for most qualified vacancies and positions, academic and/or professional, at obliterated costs.

Those who find accepting these facts unproblematic – or who even thrive or pride on them – will hear no noise; those who see the complexity of such reality but take it passively and get onboard the fastest or trendiest train will silence the noise or ignore it altogether; those who see and feel the force scheme displayed and reject it will unpack the noise into words and face the conflict. Visibilizing and dismantling the coloniality of the English curriculum that reproduces and spreads these single-minded words (theories, underpinning dictums, views) and their Euro-US-centric bandwagonism is an arduous task which I have decided to carry out within and outside the classroom, using all available material and symbolic spaces to unenslave 'the enslaved minds' (Malcolm X, 1963). This is no mild challenge since our – and our students' – minds are permanently domesticated in English be it by mass media, social networks, supranational institutions, organisms and organizations of prestige; be it locally whenever we get caught and buy into the cleansed discourse of intercultural mediation (Meyer, 1991) or interculturality both relational and functional (Walsh, 2009; 2012; 2017).

In this context, how do we optimize this reciprocally empowering dialogue, this synergy between ICT and the decolonial perspective and have it permeate our field, studies, thoughts? On rehearsing possible answers a web of connections emerged that triggered further questions, mainly amounting to the search for cognitive justice in/ from the Global South in a strongly situated yet deterritorialized fashion. I assume that this concessive 'yet' hurries a herd of possibly delayed queries: How can we take a situated locus of enunciation and still hold an itinerant view? How can we opt for bordering (*fronterización*) and exteriority-as-home yet acknowledge the drive towards a deterritorialized symbolic South-based general curriculum theory and English curriculum? How can we address the apparent paradox?

Firstly, we welcome the itchy contradiction growing out of the binary mindset which battles the internal struggle. We sustain the need to take a radical grip on our land/*suelo* and people/*pueblo* in a (Kush, 1978; 2007) sense and vein and, along with it, promote an ecology of knowledges/*saberes* (Santos, 2006a), a reconstitution of ancestral and non-modern pluriversality that rescues *all* absences from inexistence, from erasure. We see the weight of the material and symbolic occupation perpetrated by monocultures that deplete the world from the richness and vastness of social experience by Darwinist reductionist atomization of hegemonic extractivist ones. Hence, we end up all wearing identical lenses to see reality. And let us grow aware that what is real cannot be reduced to what exists (Santos, 2006a), because what exists is the surgical result of the algorithm crafted by the epistemologies of the North.

English and the English curriculum in Argentina's educational system

English is in itself an epistemic monoculture linked to epistemic fascism and is also the language of the enunciation of the category system of modern life and its respective domains and monocultures. To reconstitute and embrace the pluriversal – I argue, following Kusch (1978) – it is necessary to first ground ourselves, stop 'fearing to be ourselves and think of what is our own'[4] ([*detener*] '*el miedo a ser nosotros mismos y pensar lo propio*'), root ourselves (*arraigarnos*) in our Latin American *suelo* and re-establish the dialogue with our history, stories and ancestry. Thus, we should be able to see the destitution, the modern/colonial disruption by Latin and Spanish languages first, by Castilian imperatives, to the added complexity of a transnational gloto-political contemporary scenario having been taken over by English. Full circle. Double linguistic colonization. Even if Spanish is constitutionally our official national language, the *pachamama* – whose depth has wombed América Profunda (Kusch, 1978) – would not agree. Therefore, back to the paradox, only by first rooting on firm, rich land will the rhizome be able to display its boundaryless nature akin to ICT and become the 'I am where I think' – let us add sense – sustained by decolonial thinker Walter Mignolo (1999, 235).

Our modernity – that is not *their* modernity (Chatterjee, 1997) – has lost track of its richness, wisdom and capacity to produce its own modernity, lending itself to Westernization. This also explains the historical continuous presence of English as a school subject in the Argentinian private and public school systems since the twentieth century.

Allow us at this point the license for a clarity brush to historicize the Argentinian political and educational scenario a bit more broadly to later narrow it down to English. Following Montserrat and Mórtola (2018), in the nineteenth century the Argentinian national project, in the hands of the Generation of the 1880s,[5] had been strongly monocultural and monolingual, with a weighty emphasis laid on the elimination of otherness and wilderness, that is, *gauchos* and indigenous peoples – their languages and cultures. However, the construction of Nationality needed the 'school machinery' as a most relevant instrument to indoctrinate the population into 'habit formation, content and value transmission; also being a privileged environment for the creation of patriotic emotional endorsement'[6] (Bertoni, 1992). Therefore, the correlation of the national project in the educational area lies in Sarmiento's belief in and will to achieve the unification of the population through a nationalist aim which would simultaneously Europeanize the natives and Spanishize/Castillianize/homogenize the huge European immigration flow and their various languages and dialects – identities. This, we need to clarify, to the overall economic benefit of large landowners who rejected both indigenous settlements and immigrants' cultural/symbolic capital preservation but were keen on recruiting them all into the enslaving labour system as cheap workforce. In this respect and lacing such political goals, the Educational Law 1420 (1884), to which we owe obligatory, public, free and lay education, echoes Alberdi's idea that 'to govern is to populate' (*gobernar es poblar*) – at the expense of indigenous peoples' rights even if education functionally included them – and Sarmiento's ideas on 'civilization and barbarism' (*civilización y barbarie*[7]) which to him – in his 'civilizational' gruesome zeal – was, in fact, civilization *or* barbarism. Whatever fell into the latter was due to be either engulfed/tamed/civilized (educated) or massacred. The 'Desert Campaign'[8] led by Roca (1879–85) testifies to both and materializes in the genocide of indigenous populations (*pampas, tehuelches, mapuches, ranqueles*). Back to Law 1420 that would mandate the scope and reach of primary formal education in Argentina, we need to understand the prevalent homogenizing nation-/state-bound drive that endows it with sense and purpose and its reliance upon dominant culture – Europe and the United States – which goes well into the twentieth century. From the first government of Irigoyen (1916–22) after Saenz Peña Law (1912 – Universal Suffrage) the educational system remained obligatory, free, public and lay, with an increasingly popular spirit during the Peronist government (1946–55). However, every coup d'état – 1930, 1943, 1955, 1962, 1966, 1976 – involved the attack or loss of acquired educational rights, whether public status, gratuity or the role of the Church. In this respect, the last dictatorship (1976–82) was key to the progressive dismantling of public education in favour of liberal policies. Since the return of democracy in 1983, education – not without struggles against anti-popular, market-led measures – has remained obligatory, public, free and lay. However, from the 1960s onwards, and *in crescendo*, the state moved into a subsidiarization role, and private corporate education gained momentum.

Narrowing it down to foreign languages, Bein (2000) states that in the late nineteenth century both the teaching of French and English held a most relevant fraction of the curriculum in spite of their 'very low quality' (Juan Ramon Fernandez' report 1903 in Bein, 2000). The author also highlights that from the twentieth century to the 1990s there were loads of bicultural deals to promote target cultures. However, the presence of English in mass media in the late nineteenth and early twentieth centuries portrayed the classy gravitation of the French and English languages among socio-economic and political elites; also, English was taught privately to cater for the needs of immigrant settlers' children at English-Spanish bilingual schools. British penetration in the railway and farming business – and the state interest in them – accounted for such special policies. During the last dictatorship (1976–82) the preferred foreign language was English due to the political 'collaboration' between Argentina and the United States. With the advent of democracy (1983) the decision was to formally teach a single foreign language among English, French or Italian though English resulted – by far – the most widely taught. The massive entry of the English language into the public school curriculum took place as from 1993 with the passing of the Federal Law of Education (24195). First, in the 1960s, its teaching had been slightly introduced but still restricted to primary education since secondary education was not compulsory. Later on, in 1993, it was – as I have said – obligatorily included in the curriculum. The Federal Law of Education having failed, the year 2003 saw the birth of the National Law of Education (26206) which was regulated in 2006 amplifying the scope of English teaching to primary and secondary education. In 2007 this was further expanded from fourth form onwards both in the private and public systems. All measures meant the scalability of English (I am aware of the business jargon) at the expense of other non-native languages in the curriculum, especially debunking nineteenth-century French prevalence and early twentieth efforts.

Thus, having almost entirely displaced French, English became THE foreign language in our country, which needs to be understood against the bigger picture of coloniality/modernity, mentioned in the section 'Decolonizing the English curriculum' earlier, and the increasing gravitation of North American power, culture and lifestyle.

Bearing the heavy brunt of history, I wonder whether and how we can instantiate a decolonial itinerant curriculum of English that enables students to keep their philosophical categories, that is, not being spoken and thought by and instead use the language to enunciate themselves, name their worlds and participate in the dialogue of thoughts, contents and terms. How can we guarantee that ICT and decolonial pedagogy embrace said curriculum and resist the effects of hegemonic, single-story power that uproots any kind of belonging except the 'global' one – synonym with the market. Marketinized existences become commodities, helplessly trying to survive oppression, subalternization and suppression. Teaching English in Argentina from the messianic discourse of access, development and achievement, invisibilizing the colonial counter-benefit involved, reinforces the conception of language as an apolitical, neutral instrument that naively channels messages – puts meanings across as if it were a conveyor belt. However, as I have long been trying to raise awareness of, 'the medium is the message' (McLuhan, 1964), that is, we cannot neglect the overarching power of language in this case, beyond the content being addressed. Even if I reject the idea of language-as-means to an end that lies beyond it, I also acknowledge that McLuhan's statement does counter that very idea by placing the focus on the medium (politicized, imbued with ideologies), on language as power, control and performativity. The trap is always round the corner: not realizing that the rhetoric of modernity (control over the contents) hides the logic of coloniality (control over the terms). Managing the contents (what is said) distracts the attention from the conditions of the enunciation (the terms), that is, who defines the rules of the negotiation of meanings: who is entitled to say; what is knowledge; what knowledge is eligible to be said; who it is said to; when, where, how. Yes, the medium is the message but, doubtlessly, not all mediums are equal, not all mediums exercise and build power in the same ways. English is a suitable example to prove so, for it will locally resonate with an aspirational, carefully bred desire to be(come) the Self, to increasingly resemble a subject that proceeds by othering the Other who has already set off into a process of self-denial powered by the territorial Ego. Such Euro-US-centric machinery feeds on the Western-white-andro-anthropo-Anglo-centred colonial capitalist belief system that runs counter to pluriversality and bio/ecocentric views. Instead, it works by extraction: extractivism is affective, cognitive, linguistic and cultural. It resembles the vampirizing myth of bloodsucking creatures that weaken and dry the life out of those whose energy – vastly speaking – they hunger for.

Thus, decolonizing the English curriculum sides with a reconstitutive practice that returns life, vitality, worth to the spaces from which they were destituted before the constitution of the colonial matrix of power. A colonial language that we can use to visibilize its own coloniality and denounce and contest its normalized and normalizing effects. Let us clarify this: that we should see – on the one hand – that what is presented as natural/normal(ized) (English IS the global, international language) is not natural but follows the same determinist fallacy as the globalization phenomenon (Santos, 2006b); and – on the other hand – that we should be on the alert not to jump into the normalizing ego-epistemic market trail (English favours equality by providing common ground) – from which we have been ousted even before setting foot on – only on account of an *overwhelming majority* opting for 'the same'. Let us be clear about this: the same is strongly committed to the production and reproduction of its sameness which, in fact, lies in the hands of an *overwhelming minority*.

Decolonizing the English curriculum embraces the liberatory principles that underpin ICT and its rhizomatic construction since it does not establish hierarchies of knowledge which in turn depend on or are functional to hierarchies of power. On the contrary, these principles build a centreless system which is organized transversally, concurrently with other systems in a creative, positive interdependence. Languages are the loom, the knitting needles for the social fabric we aim to produce, and – to my view – English is but one of them. Needless to say, there is conflict and tension arising from this non-monolithic pluritopic positioning, but we welcome them into the dialogue of minds and hearts – assuming social power is made of all that – and encourage the emergence of a platform to contest the Canon (English) and the silencing of the Other. The conception of 'global' English – permeating the curriculum – as geopolitical centre reveals the most insidious problematic: the control of meanings. A South-based curriculum of English that neglects, ignores or obscures its hidden and null scope to the benefit of its washed official and taught agenda will submit to being enunciated, to having its meanings controlled, to being the puppet moved by the puppeteer's strings.

Our questions and queries are manifold: Why teach English at all? What to teach if we choose to? Shall we cage the language in a grammar and sell a boxed instrument (in the shape of coursebooks) that satisfies/suits the global market? Are we – by doing so – taking up an internationalizing stance that turns us into the 'sepoys of coloniality' (Paraskeva, 2017, 2)? Can we obediently reduce the teaching of the language of hegemonic meaning production to a quietening set of rules to be graded according to psycholinguistic criteria and taught *in tandem* regardless of place, politics and identity? What is the manoeuvre behind? Haven't we witnessed enough evidence that language is power and that modern languages have behaved in epistemically whitening ways?

This is probably our only answer amidst a large set of questions: Linguicide leads to epistemicide. By letting the coloniality of the English curriculum go inadvertently, we are underestimating its destructive agency. A language dies a slow death – or rather it is slowly killed – and the world it treasures and manifests dies with it or rather is killed with it. But let us also erase the passive voice construction that English appreciates so much and is so much complicit with modern/colonial meaning-making and the actors behind. Hegemonic power – the centre of the pattern of power (states, leaders, institutions, policies, languages) – colonizes/controls meanings in a process that is parallel to the control of money (dollar). That responds to the greed for domestication and subordination into English and preclusion of peoples' linguistic rights.

However, languages are living beings: they breathe, grow, change and strive. They have and are memories. But the coloniality of power chokes them to death not before thieving their richness to its own content. English has played such a role, in the words of James Nicoll: 'English does not borrow from other languages. English follows other languages down dark alleys, knocks them over and goes through their pockets for loose grammar.'

Therefore, mine is again a question arsenal: Who do we teach English to in our South? What contents do we teach and in whose terms? Can we address our land/*suelo* and existential address/*domicilio existencial* in an alien language? Can we find grounding/*arraigo* in its sounds, rhythms, pace, words?

My answer is yes. Building a locus of enunciation in curriculum and material design that laces language teaching to the South in terms of democratized access, permanence and termination (public does not imply non-meritocratic), contextual relevance, conceptually located anchorage, ancestral knowledges/*saberes* and sociohistorical awareness and identity. A densely knit fabric that warms our bodies, minds and souls. An *aguayo*[9] in which multicoloured strings are woven together, keeping the right tension so that a mother can hang it on her shoulders and safely carry her baby. That is why I insist on mine being a situated perspective in a broad sense, since the geo-corpopolitcal stance exceeds a view of land/*suelo* in a territorial or geographical fashion, within politically defined boundaries. However, the territory is also the defence of what is our own: the territory as body, the body as politics – bodypolitics – the female body both a sacred and depleted, ransacked territory (Abya Yala, *pachamama*), victim of extractivism, patriarchal violence and abuse since the conquest.

Situatedness turns us to the bodies in the Latin American South but also to the other bodies in Africa, Asia and the Caribbean whose present coloniality is the continuation of colonial times now beautified in the developmentalist rhetoric of modernity.

In this context, having the subaltern speak (Spivak, 1998) the language of the victimizer, how can an English curriculum not address and historicize who we are and, instead, reproduce a make-believe that whitens us and our lineage because of our 'European descent', skipping our ancestral descent?

So, is it about an anti-English, radicalized position, banning – if that were possible – English from our formal education? Is it about another fundamentalism that will seek to reproduce the steps of the linguicide perpetrated by supremacist views?

My answer is no. I will not hold a '*cidal*' position but will become and be aware and spread awareness of the complicities and the ways to break away from them. As educators in an imperial/colonial language we must teach to see the trick; we should use the classroom to show the modernity of every single story and the coloniality that made it and perpetuated it into the single one. This will surely offer students an amplified perspective into how necessary knowing and using the language of the oppressor is to contest their colonial designs. Weaponizing the English language as a collectively empowering instrument is also the path to delink, constantly underscoring the wonderful weight of epistemic disobedience. Delinking implies 'going somewhere else', and as regards the English curriculum this other place becomes a place other, away from English as an international, global, additional, foreign, target language – lingua franca, World English and World Englishes alike. It is heading for English as a language other (Baum, 2021) to decolonize the English curriculum in/from the South.

English as a language other

Inscribed in the genealogy of positions 'other' (and not other positions), from Khatibi pensée- autre (1983), Arteaga's 'an other tongue' (1994) and Mignolo's an other paradigm (2005), we name English as a language other in our quest to contribute to the emergence of a delinking space where English is no longer the language of knowledge/power. Thus, our energy as discourse and practice goes to the uncoupling of the idea of opportunity (to study, to participate in an interepistemic, intercultural environment; to nest a wish, to hold on to a dream, to treasure hope) from the idea of race, that is, to achieve equality in difference, to stop conceiving of difference as superiority/inferiority (inherently unequal) and to end the denial of otherness to instead deny the erasure and silencing of those differences where we can root ourselves. The process of deracialization exercised from the colonial difference as a dissident position in – for example –naming English as language other also provides us with a disciplinary uncoupling from the mould of modernity and the institutionalization of such difference. Regarding naming as a political act (Walsh, 2012), the language other denomination produces a syntactic break by displacing the adjective 'other' from the pre-modifying conventional, 'grammatical' position to the post-placed, anti-normative, which causes estrangement and discomfort. This pushes us to look again, reread, wonder, request clarification, search for sense variants; it stops, interpellates and transitorily suspends our common sense to seek for answers in other senses. However, the place of the language other does not get built on the denial of other ways of naming; rather, it denies itself as a disjunctive alternative (in alternation (a or b) or in exclusion (or a or b)). In fact, it is a disruptive alternative to other alternative alternatives. For this to happen, we need to find places/times other of location, enunciation and belonging. Such a border position entails looking for an alternative way to think of and imagine alternatives (Santos, 2018).

Teaching English as a language other involves doing it in the mood of knowing that we are permanently about to fall into the modern trap; it implies doing it in the awareness that having decided to delink not only does not save or free us but doubly commits us to the making of border counter-pedagogies. I believe that from pedagogies of resistance and re-existance (Walsh, 2017) we can accompany processes of awakening, of unlearning the contents and the terms of the English curriculum. ICT, in its itinerancy, allows for these processes which need to be theorized from borderspaces where English is turned into contestation, management of the terms and visibilization of the abyssal line (Santos, 2018) so that its colonial side, inhabited by the colonial difference, is no longer an absence, where the colonial wound is not an overcome past in universal history but the very reality of those who suffer racialization on a daily basis. Following Tatum (2017), 'racism is a system of advantage based on race' and we can tell whose the advantages are. English is their language and its globalization is also the product of a global class culture (mainly academic) that is usually compliant with Western scientificism power structures. Thus, teaching English as a language other acknowledges the complicities and challenges them by using the contents (available and not) and disputing the terms; intervening the production, circulation and permanence of meanings especially in modern institutions by institutional genres that weave together the rhetorical, the subjective, the social, the epistemic and the axiological. At that crossroad, further questions will queue up: who speaks? What is knowledge? Whose knowledge is spoken/taught? Why is it spoken/taught? Who receives it? And, backgrounding it all: *in what language*? Because, as I have already said, the medium is the message, and English is certainly both.

By teaching English as the global, international language of prestige, opportunity and access, we are re-epistemiciding the epistemicide.

However, we can change the rules of the game.

We can avoid teaching *by* the canon. We can avoid teaching *for* the canon. But first we need to look the canon in the eye. Second, we need to rummage into its pockets. And third, we need to name our findings in their own languages so that the curricular landscape shelters the pluriversality of minds, bodies and emotions of the world, and the 'universal canon' returns to its provinciality.

Notes

1 'The concept of gnoseology (the generation and dissemination of all knowing and knowledge to live) to reduce epistemology (the principles of knowing and knowledge to control, dominate and destitute) to its own size' (Mignolo 2020, 11).
2 The translation is mine.
3 Esta denominación es dada al continente americano por el pueblo Kuna, desde antes de la llegada de los europeos. En la lengua del pueblo Kuna, ABYA YALA significa 'tierra madura', 'tierra viva' o 'tierra en florecimiento'. La primera vez que la expresión fue explícitamente usada con ese sentido político fue en la II Cumbre Continental de los Pueblos y Nacionalidades Indígenas de ABYA YALA, realizada en Quito en 2004. ABYA YALA se configura, por lo tanto, como parte de un proceso de construcción político-identitario en el que las prácticas discursivas cumplen un papel relevante de descolonización del pensamiento, y que ha caracterizado al nuevo ciclo del movimiento 'indígena' cada vez más como un movimiento de los pueblos originarios. La comprensión de la riqueza de los pueblos que viven aquí hace miles de años y del papel que tuvieron y tienen en la constitución del sistema mundo ha alimentado la construcción de ese proceso político identitario. Recuperado de: https://www.ecoportal.net/temas-especiales/pueblos-indigenas/abya-yala-el-verdadero-nombre-de-este-continente/.
4 The translation is mine.
5 The leading class that accompanies the modernization process in which economic progress and political organization cause the emergence of a new society is known

as 'The generation of the 1880's'. It is constituted by renowned figures, ranging in age and qualifications, such as Paul Groussac, Miguel Cané, Eduardo Wilde, Carlos Pellegrini, Luis Saenz Peña and Joaquín V. González. The idea of progress in the social sphere along with advances in industrial capitalism generate an optimistic view of the human future. This view, typical of positivism, requires the elimination of the obstacles that – for the men of the 1880s – are mainly tradition, both indigenous and Hispanic, and the lack of education in the European style. https://www.elhistoriador.com.ar/la-generacion-del-80/.

6 The translation is mine.
7 Sarmiento wrote *Facundo, Civilización y Barbarie en las pampas argentinas* in 1845 from his exile in Chile. He understood that civilization was to be identified with the city, with urban life, what was in contact with the European, that is, what they understood as progress. Barbarism, on the contrary, was the countryside, the rural, the delayed, the indigenous peoples and the gaucho.
8 As war minister of Avellaneda's government, Roca organizes and carries out the Desert Campaign that is meant to be a plan of annihilation of indigenous communities through an offensive and systematic war.
9 The aguayo is a squared, multicoloured fabric typical of the Andean Bolivian region and generally used to carry babies on the back, to sit, to lay meals, to show products and so on. https://info.caserita.com/Aguayo-proceso-de-fabricacion-a71.

References

Andreotti, V. (2011), *Actionable Postcolonial Theory in Education*, New York: Palgrave McMillan.

Arteaga, A. (1994), *An Other Tongue: Nation and Ethnicity in the Linguistic Borderlands*, Durham: Duke University Press.

Baum, G. (2021), 'Diseño de materiales decoloniales situados para la enseñanza de inglés como lengua otra', *Cuadenos de La Alfal*, 13 (2): 133–68.

Bein, R. (2000), 'la situación de las lenguas extranjeras en la Argentina', *LINGUASUR*. https://linguasur.com.ar/publicaciones/articulos/la-situacion-de-las-lenguas-extranjeras-en-la-argentina/.

Bertoni, L. (1992), 'Construir la nacionalidad: héroes, estatuas y fiestas patrias, 1887–1891', en *Boletín del Instituto de Investigaciones Históricas 'Dr. Emilio Ravignani'*, Nª 5, Universidad Nacional de Buenos Aires.

Chatterjee, P. (1997), *Our Modernity*. Published by the South-South Exchange Programme for Research on the History of Development (SEPHIS) and the Council for the Development of Social Science Research in Africa (CODESRIA), Rotterdam/Dakar.

Deleuze, G. and F. Guattari (1987), *A Thousand Plateaus*, Minneapolis: University of Minnesota Press.

Fals Borda, O. (1979), *El problema de cómo investigar la realidad para transformarla por la praxis*, Texas: Ediciones Tercer Mundo.

Khatibi, A. ([1983] 2019), *Plural Maghreb. Writings on Poscolonialism*, London: Bloomsbury Publishing.

Kusch, R. (1978), *Geocultura del hombre americano*, Buenos Aires: Fernando García Cambeiro.

Kusch, R. (2007), *Obras Completes*, Rosario: Fundación A. Ross. La Paz, Plural Editores. Disponible en: http://bibliotecavirtual.clacso.org.ar/clacso/otros/20111218114130/1942.pdf.

Malcolm, X. (1963), *Message to The Grassroots*. https://www.blackpast.org/african-american-history/speeches-african-american-history/1963-malcolm-x-message-grassroots/.

McLuhan, M. (1964), *Understanding Media: The Extensions of Man*, New York: McGraw Hill.

Meyer, M. (1991), 'Developing Transcultural Competence: Case Studies in Advanced Language Learners', in D. Buttjes and M. Byram (eds), *Mediating Languages and Cultures: Towards an Intercultural Theory of Foreign Language Education*, 136–58, Clevedon: Multilingual Matters.

Mignolo, W. (1999), 'I am Where I Think: Epistemology and the Colonial Difference', *Journal of Latin American Cultural Studies: Travesia*, 8 (2): 235–45.

Mignolo, W. (2005), 'Un paradigma otro: colonialidad global, pensamiento fronterizo y cosmopolitanismo crítico', *Dispositio*, 25 (52): 127–46. Disponible en: http://www.jstor.org/stable/41491792.

Mignolo, W. (2006), 'El giro gnoseológico decolonial: la contribución de Aime Cesaire a la geopolítica y la corpo-política del conocimiento', en Aimé Césaire, *Discurso sobre el colonialism*, 197–221, Madrid: AKAL.

Mignolo, W. (2007), 'Delinking: The Rhetoric of Modernity, the Logic of Coloniality and the Grammar of De-coloniality', *Cultural Studies*, 21 (2–3): 449–514.

Mignolo, W. (2009), 'Frantz Fanon y la opción decolonial: el conocimiento y lo politico', en *Fanon, Frant, Piel Negra, Máscaras Blancas*, 309–26, Madrid: AKAL.

Mignolo, W. (2010), 'Desobediencia Epistémica (II) Pensamiento Independiente y Libertad De-Colonial', *Otros Logos*, 1 (1): 8–42. Disponible en: http://www.ceapedi.com.ar/otroslogos/2010-1.htm.

Mignolo, W. (2013), 'Geopolitics of Sensing and Knowing: On (de)coloniality, Border Thinking, and Epistemic Disobedience', *Confero*, 1 (1): 129–50.

Mignolo, W. (2015), *Trayectorias de re-existencia: ensayos en torno a la colonialidad / decolonialidad del saber, el sentir y el creer. Universidad Distrital Francisco José de Caldas. Facultad de Artes ASAB*, Bogotá: Fondo de Publicaciones, Universidad Distrital Francisco José de Caldas

Mignolo, W. (2019), 'The Way We Were. Or What Decoloniality Today is All About'. *Anglistica AION*, 23 (2): 9–22.

Mignolo, W. (2020), 'The Logic of the In-Visible: Decolonial Reflections on the Change of Epoch', *Theory, Culture & Society*, 0 (0): 1–14.

Mignolo, W. M. Tlostanova (2006), 'Theorizing from the Borders. Shifting to Geo- and Body-Politics of Knowledge', *European Journal of Social Theory*, 9 (2): 205–21.

Mignolo, W. and Vázquez, R. (2015). 'Aesthesis decolonial: heridas coloniales/sanaciones decoloniales'. in W. Mignolo y P. P. Gómez. (eds), *Trayectorias de re-existencia: ensayos en torno a la colonialidad / decolonialidad del saber, el sentir y el creer*. Universidad Distrital Francisco José de Caldas. Facultad de Artes ASAB. Bogotá, Fondo de Publicaciones, Universidad Distrital Francisco José de Caldas.

Montserrat, M. y G. Mórtola (2018), 'La Enseñanza del Inglés para las grandes mayorías nacionales en Argentina', *Revista Digital de Políticas Lingüísticas*, 10 (10): 167–91.

Paraskeva, J. M. (2016), *The Curriculum: Whose Internationalization?* New York: Peter Lang.

Paraskeva, J. M. (2017), 'Author's Response – Itinerant Curriculum Theory Revisited: On a Non-theoricide towards the Canonicide: Addressing the Curriculum Involution', *Journal of the American Association for the Advancement of Curriculum Studies*, 12 (1): 1–42.

Paraskeva, J. M. (2019), 'Justica Contra El Epistemicidio. Hacia una Breve Critica de la Razón Occidental Moderna' [Justice against epistemicide. Towards a brief critique of modern occidental reason], *Con-Ciencia Social*, 3: 157–74.

Paraskeva, J. M. (2021), *Conflicts in Curriculum Theory. Challenging Hegemonic Epistemologies*, 2nd edn, New York: Routledge.

Paraskeva, J. M. (2022), 'The Generation of the Utopia: Itinerant Curriculum Theory towards a "Futurable Future"', *Discourse: Studies in the Cultural Politics of Education*, 43 (4): 1–20.

Quijano, A. (1992), 'Colonialidad y Modernidad/Racionalidad', *Perú Indígena*, 13 (29): 11–20.

Quijano, A. (2000), 'Colonialidad del poder, eurocentrismo y América Latina', en Edgardo Lander (Comp.), *La colonialidad del saber: eurocentrismo y ciencias sociales*, Buenos Aires: CLACSO.

Santos, B. Sousa (2006a), *Renovar la teoría crítica y reinventar la emancipación social*, Argentina: CLACSO. Disponible en: http://bibliotecavirtual.clacso.org.ar/ar/libros/edicion/santos/Capitulo%20I.pdf.

Santos, B. Sousa (2006b), 'Globalizations', *Theory, Culture & Society*, 23 (2–3): 393–9.

Santos, B. Sousa (2018), *The End of the Cognitive Empire: The Coming of Age of the Epistemologies of the South*, Durham: Duke University Press.

Spivak, G. ([1988] 2010), *Can the Subaltern Speak?*, ed. Rosalind C. Morris, Columbia University Press.

Tatum, B. (2017), *Why Are All the Black Kids Sitting Together in the Cafeteria?* New York: New York Times.

Walsh, C. (2009), 'Interculturalidad crítica y educación intercultural. Ampliación de la ponencia dictada en el Seminario Interculturalidad y Educación Intercultural organizado por el Instituto Internacional de Integración del Convenio Andrés Bello, La Paz'.

Walsh, C. (2012), 'The Politics of Naming', *Cultural Studies*, 26 (1): 108–25. Disponible en: http://dx.doi.org/10.1080/09502386.2012.642598.

Walsh, C. (2017), 'Introducción. Lo pedagógico y lo decolonial: Entretejiendo caminos', en C. Walsh (ed.), *Pedagogías decoloniales. Prácticas insurgentes de resistir, (re)existir y (re)vivir. Serie Pensamiento Decolonial*, 23–60, Quito: Abya Yala.

5

Returning to the Cultural Foundations of China's Curriculum Reform

ICT and Confucian 'Wind' Education

Weili Zhao

Prelude

When I started my doctoral studies in curriculum studies with Professor Thomas Popkewitz at University of Wisconsin-Madison over ten years ago, I hoped to move Chakrabarty's (2000) well-known claim one step further. He claims that Western concepts and frameworks are indispensable and yet insufficient in explicating non-Western sensibilities. While fully complying with his statement, I wondered how it is possible then to first discern non-Western sensibilities, in my case Chinese sensibilities, before explicating them as they are on a global landscape. *Discerning* Chinese unique sensibilities is already truly challenging to me as we modern people are already subjected to, and henceforth unconscious of, a modernized-Westernized mode of thinking. Back then, my cross-cultural learning trajectory and Foucault's historical mode of inquiry provided me with a detouring strategy to access Chinese educational sensibilities. Specifically, detouring into the Western scholarship geographically and intellectually helped me access the Chinese culture from a temporary 'outside' vantage point, and detouring into the Chinese history helped me to access the Chinese present as an 'insider', nonetheless not separating East and West, past and present into binary oppositions. More importantly, my prior intellectual interest in discourse studies sharpened my sensitivity to language itself as the very cultural traces of reasoning, to borrow Heidegger's (1978) words, 'the House of being' (p. 217), rather than mere tools to express our thoughts.

    Luckily, I did *discern*, or rather encounter, some Chinese unique educational sensibilities that are nurtured prevalently yet silently within some daily schooling discourses, that is, 'school wind, teaching wind, and learning wind'. I indeed grew up with these discourses, yet I had never *seen* the cultural linkage between 'education' and 'wind'. Like other Chinese people, I tended to treat these terms as metaphorical concepts and interpret them semantically as 'school atmosphere, teaching styles, and learning manners'. In other words, I never wondered why it is historically possible for Chinese people to talk about education in terms of wind, not water, along a Foucauldian line of thinking. Since then, I followed the dancing *wind* in between history and present, and East and West, to be unexpectedly exposed to a Confucian 'wind' education as expressed in the Book of Change (*Yijing*). In other words, and as is to be further explicated later in this chapter, it can be argued that Confucius's envisioning of teaching and learning in his commentary on one Yijing hexagram can be viewed as one originary, not original, (re)source for China's educational thinking and practice. Furthermore, Chinese 'wind' can be viewed as a signature language to talk about its teaching and learning (see Zhao, 2019a, 2019b).

When I was almost done with turning my dissertation into a book manuscript in 2017, João M. Paraskeva's (2016) award-winning book, *Curriculum Epistemicide*, came to my attention. To my delight, his critique of the issue of epistemicide in international curriculum studies is insightful to my doctoral research in two senses. First, it provides a theoretical framework to opportunely contextualize my research in the broader field of (de)colonial international curriculum studies. Second, it reaffirms my Heideggerian language lens in that it does work as a powerful, albeit often neglected in the Western scholarship, decolonial tool in rendering visible Chinese educational sensibilities as they are. While I did not have time to foreground these two insights in relation to Paraskeva's itinerant curriculum theories (ICTs) in my dissertation book, *China's Education, Curriculum Knowledge, and Cultural Imprints: Dancing with the Wind* (2019), this book chapter is a good opportunity to scrutinize the linkage between Paraskeva's ICT and my own research on explicating the cultural foundations of China's curriculum thinking and practice (see also Zhao, 2019a, 2020) as below.

ICT and language as a decolonial gesture against curriculum epistemicide

One significant question commonly asked in curriculum studies is *what/whose knowledge gets taught at schools as legitimate knowledge and what/whose not* (see Apple, 2000). Yet, Paraskeva alerts us to another equally significant and yet often neglected question in mainstream Western scholarship, namely *what other forms of knowledge exist(ed) in the world outside the Western epistemological harbor*. Asking the latter question foregrounds a key issue in international knowledge (re)production, that is, the colonization of one knowledge form by another or what Santos (2007a) calls 'epistemicide'. Paraskeva (2016) proffers the term 'curriculum epistemicide' to represent a form of Western imperialism, which he argues has reached a 'quasi-irretrievable point' (p. 3) and continued to intersect with the daily praxis of schools in and beyond the West. For example, the Organization for Economic Co-operation and Development (OECD) and the United States have incurred another wave of curriculum reform global wise that intends to cultivate what OECD and the United States define as twenty-first-century core competencies or key skills. These West-Eurocentric and Anglophone discourses of 'core competencies' and 'key skills' have become dominant discourses global wise, suppressing and overwriting alternative local discourses and forms of knowledge in developing countries. It is to be noted that such phenomenon of curriculum epistemicide doesn't just happen with the core competency curriculum reform. Rather, as a form of colonialism, epistemicide 'is constitutive of, rather than derivative from, modernity' (Andreotti, 2011, 383), and 'coloniality', as the memory or legacy of colonialism, defines culture, labour, intersubjective relation and knowledge production well beyond the limits of colonialism and long after the end of a colonial administration (Maldonado-Torres, 2007).

Paraskeva argues that the happening of epistemicide is not only an effect of Western power hegemony but also anchored in a fabricated eugenic claim that Western epistemological perspective is 'unique and the only cognitive possible' (p. 3). As an effect, an epistemological disordering that treats the West as being superior to the non-West becomes a naturalized truth and myth of coloniality. One expression, for example, is that many countries in the world are still jumping on the competency-based curriculum reform wagon, hoping to go global with the more advanced West. In other words, non-Western countries are still naturally taking the Western super-discourses of 'competencies' and 'skills' as epistemologically better, reproducing Western hegemonic curriculum knowledge (above local knowledge forms) in non-Western countries before they know it. It is to be noted here that linguistic epistemicide doesn't merely mean a replacement of discourses per se. Rather, it is a killing of a mode of reasoning and a form of knowledge making that come with different cultural discourse and language. Furthermore, epistemicide is reinforced by the so-called critical theories within the Western scholarship. For example, Paraskeva (2016) argues the critical curriculum theories, as well as some postmodern and post-structural scholarship, largely presume a predominant Western modern episteme and end up becoming 'an anti-Eurocentric/Western critique from a Eurocentric/Western fundamentalist position' (p. 76). As a result, these curriculum theories not only fail to include the colossal epistemic diversities beyond the West-Eurocentric domain but also (re)produce the latter as non-existent.

To confront, and win against the war against, such epistemological imperialism in international curriculum studies, Paraskeva proposes an ICT as a new 'never stable gathering epistemological point' (p. 11), a decolonial struggle for social and cognitive justice. Upholding the understanding that 'critical knowledge starts by the critique of knowledge' itself (Santos, 1999, 205), ICT does not merely explore the classical significant curriculum question of 'what/whose knowledge gets taught at schools?' but also 'fights for (an)other knowledge outside the Western epistemological harbor' (p. 43), knowledge and epistemologies largely marginalized and discredited in the current world order. In other words, it dissolves a eugenic disordering among varied epistemes towards a 'cognitive justice' (Santos, 2007a, 2016) and 'ecologies of knowledges' (Santos, 2007b, 2016), not only recognizing the equal value of all forms of knowledge but also advocating a harmonious coexistence of varied forms of knowledge.

Simply put, ICT is itinerant, decolonial and advocates language as a decolonial tool. It is itinerant in the sense of going beyond a dichotic skeleton of West-Rest yet not romanticizing indigenous cultures and knowledges. This itinerant positioning challenges any form of functionalizing or romanticizing certain cultures and knowledge forms over others. It pushes the theorist into a pluri-directional path, allowing us not only to start anew from the beginning of the West but also from a new beginning point, that is, the non-West. The itinerant posture provides a power space in which to engage in varied sensations, fluxes and directions that attend to both globalism and localism, and hegemonic Western discourses and subaltern local counter-discourses. It is decolonial in the sense of promoting a pluriversal, not universal, cartography wherein each knot can work as a point of delinking and opening that reintroduces languages, memories, economies, social organizations and subjectivities, deconstructing Western culture and knowledge as the centre of legitimate knowledge, the arbiter of what counts as knowledge and the source of civilized or official knowledge. ICT exposes and suspends the 'darker side' of the Western modernity-coloniality of knowledge, power and being towards global 'cognitive justice', that is, 'sentient of the wor(l)ds behind and beyond the Western epistemological platform, wor(l)ds that are non-monolithic' (p. 86). Delinking itself from the yoke, the spell or the rhetoric of modernity, democracy, postmodernity or postcolonialism, all grounded in the Occident, ICT hopes to bring to the foreground 'a silenced and different genealogy of thought' (p. 80).

ICT foregrounds 'linguistic genocide' as the 'very core of the colonial and the neocolonial project' (p. 202). That is, 'the production and reproduction of hegemonic forms of knowledge are precisely the institutionalizations of a linguistic or cultural epistemicide' (p. 241). Corroborating wa Thiong's (1986) claim that language is the most important vehicle in subjugating the spiritual mindset of the colonized, Paraskeva turns language around as the very decolonial tool. Specifically, ICT questions linguistic imperialism portrayed by English and other Western imperial languages in internationalizing curriculum studies. For example, most of counter-dominant Western epistemological views neglected other linguist forms and other forms of knowledge, citing only and/or mostly English-speaking scholars and English literatures. The overwhelming majority does not know or does not value the scientific knowledge produced in other 'inferior' languages than English.

Paraskeva's claim that language is the very site of epistemicide is pertinent in re-examining China's modern language and curriculum reform since the early twentieth century at the intersection of East and West and tradition and modernity. Furthermore, language can indeed become a decolonial tool, but I would add, especially when we go beyond the traditional treatment of language as merely a linguistic system/tool and further put linguistic practices in a cross-cultural meaning-making paradigm. In the next section, I reiterate Paraskeva's (de)colonial language posture with my research on China's curriculum reform, explicating translingual practices, that is, translation, as the very site of epistemicide.

China's modern language and curriculum reform dilemma

As Paraskeva and others rightly claim, language does play an epistemicidal role in colonizing the mental universe of the colonized, especially when colonizers regulate the colonized to learn/speak the colonizers' languages to replace the latter's own languages. Things are a bit different with China and the Chinese language: Even though China was partly colonized from mid-nineteenth to early twentieth century, the modern Chinese language was not colonized or replaced by English and Chinese people still speak Chinese language. Nevertheless, as I have argued elsewhere (Zhao, 2019a, 2019b), the meaning-making rationale behind the Chinese language is indeed Westernized-modernized into a conceptual signifier-signified mode of signification. Specifically, when Western terms were introduced into China, either traditional Chinese terms are reappropriated or neologisms (compounds) of monographical characters are coined as their semantic translations. Either way, the mode of translation transfigures or overwrites the original cultural-historical senses nurtured within each Chinese character (*hanzi*) (Wu, 2014). As Bush (2008) rightly puts it, the Chinese words are not dead, but the way they are read has been transformed, that is, the modern-Western mode of signification simply eclipses and replaces the meaning-making episteme nurtured within the Chinese language terms. Accordingly, the Chinese language has become a representational system like English.

Such Westernization-modernization of the Chinese language happens along with, or is constitutive of, the Western hegemonic power expansion as well as a concomitant eugenic Western superiority versus Chinese inferiority disordering. Imprisoned by Western modernity-coloniality that the Western episteme is more 'modern, advanced, and scientific', most Chinese academics and policymakers since the twentieth century have welcomed, rather than resisted, the Western modernity-coloniality episteme (Zhang, 2013). For example, the Chinese language was often critiqued as being illogical and vague by Western scholars. This claim was corroborated by many radical Chinese scholars in the 1920s New Cultural Movement. They collectively aligned themselves to the Western science, technology and language as a eugenic norm and accordingly called to eradicate the 'backward' Chinese Confucian tradition and to Romanize the Chinese language (see Zhao, 2019b). Put differently, the Chinese intellectuals and institutions have subscribed to the murder of their own cognitive matrix (Paraskeva, 2018). This embrace of the Western modernity-coloniality episteme has indeed produced an 'academic aphasia' (Shi-xu, 2016) in post-twentieth-century China, suppressing China's traditional culture. The fact that Chinese policymakers and academics are still feverishly borrowing Western curriculum policies and practices reaffirms the long-time effect of modernity-coloniality on the colonized (Maldonado-Torres, 2007).

Nevertheless, with its rising nationalism and fast economic development in the past few decades, China is striving to recover its cultural soft power to maintain its Chinese characteristics on the global platform. Towards that end, more and more traditional-cultural discourses are being reinvoked and regenerated to counter the Western power and foreground its Chinese features. Within such a context, it is opportune to say China currently speaks a language of heteroglossia as old Chinese monographs and terms are continuously reinvoked, recombined and reinterpellated as glosses or counter-glosses of Western discourses. Such a mixture of discourses makes the expression of epistemicide more entangled and the unpacking of epistemicide more complicated. Epistemicide expresses itself less in unpacking what forms of discourses are circulating than in how the varied forms of discourses are ordered, juxtaposed, interpreted and manipulated by the Chinese academicians and policymakers. In other words, it is through unpacking the academician's and policymakers' way of understanding and reasoning the varied discourses in assemblage that we can glimpse into the operativity and expression of epistemicide. Epistemicide links itself not only to the circulating discourses but also how the modern Chinese language and schooling discourses, whether Western or traditional Chinese, are *interpreted* semantically, culturally and cross-culturally, and more importantly, in the *English* language to the international audience.

Put differently, the entangled Chinese context reiterates Paraskeva's decolonial language perspective in linkage with cross-cultural translation practices between both the Chinese and English languages and epistemes/cultures. Translation here no longer focuses itself merely on finding semantic equivalents between two language/discourse systems. Rather, as Chakrabarty (2000) rightly argues, it is through translation that cultural differences are to be rendered visible and intelligible. As an example, I share later my earlier examination into the epistemological dilemma that confronts China's current competency-based curriculum reform (Zhao, 2020), explicating how the Chinese policymakers and curriculum scholars are still subjugated to modernity-coloniality in their efforts to calibrate China's *suyang* curriculum as more than a replica of the OECD's and US competency-skill framework.

Since the 1990s, the OECD and the United States have been advocating a competency-based curriculum reform, hoping to empower students with core competencies and skills in the twenty-first century. China jumped on this wagon and released its *Core Suyang Definitions for Chinese Student Development* in 2016 as a product of a three-year, state-commissioned research project. The traditional-cultural notion of *suyang* was reinvoked as both a gloss and counter-gloss of the English terms of competency, skills and literacies. China's *Core Suyang Definitions* claims to parallel both the OCED's and US frameworks as a gesture to go global and distinguish itself from the latter in that the *suyang* framework also builds upon the Confucian tradition of *learning, body cultivation (xiushen) and governing* in nurturing holistic student development (Lin, 2016; Ministry of Education, 2016). Compared to the OECD's and US framing of competencies primarily as 'skills, knowledges, and abilities', China's *suyang* definitions encompass 'desirable character-traits (*pinge*) and key competencies-skills-literacies' as well as 'emotions-attitudes-values' (Ministry of Education, 2016). That is, China's *suyang* curriculum framework claims to be more than a replica of the Western competencies-skills model because it foregrounds elements of Confucian educational culture.

However, as I have unpacked elsewhere (Zhao, 2020), Chinese policymakers' and academics' efforts of making a Chinese characteristic competency-based curriculum are thwarted by their unconscious subjection to the modernity-coloniality, and the reinvocation of cultural *suyang* discourse is nothing but a linguistic trope. There, I examined how the *suyang* curriculum discourses are *interpreted* semantically, culturally and cross-culturally in relation to the Western discourses of competency-skill-literacy and found Chinese intellectuals, still largely subjugated to the modernity-coloniality, have subscribed to the murder of their own cognitive matrix (Paraskeva, 2018). For example, even though *suyang* is mobilized as a cultural-traditional notion with semantic registers broader than 'competency-skill-literacy', Chinese scholars commonly presume a *suyang*=competency ordering and interpret *suyang* merely as a semantic equivalent of competency (see, e.g., Chu, 2016; Cui, 2016; Zhang, 2016). The *suyang*=competency ordering well betrays scholars' subscription to the modernity-coloniality episteme of conceptual thinking, or what Foucault (1973) puts as a representational language and a signifier-signified mode of signification. This mode of signification reduces language to a trap of philology which assumes the a priori existence of grammatical arrangements in a language in which meaning is deduced from the grammatical structure.

Furthermore, China's *Core Suyang Definitions* text is replete with modern and Western introduced terms, discourses and grammatical structures, such as 'development, respect, self-regulated learning, life-long learner, critical thinking, problem-solving abilities, innovation, creativity, and sustainable development'. Even though *suyang* claims to encompass 'desirable character-traits (*pinge*) and key competencies-skills-literacies' as well as 'emotions-attitudes-values', the latter are largely treated as psychological traits, ordered in no way different from competencies-skills-literacies. Such a conceptualization of emotions-attitudes-values fails to explicate the cultural-traditional episteme that goes with a Confucian tradition of *learning, body cultivation (xiushen) and governing* in nurturing holistic student development. Basically, a Chinese Confucian holistic body-thinking episteme that possibly rests with the cultural *suyang* and Confucian teaching and learning is nowhere visible (see, Zhao, 2019a, 2020). To break apart the subjection of modernity-coloniality, I suspend *suyang* as a modern concept and read it back to su + yang, explicating further its linkage to the Chinese holistic body-thinking episteme. In so doing, I turn around language and discourse as a very decolonial tool and argue that recognizing the yoke of modernity-coloniality and the imprint of epistemicide is a first step for Chinese scholars to recalibrate China's suyang curriculum reform as more than a replica of the Western frameworks.

Thus, I would like to reiterate that, as Paraskeva's ICT rightly proffers, language indeed plays a key role in decolonizing the (re)production of international curriculum knowledge along the Western-modernity episteme but only if we retreat language not merely as a linguistic system/tool but more as an epistemic being and saying. As Heidegger (1977) rightly observes, 'language first gives to every purposeful deliberation its ways and underways. Without language, there would be lacking to every doing every dimension in which it could bestir itself and be effective' (p. 40). Seen this way, cross-cultural translingual practices like translation would become the very site of epistemicide in that the act of equalizing the semantic meanings of linguistic terms may very well cover up the cultural differences and distinctiveness that the linguistic terms possibly say. Later, I show how such decolonial language perspective has enabled me to encounter a Confucian 'wind' education as cultural foundations of China's curriculum reform and how ICT helps to re-envision my doctoral research experience (which I called Daoist onto-un-learning) (see, Zhao, 2019b, 2019c) as an itinerant curriculum (un)learning.

Historicizing China's 'wind' education as my itinerant curriculum (un)learning

Paraskeva's (2016) ICT is decolonial in the sense of promoting a pluriversal not universal cartography of knowledge wherein each knot in the genealogy web can work as a point of delinking and opening that reintroduces languages, memories, economies, social organizations and subjectivities (p. 203). In this section, I further showcase my doctoral studies on historizing China's 'wind' education as an itinerant curriculum (un)learning, which I previously call a Daoist onto-un-learning. To further out Paraskeva's invocation of ICT, I reinterpret itinerant in the sense of imploding a modernist understanding of subjectivities and language along a subject versus object disordering through a historical and archaeological detour. As Agamben (2009) argues, in archaeological inquiry, 'it is not possible to gain access in a new way, beyond tradition, to the sources without putting in question the very historical subject who is supposed to gain access to them' (p. 89).

As I introduced earlier, my doctoral research takes up a detouring-accessing cartography, detouring into the Western scholarship to gain an 'outsider' vantage point to access the Chinese educational sensibilities and detouring into the past to access the present. In the research, I assumed two roles of both researcher and learner. As a researcher, I examined into China's current curriculum reform and schooling discourses, and as a learner, I immersed myself into what I retrospectively call a Daoist onto-un-learning trajectory and unlearn what I otherwise pick up as modern knowledge and common sense. One such knowledge is an anthropocentric subject versus object disordering which orders myself as a 'subject' and my research as 'objects' (including educational practices and discourses/language). During that cross-cultural and historical learning trajectory, I found myself lost and in the hands of language, not vice versa, especially in interpreting the historical Chinese 'wind' texts. Such aporia moments decolonized my modern mindset and challenged me to rethink my own subjectivities, Chinese languages and our ordering. I call this learning and unlearning trajectory as a 'Daoist onto-un-learning' (Zhao, 2019c), which I now can reportray as an itinerant curriculum (un) learning experience with the below turning and opening moments.

First moment is my encountering of the prevalent yet silent wind-education discourses in Chinese schooling, literally put, 'school/teaching/learning wind'. This encountering delinks Chinese language from a modern representational language, asking not what 'school wind' means but how it is historically possible for wind and education to intersect in Chinese culture. It challenges the modern-Western conceptual style of reasoning and signifier-signified mode of signification as the centre of legitimate knowledge, the arbiter of what counts as knowledge and the source of civilized or official knowledge. Chinese 'wind' is more than 'air in movement' as defined by the *Oxford Dictionary*, and the Chinese language is distinct from the English language in that each monograph is constitutive of meaningful graphs/parts, unlike the meaningless English alphabetical letters. This realization provides me with a new starting point from anew, namely to start anew from a new starting point of Chinese language.

Scrutinizing the etymological roots and senses of the Chinese notion 'wind' leads to my second turning point in my itinerant learning trajectory. Namely, the Chinese 'wind' has an inherent sense of 'transforming' as the monograph etymologically states, 'wind blows, and insects get germinated and transformed within 8 days'. As Kuriyama rightly puts it, 'the fascination of the Chinese winds lay in their power to *transform*' (my italics) (1994, 23). It is this inherent 'transforming' sense that links Chinese 'wind' back to Confucian teaching and learning narratives, say, 'wind (is) teaching, wind moves and teaching transforms' (Han Preface to *Book of Odes, around 200 AD*) and 'gentleman's virtue is (like) wind and petty man's virtue is (like) grass; when wind blows across it, the grass must bend' (*Analects, around 500 BCE*). Put succinctly, the imagination of Chinese 'wind' instead looms large in and across domains of education, politics, poetry and Chinese medical body (Hsu, 2007).

Following further the dancing 'wind' finally exposed me to Confucius's own envisioning of teaching and learning as expressed in his commentary on one Yijing hexagram called *guan* (observation) with a hexagram image of wind blowing over the earth. This hexagram, itself having nothing to do with teaching and learning, zooms on one ritual scenario where the Son of Heaven washed his hands but not yet offered the sacrifice, with a pious outlook and in front of his subjects. Confucius added a couple of comments, leveraged upon the 'transforming' sense of Chinese 'wind' and envisioned it into an ideal, exemplary and contingent, teaching-learning movement that happens like wind blowing over the earth. Indeed, I was accidently exposed to the Yijing guan-observation hexagram, which I argued as an originary, not original, resource of the entire Confucian teaching and learning, and the notion 'wind' can be reviewed as the signature language of Chinese education (Zhao, 2019a, 2019b). Here, 'originary' needs to be understood in the sense that there is always something unsaid that could be further tapped, that what was said within the Chinese notion 'wind' 'prevails throughout the tradition in an originary way, is always in being in advance of it, and yet is never expressly thought in its own right and as the Originary' (Heidegger, 1969, 48–9).

To repeat, my learning experience of dancing with the 'wind' is itinerant in that it implodes my anthropocentric-modernist understanding of myself, my subjectivity and language. Rather than manipulate language as a tool, I found myself from time to time in the hands of language. For example, what does the etymological statement 'wind blows, and insects gets germinated and hatched within eight days' literally say? Why eight days? Why insects? What paralysed me was that a middle schooler would know most of the monographed Chinese characters, but when put together, I had no idea of their saying at all as words are stopped in their tracks. Such aporia-like moment disrupted my subjectivity and the presumed subject-object ordering between myself as a subject and the language as an object. Hopeless, I could only follow the dancing 'wind', listening hard to its saying.

Paraskeva's ICT provides not merely an 'alternative thinking of curriculum' but rather an 'alternative thinking of alternatives' (see Santos, 2007a). To me, here *being alternative*, say, A is alternative to B, no longer entails a clear-cut demarcation line between A and B. Rather, being alternative could involve multiple lines that both intersect and crisscross varied positionings of A, B, C and so on. My 'wind' research along a detour-and-access cartography of knowledge, language and education blurs the geographical and epistemic boundaries of East, West, past, present, human subjects and the researched objects. Instead, as ICT proffers, we theorists and researchers are thrust into a new pluriverse where to engage in varied forms of knowledge towards a cognitive justice. Within such pluriverse, language is no longer assumed to exist as a legitimized and enclosed system; meaning is no longer decided by the grammatical arrangements of statements; education is no longer about a neoliberal seeking of outcome and profit; and doing research is no longer merely to apply a pregiven framework to certain contexts. Learning with an ICT framework is more of an itinerant encountering, a decentring and recentring of various signposts, a processing, something like my dancing with the 'wind' that can only be recounted backwards rather than anticipated ahead of time.

Further implications for international curriculum studies

ICT is a much-needed decolonial gesture in current international curriculum studies that theoretically strive for cognitive diversities and differences to coexist harmoniously and yet still favour English as the internationalization language for publications. While it is not possible to use Chinese or Korean as the standard language for international publications, ICT alerts us to more authentically portray non-English forms of knowledge as they are and outside of the bracket of the English standard language. This challenge foregrounds the role that language, or rather translingual translation practices, can play in decolonizing the hegemonic reproduction of West-centric knowledge in non-Western nation states and in reinvigorating the voices of local languages and forms of knowledges. Furthermore, it challenges us to problematize the very modern mode of signification in non-Western nation states by seeking alternative meaning-making rationales.

As a decolonial gesture, ICT calls for a post-abyssal mode of thinking that no longer favours West over East, North over South, presence over absence, identity over difference and the total binary logic itself. While decentring the West-presence-identity as the arbiter of knowledge, ICT also cautions us against recentring East-South-absence-difference as the other extreme stand position. That is, ICT thinking recognizes an ecological coexistence of varying epistemological forms of knowledges around the world. As a form of decolonial thinking, it doesn't ask to begin anew in the old West-Eurocentric cartography of knowledge but to find an entirely new ecological beginning in a distinct space of knowledge.

In this alignment, my case study on unpacking China's wind education provides a new starting point to recalibrate China's current curriculum reform as it is, not as a replica of the OECD's and US frameworks and beyond a nationalism versus globalism tension and division. Furthermore, even though it is a heteroglossia of both Chinese and Western discourses and concepts, the modernized Chinese language can still be *one forgotten, muted yet living* expression of cultural wisdom. As such, problematizing the Chinese language indeed becomes a decolonial 'first and fundamental step' (Hayhoe, 2014, 315) in critiquing modern China's knowledge (re)production in general on the international platform.

References

Agamben, G. (2009), *The Signature of All Things: On Method*, New York: Zone Books.
Andreotti, V. (2011), '(Towards) Decoloniality and Diversity in Global Citizenship Education', *Globalisation, Societies and Education*, 9 (3–4): 381–97.

Apple, M. (2000), *Official Knowledge: Democratic Education in a Conservative Age*, New York: Routledge.
Bush, C. (2008), 'Reading and Difference: Image, Allegory, and the Invention of Chinese', in E. Hyot, H. Saussy and S. G. Yao (eds), *Sinographies: Writing China*, 34–63, Minneapolis: University of Minnesota Press.
Chakrabarty, D. (2000), *Provincializing Europe: Postcolonial Thought and Historical Difference*, Princeton: Princeton University Press.
Chu, H. Q. (2016), 'Hexinsuyang de gainian yu benzhi [The Concept and Meaning of Core Suyang]', *Huashidaxuebao [Journal of east China Normal University]*, 34 (1): 1–3.
Cui, Y. H. (2016), 'Suyang: Yige rangren huanxi rangrenyou de gainian [Suyang as a Contested Concept]', *Huashidaxuebao [Journal of east China Normal University]*, 34 (1): 3–5.
Foucault, M. (1973), *The Order of Things: An Archaeology of the Human Sciences*, New York: Vintage Books.
Hayhoe, R. (2014), 'Hopes for Confucian Pedagogy in China?', *Journal of Curriculum Studies*, 46 (3): 313–19.
Heidegger, M. (1969), *Identity and Difference*, trans. J. Stambaugh with an Introduction, New York, Evanston, and London: Harper & Row Publishers. (Original work published 1957)
Heidegger, M. (1977), 'The Turning', in M. Heidegger (ed.), *The Question Concerning Technology and Other Essays*, trans. W. Lovitt, with an introduction, 36–49, New York: Harper Torchbooks.
Heidegger, M. (1978), 'Letter on Humanism', in D. F. Krell (ed.), *Basic Writings*, 213–65, London: Routledge.
Hsu, E. (2007), 'The Experience of Wind in Early and Medieval CHINESE Medicine', *Journal of the Royal Anthropological Institute (N.S.)*: S117–S34. http://www.UNZ.org/Pub/HuShih-1934?View=Search.
Kuriyama, S. (1994), 'The Imagination of Winds and the Development of the Chinese Conception of the Body', in A. Zito and T. E. Barlow (eds), *Body, Subject, and Power in China*, 23–41, Chicago: Chicago University Press.
Lin, C. D., ed. (2016), *21 shiji xuesheng fazhan hexin suyang yanjiu [Study on Developing Students' Core Suyang in 21st Century]*, Beijing: Normal University Press.
Maldonado-Torres, N. (2007), 'On the Coloniality of Being', *Cultural Studies*, 21 (2–3): 240–70. https://doi.org/10.1080/09502380601162548
Ministry of Education. (2016), 'Zhongguo xuesheng fazhan suyang [Core Suyang Definitions for Chinese Student Development]', http://www.jyb.cn/basc/sd/201609/t20160914_673105.html.
Paraskeva, J. M. (2016), *Curriculum Epistemicide: Towards an Itinerant Curriculum Theory*, New York: Routledge.
Paraskeva, J. M., ed. (2018), *Toward a Just Curriculum Theory: The Epistemicide*, New York: Routledge.
Santos, B. S. (1999), 'Porque e que e Tao Dificil Construir uma Teoria Critica', *Revista Critica de Ciencias Sociais*, 54: 197–215.
Santos, B. S. (2007a), 'Beyond Abyssal Thinking: From Global Lines to Ecologies of Knowledges', *Review (Fernand Braudel Center)*, 30 (1): 45–89.
Santos, B. S. (2007b), 'Introduction', in B. de Souza Santos (ed.), *Cognitive Justice in a Global World: Prudent Knowledges for a Decent Life*, 1–12, Washington: Lexington Books.

Santos, B. S. (2016), *Epistemologies of the South: Justice against Epistemicide*, New York: Routledge.
Shi-xu. (2016), 'Cultural Discourse Studies Through the Journal of Multicultural Discourses: 10 Years On', *Journal of Multicultural Discourse*, 11 (1): 1–8.
wa Thiong'o, N. (1986), *Decolonizing the Mind*, Nairobi: East African Educational Publishers.
Wu, Z. J. (2014), 'Speak in the Place of the Sages': Rethinking the Sources of Pedagogic Meanings', *Journal of Curriculum Studies*, 46 (3): 320–31.
Zhao, W. (2019a), 'Re-Invigorating the Being of Language in International Education: Unpacking Confucius 'Wind-Pedagogy' in Yijing as an Exemplar', *Discourse: Studies in the Cultural Politics of Education*, 40 (4): 474–86.
Zhao, W. (2019b), *China's Education, Curriculum Knowledge and Cultural Inscriptions: Dancing with the Wind*, New York and London: Routledge.
Zhao, W. (2019c), 'Daoist *onto-un-learning* as a Radical Form of *Study*: Re-Imagining Learning and Study from an Eastern Perspective', *Studies in Philosophy and Education*, 38 (3): 261–73.
Zhao, W. (2020), 'Problematizing "Epistemicide" in Transnational Curriculum Knowledge Production: China's Suyang Curriculum Reform as an Example', *Curriculum Inquiry*. doi: 10.1080/03626784.2020.1736521
Zhang, H. (2016), 'Lun hexinsuyang de neihan [On the Connotations of Core Suyang]', *Quanqiujiaoyuzhanwang [Global Education]*, 45 (4): 10–24.
Zhang, X. L. (2013), *Fujian tiandixin - Rujia zailin de yunyi yu daolu [On Meaning of and Path Toward Authentic Confucianism]*, Shangai: Dongfang Chubanshe.

6

The Itinerant Curriculum Theory in the Chilean Context of Curriculum Control and Standardization

Toward a Constituent – Itinerant – Curriculum

José Félix Angulo Rasco[1]

Introduction

Thinking about the possibility of an itinerant curriculum (IC) in Chilean education requires a double exercise.[2] In the first place, it is necessary to understand and explain. However, just briefly, the curricular context in which Chile finds itself, its immediate origin in the dictatorship and the situation of solid control in which schools, teachers and the system, in general, have become stranded. In the second place, it becomes equally essential to understand the uprising of the Chilean people that took place at the end of October (2019) because it is in this historical event that there has not yet been the *presence* of an IC (in the *emergence* of a constituent curriculum.

Curriculum and education policy in Chile

It would only be possible to understand Chile's current, dominant and constituted curriculum by analysing in some depth the educational policy developed during the past thirty years, that is, since the end of the 1990s. Although it is evident that those *market policies* (Verger, 2016; Verger, Fontdevila and Zancajo, 2016) that Pinochet's military dictatorship imposed with the expectation of becoming the grand experiment – which failed (Collins and Lear, 1995) – of the free market economy, it is since the beginning of this century that it has been more clearly detected how neoliberalism has progressively become Chile's education policy as well as the subjectivity (Brown, 2015) of the political leaders, and even of a large part of the Chilean people. The first post-dictatorship governments (since 1990) of the *Concertación* adopted the economy and the education structure inherited from Pinochet, probably conditioned by the constitution drawn up by the dictator, which is still in force, and whose change, as it will be analysed later, has become an urgent demand of the least popular (i.e. of the people) 'uprising' in October 2019 (Falabella and Ramos Zincke, 2019).

We have to understand here that since the beginning of the democracy (and after the departure of the dictator), Chile has gone more deeply into neoliberalism, initially at the hands of the political parties of the *Concertación*, with the consent of the court elite as it is called by Ruiz Encina (2014, 156) and with the *political* understanding of the business community (Ruiz Encina, 2013; 2014). Neoliberalism, as it was to be expected, was radically expanded, particularly in education, with the rise to power of the ultra-liberal businessman Sebastián Piñera in 2011.

The state and the market go together because neoliberalism needs the structures of the state not only to impose legitimate neoliberal policies but also to cover market deficiencies. It is about an entrepreneurial government (Osborne and Gaebler, 1994, 64). The state becomes highly invasive: 'Now, the state exerts a higher control on health, education, and the arts than in the era of labor collectivism' (Gray, 2010).

At the same time, in Chile, the state also adopts a subsidiary role, which remains intact until today. A subsidiary state does not guarantee rights (Ruiz Encina, 2014) but delivers resources which are in turn capitalized by the market, as it happens with *vouchers* (Angulo and Redon, 2012; Ruiz, 2013; 2014; 2019; Bellei, 2015; Verger, Fontdevila and Zancajo, 2016), that by delivering those resources using subsidies on demand, 'the state becomes the main responsible for private educational expansion' (Ruíz Encina, 2014, 97). In this way, Chile is one of the countries which has applied more *voucher* policies, not only at a national scale but it has also been using them for more than thirty-four years at all school and university levels (Ruíz Encina, 2014, 97).

Chile: The road to the evaluative state

In what follows, I would like to focus precisely on the role of institutional gendarme that the Chilean state adopts in education rather than on its part of subsidiarity. The reason is simple. Assuming that in Chile, it was the dictatorship that imposed neoliberal policies, after it, the governments that emerged from the plebiscitary democracy became a kind of gendarme or guardian of their compliance. Not only did they continue along the path of neoliberalism, but in education (as well as in public health or pensions), they deepened and increased their implementation; in addition, in education, a susceptible area and a primary sphere of profit (Olivia Mönkeberg, 2013), they have been making use of a narrow and Manichean version of quality and equity. Thus, the state has been transformed into what Neave (1990, 8, 1994)[3] called an evaluative state based on solid accountability mechanisms (Parcerisa and Falabella, 2017).

The evaluative state has been taking shape since 1990 through a series of laws and legislative instruments as the following ones:

- National System of Teacher Performance (SNED), Law 19.410 of 1995. Through this system, subsidized school centres with the best evaluation results are granted,

at least for two years, the 'Subvención por Desempeño de Excelencia' (Schools Excellence Fund) to deliver remuneration incentives to teachers and education assistants.
- Preferential School Fund (Law 20.248) of 2008 establishes the school classification based on the outcomes as the primary criterion of support and the consequences for the schools in case of non-compliance with the selected achievements, even leading to their closure.
- General Law of Education of 2009 (Law 20.370) offers an institutional frame to control and take charge of the quality of education.
- The National System for Quality Assurance (SAC) for Early, Basic, and Secondary Education and its Auditing, Law 20.529 of 2011 (renewed and modified in 2019).

This set of laws, I repeat, gradually consolidated an evaluative state based on the Accountability and Performance Evaluation for schools (Angulo, 2014; 2020). From all of these legislative instruments, it must be highlighted that the General Law of 2009, which did not modify some essential aspects of the previous law passed by the dictatorship (Osandón et al. I, 2018, 29), sets up the Agency for Quality Education, an agency that becomes the institution to apply SIMCE standardized tests,[4] which de facto regulates accountability in education, classifies schools and imposes modification to those that do not reach the expected results. As a result of this law, in April 2012, the Curricular Guidelines for Primary Education and the 7th and 10th Grades of Secondary Education were approved. The approval of these curricular bases is critical, as they do not only represent the continuation of the historical model of a curriculum based on objectives that were already established in Chile through the import of the ideas of Bloom and Tyler (Redon, 2016; Osandón et al., 2018) since the 1960s, but they also constitute a crucial element in the process of standardization and maintenance of the evaluative state and of accountability in Chile. Osandón et al. (2018, 32) have identified several key elements of these curricular bases:

- A rapid and considerable increase of learning objectives in every subject stated with a robust operational sense has been confirmed.
- The objectives, and by extension, the curricular bases, are organized and written with the implementation of the internal and external standardized tests in mind. First, by emphasizing the objectives as minimum contents to be achieved, they connect and facilitate their adaptation to the SIMCE standardized internal tests. Second, because they are made to be adapted to the demands of external and international standardized tests such as PISA, PIRLS and TIMSS (Álvarez Rojas, 2018).
- The bases are focused on the subjects of language, mathematics and sciences.

However, the legislative instrument that closes this perverse circle is the Law for Quality Assurance (Angulo, 2018; 2022; 2020). This law was enacted under the first mandate of the first government of the businessman Piñera and has remained with slight variations. The law above was published to ensure the quality of the education system and equity. Although quality is not clearly defined in this law, since it vaguely states that it will include educational principles of a comprehensive nature, it does emphatically state in Article 3 that such quality is related to the fulfilment of student learning standards, which are associated with the general objectives of the law and to other quality indicators and performance standards of educational institutions and their supporters.[5] Equity is related to all students having the same learning opportunities, meaning all students acquire basic content standards.

In an official document on Chilean education indicators, the following can be read:

> The focus of public policies in primary education is currently on equity, specifically on raising the quality of the education provided so that all students can access both suitable learning and environments for the optimal cognitive, social, and physical development of children, regardless of the level of resources of the families or the type of school attended. (MINEDUC, 2018, 34)

Note here the coincidence among equity, quality and learning standards. Equity is based on raising the quality of education, which is based on achieving access to essential learnings. Just for basic learning, they are and should be the same for everyone. Equity translates into homogenization in the same way as quality does. As a report from the Chilean Teachers' Association points out, 'trying to ensure equity through the equality of cumulative contents and fragmented and decontextualized skills, as the standard provides it [. . .], does only deepen inequalities and the lack of cultural relevance of the school' (CPCh, 2017, 7).

Quality assurance depends on measurable results per the established minimum and essential curricular contents. Article 2 adds the confluence of external tests of a census nature (SIMCE) and accountability, adding legal consequences and a regime of sanctions for non-compliance with what is established and stipulated.

Here, we have a demonstrative system related to the Global Education Reform Movement (GERM), indicated by Shalberg (2016), which strengthens the state as evaluative and controller among all its characteristics. All the components of the education system, people and professionals, the curriculum, the organization of schools, the students' lives and even the country's expectations concerning the 'importance' of education, are left subsumed under evaluative control. Nothing, absolutely nothing, has been and is more critical in Chilean education until now than the implementation of the SIMCE standardized tests and the achievement of quality through the performance measured by them.

Therefore, the crucial question is whether an IC is conceivable in such a context. The direct answer would be no. An IC in the current Chilean situation would be inconceivable. However, there is an opportunity that the Chilean people themselves have opened in October 2019: that of the constituent process. Nevertheless, before going any further with this argumentative line, I would analyse what is or, instead, what an IC means.

The theory of an itinerant curriculum: An option for Chile?

After this minor revision of the curriculum policy in Chile in the past twenty years, we would have to ask ourselves two things: Is it possible to conceive an IC and a theory of the IC in such a panoptic context subject to surveillance and control? I am convinced that the affirmative answer comes precisely from the Chilean social movements and the changes that such (student, popular, and citizen) movements have strongly favoured since October 2019 (Inzunza et al., 2019). However, first, we must make an effort to outline to some extent what we mean by or what the itinerant curriculum theory (ICT) is to see at least how an IC can connect with the changes demanded in Chile today. Here, it is necessary to make a warning.

The idea of ICT is a fortunate creation of J. M. Paraskeva. This idea has been developing for more than ten years, since at least the publishing in 2011 of *Conflicts in Curriculum Theory, Challenging Hegemonic Epistemologies*, after being introduced several years before in academic spaces – AERA – USA, AACS – USA and ANPEd – Brazil. The argumentation and discourse that Paraskeva (2011; 2016a; 2016b; 2021; 2022a; 2022b; 2023) develops on ICT is, in the way the author himself has been constructing it (*more poiesis*), strongly interwoven with the authors and the ideas and conceptions that act as their support and foundation. For this reason, it becomes immensely complicated to separate the views from the references; we will try to limit ourselves to his key ideas, excluding the references that the author uses as much as possible.

Against the curriculum canon

One of ICT's key and initial points is its distancing – or, as Paraskeva deliberately calls it, *disrespect* – as its criticism of the curricular *canon*. It is not about providing another perspective; it is about stating that the canon is not relevant and unnecessary and that the canon, the established curricular approaches, whatever they were, must be challenged. It is a matter of dismantling the epistemological and discursive orthodoxy that nourishes and supports the curricular canon (2011, 175, 2016a, 266, 2016c, 131). This lack of respect entails dismantling Eurocentrism, the epistemological codes and conceptions of the culture that nullifies and forecloses on its reproduction (foreclosure). The ICT aims to place the curriculum, or rather curricular thinking, in a diametrical perspective[6] (Paraskeva, 2011, 175, 2022a) that does not correlate with 'any disciplinary grid that ossifies Modern Western Eurocentric epistemological platform' (2020, 113).

However, the ICT goes beyond a deliberate disrespect of the canon; it represents a 'struggle against epistemological orthodoxy', and it attempts, following Sousa (2005), 'to bring scientific knowledge face-to-face with non-scientific, explicitly local knowledges, knowledges grounded in the experience of the leaders and activists of the social movements studied by social scientists' (Paraskeva, 2011, 2022a).

It is a movement representing a turn, an authentic epistemological rupture (Bachelard, 1994; Bourdieu, Chamboredon & Passeron, 2003), by leaving out the typical topics and places where curricular practice and discourse have been circulating.

Epistemological turn

The first element in this process of radical change in curricular discourse and thinking is found in the transformation of the language used to talk about the curriculum, something that was early proposed by Huebner (1999) (Paraskeva, 2016b, 189, 2021, 2022b, 2023). Here, transforming language also entails changing thinking, moving it away from the abyss and the absence it produces: the absence of humanity (Paraskeva, 2011, 2022a).

Furthermore, it is these absences, the acceptance or the blindness to abyssal thinking, that generate epistemicides: the annulment of other ways of thinking and talking about the world, culture, education and the curriculum. 'The struggle against epistemicides consolidates a kind of new curriculum revisionism that challenges frameworks, claiming that the authority of particular discourses and hierarchies need identities, rights, subjectivities, and experiences [. . .] A new epistemological intrans-discipline – based on epistemological disobedience – will allow us to understand more accurately our struggles for pedagogies' (2016b; 2021, 2022b, 2023). Thinking in a non-abyssal way also leads to a post-abyssal epistemology that expands the ecology of knowledges that rescues those knowledges marginalized, trampled or discredited by discourse and canonical thinking. 'Post-abyssal thinking while [. . .] implies a radical break with modern Western ways of thinking and acting, such break does not mean slurring specific modern Western impulses' (Paraskeva, 2016b, 242).

> I argue that alternative thinking of alternatives implies learning to unlearn, a decolonial take that aims at a general epistemology of the impossibility of a general epistemology. Not to walk away but to crossover the abyssal lines to produce a non-abyssal thinking. This is undeniably a challenging task. (Paraskeva, 2016b, 241)

Deterritorialization as Itinerancy

Thinking of the unthinkable, then, crossing over and not being crossed over by abyssal thinking, requires, and this is a crucial point, an itinerant posture. Why? Because it is necessary to find a place beyond the established, beyond the canon, beyond Eurocentrism or Occidentalism. Founding a new language requires reversing epistemicides; changing epistemology implies finding the sense of the new place from which to speak, an entire and ecologically diverse place. Therefore, the curriculum theorist is a *constant migrant*. However, finding a stable place is less important than going along the places; it is not a matter of establishing a new epistemology as if it were a new dogma; it is about accepting a changeable and diverse epistemology. Acknowledging the diversity of epistemologies is avoiding epistemicides. 'It requires an itinerant posture. It requires thinking the unthinkable. It implies daring to find a location beyond Eurocentrism, beyond Occidentalism; it implies defying not just the subalternization of particular forms of knowledge' (Paraskeva, 2016b, 242). The IC is a 'destabilizing epistemology that aims to defamiliarize the canonic tradition of monocultures of knowledge' (2020).

Itinerancy is the acceptance of the multiple spaces and places from which to think and understand new epistemologies. The term *corazonar,* by Sousa, spreads here in the embracement to the rhizomatic sense of the curriculum. An IC is not a curriculum of the non-spaces but of the multiple spaces,[7] the various places where identities flourish and stories are and occur. Paraphrasing Jack Goody (2006), we must travel to reach its acknowledgement to avoid the theft of history, that is, histories. The IC goes along those histories, multiple symbolic worlds and diverse and distinct epistemologies. 'Deterritorialized curriculum theory is exploring new ways of thinking and feeling and finding ways to produce new and different purposes of mind' (2011, 194). As mentioned earlier, the rhizomatic sense is associated with diversity, with the diverse. The rhizomatic reason breaks dichotomies, goes beyond 'beginnings and endings'; the IC 'is an approach that is born of the multiplicity on immanent platforms' (Paraskeva, 2016b, 270) and is 'profoundly sentient of the multiplicities of lines, spaces, and dynamic becomings' (2016a, 271, 2022a).

In turn, Paraskeva emphasizes that ICT needs to be understood as *poiesis*. 'ICT is a poesis that itinerantly throws the subject against the infinite of representation to grasp the omnitude of the real(ity) and the rational(ity), thus mastering the transcendent. Being more *poiesis* than just theory (and not because it is less theory), its itinerant position epitomizes a transcendent nomadography, which is not transcendental' (2019, 24). But is it only *poiesis*? Let us remember that the notion of *poiesis* is connected to that of praxis. Both are linked to making to production. However, while *poiesis* denotes every activity that would mean the passage from non-existence to existence and presence, such as artistic 'production' or creation, the praxis involves the will of action.

Thus, ICT is not just a *poiesis* that leads curricular thinking and, hence, educational thinking from non-existence to presence, recognizing the epistemologies, symbolic worlds and stolen history as an act of creation. In this way, ICT widens and empowers the role of praxis, of educational action. I want to stop here for a moment. The relevance of linking *praxis* to the *poietic* sense of ICT lies in its political orientation. I mean that ICT is not a mere and new theoretical discourse but also forms a practice, a transformation. Its critical nature lies in the assumption of diverse epistemologies, the multiple spaces it can acknowledge and give place to and the very action of change and transformation of education. Educational *praxis* can be based on *poiesis* insofar as it implies going from non-existence to presence, but it does not stop here; as praxis, it also involves the struggle for that created presence, the fight for the recognition and dignity of that presence. Therefore, ICT is based on the exercise of 'citizenship and solidarity' (2020, 2021, 2022b, 2023).

The ICT does not forget as praxis; it could not without denying itself (2016a; 2016b, 266). The IC is 'an act of social and cognitive justice' (2016a, 281, 2021, 2022a, 2022b, 2023). 'Deterritorialized curriculum theory that privileges the cult of difference implies the need to understand education as a set of relationships in which the personal and political plays a leading role' (2016a, 268–69, 2021, 2022a, 2022b, 2023).

In conclusion, the curriculum as itinerancy introduces a new post-abyssal momentum in the field and inaugurates a decolonial turn; it is related to the fact that the curriculum is not a canon or a fixed 'object', a standardized monolith for schools; itinerancy implies variation. Every school has to carry out its itinerary, not identical to the others, perhaps asymptotic, perhaps divergent, but never the same. Itinerancy aims to obliterate the trite customs and topics of the curriculum: the objectives or competencies, the conventional subjects and their hermetic classification. At the same time, itinerancy fosters the search that students must make for themselves, for the world, for injustices, for epistemological subjugations on which a large part of the supposed canonical knowledge is based, for the obliviousness of the other and other epistemologies, for even their ways of seeing and understanding the world. This is not just a question of simply accepting them but of critically analysing them, recognizing them, identifying them and making them the object of analysis.

The IC challenges teachers, schools, students and communities to think for themselves, to choose their variation, their route, to extend epistemology, to open it up to other possibilities, to develop pedagogical imagination in practice, to go beyond what is given, to recognize where to start without having the objective or final result defined. It challenges us to forget that the curriculum is justified by particular learnings by outcomes; the curriculum is a space, it is not a passage; it is contrary to the non-space, it is a shared space for epistemological, human and affective encounters (Huebner, 1999). The IC urges us not to compare schools by their productive results but to understand them in their actions, becoming and diversity. The IC encourages us to think about qualities rather than quality.[8] The IC is a space for dialogue, conversation, debate, inquiry and openness. The IC does not give the floor to the subordinate (Spivak, 2011), something that would be a colonial act in itself: in the IC, the subordinate, the emigrant, the different, the other takes the floor and turns it into an act. It takes its epistemology and endorses it; it shows it is facing other epistemologies and strikes up its dialogue with them and among them, not in solitude but in collectivity. The IC is not an act of one person alone; it is a collective act, an idea that has no sense without the others. For this reason, the IC is a *constituent curriculum*.

A constituent curriculum as an itinerant curriculum: Prolegomena to a constituent process

At the end of October 2019 (between the 14th and 18th), Chilean secondary students started to evade paying for the Santiago Metro (underground) ticket in protest of the recent rise of 30 pesos.[9] One of their first slogans was 'to evade, not to pay, another way to fight', because secondary students who jumped through the turnstiles without paying made evident a latent malaise in Chilean society: the enormous inequality, the private indebtedness of families,[10] corruption and the prevailing injustice (Fazio, 2016; Tromben, 2016; Guzmán and Rokas, 2017). The student protest expanded from Friday the 18th, starting with demonstrations in the main underground stations in Santiago (those with the largest turnout), continuing with casserole protests in some communes of the same city, burning some underground stations and looting shops and supermarkets. The protest gradually became national, from the North to the South of the country, but with enormous intensity in Santiago, Valparaíso and Concepción. It lasted for months until the arrival and spread of the pandemic; Chile experienced one of the most significant social 'outbreaks' since democracy was restored in 1990 (Garcés, 2020, 13). This mobilization that 'leads' to the outbreak has two characteristics: its enormous spontaneity and its transversality. Concerning the former, the mobilization occurs without a central organizer or known organic structures. Transversality teaches us that although it was once again the secondary students who started various social movements, the existing ones joined the protest, generating – both of them – 'their processes of organization and public expression' (Garcés, 2020, 12). The outbreak of 2019 reflected a deep malaise. As one of its most chanted slogans pointed out, it was not about 30 pesos (the rise in the price of the underground) but thirty years of constant injustice and inequality (Garcés, 2020). The conservative and neoliberal government of Sebastián Piñera responded by declaring an emergency state and taking the army out to the streets. However, to its surprise, the mobilizations continued, occupying squares with marches and casserole protests in communes and neighbourhoods. The demonstrations, which could not stop the enormous repression carried out by the 'carabineros' (Chile's national policemen) and the army together, controlled the presence of the pandemic.

The October 2019 popular uprising is not an isolated event. Between 1983 and 1987, there were twenty-two national days of protest (Salazar, 2011, 15). The most recent ones are those of the Mapuche movement at the end of the 1990s (which continue)[11] and the current student movements: the so-called 'mochilazo' of 2002, the penguin revolution of 2006 (Bellei, 2015) and the movement for public education in 2011 (Arrué, 2012). We must also include the protests of 'No + AFP' (No more AFPs) since 2016,[12] the feminist May of 2018, the socioenvironmental struggles for water and the preservation of Chile's natural heritage and the teachers' strike in 2018.

The popular uprising of October 2019 demanded, as we have just pointed out, a profound change in Chile's economic and social policy – a change that for all the actors involved was represented by a *new constitution for* Chile that would nullify the constitution in force which was drawn up during the dictatorship of Pinochet – a constitution that was created precisely to maintain injustice and inequality and to legitimate neoliberalism. The new constitution demanded implies the establishment of a *constituent process*.

Before explaining what a *constituent process* involves, it is necessary to remember that, here too, Chile has a long *constituent* tradition that goes back to its independence as a colony and its instauration as a country and to the fruitless effort to approve a constitution that is the product of popular constituent power. As Salazar has shown (2009, 2011), in two hundred years of history, 'the (mercantile) ruling class has never admitted, by self-interest and conviction, any *public exercise of constituent power*' (Salazar, 2011, 29); but neither has the official political left, which only names and admits it when it can lead it by appropriating it (Ruíz, 2013, 2019). Salazar highlights two relevant social citizenship mobilizations between the nineteenth and twentieth centuries. In 1822, a constituent process, which was not only against the criminal dictatorship of Bernardo O'Higgins, started; it finished in 1829 with the approval of a political constitution. Almost 100 years later, in 1918, it was decided to replace the oligarchic regime of the time (inherited from the famous defeats of the previous century) with a National-Developmental Popular State, for which a Constituent Assembly of Workers and Intellectuals was convened in 1924 (Salazar, 2012, 31–2).

Both events in 1822 and 1924 arose from social and political traditions that likewise had been based since the sixteenth century when the Chilean people organized themselves outside the metropolis in neighbourhood assemblies or open cabildos that consolidated a self-government tradition. These cabildos were direct and local organs of popular sovereignty (Salazar, 2012, 36), bringing chacareros,[13] ranchers, landowners, labourers, artisans, miners, teachers, scribes, bailiffs and militiamen. The key here is double: On the one hand, the constituent power needs a diversified social power (Salazar, 2011, 74); on the other, its primary substance is found in self-generated social culture (Salazar, 2011, 75).

Although historically, these self-generated processes finally succumbed to the power of the (oligarchic, military and political) elites owning the Chilean state, the memory of this form of social and political organization, this citizen social memory, has remained through the 'underground historical-cultural processes, filtered from subject to subject under the political space monopolized by the State, almost always invisible to the law.... They are far-reaching historical weapons ... it is the way popular sovereignty works: through slow cultural movements subsidized underground. They are consolidating and undermining. It is the popular "mole" of history' (Salazar, 2011, 55). Since October 2019, the Chilean people have been organizing and gathering in cabildos, formed by diverse social actors, throughout the territory of the country. The cabildos had the purpose of beginning to discuss, as they did in 1828, the terms of a new constitution for Chile. In this sense, the cabildos were and are the primary organization of the constituent process.

The constituent process

What is a constituent process? Like any other constitution, the Chilean constitution finds its meaning in providing rules for organizing the citizenry and their life in a country in its various aspects. It shapes a framework of primary and general rules; from these rules or under this *framework*, it approves and creates laws closer to the immediate needs of the country and the citizens. However, in addition to shaping norms and rules, a Constitution shapes the political power that rules the country: it determines political decisions. A constitution and a country's institutions (including legislative chambers, political parties, the judicial structure, etc.) constitute power. Such political power, as emphasized by Atria et al. (2020, 12), is not a natural power but an artificial one. 'Its existence poses a legitimization problem.' The legitimization of such power comes from the constituent power of the people. Let us stop here. The constituted power – the military forces, the oligarchy and the politicians attached to the dictatorship – approved the Constitution of dictator Pinochet. Subsequently, this Constitution was accepted by the constituted powers in Democracy. In both cases, there was a lack of constituent legitimacy. Let us repeat it: Only the sovereign people can justly legitimize.

> What is relevant is the distinction between constituent and constituted power, between the power to decide on the form and the manner of exercising power and the power which is based on a decision already taken on the form and the manner

of exercising power and which, therefore has a blind spot: it cannot challenge that decision, it cannot challenge the Constitution. The constituted powers are normative powers. (Atria and Wilenmann, 2020, 13)

We must understand that the current powers and constituted institutions, even in a democracy, lack the legitimacy to challenge the Constitution to revoke it precisely because they are and have been formed under the legal instrument that justifies them. On the contrary, 'the constituent power, being a formless power, not being a normative power, a power without shape, is just the only one which can challenge and elaborate a new Constitution; because, the constituent power is the power in sufficient quantity to make a constituent decision, a new fundamental decision on politics' (Atria and Wilenmann, 2020, 16).

Decisions on constituted powers are the measure of the facts and rules and the measure of the acts. When a constituted power breaks in, the relationship between facts and norms that characterize normality is reversed. The norms stop being the measure of the facts, and the facts become the measure of the norms. (Atria and Wilenmann, 2020, 17–18)

The constituent power holds the reins of the action. It creates the political facts through a constituent process. A process in Chile was structured in the wake of the underground tradition that has been constant throughout its history through diverse and multiple cabildos all over the country. The constituent power is a rational power based on constituent deliberation (Salazar, 2009).

The IC as a constituent curriculum

Chile's current curriculum, constituted and governed by a control system that is justified through a perspective on quality that only understands standardized tests and the very standardization of the curriculum, closes any pathway to thinking about an IC. In the same way, as Chilean people are demanding a constitutive process that nullifies the past Constitution and allows a new Constitution to be drawn up, discussed and proposed through cabildos or any other type of popular organization, Chilean education, in these moments, requires a profound social change, popular rebellion and popular demands; it needs to rethink a new curricular framework constitutively. However, this is not enough. The possibility of a constituent curriculum cannot be understood or even conceived without social and citizen participation; active participation allows the flow of itinerancy by contributing particular and distinctive cultural elements to the curriculum by remodelling it interactively. As Salazar has pointed out, 'constituent power needs diversified social power' (2011, 74). The constituent process requires schools to be accepted as cabildos in their own right so that they create and constitute their curriculum. The constituent curriculum will be the process of an ongoing famous dialogue. The facts, the actions and the educational *praxis* at schools will make possible a curricular space and the sense of constituent education to emerge by *poiesis*; in this way, each school in itself being the political epicentre of such a constituent process, thus that extent, the curriculum would be itinerant, it would be epistemologically diverse, far from the abyssal discourse and, what may be more important, free from the panoptical control currently exercised over it.

Notes

1. Member of the UNESCO Chair in Democracy, Global Citizenship, and Transformative Education Catholic University of Valparaiso, Chile & University of Cádiz, Spain.
2. This work was funded by CIE160009 and Fondecyt 1221625.
3. Neave defines the evaluative state as a 'general rationalization and redistribution of functions between the center and the periphery, in such a way that the center maintains the overall strategic control, using fewer, but more precise, policy levers constituted by the assignment of missions, the specification of goals for the system and the operationalization of criteria related to the quality of the product' (Neave, 1990, p. 8).
4. These standardized tests have been applied as a census – to all the schools – at primary levels (second and eighth grades) and secondary levels (third and fourth grades) since 1988. The test has been extended in the past twenty years by incorporating new subjects and adding personal and social development indicators.
5. The law euphemistically uses the concept of the *holder* instead of the establishment's owner. We want to remember here that in Chile, there are three types of establishments for primary and secondary education: private, subsidized (they have an owner/holder and receive funds – vouchers – from the state) and municipal schools.
6. From the Greek δύναμις *dýnamis* 'strength' and *geno*: that stimulates physical vigour (Paraskeva, 2020).
7. Here, I differ from Paraskeva's interpretation of the idea of non-place by Marc Augé (1993). A non-place is a place of passage where one does not stay, where one does not communicate and where one does not speak. Augé defines it as follows: 'Non-places are the necessary facilities for the hasty circulation of people and goods (motorways, crossroads, airports) like the means of transport themselves or the large shopping centres. Also, the long-lasting transit camps where the planet's refugees are stationed' (41). Bauman (2004:111) retakes this idea from Augé and amplifies it: 'A non-place is a space deprived of symbolic expressions of identity, relationships or history: examples include airports, highways, self-contained hotel rooms, and public transport.'
8. The concept of 'qualities' comes from the educational indicators developed by the government of Evo Morales in Bolivia.
9. 30 Chilean pesos are equivalent to 0.039 dollars and 0.034€.
10. The debt of Chilean families, according to the Central Bank, amounts to 79.9 per cent of the annual household disposable income. See https://www.cnnchile.com/economia/banco-central-deuda-hogares-754-ingresos-disponibles_20200706/.
11. One of the most terrible recent episodes against the Mapuche people is the murder of Catrillanca on 14 November 2018, in the Mapuche community of Temucuicui, a Mapuche community 600 kilometres to the South of Santiago, by the Carabineros Special Operations Group. See https://es.wikipedia.org/wiki/Camilo_Catrillanca#:~

:text=Catrillanca%20fue%20asesinado%20por%20un,Policiales%20Especiales%20de%20Carabineros%20llamada%20%C2%AB.

12 The AFPs are Pension Funds Administrators, forcibly imposed on Chilean people by the Dictatorship of Pinochet (Rivadeneira Martínez, 2018).

13 Chacarero is the owner of a chakra. A chakra is a small rural property. Today in Chile, the term is often used in a derogatory way, as when it is said that 'algo se chacreó' means something became popular or vulgar.

References

Álvarez Rojas, G. (2018), 'Requerimientos de la racionalidad neoliberal al sistema educativo: Reforma escolar y curriculum en el Chile posdictadura [Requirements of Neoliberal Rationality to the Educational System: School Reform and Curriculum in Post-Dictatorship Chile]', in C. Ruiz Sneider et al. (ed.), *Privatización de lo público en el sistema escolar. Chile y la agenda global de educación*, 317–37, Santiago: LOM.

Angulo Rasco, J. F. (2014), 'Los test estandarizados como estrategia neoliberal de sometimiento [Standardized Tests as a Neoliberal Submission Strategy]', *Trabajadores de la Enseñanza*, 348: 38–41.

Angulo Rasco, J. F. (2015), In Search of the Lost Curriculum. In J. M. Paraskeva and S. R. Steinberg (eds.), *Curriculum: Decanonizing the Field*, 137–55, New York: Peter Lang.

Angulo Rasco, J. F. (2018), *Breve introducción a tres conceptos importantes*, Valparaíso: Centro para la Investigación en la Educación Inclusiva. PUCV.

Angulo Rasco, J. F. (2020), 'Standardization in Education, a Device of Neoliberalism', *Journal for Critical Education Policy Studies*, 18 (2). http://www.jceps.com/wp-content/uploads/2020/10/18-2-7i.pdf.

Angulo Rasco, J. F. (2022), 'Sobre y Contra la Prueba Estandarizada SIMCE [About and Against the SIMCE Standardized Test]', in J. F. Angulo Rasco and C. Bernal (Coords.), *Las pruebas estandarizadas en educación. ¿De qué estamos hablando?*, 93–106, Madrid: DYKINSON.

Angulo Rasco, J. F. and S. Redon Pantoja (2012), 'La educación pública en la encrucijada. La pérdida del sentido público en educación [Public Education at the Crossroads: The Loss of Public Sense in Education]', *Estudios Pedagógicos*: 61–85. http://doi.org/10.4067/S0718-07052012000400003.

Arrué, M. (2012), 'El movimiento estudiantil en Chile (2011–2012): una lucha contra la discriminación', *Amérique Latine. Histoire & Mémoire. Les Cahiers ALHIM*, 24. http://journals.openedition.org/alhim/4388.

Atria, F., C. Salgado and J. Wilenmann (2020), *El proceso constituyente en 138 preguntas y respuestas [The Constituent Process in 138 Questions and Answers]*, Santiago: LOM.

Augé, M. (1993), *Los no lugares: Espacios de anonimato: Una antropología de la sobremodernidad*. Barcelona: Gedisa.

Bachelard, G. (1994), *La formación del espíritu científico [The Formation of the Scientific Spirit]*, Buenos Aires: Siglo XXI.

Bauman, Z. (2004), *Liquid Modernity*, México: Fondo de Cultura Económica.

Bellei, C. (2015), *El gran experimento. Mercado y privatización de la educación chilena [The Great Experiment: Market and Privatization of Chilean Education]*, Santiago: LOM.

Bourdieu, P., J. C. Chamboredon and J. C. Passeron (2003), *El oficio de sociólogo [The Profession of Sociologist]*, Madrid: Siglo XXI.

Brown, W. (2015), *Undoing the Demos: Neoliberalism's Stealth Revolution*, New York: Zone Books.
Colegio de Profesores de Chile (2017), *Diagnóstico. Nuestra visión sobre la educación chilena*. Working Paper DEP-CP 2017, Santiago.
Collins, J. and J. Lear (1995), *Chile´s Free-Market Miracle: A Second Look*, Oakland: The Institute for Good and Development Policy.
Falabella, A. and C. R. Zincke (2019), 'La larga historia de las evaluaciones nacionales a nivel escolar en Chile', *Cuadernos Chilenos de Historia de la Educación*, 11: 66–98.
Fazio, H. (2016), *Mecanismos fraudulentos de hacer fortuna. Mapa de la extrema riqueza 2015 [Fraudulent Mechanisms to Make a Fortune: Extreme Wealth Map 2015]*, Santiago: LOM.
Garcés, M. (2020), *Estallido social y una nueva constitución para Chile [Social Explosion and a New Constitution for Chile]*, Santiago: LOM.
Goody, J. (2006), *The Theft of History*, Cambridge: Cambridge University Press.
Gray, J. (2010), *Review of The Neoliberal State*, by Raymond Plant. New Statesman, 7 January (n.p.).
Grez, S. and F. por la Asamblea Constituyente (2015), *Asamblea Constituyente. La alternativa Democrática para Chile*, Santiago: América en Movimiento.
Guzmán, J. A. and J. Rokas (2017), *Empresarios Zombis. La mayor elusión tributaria de la élite Chilena [Zombie Entrepreneurs: The Greatest Tax Avoidance of the Chilean Elite]*, Santiago: Catalonia.
Huebner, D. E. (1999), *The Lure of the Transcendent: Collected Essays by Dwayne*, London: Lawrence Erlbaum Ass.
Inzunza, J., J. Jenny Assael, R. Cornejo and J. Redondo (2019), 'Public Education and Student Movements: The Chilean Rebellion Under a Neoliberal Experiment', *British Journal of Sociology of Education*, 40 (4): 490–506. http://doi.org/10.1080/01425692.2019.1590179.
MINEDUC (2018), *Ciclo de Mejoramiento en Establecimientos Educacionales. Orientaciones para la elaboración del Plan de Mejoramiento Educativo 2018*. Santiago de Chile.
Neave, G. (1990), 'La educación superior bajo la evaluación estatal', *Universidad Futura*, 2 (5). México.
Neave, G. (1994), 'El Estado evaluador', *Mejoramiento de la calidad académica de la U.N.L*, Cuadernillo nº1. Univ. Nac. del Litoral, Santa Fe.
Oliva, M. T. and F. Gascón (2016), 'Estandarización y racionalidad política neoliberal: bases curriculares de Chile [Standardization and Neoliberal Political Rationality: Curricular Bases of Chile]', *Cad. Cedes, Campinas*, 36 (100): 301–18.
Olivia Mónckeberg, M. (2013), *Con fines de Lucro [Only For Profit]*, Santiago: Debate.
Osandón, L. et al. (2018), 'Estado, mercado y curriculum escolar: la experiencia chilena (1964–2018) [State, Market and School Curriculum: The Chilean Experience (1964–2018)]', Oficina Internacional de Educación, UNESCO.
Osborne, D. and T. Gaebler (1994), *La reinvención del gobierno. La influencia del espíritu empresarial en el sector público*, Barcelona: Paidós.
Paraskeva, J. M. (2011), *Conflicts in Curriculum Theory: Challenging Hegemonic Epistemologies*, New York: Palgrave MacMillan.
Paraskeva, J. M. (2016a), 'Epistemicides: Toward an Itinerant Curriculum Theory', in J. M. Paraskeva and S. R. Steinberg (eds), *Curriculum: Decanonizing the Field*, 261–89, New York: Peter Lang.
Paraskeva, J. M. (2016b), *Curriculum Epistemicide: Toward an Itinerant Theory*, New York. Routledge.

Paraskeva, J. M. (2016c), 'Desterritorializar: hacia una Teoría Curricular Itinerante', *Revista Interuniversitaria de Formación del Profesorado*, 85 (30.1): 121–34.

Paraskeva, J. M. (2019), 'Itinerant Curriculum Theory Revisited don a Non-Theoricide Towards the Canonicide: Addressing the "Curriculum Involution"', *Journal of the American Association for the Advancement of Curriculum Studies*, 12 (1): 1–43.

Paraskewa, J. M. (2020), 'Teoría del Curriculum Itinerante: una Declaración Epistemológica de Independencia [Itinerant Curriculum Theory: An Epistemological Declaration of Independence]', in R. Espinoza Lolas and J. F. Angulo Rasco (Comps.), *Conceptos para disolver la educación capitalista*, 107–26, Barcelona: TerraIgnota.

Paraskeva, J. M. (2021), *Curriculum and the Generation of Utopia*, New York: Routledge.

Paraskeva, J. M. (2022a), *Conflicts in Curriculum Theory*, 2nd edn, New York: Palgrave.

Paraskeva, J. M., ed. (2022b), *The Curriculum: A New Comprehensive Reader*, New York: Peter Lang.

Paraskeva, J. M., ed. (2023), *Critical Perspectives on the Denial of Caste in Educational Debate*, New York: Routledge.

Parcerisa, L. and A. Falabella (2017), 'La consolidación del Estado evaluador a través de políticas de rendición de cuentas: Trayectoria, producción y tensiones en el sistema educativo chileno', *Education Policy Analysis Archives*, 25(89). http://doi.org/10.14507/epaa.25.3177.

Redon, S. (2016), 'Voices of the Curriculum to the South of Latin America: The Subject, the History, and the Politics', in J. M. Praskewa and S. R. Steinberg (eds), *Curriculum: Decanonizing the Field*, 583–607, New York: Peter Lang.

Rivadeneira Martínez, C. (2018), *Aquí se fabrican pobres. El sistema privado de pensiones chileno [They Are Poorly Made Here: The Chilean Private Pension System]*, Santiago: LOM.

Ruiz, C. (2013), *De nuevo la sociedad [Society Again]*, Santiago: LOM.

Ruiz, C. (2014), 'Lo público y lo estatal en el actual problema de educación', *Revista Anales* (7): 95–105.

Ruiz, C. (2019), *La política en el neoliberalismo. Experiencias latinoamericanas [Politics in Neoliberalism: Latin American Experiences]*, Santiago: LOM.

Salazar, G. (2002), *Función perversa de la 'memoria oficial', función histórica de la 'memoria'social': ¿cómo orientar los procesos auto-educativos? (Chile, 1990–2002) [Perverse Function of 'Official Memory', Historical Function of 'Social Memory': How to Guide Self-Educational Processes? (Chile, 1990–2002)]*, Universidad de Chile. Archivo Chile. Centro Estudios 'Miguel Enríquez': CEME.

Salazar, G. (2009), *Del poder constituyente de asalariados e intelectuales (Chile, siglos XX y XXI) [Of the Constituent Power of Wage Earners and Intellectuals (Chile, 20th and 21st Centuries)]*, Santiago: LOM.

Salazar, G. (2011), *En el nombre del poder popular constituyente (Chile, siglo XXI) [En el nombre del poder popular constituyente (Chile, siglo XXI)]*, Santiago: LOM.

Salazar, G. (2012). *Movimientos sociales en Chile: Trayectoria histórica y proyección política*, Santiago de Chile: Uqbar editores.

Santos, B. De Sousa (2005), *Conocer desde el Sur: para una cultura política emancipatoria*. Lima: Fondo Editorial dela Facultad de ciencias Sociales. Programa de Estujdios sobre Democracia y Transformación Global.

Santos, B. De Sousa (2009), *Una epistemología del SUR [An Epistemology of the SOUTH]*, México: Siglo XXI Editores.

Santos, B. De Sousa (2013), *Descolonizar el saber, reinventar el poder [Decolonize Knowledge, Reinvent Power]*, Santiago: LOM.

Santos, B. de Sousa (2019), 'Más allá del pensamiento abisal: de las líneas globales a las ecologías de saberes [Beyond Abyssal Thinking: From Global Lines to Ecologies of Knowledge]', in M. Paula Meneses et al. (Comp.), *Construyendo las Epistemologías del Sur Para un pensamiento alternativo de alternativas, Volumen I [Constructing the Epistemologies of the South for Alternative Thinking of Alternatives, Volume I]*, 585–620.

Spivak, G. C. (2011), *¿Puede hablar el subalterno? [Can the Subordinate Speak?]*, Buenos Aires: El cuenco de plata editores.

Tromben, C. (2016), *Crónica secreta de la economía Chilena [Secret Chronicle of the Chilean Economy]*, Santiago: Ediciones B.

Venegas, J. I. (2016), *¿Por qué los jóvenes chilenos rechazan la política? Desafección política juvenil en el Chile postransición [Why Do Young Chileans Reject Politics? Youth Political Disaffection in Post-Transition Chile]*, Santiago: Ril Editores.

Verger, A. (2016), 'The Global Diffusion of Education Privatization: Unpacking and Theorizing Policy Adoption. en K. Mundy, A. Green, B. Lingard, and A. Verger (eds), *Handbook of Global Education Policy*, 64–80, Chichester: John Wiley & Sons. https://doi.org/10.1002/9781118468005.ch3.

Verger, A., C. Fontdevila and A. Zancajo (2016), *The Privatization of Education: A Political Economy of Global Education Reform*, New York: Teachers College Press.

Zambrano, U. M. (2019), 'Las nociones de *poiesis*, *praxis* y *techné* en la producción artística', in *Index revista de arte contemporáneo*. INDEX #07, Quito: PUCE.

7

Itinerant Curriculum Theory in the Turkish Context

Fatma Mizikaci

As a Turkey-born scholar, my ancestry, legacy and social-historical position shaped my experiences within the dichotomies of the thoughts and knowledges of the West and the East, the North and the South, the religious and the secular. This is a confusing situation rather than comforting in a context that normalization of the abnormal becomes normal. What any colleague of mine may recall that daily life may be a scene for right-left conflicts, street fights of the late 1970s, the 1980 military coup d'état, police troops at the campus in 2000s, discharge of professors, students marching for their democratic rights, Gezi resistance in 2013 and so on. Challenges on education, youth and social justice have been significant stimulus of these conflicts and struggles. Such overt resistances against the hegemony of any kind of oppression, any authoritarianism of the twenty-first century, any colonization of thought are linked to the ones in the history of this land, that is, resistance for emancipation, social justice and cognitive justice.

The Turkish anti-colonial revolution emerged as the rejection of Ottomanism and Euro-British colonialism in the beginning of the twentieth century. It was characterized as social mobilization for emancipation, therefore education was given utmost importance as the engine of change in the transition period. In the foundation of Turkish Republic in 1923, education was deemed public sphere as it was stated in the founding principle 'sovereignty unconditionally belongs to the nation/public', as opposed to its earlier Ottoman version, and achieved its higher goal of social unity. It persisted after major changes in the following period until early neoconservative, neoliberal upsurge in the 1950s that fully legitimized by the coup d'état in 1980.

This chapter is organized over three main discussions that landmark curriculum theorizing in terms of itinerant curriculum theory (ICT): First section examines the late Ottoman historical context, which had been demarcated with Islamic education for ages together with the modern education thought in the Western type of schools including missionary ones. Second section is devoted to the Turkish anti-colonial revolution as a social mobilization against reactionaryism of the Ottomans and colonialism of the Europe-America circle. Finally, a discussion of the third era, what I call 'recolonization of curriculum', takes place referring to the wed of neoliberalism with political Islam and the distorted education system with its curriculum knowledge and methodology.

Within this broader context, the discussion is anchored in the discourse of geopolitical and historical identifications as an essence of ICT. Any narrative of the Global North, the Global South, the West, European or Eurocentric, Eastern or Oriental (Paraskeva, 2016, 2017; Santos, 2014; Oliveira, 2017; Said, 1979; Berkes, 1998; Mardin, 1991; Gurnah, 2002) has significant assumptions to understand epistemologies and 'epistemicide' in Turkey. Paraskeva claims many nations educate their generations with a hegemonic US-centred, Anglophone and Eurocentric curriculum historically made of a knowledge set accepted as superior to non-European or non-US knowledge which is ignored or silenced (2020). This has applied in Turkey in many occasions together with Islamic education of Ottoman time and political Islam of the recent government. Thus there is need for broader understanding of a non-conformist curriculum theory. No struggle for social justice can be separated from struggle for cognitive justice which brings out knowledge in either hegemonic or emancipatory form (Paraskeva, 2018). Santos (cited in Paraskeva, 2018), on a similar ground, discusses the link between the social and the scientific, separation of science from social that characterizes hegemonic knowledge and emancipatory knowledge. The ecology of knowledges occurred in the circles of the East and the West, European and non-Europe, civilized and wild has a more profound generis beyond dichotomies. Perspectives on the variance of knowledges and the truth's itinerancy as a curriculum theory can provide substantial understanding for curriculum theorists, practitioners, educators and teachers. A stage of a new theory is that the colonial knowledge and its terrain has been bankrupted and the global order is hard-lived (Paraskeva, 2018; Santos, 2014; Carrales & Suárez-Krabbe, 2021). Therefore, different communities of knowledge across the globe are increasingly coming together, rejecting the Westernised monopoly of knowledge and engaging in debates around pressing issues. According to Paraskeva (2017) and Santos (2014) an important challenge in relation to epistemologies has been advanced. This analysis is more than relevant for Turkey as it has been standing in the heart of the discussions of West/anti-West, Muslim/non-Muslim, religious/non-religious, secular/religious and rural/urban discourses. It is also a relevant analysis that how preexisting collective memory of knowledges was killed, silenced or ignored by the present upsurges. Thus any discussion on epistemologies should take place on the grounds of not only domination but also a systematic exclusion of knowledges.

Forgetting the past: The Ottoman Empire

Looking back to the roots of education as a colonial device in the Ottoman Empire/ Ottoman State (1453–1923) we can see that the *raison d'être* of colonization and domination did not work in parallel with the ideals of civilization and faith of Islam. Lewis analysed the empire's colonial ideals as follows:

> The Ottoman state had been born on the frontier between Islam and Byzantine Christendom; its leaders and armies had been march-warriors in the Holy War,

carrying the sword and the faith of Islam into new lands. The Ottoman ghazis and dervishes, like the pioneers and missionaries of the Americas, believed themselves to be bringing *civilization* and *the true faith* [my italics] to peoples sunk in barbarism and unbelief – and like them reaped the familiar rewards of the frontier-warrior and the colonist. (1958, 117)

Neither it happened likewise with Eurocentric canon (Paraskeva, 2017), as education was not prioritized and too much politicized conditions were non-existent for the Ottoman Empire to create a world for Ottoman-centric epistemology. Neither cultural imperialism in the imperial lands nor epistemologies valuation in the own land was reached. After glorious centuries of well-being in creating and valuing knowledge accumulation, the empire had to face malady of social disintegration along with drawbacks in the complexities of the world order of the time. In the larger areas of influence of the empire, multicultural features and their knowledge had not been valued in education. In schools these cultures are either ignored or silenced by Islamist Ottomanist content. What we have is the invisibilization of pre-Islamic epistemologies. As an example archaic Turks such as Uyghur and Oghuz tribes had built up a literary culture for acculturation of values and social life. The first known pre-Islamic *Book of Grandad Korkut* written in Sogd alphabet, for example, can be the first pedagogical work with its depicted twelve stories teaching values and morals. In the narratives Grandad Korkut, an old wise man, was an unchallenged authority, symbol and speaker of the ethos, honour, conscience, faith and devotion to the Khan, Prince and people. An early Islamic literary work was *Kutatgu Bilig* (Ethics of Happiness) by Yusuf Has Hacib (1069), which carries influences of Islamic faith in social life. One can see this influence on the value of women in society. While in pre-Islamic era women had been powerful respectful authorities in society, in the book women were attributed secondary status with the newly adopted religion. The first cyclopaedic dictionary was *Divan-ü Lugat-it Turk* by Mahmut of Kasghar (1072–4) aimed to teach Turkish to Arabic-speaking people. None of these books included scholastic or formal teaching but references to toilet training, lullabies, nursing and so on (Güvenç, 1998, 9–11). The legacy of this literary culture of the pre-Islamic and early Islamic era could not be transferred through formal education. Yet, culture of learning was alive and multicultural peoples of the Empire lived in silence in their own value systems as they adapted, negotiated and experienced their 'dissonant' knowledges. This can be regarded as the beginning of a 'virtual disappearance of narrative history from the curriculum . . . that ends in realms of forgetting . . . realms of ignorance, since there will have been little to forget' (Connerton, 2009, 3).

It is a general pattern that colonization penetrated in two ways in the Ottoman Empire; one was the Islamist Ottomanist ideology which structured the religious school curriculum; another was authorizing foreigners mainly Europeans[1] and Americans to function and install their school models and curriculum in the country. There were schools for the Muslim children teaching Islamic faith, Quranic verse and Ottomanism (unconditional loyalty to the empire) in the annexes of the mosques. The method was rote memorization of Quran in Arabic with strict discipline. The state did not interfere or inspect these schools as long as they teach

Ottoman-Islamic ideology. State military schools were modelled from Europe, in the eighteenth century. French (and later) German forms of schooling influenced the organization and curriculum of these schools. *Enderun*[2] located in the palace territory had a special curriculum including teaching of Turkish-Islamic tradition for acculturation of the non-Muslim boys who were brought from the imperial taxation territories.

Medrese that marked an epoch from eleventh to nineteenth century were the places opened in the time of Great Seljuk Dynasty (1040–1157) (Peacock, 2015); they had witnessed major changes throughout the centuries and finally the demise of own. Their curriculum included Islamic theology, philosophy, logic, mathematics, history, law and languages. Arabic, Persian and Turkish languages were used for different courses in teaching. Later periods witnessed abolition of philosophical discussions and science texts as they were considered sinful and harmful to Islamic faith. Nonetheless, Muslim thinkers such as Avicenna (Ibn Sina), Averroes (Ibn Rusd), Ibn Haldun and Al Farabi, renowned for world's scientific and philosophical knowledge accumulation, were studied as the major epistemological foundation of *medrese* curriculum.[3] The founder of modern middle age science Avicenna (Ibn Sina) and his original epistemological theory became the philosophical curriculum in the *medrese*. His books *El-Kanun fi't-Tıb* (The Canon of Medicine) and *Kitabü'ş-Şifa* (Book of the Cure) were major curriculum in medicine schools in the West for ages (Britannica, Gutas, 2020). Similarly, Averroes (Ibn Rusd) had been a significant epistemological base with his commentaries and summaries of the thoughts of Aristoteles and Plato. His examinations on philosophy and religion, especially his critics on Plato's 'philosopher-king', created considerable discussions in intellectual circles of *medrese*. Ibn Khaldun, another Islam philosopher and historian, made a historical analysis of human societies and critics of Greek philosophers Aristoteles and Plato in Muqaddimah.[4] Muqaddimah consisted of six chapters and in the sixth there is a section entitled education and teaching where he examined education as a social phenomenon that has a social impact on people; he also compared various teaching methods such as lecture, discussion and demonstration (Süngü, 2009, 23, 45; Ülken, 1992). Knowledge created by these scholars accumulated throughout the ages in the Arabic, Asian and North African regions and had expanded in *medrese* curriculum until the dogmatic and political interference from the religion circles and the sultans of the empire. Accumulation of knowledge had been interfered by bans, abolishment, burning of holographs, manuscripts and exiles of scholars as well as bans on translation and commentaries. Some branches of science were considered harmful and were not taught deliberately. No book printed. The printed books were banned. As teaching of Islamic doctrine and Ottoman ideology dominated over philosophy, math and science courses, intellectual characteristics of these institutions disappeared. As time went by, these schools quitted appealing to large communities of the empire even in the Muslim neighbourhoods (Mizikaci, 2006; İnalcık, 2003; Berkes, 1998). The fanaticism of the *medrese*, the disrespect of the dervish lodges to lay people created two opposing forces that destroy each other, and in the last century these institutions grown out of love and respect in public. The educated and the people became two differing groups in society. The genres of satire, criticism and humour did not develop in *medrese* but in public. Different cultural identities conveyed knowledge within their communities while they kept interaction among different religious and cultural neighbours (Lewis, 1961; Feroz, 1993; Güvenç, 1998). Within and beyond the singularity of the *medrese* fact, the knowledges, ideas and social realities had continuously been befallen in antinomies: intelligentsia or public, West or East, old or new, tradition or modern, local or universal, even as Arabic or French. By time, public's legacy was delinked from public, learning from wisdom was lost, wisdom was replaced by school knowledge as scholastic and formal education penetrated.

Interference and indifference on school curriculum played a role to segregate between the educated and not educated, later conceptualized as centre-periphery theory in Shils (1961) and Mardin (1973). Islamic doctrine did not apply to public pedagogy, and institutionalized teaching of religion did not, in any simple way, translate from Quran to public's imagination. It was rather a hierarchical order of rules to transfer without meaningful justifications in life. One of the factors that led the empire to an end was the orthodoxy of Islamic traditions (including education) and the absence of new creative impulses in the intellectual and cultural life (Lewis, 1958). A great mosaic of the cultures of the Ottoman *Millets* (nations), Muslims, Jews and Christians, had lived in the lands of ancient civilizations of Central Asia, Asia Minor, Mesopotamia, Trojan, Hittites, Arabs, Persians and Africans. An incontestable extensive heritage of knowledges conveyed through generations from antiquity to present (Lewis, 1961; Güvenç, 1993). For state schools and *medreses*, ignorance of this kind of knowledge was a 'superiority'. For instance, the Islamic discourse has a concrete opposition to Shamanist discourse and anything related to pre-Islamic culture. However, in public life, religious and cultural traditions such as healing rituals, folk tales, music and dance attributed to Islamic tradition are associated with Shamanism and accumulated for generations. Zarcone points out, 'under the pressure of Islam, since the seventh and eighth centuries, Shamanism had undergone many transformations in order for its pagan character to be veiled behind Muslim symbols and gestures' (2017, 169). A considerable amount of research work and publications show how Shaman, Islam and Sufi cultures are interrelated for centuries in the larger regions of Central Asia, Northern Asia, Siberia, the Balkans, Middle East, Africa and Indonesia.[5] On this rich background, we can see how pre-Islamic culture is mixed and conveyed in public narratives. These are the narratives such as 'public saying, epic, legend, fairy tale and folk tale' characterized by the narrator's own interpretations of the narrative with a particular discourse and context. Learning through the 'folk narrative context' serves as an essential part of education widespread and freely (Cemiloğlu, 2006; 264–6). For example, talisman and magic, heroic characteristics, fun and humour, patterns of love and marriage are learned in a hidden way in these narratives. Narrator's interpretation is conveyed with his words, music, posture, mimicry and gestures, for example, what is approved or disapproved morally as a social code. Then it turns into a theatric performance as an element of learning. Undeniably, at present these cultural elements in official curriculum are disconnected from its context and serve as a device in objective oriented curriculum.

Curriculum in between modernity and Islam

Modernization movements which have a long history back to the eighteenth century emerged as economic, political and sociocultural change and as an indicator of development, especially for non-Western countries (Santos, 2007, 2014; Paraskeva, 2016, 2017, 2018). In the flow of changes in Europe, Ottoman Empire had to enact major educational reforms in schooling and curriculum. The idea of *Cameralism*[6] introduced a state-controlled economy, and its reflections in education could relate to curriculum standard of Bobbit as he stated, 'curriculum must serve the larger public welfare, albeit in an almost entirely economic way' (1982). This was not only introducing a state-based economy in the empire but also education and schooling as the instrument to the establishment of this idea. For *Cameralist* policy, education was a tool to create a strong middle class to provide competencies beyond literacy for the subjects. Therefore, modern schooling was based on social efficiency curriculum with state economy and social unity emphasis. The organization and curriculum of modern schools were thus portrayed as European school model. Similar practice works for American society to socialize youth into the adult work and citizenship roles in order to reproduce the existing social class hierarchy in succeeding generations of Americans (Apple, 1979; Kliebard, 1968; Bobbit, 1982).

Westernism also refers to the ideal to reach to the 'superiority' of European civilization with integrating their values and practices. The concept has been used interchangeably with the terms of development, progress, modernism and civilization in Turkish education literature (Mardin, 1991; Berkes, 1998; Ülken, 1992) in a similar way it was addressed in Paraskeva (2017), Santos (2007) and Giroux (2010). The advocates of Westernism esteemed Western value system against reactionary Islamic principles. The low state of women in Islamic principles has always been a powerful argument in defending Western modernity. For instance, an Ottoman thinker, Abdullah Cevdet, was a pure Westernist who believed that Western civilization should be adopted in its entirety, that is, 'with its roses and thorns' (Heper, 2012, 140). These ideas had grounded justifications in the state's religious tradition (*Sheria*[7]) – reactionary movements and illiteracy among villagers. As Mardin claims, the term Westernism itself was mostly used to name the views of those who want to imitate the West in every respect (1991). Consistent with the 'concept of development', as Santos (cited in Paraskeva, 2018) addresses, Ottoman Empire became a part of the Westernization of the world project, that is, 'making the rest of the world conform to the economic, socio-cultural, and political norms that have developed in the West' (2007, 318). According to Berkes the West had always been a reality of the Turks without alternative:

> Turkey had already been touched by the impact of the West. There had been signs in the 18th century that, in spite of resistance, the idea of Turkey having to adapt itself to the requirements of European civilization continuously gained ascendency. But neither in political organization, nor in social life or cultural and intellectual spheres, can we find any substantial change in the older Ottoman system, which was then in a state of corruption and disorganization. (1998, 378)

In the meantime, foreign schools (European and American) spread all over the country in a range from American Academy for Girls to Liceo Italiano di Istanbul; from Lycée Saint-Benoît d'Istanbul to Deutsche Schule Istanbul (Earle, 1929). Undoubtedly, curriculum of these schools had no recognition of the 'other' while existing in the other's land, that is, 'Orient' in Said (1979), the 'invisible' in Santos (2007) and 'non-western Epistemes' in Paraskeva (2016; 2022). In the meantime, American missionary schools were given privilege by the sultan. Muslims could not go to these schools for two reasons: first a Muslim should be strictly tied to his Islamic faith. Second, Abdulhamid's Sharia policy was to prevent the diffusion of learning and spread of liberal thoughts in the Muslim population (Orvis, 1915, 20).

Orvis who was a missioner at that time for the American Board of Commissioners for Foreign Mission in Turkey wrote this:

> Turkey was occupied by these schools, and the great desire for Western education had overcome the prejudice of many Muslims and in spite of the Christian religion being taught in the schools the number of Turkish (Muslim) students in the American College had increased to 429 in the year 1914. (1915, 21)

The fact that the country had long been occupied by European and American schools was related to capitulations.[8] In *Nutuk*,[9] Atatürk addressed, 'there was 25 missionary schools only in *Sivas* province' (1927, 70). Foreign schools were training not only Christian missionaries but also believers of Western ideals and individualism on a structure that 'student activities were encouraged and all the life of the school was permeated with an ethical aim to which the religious instruction was closely related'; similarly 'teacher training work had a large influence on religious education' (Orvis, 1915, 37–8). Bible study and Christian service were in the centre course of study in different types of foreign schools from kindergartens to schools for the blind and deaf, from teacher training to industrial/technical schools. In the meantime, colonialism was fulfilling its conception of the other as object, and consequently the non-recognition of the other as subject (Santos, cited in Paraskeva, 2017), here of the Muslims in their own homeland.

Modernity versus Islam dichotomy occurred by way of curriculum and organization of the schools in the country. In both Islamic and Western types of schooling curricular epistemologies embraced, enacted and perpetuated were never innocent or neutral (Paraskeva, 2016, xiii). Regardless of religious faith, socio-economic status parallel with urban versus rural dichotomy became determiner in one's accessing to education. On the one hand there was a large majority of Muslim kids who were obliged to go to outdated schools to memorize Quran in Arabic; on the other hand there were such privileged schools under the auspices of European states and the sultan. Villagers and the poor families had no choice but religious education for their children. The following eras recurrently would witness the production of segregation and social injustice through education and cognitive injustice in an epistemological platform characterized by border thinking or abyssal thinking (Santos, 2007). The epoch also remarked delinking communication across generations, detaching human culture from the youth by way of education.

Anti-colonial revolution of the Turks

In the beginning of the twentieth century a revolutionist upsurge paved way for progressive education based on scientism, secularism and education for all principles. On this ground, Baltacıoğlu, an advocate of modern education and known for his revolutionary ideas, claimed that 'nature of revolution requires not only introduction of new ideas but also invalidation of the past ideas (that of Ottomans)' (1942, 9). He was representing the ideas against the cosmopolitan, individualized Ottomanist understanding in education. He proposed a social school model (*İçtimai Mektep*) which integrated the idea of scientific principle of modern Turkey with Einstein's positivist science, Bergson's philosophy, Freud's psychology (and Watson's) and Durkheim's sociology so that he advanced the idea of social democratic and independent education model (1942, 357–8). Fully integrated with scientific basics, social school is an education model where human personality starts life in the community, in its real environment, by working and producing real products. Only with scientific knowledge and cognitive skills, can a person be citizen of his society. *Scienticism* for modern Turkish education idea is valued as its superiority to human in universe, particularly as its superiority (with its rationality) to religion. 'Science must be linked to citizenship. A citizen is a person of knowledge', as it is seen in a similar practice in India (Shiv Vasvanathan, 184, cited in Santos, 2007). Science is a pathway to rationalism – a unique way to distant religious dogmatism which left the country behind the West (Berkes, 1998; Lewis, 1961; Feroz, 1993). Atatürk in his statement 'In the human world, until the expertise and deep knowledge of religion is immaculate and perfect free from all superstitions with the lights of technique of true science, the actors of the religious play will be found everywhere' (1927) was defining a guide for curriculum knowledge which was not religious but scientific. For the Turkish people, this was the only way to read the wor(l)d in a Freirean word and 'that all education in the broadest sense was part of a project of freedom' (Giroux, 2010).

Geometry textbook and curricular epistemology

Along with the *script revolution*[10] the Turkish Language Convention initiated neologism studies for the adaptation of the Latin script into Turkish in sciences and disciplines such as medicine, geology, astronomy, mathematics, physics, chemistry, technology, history, linguistics, language and literature, social sciences, fine arts, sports, roads and vehicles. Following the detailed analysis of syntax, morpheme, phonology, etymology and grammar, the words and phrases in their original language were formulated or reformulated in Turkish. In the new Turkish, Atatürk wrote a secondary school geometry book for teachers[11] first published in 1937 (Atatürk, 2020).

The new Turkish Republic situated itself a part of Europe and adopted the definition of modernism as Dussel defined that 'an emancipation, [a] way out, from immaturity by means of reason, understood as a critical process that offers humanity the possibility of new development' (2000, 469). This idea of Turkish modernity sees the Western civilization as the primal centre, where Turkey historically belongs to (Mignolo, 2008; Berkes, 1998; Karpat, 1973). Parallel to this, as 'being the center of world history achieved from state, military, economic, and philosophical perspectives' (Dussel, 2000, 249), Turkey has become a role model of modernity in the Central Asia and some parts of the Middle East and South Asia. This power of being a model to the East originates from its East belonging, its pre-Islam and Islam culture and the way it integrates into the West. With this background, it can be seen that Western modernity was an integrated piece of the mosaic and meant secularism, emancipation and power, not necessarily the European-made one.

Parallel to scienticism and Westernism, laicism constituted the national education and a dogma-free social life. Berkes claims, 'The basic conflict in secularism is not necessarily between religion and the world, as was the case in Christian experience. The conflict is often between the forces of tradition which tend to promote the domination of religion and sacred law and the forces of change' (1998, 6). This definition worked for education in explaining the conflict between religion and emancipation especially in curriculum knowledge. So the tension between indoctrination of religion and progressive scientific way of thinking in curriculum has ever remained since then. Turkish nationalism is a wed of Turkishness ideology to Western modernity; in a broader context it is a disconnection movement from the Islamic past – a unification of Turkey with Europe. According to Feroz, 'Turkishness involved pride in the history and traditions of Anatolia ("the cradle of civilisation") both of which had to be rediscovered or even manufactured. But Turkishness was also defined in contrast to the rest of the Islamic world, thus the emphasis on secularism, or at the very least a Turkish Islam' (1993, 78).

Through a centralized national curriculum

The segregated social structure and its reflection in schooling ended with the Law of Unification of Instruction in 1924 which abolished religious education in state schools (secularization of education), closed foreign missionary schools and unified education under the Ministry of Education. Radical changes in education were a part of social-cultural revolution acknowledged as fundamentals of national independence from imperialism, which lead a process of nation state building with its universally valid, legal, political and economic domains to make a modern social order (Santos, 2014) mingled with national culture. Among the intelligentsia, supremacy of scientific knowledge and rationalism was acknowledged and promoted by integrating it with the Turk's language, tradition, history and culture. Linking Eurocentric episteme with that of the Turk's might have been a unique struggle and therefore model of the new republic. The struggle was not only against a colonial Western education but also against an internal colonial imperial tradition. The role of Turkish intelligentsia though, as a power to recognize and integrate the modern education thought, has been worthwhile. Chomsky defines this type of intelligentsia as 'they serve as mediators between the social facts and the mass of the population: they create the ideological justifications for social practice' (2007, 4). In the Turkish context, intelligentsia should be regarded as having an additional role as the engine of social mobilization, the ideological constructor of social mobilization for emancipation from reactionarism of the Ottoman State and the colonization of foreign schools. Novels of the republic era, for example, presented social themes, lives of modern and traditional women and men, family life in urban and rural milieu with a social realist approach for the construction of cultural memory. This was also a translation period; a large collection of classical works, novels and poets of European, American and Soviet authors was translated into Turkish. Similarly, historiography was given utmost importance and a Turkish history writing process was supported. All efforts were about to relink the social with the intellectual in a public sphere. Education unconditionally had to be a public issue on the national grounds. However, it was again stigmatized as an era of forgetting that inherited in modernity as Connerton argues, 'To say that modernity is characterized by a particular type of forgetfulness is to presuppose a conception of remembering. Remembering, therefore, needs to be delineated to make clear the meaning of forgetting' (2009, 4). This was observed more visibly in history curriculum that was to define order of the things to be remembered and learned. Overall it was a nation state building process originated in Europe, as Mizikaci identifies:

> Education systems serve the nation state by creating . . . 1) a shared experience as students developing a sense of nationhood; 2) a common culture through teaching a national history and literature; 3) emotional loyalty to the state through patriotic exercises such as flag, salutes and nationalistic rhetoric and song; and 4) a citizenry that accepts the legitimacy of the government and their own political role within the system. (2017c, 39)

The cement of Turkish nationalism offers profound thought schools such as Turkism, Westernism, Islamism and Euro-Asianism – the idea that Turks ethnically belong to Asia and a larger family of Eurasia and it should politically be close to Soviet Socialism. The long-lasting studies of the Soviet Turcologs have linked the ancient history and civilizations of Turks to that of Soviet and Asia. Parallel to these new knowledge, new discoveries in Anatolia added the Sumerians, the Trojans and the Hittites in Turkish nationalism (Lewis, 1961).

In the long run the quest of curriculum epistemologies remained unanswered especially in curriculum scholarship of Turkish academia. In the early 1970s Selahattin Ertürk, who studied at Colombia and the founder of the curriculum development division at Hacettepe University (Ankara), was one of the first advocates of curriculum development in a systematic, scientific, goal-oriented Tylerian way in Turkey. Another curriculum scholar Fatma Varış, who studied in Florida University in the United States, founded the curriculum department at Ankara University. Ertürk's (1972) and Varış's publications (1989) were not only the first academic works in Turkish curriculum field but also they founded the school of curriculum thought in Turkey. Both Ertürk and Varış positioned themselves on scientific management side of curriculum development with a goal-oriented approach. Both analysed and discussed source, level, order, relationship, organization and assessment of goals in curriculum development. How to systematize curriculum elements in order and how to assess goals and objectives were the main consideration. Ertürk addressed content of curriculum as subject matter, with no reference to epistemology or knowledge (1972). Knowledge is considered as an inert component of curriculum, a critic-proof divine ingredient; its source is not discussable, questionable or criticized as it was decided by the authorities in a scientific way. Ironically, both curriculum scholars in their later works questioned problems of the society and challenges in education and schooling; both connected social disrupts with education in a broader sense. For instance, Ertürk criticized 'transferism' as a habit of Turks that is transferring(!) Western education thought and methodology, which eventually lead us to a monistic system (1988, 13). He predominantly disconnected elite's conflict from social conflict, a typical intellectualism, placing severe distinction between the intelligentsia and the social.

Recolonizing knowledge in a neoliberal era

In *Another Knowledge Is Possible*, Santos (2007) draws attention to silenced and absenced knowledge upon which Paraskeva (2018) introduces ICT. Following their proposals, I will continue with a discussion of dangers of 'localized knowledge created for political interests as a superior discourse delivered on tradition, religion and nationalism domains. Within a neoconservative and neoliberal context, soon after the 1980 coup d'état, a Turkish-Islamic statement – a made ideology of a Turkist-Islamist character – has been prioritized over Western imported knowledge and as an alternative to colonial Western ideology which has a long story stigmatized as non-Muslim and non-Turk in the country. With an Article (code 24 of 1982 Constitution) a course titled 'Religious Culture and Moral Knowledge' teaching mainly Sunni Islam became mandatory in primary and secondary schools. Courses function as another way of colonization, Islamization and monoculturization by demarcating the borders and content of curriculum knowledge. Not surprisingly the Turk-Islam ideology neither has an aim to dialogue 'among knowledge for equality of opportunities to the different kinds of knowledge or an invitation to build a more democratic and just society and at decolonizing knowledge and power' (Paraskeva, 2011, xx). Exclusion of the other is a norm in such a monoculture knowledge. The Turkist component of the couplet inevitably excludes the other and their knowledge. The Islamist component, on the other hand, is a propaganda tool of power relations.

'Production' of curriculum knowledge on the principle of 'what is good for the country is good for the people' is the voice of hierarchy, authority and domination (Chomsky, 1996; Paraskeva, 2011; Santos, 2014); it talks for people in the name of people. This is also what progressivists missed out in their claim that progressive education would be the solution to fight with dogmatism and regressivism. And this disconnection together with fear of dogmatism and perception of threat on secularism turned the field of curriculum into a pool of '-isms' in a narrow arena, and a monologue. The legacy of the state tradition, the habit of statism dominates the social domain, academia and education. A metaphor for the word State 'the father State' in Turkish must explain the degree of 'maleness of the state. The popular saying 'flesh is yours, bones are mine' is addressed to teacher when a kid begins school and exemplifies the trust in authority in public education (Mizikaci, 2017a). What happens if the most trusted father state becomes authoritarian? In such a culture, however, when state is in the hands of market-driven policies of authoritarians, any concern for the public good is abandoned, public imagination is killed (Giroux, 2021). All these eventually construct and legitimize a process of delinking school from society (Mignolo, 2008) and creating a legitimate culture (Apple, 1979) for thinking about knowledge of curriculum through curriculum. This is what happened in Turkey with anti-secular and anti-intellectual policies of the right-wing conservative and Islamist parties. The Islamist threat to the secular state not only risks the progressive foundations of the Turkish Republic but also causes social disintegration and delink the social reality from school. After the 1980 coup d'état, political Islam in cooperation with neoconservative and neoliberal policies has targeted education, and in public's eye this was an attack, if not a threat, to secular curriculum knowledge, public education, social justice and right to education, all had been guaranteed by the anti-colonial revolution laws. Indoctrination of political Islam is actualized by opening *Imam-Hatip* schools or converting normal schools into *Imam-Hatip*[12] schools. Having increased the number of these schools in the neighbourhoods, poor families are forced to send their children to these schools while well-off families can afford private schools with secular curriculum and modern education facilities. Secular education became a commodity. Religious foundations *tarikat* and *cemaat* supported with state funds function in education to remantle Islamic curriculum in schools. According to Çakmak (2009), the curriculum of these schools is 'designed to provide a fundamental correct knowledge and understanding of Islam, does not produce religious Muslim generations; instead, it produces new Islamist generations'. The influence of political Islam on curriculum is beyond becoming a curriculum issue, as Çakmak continues:

> students and graduates of these schools try to relate and apply their knowledge of Islam not only to their private lives but also to public life, violating the secularist principle which aims to establish a system of beliefs and rituals confined to the relationship between God and the individual. In other words, religious education infuses Islamist views into the character and personalities of students of the *Imam-Hatip* schools, possibly leading to an Islamization of the regime. (839)

Consequently, Turkey has to face dichotomies of knowledge in the circles of political Islam and neoliberal principles. Curriculum revisions are done on the base of skill-based, test-oriented, competitive, individualized principles. In its broad sense, curriculum work is distanced from public sphere and got closer to neoliberal Islamist policies:

> The curriculum development approach adopted has been transformed into an approach that legitimizes the demands of globalization, business and corporate while obscuring the social reality and the reality of education, school, teacher and student. This is the result of a product-oriented approach. Accordingly, students are the product to be equipped with predetermined features, and teachers are the agents responsible for creating this product in the best way, and the school has

one of the key functions in this transformation business by providing appropriate management conditions. (Mizikaci, 2017b, 7)

History curriculum is portrayed with Ottoman 'victorious' past, as it serves to historical reconstruction rather than constructing social memory (Connerton, 1989). Mathematics curriculum has priority in society as success in math in high-stake testing is regarded as a key to better jobs. Curriculum field is engaged in curriculum design and disciplinary content issues; most of the critics from the curriculum scholars are about lack of expertise in designing national curriculum and insufficient teaching of disciplines. Instructional design and methodological challenges in teaching are common research subjects among curriculum researchers and in dissertations. Academia apparently avoid discussing paradoxes of curricular paradigms such as disciplinary versus epistemological, skills versus conscience, wisdom versus information, poor versus well off.

Apart from micro thinking of curriculum issues, challenges are linked to immigration, human trafficking, wars, social distress and polarization that the school and the curriculum are not insensitive (Paraskeva, 2017). According to a UNHCR report, Turkey hosts about 2 million refugee children, about 450,000 of whom are deprived of education rights (2017). Geographical bias and EU's immigrant policies are creating overwhelming load on Turkey's schools. As an abrupt Covid-19 pandemic is not health crisis but the imposition of transformations by the alliance of conservative modernization in political, economic and social grounds in an *epistemological fog* (Apple, 2022, 56). The post-pandemic era forces us new thinking to decode the codes of the new epistemological *fog*. Russia's attack on Ukraine forces us to rethink the versions of the truth and lies in the turmoil of discursive complexities. According to Paraskeva, 'the true question is not how conflict might be abolished but how humanity might learn to live with it and transform it into a productive step forward for freedom' (2011, 12)

It has turned into an age of false promise as 'the modern promise of equality collides with massive disparities of power, education, status and property ownership' (Mishra, 2017, 31). Another false promise is that of rationalism, according to Giroux, 'rationalizing everything down to its lowest common denominator so that pedagogy is reduced to a force of enormous oppression that excludes questions of ethics, social responsibility, justice, power, values and the elements of a democratic vision' (2022, 19–20). Turkey is at a turning point with this background of struggles which provide a deep learning for us to demand for a just society. Curriculum needs to understood and examined within the dynamics of ideological production in which categories, such as culture, politics and economy intersect with class, race, and gender dynamics, each one exhibiting relative autonomy (Paraskeva, 2022, 349). Especially the invasion of Turkish anti-colonial revolution discourse by the political Islam in cooperation with so-called global knowledge and skill in curriculum should be challenged by ICT. Turkish landscape is a landscape of epistemological diversity. I believe the children, the youth, the adults and the elderly of this country proved that they belong to this epistemological diversity during the Gezi resistance in 2013, which started in Istanbul and then spread to provinces of Turkey and Turkish diaspora and lasted for about three months. Gezi was a democracy demand for freedom of speech, for recognition of cultural, gender, life diversity, for social justice. It started to prevent trees from being cut in the Gezi Park but reached beyond its naïve aim and turned into a social movement and showed us new knowledge is possible, which centres affective reaction to global knowledge and skills discourse as in Paraskeva's proposed ICT and as Santos's call for cognitive justice. What does ICT speak to Gezi resistance? It seems the way ahead will lead us to think similar questions. The way to walk forward the future is inevitably, undeniably that. No ideology, no dichotomy, no political view and unfortunately no academia will be dealing this question to the(ir) end. Ultimately, ICT is an opening to reorient educational thinking to the rich cultural history of the present, human's lead and its balance within the epochs discussed. A curriculum theory in association with sociology of absence needs to depict the parameters of ignorance of cultures and knowledges of components as a value system, as episteme.

Notes

1 An increase was witnessed in the number of German, French and Italian schools during and after the First World War.
2 In Persian, it means 'inner sections of the palace'. The name of the royal school in Ottoman Empire.
3 For a detailed discussion of present *medrese* curriculum see Uzma Anzar (2003). Islamic education: A brief history of *medrese* with comments on curricula and current pedagogical practices.
4 Was banned by Abdulhamit II because he thought the book included too liberal subjects.
5 See Shamanism and Islam: Sufism, healing rituals and spirits in the Muslim world by Zarcone, T., & Hobart, A. (Eds.) for a concise collection.
6 *Oxford Dictionary* meaning: An economic theory prevalent in eighteenth-century Germany, which advocated a strong public administration managing a centralized economy primarily for the benefit of the state.
7 State system based on Islamic law.
8 Economic activities of the foreigners using the national sources by given large privilege.
9 The renowned address on the Turkish War of Independence. The speech was given by the founder of the Turkish Republic, Mustafa Kemal Atatürk, in the Grand National Assembly of Turkey between the 15th and the 20th of October, 1927. First published in Turkish in 1927.
10 Adaptation of the Latin alphabet in Turkish.
11 Atatürk never claimed authorship on the book.
12 Schools that train *imam* (priest in a mosque) and *hatip* (preacher) with Sunni Islamic curriculum content and method. Generically these works are fulfilled only by men. So a woman cannot be a priest or preacher. However, girls have been enrolled in these schools since 1960. Graduates, if not continue to higher education, are recruited in state and private jobs.

References

Anzar, U. (2003), *Islamic Education: A Brief History of Medreses with Comments on Curricula and Current Pedagogical Practices*. Paper for the University of Vermont, Environmental Programme.
Apple, M. W. (1979), *Ideology and Curriculum*, Boston: Routledge.
Apple, M. W. (2022), 'Critical Analysis and the Covid-19 Crisis: An Interview with Michael W. Apple', in F. Mizikaci and E. Ata (eds), *Critical Pedagogy and the Covid-19 Pandemic: Keeping Communities Together in Times of Crisis*, London: Bloomsbury Publishing.
Atatürk, M. K. (1927), *Nutuk* (translated into new Turkish by Zeynep Korkmaz).
Atatürk, M. K. (2020), *Geometri*, İstanbul: Türkiye İş Bankası Kültür Yayınları.
Baltacıoğlu, I. H. (1942), *İçtimai mektep*. Ankara: Milli Eğitim Basımevi.
Berkes, N. (1998), *The Development of Secularism in Turkey*, 2nd edn, 407, London: C. Hurst & Co. Publishers.
Bobbit, F. (1982), 'The Social Efficiency Movement Reconsidered: Curriculum Change in Minneapolis, 1917–1950', *Curriculum Inquiry*, 12 (1): 9–33.
Çakmak, D. (2009), 'Pro-Islamic Public Education in Turkey: The Imam-Hatıp Schools', *Middle Eastern Studies*, 45 (5): 825–46.
Carrales, J. C. F. and J. Suárez-Krabbe, eds (2021), *Transdisciplinary Thinking from the Global South: Whose Problems, Whose Solutions?* New York: Routledge.
Cemiloğlu, M. (2006), 'Eğitim bilimi açısından örtük program ve halk anlatılarının örtük program bağlamında değerlendirilmesi', *Uludağ Üniversitesi Eğitim Fakültesi Dergisi*, 19 (2): 257–69.
Chomsky, N. (1996), 'Consent without Consent: Reflections on the Theory and Practice of Democracy', *Clevland State Law Review*, 44 (4): 415–37.
Chomsky, N. and Ronat, M. (2007), *On Language: Chomsky's Classic Works Language and Responsibility and Reflections on Language in One Volume*, New York: Pantheon Books.
Connerton, P. (1989), *How Societies Remember*, Cambridge: Cambridge University Press.
Connerton, P. (2009), *How Modernity Forgets*, Cambridge: Cambridge University Press.
Dussel, E. (2000), 'Europe, Modernity and Eurocentrism', *Nepantla: Views from South*, 1 (3): 465–78.
Earle, E. M. (1929). 'American Missions in the Near East', *Foreign Affairs*, 7: 398–417.
Ertürk, S. (1972), *Eğitimde Program Geliştirme*, Ankara: Yelken Yayınları.
Ertürk, S. (1988), 'Türkiye'de eğitim felsefesi sorunu', *Hacettepe Üniversitesi Eğitim Fakültesi Dergisi*, 3 (3): 11–16.
Feroz, A. (1993), *The Making of Modern Turkey*, New York: Routledge.
Giroux, H. A. (2010), 'Rethinking Education as the Practice of Freedom: Paulo Freire and the Promise of Critical Pedagogy', *Policy Futures in Education*, 8 (6): 715–21.
Giroux, H. A. (2021), 'The Public Imagination and the Dictatorship of Ignorance', *Social Identities*, 27 (6): 698–717. http://doi.org/10.1080/13504630.2021.1931089.
Giroux, H. A. (2022), 'An Interview with Henry Giroux: Cultural Studies and Pandemic Pedagogy', in F. Mizikaci and E. Ata (eds), *Critical Pedagogy and the Covid-19 Pandemic: Keeping Communities Together in Times of Crisis*, 15–28, London: Bloomsbury Publishing.
Gurnah, A. (2002), *By the Sea*, London: Bloomsbury.
Gutas, D. (2020), *Greek Philosophers in the Arabic Tradition*, New York : Routledge.
Güvenç, B. (1993), *Türk kimliği [Turkish Identity]*, Ankara: Kültür Bakanlığı Yayınları.

Güvenç, B. (1998), *History of Turkish Education*, Ankara: Turkish Education Association.
Heper, M. (2012), 'Kemalism/Atatürkism', In *The Routledge Handbook of Modern Turkey*, 139–48, New York: Routledge.
İnalcık, H. (2003), *Şair ve Patron: Patrimonyal Devlet ve Sanat Üzerinde Sosyolojik Bir İnceleme*, Ankara: Doğu Batı Yayınları.
Karpat, K. (1973), *An Inquiry into the Social Foundations of Nationalism in the Ottoman State: From Social Estates to Classes, from Millets to Nations*. (Research Monograph number 39.) Princeton: Center of International Studies, Woodrow Wilson School of Public and International Affairs, Princeton University.
Kliebard, H. M. (1968), 'The Curriculum Field in Retrospect', in P. W. F. Witt (ed.), *Technology and the Curriculum*, 69–84, New York: Teachers College Press.
Lewis, B. (1958), 'Some Reflections on the Decline of the Ottoman Empire', *Studia Islamica*, 9: 111–27.
Lewis, B. (1961), *The Emergence of Modern Turkey*, London: Oxford University Press.
Mardin, Ş. (1973), 'Center-Periphery Relations: A Key to Turkish Politics?' *Daedalus*, 101 (1): 169–90.
Mardin, Ş. (1991), *Türk modernleşmesi. Makaleler IV*, Istambul: İletişim yayınları.
Mignolo, W. (2008), 'The Geopolitics of Knowledge and Colonial Difference', in M. Morana, E. Dussel and C. Jauregui (eds), *Coloniality at Large: Latin America and the Postcolonial Debate*, 225–58, San Antonio: Duke University Press.
Mishra, P. (2017), *Age of Anger: A History of the Present*, New York: Farrar, Straus and Giroux.
Mizikaci, F. (2006), *Higher Education in Turkey*, Bucharest: UNESCO.
Mizikaci, F. (2017a), 'Introduction', in F. Mizikaci, G. Senese, S. Gorman and Y. T. Cakcak (eds), *The Language of Freedom and the Teacher's Authority: Case Comparisons from Turkey and the United States*, xx–xxv, New York: Lexington Books.
Mizikaci, F. (2017b), 'Askıya Çıkarılan Taslak Programlar ve Düşündürdükleri', *Eleştirel Pedagoji (Critical Pedagogy)* (50): 1–8.
Mizikaci, F. (2017c), 'The Role of Education and Ideology in Re-Building Nation-States in Post-Soviet Societies', in A. Friedli, A. Gohard-Radenkovic and F. Ruegg (eds), *Nation Building and Identities in Post-Soviet Societies: New Challenges for Social Sciences*, Vol. 47, 37–54, Wien: LIT Verlag Münster.
Oliveira, I. B. (2017), 'Itinerant Curriculum Theory Against Epistemicides: A Dialogue Between the Thinking of Santos and Paraskeva', *Journal of the American Association for the Advancement of Curriculum Studies (JAAACS)*, 12 (1): 1–22.
Orvis, S. W. (1915), *Religious Education in American Schools in The Ottoman Empire* (Doctoral dissertation, The University of Chicago).
Paraskeva, J. M. (2011), *Conflicts in Curriculum Theory: Challenging Hegemonic Epistemologies*, New York: Palgrave Macmillan.
Paraskeva, J. M. (2016), *Curriculum Epistemicide: Towards an Itinerant Curriculum Theory*, New York: Routledge.
Paraskeva, J. M. (2017), 'Itinerant Curriculum Theory Revisited on a Non-Theoricide Towards the Canonicide: Addressing the "Curriculum Involution"', *Journal of the American Association for the Advancement of Curriculum Studies (JAAACS)*, 12 (1): 1–43.
Paraskeva, J. M. (2018), *Towards a Just Curriculum Theory: The Epistemicide*, New York: Routledge.
Paraskeva, J. M. (2020), *Curriculum and the Generation of Utopia: Interrogating the Current State of Critical Curriculum Theory*, New York: Routledge.

Paraskeva, J. M. (2022), 'The Generation of the Utopia: Itinerant Curriculum Theory Towards a "Futurable Future"', *Discourse: Studies in the Cultural Politics of Education*, 43 (3): 347–66. http://doi.org/10.1080/01596306.2022.2030594.
Peacock, A. S. (2015), *Great Seljuk Empire*, Edinburgh: Edinburgh University Press.
Said, E. W. (1979), *Orientalism*, New York: Vintage.
Santos, B. (2007), *Another Knowledge Is Possible*, London: Verso.
Santos, B. (2014), *Epistemologies of the South: Justice Against Epistemicide*, Boulder: Paradigm.
Shils, E. B. (1961), *Centre and Periphery: In the Logic of Personal Knowledge: Essays Presented to Michael Polanyi*, 117–30, New York: Routledge & Kegan Paul.
Süngü, A. (2009), *İbn Haldunun eğitim felsefesi*. Unpublished Master's thesis, Süleyman Demirel Üniversitesi Sosyal Bilimler Enstitüsü.
Ülken, H. Z. (1992), *Türkiye'de çağdaş düşünce tarihi*. Ülken Yayınları.
United Nations High Commissioner for Refugees. (2017), 'Figures at a Glance', http://www.unhcr.org/figures-at-a-glance.html.
Varış, F. (1989), 'Eğitimde Program Geliştirmeye Sistematik Yaklaşım', *Ankara University Journal of Faculty of Educational Sciences (JFES)*, 22 (1): 7–12.
Zarcone, T. (2017), 'Shamanism in Turkey: Bards, Masters of the Jinns, and Healers', in T. Zarcone and A. Hobart (eds), *Shamanism and Islam: Sufism, Healing Rituals and Spirits in the Muslim World*, London: Bloomsbury Publishing.

8

Leaving the United States in Fear and Tears

Young Chun Kim's Lonely but Brave Scholarship as a Critical Text of Decolonizing Curriculum Studies

Jung-Hoon Jung

The poet, Sang-hwa Yi, wrote the poem 'Does Spring Come Even to the Stolen Fields?' in 1926, during the Japanese colonial period (1910–45). Lamenting the situation Korean people faced, he expressed a strong hope and desire for decolonization and freedom. The colonial period ended long ago. Yet, in academia, Koreans still observe a strong Western influence. What would Sang-hwa Yi (2018) say for the scholars whose fields have been colonized and those who struggle for decolonization? How shall we, as the poet's descendants, act and live to see the bright light on our green grass of the field? In this chapter, I discuss how such efforts can be made through studying the scholarship of a Korean curriculum scholar, Young Chun Kim, whose academic life has been similar to the poet. His scholarship and academic journey may read as an example of how postcolonial curriculum studies can be pursued in a non-Western country.

The scope of curriculum studies has expanded from pre-occupation to curriculum development since the emergence of the field. In the 1970s, the discourse has been reconceptualized and increasingly become interdisciplinary. Then, in the recent decades, it has expanded by internationalization (Pinar, 2014; Gough, 2007). As Paraskeva (2016) notes, 'around the world, curriculum – hard sciences, social sciences, and the humanities – has been dominated and legitimated by prevailing Western Eurocentric Anglophone discourses and practices' (p. i). The current move aims to acknowledge regional curriculum views, local knowledge and concepts and indigenous interpretations of curricular concepts and practices. Informed by Boaventura de Sousa Santos (2009), João Paraskeva supports such efforts, claiming that the field has been predominantly Western with *epistemicides* in terms of colour, gender, culture and world view. Paraskeva (2016) invokes 'intellectual decolonization [from non-Western perspectives, epistemologies, ethics, and worldviews] because the models of the Eurocentric critique of Eurocentrism not only do not cease to be Eurocentric, but [. . .] are also not sufficient to describe the realities beyond the Occidental framework' (p. 67). For Paraskeva, the task of decolonizing curriculum discourse requires fighting 'for cognitive diversity and justice' and 'for (an)other knowledge outside the Western epistemological harbor' (2016, 43).

I live in South Korea, and my field is curriculum studies. I have an opportunity to deliberate on what decolonizing curriculum studies and ICT means in the South Korean context where 'pedagogy has been shaped and continuously influenced by American and other Western epistemologies, given the historical configuration between Korea and the United States' (Kim, 2005a, 59). The works of Pinar, Paraskeva, De Sousa Santos and Fanon resonate with me, and I am concerned with Audre Lorde's (1984) statement, *The Masters' Tools Will Never Dismantle the Master's House* (Lorde, 1984), and Spivak's 'the subaltern cannot speak' (1988, 104). If I agree, at least in part, with Lorde and Spivak, my task of decolonizing Korean curriculum studies faces a double challenge: to develop the tools to dismantle the master's house and to create intellectual spaces where virtues of alterity and incommensurability may thrive. This task cannot be achieved alone. Yet, someone must lead the way. For this challenging and necessary task, I examine an exemplary scholar's work from the perspective of decolonization curriculum studies in South Korea.

Young Chun Kim is a professor in the Department of Education at the Chinju National University of Education in South Korea. He is a curriculum scholar whose research areas include curriculum theory, postcolonial curriculum studies, qualitative research and cultural studies. He earned his PhD from the Ohio State University under the supervision of Patti Lather. He authored more than forty books in the areas of curriculum studies, qualitative research, multicultural education and shadow education. He has won five national book awards from the Research Foundation of Korea and the Korean Department of Education and Culture. In addition to taking a leading role in Korean curriculum and education research in South Korea, Kim has participated in global curriculum studies since 2000, and his articles on reconceptualizing Korean curriculum studies and on curriculum studies as postcolonial texts have appeared in North American journals.

Why did Kim leave the United States in fear and tears? He had eagerly left for the United States to become 'American-like' (Kim, 1997, 7), and he was desperate to master American academic knowledge. Yet, he realized that neither could he become American-like nor white. Finishing his PhD, he was immersed in sorrow, as his identity could not be changed, and his mimicry academic identity was bound to crash. Knowing he was too Americanized in terms of scholarship, he questioned in fear whether he could lead an independent life without completely resorting to his academic roots. Kim (2020) recalls a kind of anxiety that Lacan talked about. Yet, given his accomplishments, Kierkegaard's concept of *Begrebet angst*, the 'dizziness of freedom' (Park, 1999, 197), an existential status where new forms of life are possible, might be more applicable. The academic journey portrayed in this chapter examines, as a critical text of postcolonial curriculum research, the works of a scholar who overcomes the fear and anxiety he faces as a person whose mentality was colonized by the West.

Echoing Kester and his colleagues (2020), I consider Kim as a leading scholar and theorist with a Southern or Eastern perspective that enabled new findings to emerge in ways that were not possible under the colonized academia. Reviewing Southern and Eastern scholars' efforts in the discourse of decolonization, Kester et al. (2020) ask 'what new findings might be produced' if scholars theorize through the work of Kim and other non-Western or non-European. Young Chun Kim's scholarship provides us with an example of how postcolonial curriculum studies can be conducted and how it can contribute to curriculum studies. In the following, I review Kim's contributions to the field and the significance and implications of his scholarship.

Recontextualizing postcolonial discourse in curriculum studies

Extracting postcolonial texts, concepts and meanings from Western postcolonial discourse, Kim investigates its situated applicability and the challenges faced by those pursuing postcolonial studies and practices. In performing such conceptual and theoretical works, Kim aimed to chart his (and Korean) ways of decolonizing curriculum studies in South Korea from a historical perspective. He conducted intensive analyses on the development of Korean curriculum studies as well as the postcolonial, international discourse of curriculum studies.

Since the beginning of his academic life, Kim has written about the colonization of educational theories, practices and institutional structures, as detailed in his works such as 'Postcolonialism and Reconceptualization of Korean Curriculum Studies' (Kim, 2005a). Informed by 'curriculum studies as postcolonial text' (Pinar et al., 1995), Kim discussed the possible boundaries and contents for postcolonial curriculum studies: 'how can curriculum studies in Korea be reterritorialized or reconceptualized in order to increase decentered consciousness and decolonized minds?' (Kim, 2005a, 70). To address this question, Kim first explained how Korean scholarship has been colonized in three phases. The first phase, as Kim explains, was the application of a 'curriculum of translation'. That is, Korean curriculum studies were primarily focused on reading 'popular books and scholarly articles written in America, translat[ing] them into Korean' (Kim, 2005a, 59). The leading scholars who studied in the United States 'contributed to the establishment of a colonized culture of Korean curriculum studies' (p. 59). The second phase involved the 'curriculum of abstract theories'; research on American curriculum theories was considered 'the most important academic activity' (p. 60). Such studies were valued more than formulations of Korean practices, as Korean curriculum scholars were eager to 'detect new US research themes (trends), then adapt them as legitimate topics for Korean curriculum studies' (Kim, 2005a, 59). In describing this strong tendency, Kim used the phrase 'first come, first served' to indicate the competition, yet this line of work was mere adaptation: 'Korean practices were relatively ignored and made invisible in Korean pedagogy' (Kim, 2005a, 60). For the third phase, Kim discusses the 'curriculum of domestication': 'Korean scholars' minds and consciousness were arrested by phantoms of US practices, inscribing us [Korean scholars] as subordinate to US scholars' (Kim, 2005a, 60). Kim believed that such candid self-critical analysis was 'necessary as the first step in [deterritorializing] Korean curriculum studies from America and in searching for strategies of resistance, toward the formulation of decolonized curriculum practice' (Kim, 2005a, 59). To theorize a Korean curricular concept using the birth myth of Korea, Kim suggested:

> Ungnyo was the mother of the founder of Korea, described in the 2003 B.C. Korean myth called 'Dangun (King of Korea)'. She was a wild bear but became human after enduring 100 days of cold and hunger, praying in a dark cave. She represents the power of endurance, production, and creation. Also, it is a symbolization of Koreans' abilities to create something new from nothing on the planet. (Dangun Synwha: Myth of the Foundation of Korea) (Kim, 2005a, 66)

In addition, Kim emphasizes the hongikingan ideology, that is, an ethical and existential view to benefit all people. Yet, this indigenous notion of curriculum was not appreciated by not only Western but also Korean readers. Nonetheless, Kim has desperately worked to bring forward Korean culture and history into the discourse of curriculum studies.

Five years after this text, Kim (2010) published 'Transnational Curriculum Studies: Reconceptualization Discourse in South Korea'. This article provided an intensive historical review of Korean curriculum studies, with a focus on the 'reconfiguration of Western discourse in terms of local and regional knowledge' (Kim, 2010, 531) from the perspective of 'reconceptualization discourse' (Pinar, 1975). The scholarly value of the article is that it 'authentically demonstrate[s] their [Koreans'] own localness' (Gough, 2013, 68). Informed by his 2005 article, Kim analysed the development and complexity of Korean curriculum studies. He understood that reconceptualization discourses, notwithstanding their Western origins, 'has enabled Korean scholars to shift their attention away from Western curriculum theory to the formulation of Korean theory focused on Korean practice' (Kim, 2010, 542) in three ways: stimulation of a complex and diverse understanding of curriculum; generation of alternative research methodologies; and inspiration for research on Korean curriculum practices. Kim identified this movement as the 'Koreanization of reconceptualization discourse' (Kim, 2010, 542), as it brought attention to Korean educational culture and phenomena such as *hakbeol* (Lee, 2003), *hakwon* (Kim, 2007) and other Korea-specific practices (Oh, 2008; Park, 2003). In the conclusion of the article, Kim discusses the value of this kind of analysis from two important perspectives. First, 'the value of composing local tales goes beyond the simple narration of intellectual history and advancement; potentially, it functions to usher in a future era of post-Western curriculum studies' (Kim, 2010, 547) by making the international curriculum discourse more 'hybrid' (Lather, 2006, 52), as curriculum scholars in different countries work to 'produce different knowledge and produce knowledge differently' (p. 52). Second, such work can 'constitute projects of self-discovery' that enables one 'to appreciate and develop one's own situated ideas and perspectives in the formation of new curriculum knowledge' (Kim, 2010, 547).

Following the 2010 article, Kim worked to provide a concrete example of Koreanized postcolonial study. 'Elusive Images of the Other: A Postcolonial Analysis of South Korean World History Textbooks' (Kim, Moon and Joo, 2013) is a critical discourse analysis of Korean high school textbooks from the perspective of cultural imperialism, informed by postcolonial theories such as that of Fanon, Said, Foucault, Spivak and Freire. Kim and his colleagues focused on two themes: how the Discovery of New Trade Routes and the Industrial Revolution are represented in Korean high school textbooks and how they are taught. Their analysis is based on four criteria that they developed, informed by postcolonial theories: (1) constructions of subject/Other, (2) discourses of inclusion/exclusion, (3) silencing of voices and (4) narratives of re/colonization. Their analysis revealed that despite Korean scholars' efforts to move away from colonized history and historical perspectives, 'the dominant textbooks and teaching practices continue to project colonial and Eurocentric epistemologies and to control knowledge production' (Kim, Moon and Joo, 2013, 219). For instance, Columbus's discovery represented in Korean textbooks carries 'a sense of Eurocentrism, and allowed Europeans to make sense of the world from their own perspective' (Kim et al., 2013, 227). Questioning the discourse of *discovery*, the authors argued that America was not discovered by Columbus, as indigenous people already resided on the land. By representing a Eurocentric world view in the textbooks and teaching in the same fashion, they argued that Korean history education remains colonized. Based on this study, Kim and his colleagues argued for 'the need to pluralize historical consciousness' (Kim et al., 2013, 241).

The latest, key conceptual and theoretical work of Young Chun Kim on postcolonial discourse is 'Key Themes in Postcolonial Curriculum Studies' (Joo and Kim, 2017). This study further develops Kim's 2005 article. They first provide how research trends have changed in the past four decades, beginning with identifying how colonial minds and epistemologies have been implemented in schooling and school curriculum (Said, 2012; Coloma, 2009); complexification of theoretical discussion in the paradigm (Dey, 2010; Ghosh, 2008); and pursuing possible postcolonial curricular practices (Subeedi and Deza, 2008; Sleeter, 2010). Based on the historical review, Kim and his colleagues identified five key themes in postcolonial curriculum studies: (1) investigation of the colonized aspects of the school curriculum; (2) ideological analysis of schooling and classroom instruction; (3) developing curricular practices to promote postcolonial minds and resistance; (4) research and theorization from indigenous curriculum phenomena; and (5) self-critique of the colonized research tradition and approaches in curriculum studies.

Kim's postcolonial scholarship has recently begun to be recognized as Kevin and his colleagues perceive him as a leading figure in South Korea, evaluating his scholarship as important as that of postcolonial scholars in other countries such as Anibal Quijano from Peru, Boaventura de Sousa Santo from Portugal, Gustavo Esteva from Mexico and Kuan-Hsing Chen from Taiwan (Kevin et al., 2020; Connell, 2020). Kim suggests curriculum research themes that he has endeavoured to contribute to the literature over the past three decades, such as reconstruction of the images of Korean education and curriculum theorization through a situated understanding of Korean educational phenomena, which could not have been achieved by Western scholars.

Reconstructing the images of Korean education

From the inception of his academic career, Kim has questioned, 'Why is not there much Korean educational theories and discussions to explain and to understand

Korean schools and classrooms in Korean curriculum studies?' (Kim, 1997, 316). He diagnosed Korean curriculum studies as a colonized field where Western theories and knowledge are tested, which conceives Korean education as peripheral. His criticism was driven by the dominance of quantitative research methodologies in educational studies, predominantly informed by positivism and scientific approaches. As an anecdote to rectify the academic culture and colonized status of educational studies, he saw *hope* in qualitative research methodologies and was mesmerized by their potential for the 'social construction of reality' and 'discovery' (Kim, 1997, 318).

His academic career began with producing indigenous images of Korean education, using his expertise in qualitative methodologies. At the end of his oral defence for his PhD, he was asked, 'What do you want to do, once you return to South Korea?' (Kim, 1997, 12). He replied, 'Rather than being a consumer of the knowledge produced by Western scholars such as Pinar and Apple, I will conduct Korean indigenous curriculum research, and in doing so, I will conduct contextualized empirical research that explains Korean schooling, culture, and practices' (p. 12). He kept his promise, as Table 1 shows:

As Table 1.1 shows, Kim's efforts to reconstruct the image of Korean education span various research topics such as the culture of schooling, students' and teachers' lives and the culture of Korean education. The works pioneered scholarly attention on the

Table 1.1 Young Chun Kim's Representative Empirical Studies on Korean Education

Culture of Schooling
Tales of Four Schools: Classroom Life and Instruction of Korean Elementary Schooling (Kim, 1997).
Curriculum Practice
A Midnight Summer: Narrative of Fantasy and Fall of the Korea National Seventh Curriculum Reform (Kim et al., 2009).

Teachers' Lives and Experience
Ugly Duckling: The Lives of Korean First-Year Elementary Teachers (Kim, Jung and Lee, 2006).
Starry Night 1: Korean Teachers' Lives and Their World (Kim, 2005b).
Starry Night 2: Korean Teachers' Lives and Their World (Kim, 2005c).

Multicultural Education
'Lives and Education of Students of Korean Multicultural Families: Reconstruction of Live History Voices' (Kim, Lee and Whang, 2012).
The Darkest Eyes: The Life Histories of Five Children of Korean Multicultural Families (Kim, 2011).

Shadow Education
Shadow Education and the Curriculum and Culture of Schooling in South Korea (Kim, 2016).
Shadow Education as Worldwide Curriculum Studies (Kim and Jung, 2019).
Korean Father Dies but Hakwon (Private Education Institute) Will Never Die: What US President Obama Did Not Know about the Secrets of International Success of Korean Education (Kim, 2012).
Alternatively, Send Your Children to Hakwon (Kim, 2008).
'What Makes Students World-Class Learners: Postcolonial Narratives against the Dominant Discourse about Korean Education' (Kim and Jung, 2019).
'The Education of Academically Gifted Students in South Korea: Innovative Approaches in Shadow Education' (Kim, Jo and Jung, 2020).
'Integrating Shadow Education with Public Schooling: South Korean Students' Transboundary Learning Culture for Academic Success'.

importance of understanding the reality of the practice and culture of Korean education from an insiders' view. The foci of the works were to identify the characteristics of Korean educational phenomena and, most importantly, to show how they are different from those of the West. *Tales of Four Schools* (Kim, 1997) is arguably the first work, over the past fifty years of modern educational research in Korea, that vividly portrayed what was happening in Korean school classrooms. Informed by Jackson's *Life in Classrooms* (1968), the work has not only ignited qualitative study in school lives in academia but also inspired teachers to understand their lives and practices; Kim mentions that he received an e-mail from a teacher stating the teacher 'would not use corporal punishment anymore after reading the portrayal of a teacher's behavior in the book [. . .] this book had influenced him more than any other in-service training program' (Kim, 2010, 538).

Starry Night: Korean Teachers' Lives and Their World series (Kim, 2005b, 2005c) portrayed the daily lives of Korean teachers (Kim, 2005b). The books provided different narratives and meanings of Korean teachers, different from the classic works such as *First Year Teacher: A Case Study* (Bullough, 1989) and *Schoolteacher: A Sociological Study* (Lortie, 1975). Like the swirling sky and relatively calm village in Van Gogh's painting, Kim's portrayal of teachers' lives is multilayered, ironic and sometimes contradictory. Criticizing the traditional perspective of curriculum that has been predicated primarily on functionality in South Korea, the works contributed to the turn from process-product research paradigms to 'understanding curriculum' (Pinar et al., 1995) in South Korea. Acknowledging that teachers' attitudes are heavily influenced by their everyday school environment and practices, Kim's work, for instance, reports that some teachers with higher expectations from students sacrifice their educational beliefs over peer pressure and the hierarchy of the school bureaucracy. Actively participating in and leading the historical turn towards understanding the curriculum, Kim argues through his works that 'without knowing about teachers' individual, social, and cultural lives, it is not possible to formulate suggestions that might lead to curriculum improvement' (Kim, 2010, 541).

The Darkest Eyes: The Life Histories of Five Children of Korean Multicultural Families (Kim, 2011) revealed the distinctiveness of multicultural education in South Korea, which is different from that of the West. 'The Darkest Eyes' metaphorically emphasizes the essential difference in terms of the real issues of multicultural education in South Korea. Kim took the title from Toni Morrison's (2007) *The Bluest Eye*. While blue eyes are considered as normal and ordinary – a way of discriminating based on pupil colours in the United States as Morrison narrates – so are black eyes in South Korea, a situation that multicultural families and students face in Korean schools and society. The book questions 'the Koreans' who believe they are truly Korean, to think about the bias, presuppositions and perhaps racism embedded in their unquestioned, ordinary gazes, words, gestures and behaviours.

A Midnight Summer: Narrative of Fantasy and Fall of the Korea National Seventh Curriculum Reform (Kim et al., 2009) contains a series of stories on how the seventh national curriculum reform failed in public schooling. Revealing teachers' daily curriculum practices, their criticism on the national curriculum and the practical challenges they faced every day, this book is a testimony of how the importation and implementation of Western, or simply American, curriculum into the Korean context is unquestioned. It was a disaster, as the title expresses, in that teachers were not equipped with practical tools for process-based evaluation, a differentiated curriculum and the changed evaluation system both for school grades and upper school selection. The central argument Kim made in the book is that curriculum renovation will fail if it ignores the realities of Korean students, teachers and schools. Yet, such institutionalized approach continues, as the power of developing and changing the national curriculum is possessed by the government, as I critiqued elsewhere (Jung, 2017).

In the recent years, Kim's research focus has been on shadow education, commonly known as private supplementary tutoring. He published many articles and several books on this research topic; representative works are included in Table 1.1 (Kim, 2007, 2008, 2012, 2016, 2019). With these works, Kim highlighted a Korean educational phenomenon, as it is the strongest in terms of intensity and diversity of the forms (Kim and Jung, 2019), as an academic area of curriculum studies, which has not been considered as one for curriculum research. His first book on hakwon, private tutoring institutes that are often called cram schools, is *Secrets of Academic Success of Korean Students: Stories of Hakwon* (Kim, 2007). In this book, Kim revealed the realities of students' learning experiences at hakwon and discussed what makes *hakwon* (private institutes) better than *hakkyo* (public schools) in helping students attain academic success. Kim (2007) provides four major characteristics in terms of hakwon's effectiveness: (1) the emphasis of learning by repetition; (2) a tracking system equipped with individualized instruction; (3) continuous and holistic assessment; and (4) providing information on student's progress for students and their parents. This book and his following books such as *Alternatively, Send Your Children to Hakwon* (Kim, 2008) and *Korean Father Dies but Hakwon (Private Education Institute) Will Never Die* (Kim, 2012) reveal why Korean students evaluate these institutes as better places of learning than schools. Based on his studies, Kim's standpoint is that '*hakwon* needs to be studied as an important regional curriculum issue' (Kim, 2010, 544), because such practices are highly popular in South Korea and other countries such as Japan, Taiwan, China and Singapore. Beginning with his first book and in his publications in the following years, Kim expanded his study, going beyond the national boundary of South Korea. His first English book on this topic, *Shadow Education and the Curriculum and Culture of Schooling in South Korea*, presented to readers in the West how Korean students learn in the shadow education space. This work paved the way for his recent scholarly efforts to theorize the phenomenon from the perspective of curriculum studies.

To reconstruct the images of Korean education, Kim has been working to produce narratives, knowledge and theories of Korean education from indigenous perspectives. As many postcolonial theorists (Briggs and Sharp, 2004; Gandhi, 2019) and curriculum scholars (Pinar, 2014; Gough, 2007) argued for the significance of producing indigenous or local knowledge, Kim's line of work can be characterized as the 'reconstruction of marginalized knowledge' (Gandhi, 2019) that rejects being the 'inferiority of the other' (Quijano, 2000). Creating new non-Western narratives is an approach that breaks away from the colonized tradition and legacy and provides a new vision for the field (Ashcroft, Griffifth and Tiffin, 1989; 1998). In this vein, Kim and Joo argue that 'to be truly decolonized, we need to get away from importing knowledge by which we might be brainwashed. Rather, we must empower ourselves with abilities to study local traditions and cultures and produce our own knowledge to theorize on' (Joo and Kim, 2017, 238). In a personal communication with me, Kim said, 'What they [scholars in the West] believe they know may not be valid for us. We must conduct ourselves by a different logic by which we should be able to tell them what we see, experience, and understand can be different from theirs.' In doing so, Joo and Kim further argued that the production of indigenous knowledge is a way to make the silenced voices heard, which might challenge Western epistemologies and world views. As Fanon (1968) argued, the recuperation of the colonized psyche must be fundamentally based on 'the reality' of the local. This reality can be understood only when marginalized people begin to conceive their subjectivity, practices, daily lives, cultures and traditions as essentially valuable – at least as valuable as those imported from the West. Then, what should one do with the renewed understanding? What Kim did was to move towards developing curricular/educational concepts.

Internationalization of non-Western/ postcolonial curriculum phenomena

As a curriculum scholar in the East, Young Chun Kim's postcolonial research has contributed to creating non-Western curricular educational concepts. Critiquing the colonized research culture of curriculum studies in Korean academia, Kim has emphasized the significance of curriculum theory through Korean indigenous curriculum phenomena (Kim, 2005a; Joo and Kim, 2017). This kind of curriculum research is an effort to theorize alternative, non-Western curriculum approaches based on the indigeneity of the local (Tuck and Yang, 2012). As such, marginalized knowledge can be found, as Briggs and Sharp (2004) have also argued. 'Whether or not it has been acknowledged by the Eurocentric mainstream', as Battiste (2002, 4) argued, 'indigenous knowledge has always existed' (p. 4). Such knowledge includes world views, customs, traditions and intellectual legacies that have been generated from distinctive historical and cultural contexts (Hart, 2010). Thus, the task for non-Western scholars is to 'reveal the wealth and richness' (Battiste, 2002, 4) of such knowledge.

The work Kim has produced in this line is featured in two categories. The first is to develop a Korean curriculum and educational concepts based on the history, culture and educational environment of South Korea, and the second is curriculum theorization for international curriculum discourse as a non-Western scholar. The representative concepts he theorized include *Ungnyo curriculum* (Kim, 2010), *the darkest pupils* (Kim, 2011), *super-education* (Kim, 2016), *shadow curriculum* (Kim and Jung, 2019) and *trans-boundary learning culture* (Kim and Jung, 2019).

For the advancement of the international curriculum discourse, Kim theorized a new kind of curriculum, *shadow curriculum,* which he defined as a 'supplementary curriculum out of schooling provided by educational business industries that is intended to improve academic success among individual students in formal education'

(Kim and Jung, 2019, 150). Kim's interest in this research topic (private supplementary tutoring) was sparked by his mundane, daily life observations. One day he said hello to a boy whom he often encountered in the elevator of his apartment. He asked the boy where he was going. 'I am going to *hakwon*', replied the boy. Kim asked the boy, 'Is it not hard for you to go to *hakwon* and study after school?' Contrary to what he expected, the boy said, 'No, it is a lot of fun actually.' At that moment, his self-critique was activated, contemplating that he may have had a biased perception about shadow education. Then, he began conducting research on this educational phenomenon. He immediately found that 'Korean students evaluate these institutes as better places of learning than school' (Kim, 2010, 544), and 'even though most Korean students attend *hakwon* every day, this national phenomenon has never been researched in curriculum studies, perhaps because it has never been discussed as an important theme in Western fields of education' (p. 544). In the past two decades, Kim published several books and articles. Besides the concept of the shadow curriculum, he has been theorizing cognizant concepts related to shadow curriculum such as the 'trans-boundary learning culture' (Kim and Jung, 2019) and 'super-education' (Kim, 2016).

Working through Korean language is necessary for Kim, as he argued that 'the language of US curriculum theories profoundly influences our ways of seeing and determining what and how we can see/not see in Korean education' (Kim, 2005, 66). Kim further argued that the curricular language adopts function as 'an effective control apparatus to regulate our academic boundaries' (p. 66), and Ungugi (1986, 9) argues that 'bullets destroy a colonizer's body but language is the means of controlling our minds'. In the same vein, Kim argues:

> We must formulate concepts and theoretical expressions to represent the indigenous meanings of a phenomenon [which] can only be conducted by Korean scholars. When Korean scholars successfully accomplish this task, they will become the originators of a new Korean curriculum language, both indigenous and reflective of our in-depth knowledge of Western curriculum scholarship. As the phrase, 'the Empire writes back' indicates, we will increase our own independent power to create new Korean curriculum theories, providing both a competing language and a complementary curriculum language. (Kim, 2005, 67)

To work for the power of language, Kim argued earlier that 'the first way is to take historical ideas from Korean (and, more broadly, Asian) knowledge and epistemologies' (p. 68). Keeping the promise he made in his doctoral dissertation, Kim has worked to create curricular concepts with a Korean perspective and by studying Korean educational phenomena. By developing curricular concepts based on the Korean language and context, Kim has worked to fight against 'epistemicide' (Paraskeva, 2016), that is, a kind of academic tendency to suppress the creation of alternative knowledges in curriculum studies discourse. Working against epistemicide is 'so crucial for the [more just] curriculum field' (Paraskeva, 2016, 1).

Writing non-Western tales and theorizing outside the Western context can 'constitute a moment of cultural resistance [. . .] to decolonize curriculum studies, ushering in, perhaps, a postcolonial curriculum studies' (Kim, 2010, 548), as Ashcroft,

Griffifth and Tiffin (1989) powerfully argued in *Empire Writes Back*. Through his research on shadow education and his curriculum concept, shadow curriculum,[1] Kim has shown that non-Western scholars also have abilities to create knowledge that may inform international academia. Kim thought that shadow education discourse has been dominated, at least led, by Western scholars; however, he believed that the phenomenon can be and shall be led by Korean or East Asian scholars because it has been the most prominent and intense in these countries (Kim, 2016). As discussed earlier, one of the reasons why the phenomenon shall be studied by local scholars is the problem of language. For example, Kim critiqued the use of *hagwon* that refers to private tutoring institutes in Korea. Since it is Korean language, Kim wanted to correct it as *hakwon,* as it is closer to Korean pronunciation (Kim, 2016).

Conclusion: Towards simulacra curriculum studies

To conclude this chapter, I would like to revisit Lorde (1984) and Spivak (1990). Can non-Western scholars dismantle the power or inertia of the epistemicide of mainstream curriculum discourse? How can we centre the decentred Korean, non-Western, epistemologies, cultures, histories and educational/curricular phenomena? What can the readers learn from Young Chum Kim's scholarship about how postcolonial studies can be conducted, especially when they cannot completely abandon the tools, research methodologies, concepts and theories of the West?

Kim (2005) discussed the concept of 'ironic validity' and 'simulacra validity' to emphasize the importance of local discourse, that is, studying/answering Korea's own curriculum questions. Deleuze understood simulacrum as a 'becoming-unlimited' and/or 'difference in nature' in working with difference between copies (Deleuze, 1994). For Kim, what is true, validated and represented is always simulacra that reveals resemblances and difference. Only difference between things, entities, concepts and phenomenon testifies that they are not identical. Representation by a specific perspective and theory is always challenged by different approaches in terms of languages, cultures and methodologies. In the same vein, when studying the topic of multicultural education, such as studying immigrant students and their families, the understanding of Korean researchers is always limited and risks producing false representation because of the linguistic barrier they have, as discussed in *The Darkest Eyes* (Kim, 2011). In doing so, Kim intends to promote 'simulacra curriculum discourse' to be constantly mutable, rather than simply a merely reproduced species of national curriculum studies.

The efforts discussed in this chapter may be summarized as a struggle for making one's own voice heard while creating spaces where that voice can be heard. As Spivak (1988) argued, 'the subaltern cannot speak. There is no virtue in global laundry lists with "woman" as a pious item' (p. 104). We must question who gives the authority to give power to the subalterns to speak and who creates academic as well as public spaces and opportunities for the emergence of the unspoken or unheard. Kim (2016) encourages Korean curriculum scholars to be aware of how Korean education has been seen as subaltern, by not only others but also Koreans. His response to Spivak's (2003) famous question, *Can the Subaltern Speak?*, is that we should not ask whether we can use our own voices but instead realize that using our own voices is our 'responsibility' (Kim, 2016, 12), especially through historical investigation that might reveal how we have arrived at the status quo and how conceptions and practices of Korean education could be constructed otherwise.

I would like to conclude this chapter with a phrase that supported Kim's life and scholarship in the far East; it is staged in the Sutta-nipāta, primitive Buddhist scriptures: 'Go alone like the horns of an ox.' It means to boldly and bravely follow one's beliefs and resolutions. Kim's scholarship may be read as an example in that he continuously questions what counts as knowledge and research topics.

Note

1   A chapter about shadow curriculum will be included in the *Encyclopedia of International Education* published by Elsevier in 2022.

References

Ashcroft, B., G. Griffifth and H. Tiffin (1989), *The Empire Writes Back: Theory and Practice in Post-Colonial Literature*, London: Routledge.

Ashcroft, B., G. Griffifth and H. Tiffin (1998), *Key Concepts in Post-Colonial Studies*, New York: Routledge.

Battiste, M. (2002), *Indigenous Knowledge and Pedagogy in the First Nations Education: A Literature Review with Recommendations*, Ottawa: Indian and Northern Affairs Canada.

Briggs, J. and J. Sharp (2004), 'Indigenous Knowledge and Development: A Postcolonial Caution', *Third World Quarterly*, 25 (4): 661–676.

Bullough, R. V. (1989), *First Year Teacher: A Case Study*, New York: Teachers College Press.

Coloma, R. S., ed. (2009), *Postcolonial Challenges in Education*, Vol. 369, New York: Peter Lang.

Connell, R. (2020), *Southern Theory: The Global Dynamics of Knowledge in Social Science*, New York: Routledge.

Deleuze, G. (1994), *Difference and Repetition*, New York: Columbia University Press.

Dey, G. J. (2010), *Fanon and the Counter Insurgency of Education*, Boston: Sense Publishers.

Fanon, F. (1968), *The Wretched of the Earth*, New York: Glove Weidenfeld.

Gandhi, L. (2019), *Postcolonial Theory: A Critical Introduction*, New York: Columbia University Press.

Ghosh, R. (2008), 'Racism: A Hidden Curriculum', *Education Canada*, 48 (4): 26–29.

Gough, N. (2007), 'Changing Planes: Rhizosemiotic Play in Transnational Curriculum Inquiry', *Studies in Philosophy and Education*, 26 (3): 279–94.

Gough, N. (2013), 'Thinking Globally in Environmental Education: Implications for Internationalizing Curriculum Inquiry', in W. F. Pinar (ed.), *International Handbook of Curriculum Research*, 53–72, New York: Taylor & Francis.

Hart, M. A. (2010), 'Indigenous Worldviews, Knowledge, and Research: The Development of an Indigenous Research Paradigm', *Journal of Indigenous Social Development*, 1 (1A): 1–16.

Jackson, P. (1968), *Life in Classrooms*, New York: Teachers College Press.

Joo, J.-H. and Y. C. Kim (2017), 'Key Themes in Post-Colonial Curriculum Studies', *The Journal of Curriculum Studies*, 35 (4): 231–57.

Jung, J.-H. (2017), 'A Note on the Centrality of Knowledge and Experience for Curriculum Development', *Journal of Education & Culture*, 23 (5): 517–45.

Kester, K., L. Sweeney, C. Chang, M. Watkins and J. Cha (2020), 'Decolonizing Higher Education: Practical Examples from International and Intercultural Educators in Korea', *The Korea TESOL Journal*, 16 (1): 27–53.

Kim, Y. C. (1997), *Tales of Four Schools: Classroom Life and Instructions in Korean Elementary Schooling*, Seoul: Munumsa.

Kim, Y. C. (2005a), 'Post-Colonialism and Reconceptualization of Korean Curriculum Studies', *Journal of Curriculum Theorizing*, 21 (1): 57–75.

Kim, Y. C. (2005b), *Starry Night: Korean Teachers' Lives and Their World I*, Seoul: Munumsa.

Kim, Y. C. (2005c), *Starry Night: Korean Teachers' Lives and Their World II*, Seoul: Munumsa.

Kim, Y. C. (2007), *Secrets of Academic Success of Korean Students: Stories of Hakwon*, Seoul: Brenz.

Kim, Y. C. (2008), *Alternatively, Send Your Children to Hakwon*, Seoul: Academy Press.

Kim, Y. C. (2010), 'Transnational Curriculum Studies: Reconceptualization Discourse in South Korea', *Curriculum Inquiry*, 40 (4): 531–54.

Kim, Y. C. (2011), *The Darkest Eyes: The Life Histories of Five Children of Korean Multicultural Families*, Seoul: Academy Press.

Kim, Y. C. (2012), *Korean Father Dies But Hakwon (Private Education Institute) Will Never Die: What US President Obama Did Not Know about the Secrets of International Success of Korean Education*, Seoul: Academy Press.

Kim, Y. C. (2016), *Shadow Education, Curriculum, and Culture of Schooling in South Korea*, New York: Palgrave Macmillan.

Kim, Y. C. (2020), Personal Communication.

Kim, Y. C. and J. H. Jung (2019), *Shadow Education as Worldwide Curriculum Studies*, New York: MacMillan.

Kim, Y. C., J. Jo and J. H. Jung (2020), 'The Education of Academically Gifted Students in South Korea: Innovative Approaches in Shadow Education', *European Journal of Education*, 55 (3): 376–87.

Kim, Y. C., J. Jung and Y. Lee (2006), *Ugly Duckling: The Lives of Korean First-Year Elementary Teachers*, Seoul: Munumsa.

Kim, Y. C., D. Lee and C. Whang (2012), 'Lives and Education of Students of Korean Multicultural Families: Reconstruction of Live History Voices', *Journal of Multicultural Education*, 5 (1): 137–54.

Kim, Y. C., H. Y. Lee, H. C. Lee and J. H. Choi (2009), *A Mid-Night Summer: Narrative of Fantasy and Fall of the Korea National Seventh Curriculum Reform*, Paju: Academy Press.

Kim, Y. C., S. Moon and J. Joo (2013), 'Elusive Images of the Other: A Postcolonial Analysis of South Korean World History Textbooks', *Educational Studies*, 49 (3): 213–46.

Lather, P. (2006), 'Paradigm Proliferation as a Good Thing to Think with: Teaching Research in Education as a Wild Profusion', *International Journal of Qualitative Studies in Education*, 19 (1): 35–57.

Lee, J. K. (2003), *Korean Credential and Hakbeolism: Origin and Development*, Seoul: Jipmoondang.
Lorde, A. (1984), 'The Master's Tools Will Never Dismantle the Master's House', *Sister Outsider: Essays and Speeches*, 1: 10–14.
Lortie, D. C. (1975), *Schol Teachers: A Sociological Study*, Chicago: University of Chicago Press.
Morrison, T. (2007), *The Bluest Eye*, New York: Random House.
Oh, W. (2008), *Educational Exodus: Korean Children Go to USA and Canada for New Education*, Seoul: Kyoukkwahaksa.
Paraskeva, J. M. (2016), *Curriculum Epistemicide: Towards an Itinerant Curriculum Theory*, New York: Routledge.
Park, C. (1999), 'A Comparative Study of the Concept of Dread of Heidegger and Kierkegaard', *Journal of Time and Philosophy*, 10 (1): 188–219.
Park, N. (2003), *Korea in Educational War*, Seoul: Jangmi Press.
Pinar, W. F. (1975), *Curriculum Theorizing: The Reconceptualists*, Berkeley: McCutchan Publishing Corporation.
Pinar, W. F. (2014), *International Handbook of Curriculum Research*, New York: Routledge.
Pinar, W. F., W. M. Reynolds, P. Slattery and P. M. Taubman (1995), *Understanding Curriculum: An Introduction to the Study of Historical and Contemporary Curriculum Discourses*, New York: Peter Lang.
Quijano, A. (2000), 'Coloniality of Power and Eurocentrism in Latin America', *International Sociology*, 15 (2): 215–32.
Said, E. W. (2012), *Culture and Imperialism*, New York: Vintage.
Sleeter, C. (2010), 'Decolonizng Curriculum', *Curriculum Inquiry*, 40 (2): 193–203.
Santos, B. D. S. (2009), 'If God Were a Human Rights Activist: Human Rights and the Challenge of Political Theologies Is Humanity Enough? The Secular Theology of Human Rights', *Law, Social Justice & Global Development Journal (LGD)*, 1: 1–42.
Spivak, G. C. (1990), *The Post-Colonial Critic: Interviews, Strategies, Dialogues*, ed. S. Harasym. New York: Routledge.
Spivak, G. C. (1988), *In Other Worlds: Essays in Cultural Politics*, New York: Routledge.
Spivak, G. C. (2003), 'Can the Subaltern Speak?' *Die Philosophin*, 14 (27): 42–58.
Subeedi, B. and S. L. Deza (2008), 'The Possibilities of Postcolonial Praxis in Education', *Race Ethnicity and Education*, 11 (1): 1–10.
Tuck, E. and K. W. Yang (2012), 'Decolonization Is Not a Metaphor', *Decolonization: Indigeneity, Education & Society*, 1 (1): 1–40.
Ungugi, T. (1986), *Decolonizing the Mind: The Politics of Language in African Literature*, London: James Currey.
Yi, S. H. (2018), *Does Spring Come Even to the Stolen Fields?* Seoul: Designeum.

9

A Possible Utopia for Cognitive Justice

Towards an Itinerant Curriculum Theory as a *Deterritorialized* Critical Pedagogy

Rosa Vázquez Recio

Possible worlds, available realities and unforgivable forgetfulness

There is not a single world, not a unique available reality, as there is not just one single omission. They are numerous and can be counted, not just by the one and only recognized, legitimized and authentic reality which belongs to the unique World but also by those available realities incardinated in diverse and possible worlds, rich in knowledge, experiences, relationships. This demarcation between the one/unique and the diverse/plural is a feature which characterizes and defines our present (not devoid of its past neither unconnected to its future). This feature influences everything, and education is not a separate case. In view of this fact, it makes perfect sense to ask ourselves about critical pedagogy, which cannot be just anyone but one which questions *deterritorialization*. A question that is necessary for the achievement of cognitive justice (and other types of justice with which it is connected). This is not an innovative task, but it appears to be so in view of the condition in which, in general, the *worlds and realities* are and particularly those that belong to education.

At the present time we are immersed in a crisis; it is not just a health crisis but also a crisis of diverse nature, which share the lexeme of inequality, injustice and exclusion. In a world of technological advances as the one we live in, it must be taken into account the fact that inequalities are increasing as well as people at risk of social exclusion and children at risk of poverty, and they need careful consideration; they cannot sink into oblivion. Oddly enough, further progress does not minimize inequality, poverty or exclusion, but all the contrary. These consequences caused by structural factors have *faces* and their own ways of being in the world, which are not those recognized as legitimate. Those faces are the faces of the homeless, of those living in subhuman settlements, in impoverished neighbourhoods and so on. The current crisis has brought to light the weaknesses of the education systems, the inoperative character of the official (hegemonic) curriculum, the lifelong rights of private schools, the technocracy of management, the face of authoritarian democracies, the interests of ultra-conservative sectors, the supremacy of the markets, politics as *business*, and violence as an instrument of legitimate management. However it also highlighted, and the importance of the public and the value of the common good. As Therborn (2015, 11) points out inequalities imply a 'violation of human dignity' and, with it, injustices. Oblivion or disregard towards the specific circumstances of social life makes poverty, misfortune, helplessness and marginalization to be unfairly recognized as an individual responsibility (Young, 2011) and not as a collective one. It has been established as a rule that the causes of poverty are not social but personal, individual. It has been neoliberal ideologues who have provoked that turn in the responsibilities of the state, from the institutions to individual responsibility. Consequently, the structural and intersectional analysis which allows injustices (cognitive, social, etc.) is disqualified, and therefore the possibilities to end them up are limited, not to say non-existent. Depoliticization leads to the belief that social, economic and educational problems are the responsibility of the individual, hence people must look for solutions through 'self-help catechisms'. Self-help is based on individual autonomy and on the capability of everyone to make themselves in a world that cannot change – according to neoliberal ideology. Psycho-politics (Han, 2014) helps, as it involves 'the practice of domination over the citizens in a subtle and covert way' (Vázquez Recio, 2018, 88). But that idea that makes us believe that 'I can' is a way of making the citizens believe that they have the power, when actually this is not the case: it is 'apoliticism' (Santos, 2014, 17) which is used to reinforce dominant power relations. 'Social fascism' and 'democratic societies' coexist (Escobar, 2004, 89).

Human rights are affected. They are being violated. The agents of the colonialist, patriarchal, individualist, neoliberal and capitalist global order are the executors of such an action, although this attack is not the same for all the possible worlds and available realities. From its legitimacy, they define an abyssal line (Santos, 2007, 2009, 2010) between 'human rights' and 'non-human rights', justified from the differentiation of those who are on each side of that line. Those on the *non-human* side are the subordinate, the powerless groups, the dominated, the excluded, the *nobodies*, who, in turn, are exempted from the principle of citizenship; they are, consequently, without-citizenship people. Therefore, they become *non-citizen* people with *non-human* rights. They are *non-citizenship* people with *non-human* rights, they are non-people, non-being (Fanon, 2009). The maintenance of that line of thought is necessary in order to guarantee the positions of power erected in the complex weft of relations and naturalized hierarchies which result in inequalities, equally naturalized, which function with dehumanizing logics and with the denial of dignity. This line of thought is built as a barrier 'in reality not to fear competition from those it exploits and despises' (Fanon, 1999, 128). This situation requires a turn which is only possible from the pluriverse of experiences, practices, ways of living and ways of being in the world (Santos, 2009). It requires counter-hegemonic action in order to achieve a fairer and more decent society (Santos, 2014). For that purpose, the epistemic support which shapes human rights as absolute universals is no longer valid; such rights must be assumed as *situated universals* (Auat, 2011), as bearers of non-hegemonic languages, so as to face a liberatory and emancipatory hermeneutics, and of human rights incarnated in the subject and in the land they belong to. They have geo-politics and corpo-politics (Haraway, 1988, 1995; Quijano, 1992; Césaire, 2006; Dussel, 2007; Mignolo, 2006, 2010; Fanon, 2009). This turn needs of the respectful exercise of 'communicative freedom' (Benhabib, 2008), in addition to communication and action: 'It is necessary to be recognized as a member of an organized human community in which your words and your acts situate yourself within a communication and interaction social space. You possess a "right", that is, a moral requirement to be recognized by others as "a person who carries their own rights" with a legitimate claim to a legally instituted bill of rights' (p. 190). In this searching of an alternative that this turn represents, it is key 'from where' it is assumed, as the 'location' (Dussel, 2007), that 'from where', 'indicates the hermeneutic action through which the observer is (committedly) "situated" in some socio-historical "place", as a subject of enunciation of a discourse, and therefore it is the place "from where" controversial questions are posed [...]. This critical attitude of trying to obtain the highest possible degree of reflexivity over the "place" from where the discourse is enunciated (the *locus enuntiationis)* should be maintained as a permanent position' (p. 15).

Equality gaps are a proven fact. Behind educational, social and economic inequalities it is found (financial, cognitive, social, etc.) capitalism and other systems of oppression which exert the power of classism, colonialism, supremacism, patriarchy, xenophobia and so on. These have their path determined: to dominate, to oppress, to exploit those who are attributed an alleged inferiority (of social class, culture, ethnicity, gender, etc.), and they are just useful to guarantee the survival of the fittest (those with power, wealth, etc.). This useful dependency, however, occurs in an indirect manner due to the intervention mechanisms of financial capitalism which make us think that the enrichment of some and the impoverishment of others have nothing to do with each other (Bauman, 1998, 72), although those who are 'down', those who are 'out', those who are *nobody* are the ones who are harmed. An achievement which has been successfully reached by neoliberal and neoconservative agents.

UNICEF (2017, 1) notes that the 'digital divides also mirror prevailing economic gaps, amplifying the advantages of children from wealthier backgrounds and failing to deliver opportunities to the poorest and most disadvantaged children'. The digital divide only reflects the existence of other gaps – social and economic gaps between men and women, rich and poor people, urban and rural areas, Europeans and Africans, families with cultural resources and those without them, or with education and without it, and so on, and all the intersections that can occur among these possibilities. The inequalities attached to the various gaps have an intersectional character, revealing the interrelations that exist at individual, social and institutional levels (Hill Collins and Bilge, 2016). This is a compelling reason to assume a commitment to critical dissidence that breaks with the vision of the hegemonic power which makes the subjects exclusively responsible for their failures, their poverty, their unemployment and so on and which justifies them under 'Impossibilism' (Pucciarelli, 2005). This ideology only recognizes as valid and legitimate the alternatives offered by the domination systems (neoliberal, capitalist, colonialist and patriarchal), which favour dominant elites, dismantling at the same time, in order to make effective their purpose, any attempt of political project related to social transformation in which the subalterns, the oppressed, the ignored and the subordinates have a key role. They have been evicted from the epicentre of the relevant processes of democratization and from the construction of a fairer and more caring world. There cannot be a construction in terms of justice, redistribution and recognition if the 'Others' are left 'out' of the spaces of transformational and emancipatory decision-making and action. 'The "voice" of indignation remains alone' (Pellizzetti, 2009, 32). As Bilge (2013, 407) points out, 'neoliberalism denies certain preconditions that lead to structural inequalities; as a consequence, it is pleased to dismantle policies and discredit those movements concerned with the structures that generate injustice', without forgetting that such policies have appropriated inclusion, justice and equity in their eagerness to construct 'achievement-subjects' (Han, 2012) for a society that requires the best and most successful entrepreneurs, the most competitive ones.

These gaps which act as axes do not impact independently; on the contrary they act as a 'tangle' which intersects some moments and situations in the life of people, of students. This connection of interdependency among the axes is not equally reflected in all of them, because they are linked to the own experiences of every person. For that reason, homogeneous and standardized patterns cannot be adopted in order to understand those experiences. The impossibility comes from the fact that the *universal or objective subject* as an *abstract entity* (typical of the traditional model in Western science) does not exist. Giving value to such experiences is to validate the constituent narratives of the subjects, and to assume them as valid and legitimate knowledges which represent an epistemology incarnated in them, in those who undergo and suffer exclusion, inequality and marginalization. To recognize this epistemology is to legitimize a way of being in the world, and this way of being is not transferable, generalizable or inferior to any other. If we do not recognize it, we would be defending the supremacism, not just of modern scientific knowledge, of Western knowledge, of Northern knowledge but also of the knowledge of those who do not suffer exclusion, marginalization and segregation. This recognition obliterates any hierarchy and subordination relationship, preventing the definition of categories with which to classify. The possible worlds and the available realities are infinite: all of them are situated epistemic experiences, which bring an enrichment and never a loss, because 'they begin to dialogue in a transmodern pluriverse where each aesthetic culture dialogues and learns from the others, including modernity itself (certainly deprived from its universality and situated as a highly developed particularity, certainly)' (Dussel, 2018, 34). It is enough to assume different ways of knowledge and of incardination in the world, as well as to construct new inclusive categories of analysis in which the epistemologies-others/border epistemologies (Mignolo, 2000, 2008, 2010; Dussel, 2018), 'which have been suppressed, denigrated, despised' (Vázquez, 2016, 80), have political participation in a relational, dialogical and common-union dimension. It is not to speak, to explain or represent in the name of those epistemologies-others; the error would persist. The presence that gives it a place does not eliminate the hierarchical relationship among knowledges, because an *'epistemic detachment'* (Mignolo, 2010, 15) does not take place, a 'break and fracture, a moment of opening' (Mignolo, 2008, 252). Thus, it is not a given presence but a presence that gains plenitude when the 'own voice' is heard: 'listening beyond the frameworks of modernity may give birth to a kind of rooted and relational critical thinking' (Vázquez, 2016, 92). From this assumption, 'the political praxis of subaltern groups' (Escobar, 2004, 92) would be the trump card to review and reconstruct new explanatory, comprehensive and transformational frameworks for our reality and our world.

Educational inequalities and deficiencies need to be urgently addressed in the face of increasingly suffocating structural conditions that bring about the loss of basic public services. On the one hand, it is necessary to generate transformation processes, because 'the price of silence is paid in the hard currency of human suffering' (Bauman, 1998, 5) and on the other to assume 'local policies [that] constitute an emerging kind of politics, a new political imaginary in which to state a logics of difference, and a possibility which develop a multiplicity of actors and actions that take place in daily life' (Escobar, 2004, 96).

Within this ethical and political project, education becomes a way to achieve a fairer and more respectful world, and in this project, critical pedagogy would have a relevant place. In this respect, a question arises: does it have it? On the one hand, hegemonic power spaces and dominant discourses protected by the market, quality and academic performance, and a false idea of equality, and cognitive and social justice have been *good* 'veil makers' (Nietzsche, 2002), as far as they have accomplished their purpose of mitigating and weakening the agents of 'pedagogical revolution' (McLaren, 2012). On the other hand, it gives the impression that it has remained as a stronghold of itself and for itself, as the result of a 'particular intellectual elitism' (López Facal, 2004, 98) which has surrounded it; neither has it played much in its favour to believe that the discourse of critical pedagogy would result, de facto, in critical practices. Has critical pedagogy been left to 'Northern' epistemologists? Has it abandoned its political, social and emancipatory function?

Critical pedagogy: Traps, silences and new omissions

The emotional axis of neoliberalism, with its 'happiness industry' (Cabanas and Illouz, 2019), has become a key piece for transformation in citizens' ways of feeling, being and thinking. Language, with its rich playing possibilities, has played a relevant role, precisely because it is capable of 'stimulating certain emotions' (Cassier, 2004, 335). As a result of the language game it is being played with language, it is experiencing a resignification or emptying with a loss of its constituent referents. As an effect of this practice, many words are reduced to ornaments exhibited in 'discursive displays'. It is possible to think that this is what has happened to the word 'criticism'. It seems that by introducing it in the discourses which question the educational and social system, critical pedagogy is already being done. This reiterative reappearance of the word 'criticism', in these times in which criticism is suffocated by neoliberal, neoconservative and far-right discourses, has a low impact, and it is confirmed by the fact that we keep recognizing the existence of educational inequalities and injustices, intersected with others which occur at other levels (social, economic, cultural, political, ethnic, etc.). There is nothing worse to fight hegemony and relations of dominance than making critical pedagogy a 'placeholder', or an 'all-purpose concept'. Where does critical pedagogy look at?

If we look at educational realities, we continue to see the existence of a student body which still remains outside the educational system; there are students 'without-system' (Vázquez Recio and López Gil, 2018). Many elements intervene in this educational abandonment, being the curriculum the one which reveals itself significantly. The curriculum is condemned by disciplinary academicism that despises the diversity of knowledges (which go beyond scientific knowledge) and non-hegemonic and popular cultures; it depreciates the value of the diverse and different and silences those who belong to minority (powerless) groups and organizations and subordinates. It is an hegemonic curriculum tailored to the interests of those who place knowledge and education at the service of the economy of financial capitalism (nothing new since education and economic development were twinned), and in order to achieve it, they put pressure on education systems (Williamson, 2019). The OECD, the IMF, the WM the WTO need to strengthen both their economic and political power. This instrumentalization of the education systems, and all what they involve, becomes a requirement for cognitive capitalism which controls valid and profitable knowledge. Yes, it does so!, and according to Vercellone (2004, 66), 'knowledge production becomes the main bet of capital valorization', then it is defined as the way to obtain economic and political power by those who manage capital with the aim to ensure their benefits. The curriculum is not managed separately from the market interests, thus it becomes one more commodity for neoliberal business which functions according to the image of an *iceberg*: the visible part is what is made official as a common curriculum to please the citizens, its 'face' in front of society, and the invisible one is where the 'control unit' is in charge of making the curriculum meet the needs of neoliberal economy and financial capitalism. There is a structural relation between economy and education, typical of the 'global education industry' (Amaral, Steiner-Khamsi and Thompson, 2019), that does not only involve the privatization of education but also the redefinition of its meaning. In this turn, the curriculum fulfils its mission as a mechanism of cultural and social reproduction and control; it is neither neutral nor naïve, and it exerts a prophylactic action in order to protect legitimated knowledge (authentic, valid and profitable).

From this framework of commercialized curriculum, cognitive justice stays cracked, since cognitive capitalism is in charge of deciding what is valid, profitable and beneficial for the economic power incarnated in the structures of domination. Knowing about Romani people, nomadism and transhumance, the LGBT community, the technological warfare, human trafficking, the destruction of the Amazon, Sephardic culture, poverty[1] and so on. What capital do these knowledges bring? These, and others, would fall into that set of knowledges 'which are aims by themselves and which – precisely because of their free and uninterested nature, far from any practical or commercial link – can exercise a key role in the cultivation of the spirit and in the civilian and cultural development of humankind' (Ordine, 2013, 9). They are not 'useful' knowledges, as they have no interest for the OECD, the WM and the WTO, and if they have no interest for these organizations, here their possibilities within the curriculum are finished. The realities displaced to their margins are left outside of all recognition; if any, it would be the one which is nourished by stereotypes and prejudices, the one which stigmatizes and makes different its reality. They are abject worlds, experiences and realities which remain excluded, suffering an oppression as an effect of the processes of structural power and of domination, which consist of unquestioned norms, symbols and habits. Invisibility mutes the existence of what shapes the 'other'; it is a way to cover up 'the way in which the characteristic perspectives of dominant groups claim universality and help to justify their hierarchical structures' (Young, 2000, 167). As Young (2000, 243) points out, 'the abject provokes horror and disgust because it shows the border between the self and the other, which is constituted and is fragile, and threatens to dissolve the subject by dissolving the distance.' Dissolving the subject and the realities is a way of threatening the privileged and those territories which are pregnant with privileges. The abject is the enemy, the 'other'.

The managers of academicism reinforce their hegemony thanks to the control they have over the sources, the codes, the symbols and the history; they make the curriculum an 'imposed' (Ricoeur, 2004, 116), authorized and official memory. Besides, these managers have the capability to control both what they recognize and legitimize as well as what they forget and exclude. That curriculum turns out to be a kind of *heterotopia* which juxtaposes two realities; on the one hand, the authorized and official curriculum is addressed to all the students at a certain educational level and, consequently, it is assuming the available and possible worlds, but, on the other hand, that curriculum does not have the virtue of including that whole, that is, those realities which are not within that exclusive group that it represents: a Spanish gypsy boy 'shares' the same authorized and official curriculum with a Spanish non-gypsy boy; nonetheless, that gypsy boy is not 'inside', this boy does not have recognition as a political subject: his world, his experiences, his history are repelled by the hegemonic epistemology that carries the legitimized curriculum which acts as an oppressor. In this way, 'it imposes the dominant ideology which makes possible an unequal order to be experienced spontaneously as a necessary and unquestionable order' (Lerena Alesón, 1989, 91–2). That ideological imposition needs the educational and social practices to be recognized as the only possible and valid ones, to function, in turn, to accomplish the task of excluding those delegitimized, inferior (those from other groups, ethnics, cultures, religions, etc.) practices, and 'by excluding groups and social practices, they also exclude the knowledges used by those groups to carry out those practices' (Santos, 2009, 12). That task refers directly to what Santos (2009, 2010) calls *epistemicide*, since there is a destruction of those knowledges which are different to the recognized ones (hegemonic, dominant), there is a discredit of the expelled or not recognized knowledges, and when they are mentioned it is just to occupy a subordinate, inferior place. It is a *curricular and educational epistemicide* (Paraskeva, 2011, 2016a, 2016b, 2018): 'There is no need to mention how the education system in general, and the curriculum in particular, are both profoundly involved in that said epistemicide. By identifying certain kinds of knowledge as "official", education participates in an absolute epistemicide' (Paraskeva, 2018, 197). The excluded and silenced realities (Torres Santomé, 1993, 1994, 2017) *have no curriculum as a territory* in which they can recognize themselves in terms of equity and cognitive justice (and consequently, social, educational, etc.) – realities which are *'out of place'* (Cresswell, 1996) at the same time as they are inside. Their *'funds of knowledge'* (Moll, Amanti, Neff and González, 1992; Moll, Tapia and Whitmore, 2001; González, Moll and Amanti, 2005) do also remain outside that curricular and educational scenario which does only validate hegemonic disciplinary knowledge. This expulsion clearly deprives 'students of the opportunity to know, at first hand, the current social diversities, the possibility of living together and the ability to question the differences in a discursive manner' (Sánchez Bello, 2018, 36). This epistemicide is not free; it seeks the reward of leaving out the 'useless' who are not very profitable. With such a deed, cognitive injustice is served.

The curriculum *epistemicide* (Paraskeva, 2016) that denies what is denied is only possible to be carried out under the codes of a pedagogy of cruelty (Segato, 2018), which may become a pedagogy of 'barbarity'. Does the triumph of this one leads to the decline of critical pedagogy? Where has it looked at? Those who suffer exclusion, inequality, marginalization and oppression have been left orphans in the processes which look for the 'good' education – in the oblivion of the promised land of equality. A promise which is violated from the moment that it is being used as a cover to perpetuate the concealment of the origin of injustices and inequalities based on gender, ethnicity, social class and so on (Hill Collins and Bilge, 2016). Structural violence goes on acting under the window of equality, leading subjects to accept their position in social hierarchy, and it should come as no surprise when educational systems are constituted as 'the instance which has most fought to impose the idea of *homo hierarchicus*' (Lerena Alesón, 1989, 19). Critical pedagogy is necessary; this is the first step. Critical pedagogy as a political and emancipatory project cannot leave aside the harsh realities experimented by those people and organizations (powerless) under the relations of domination and subordination that shape the institutionalized dimensions and structures (Giroux, 1992, 2001, 2005). It cannot fall into the trap of its commercialization before the reiterative use of 'criticism'.

To escape that epistemic violence – structural violence – for the sake of cognitive justice and, in turn, social justice, the construction of a 'critical curriculum' (Paraskeva, 2011) that flees from disciplinary academicism, must address the complexity of the human being and recognize the pluriverse existent and available realities, knowledges, and the possible worlds. It is to bet for an 'itinerant curriculum' (Paraskeva, 2016a, 2016b, 2018, 2019) that will constantly question the kinds of subordination that generate inequity, segregation and exclusion, preventing educational Darwinism to become the norm; it is also to bet for 'curriculum deliberations' (Liston and Zeichner, 1987, 130). Education for liberation is the base of this revolutionary practice. This is a critical curriculum which, in order to fulfil its task, demands the critical revision of critical pedagogy. The unfulfillment of its task, 'the goal of critical pedagogy was a critical democracy, individual freedom, social justice, and social change – a revitalized public sphere characterized by citizens capable of confronting public issues critically through ongoing forms of public debate and social action' (Ellsworth, 1989, 300), is revealed in the light of epistemicide practices which develop *for the sake* of the official curriculum and educational institutions; social and cognitive justice remains disarmed.

Critical pedagogy, which must be liberating, has been left at the level of 'theoretical liberation', since realities keep being silenced and different ways of seeing and being in the world keep being excluded. This is a space for theorization that has not entered the practice, nor has it allowed practice to take direct part in those very processes of critical pedagogy. Perhaps, the reason lies in the fact that critical pedagogy becomes inclusive at its discourse level but exclusive in the field of praxis. If this is the case, does it not become a dominant critical pedagogy which falls into the trap of domination? And does it not operate 'at [a] high level of abstraction' (Ellsworth, 1989, 300)? It is the ghostly relationship between theory and practice (Santos, 2009, 2010) not far from Gil's phenomenon of 'involution' (2009, cited by Paraskeva, 2018, 2019). Therefore, from the recognition of its value, critical pedagogy must be rethought according to conscientization (Freire, 1970) and resistance (Giroux, 1985, 2001, 2016).

Deterritorialized critical pedagogy *for an itinerant curriculum*: A possible utopia

In this world dominated by neoliberal, conservative and extreme right thinking which has permeated the common sense of citizens in a scenario of (capitalist) social (dis) welfare, it is necessary not to relinquish utopia. Its rejection is justified, sometimes, by its imaginary, not very rational or unreal character. But the utopia does not stop being a subversive, restless, non-conformist, revolutionary horizon, which does not adapt to standardization. And its qualities are enough to recognize that there are alternatives. There are possibilities, although the excessive bureaucratization, technification and commercialization achieved have depoliticized the issues and problems which require social and collective answers, making them individual ones. The political weakening is an evidence of the 'weakness of our will [that] speaks about the power of the vice that dominates us [. . .]. That is equivalent to being increasingly submissive to the power that crushes us or drowns our possibilities to react and fight' (Freire, 2006, 55). This weakness can be overcome with doses of utopia.

Within the margins of neoliberal and conservative educational policies, a tailored curriculum is adopted, which excludes, silences, devaluates and recognizes as illegitimate those cultures, knowledges, experiences of powerless peoples and groups, those who have '*non-human* rights'. Educational proposals are technified, self-management and the entrepreneurial self are encouraged, knowledge production is merely promoted from a technical (and not an ethical-political) perspective, accountability is sacralized, the democratic pillars of schools are fractured, formal power in school institutions is fortified (economical, political, cultural and social knowledges and systems), keep being given a hierarchical structure and the structural conditions that generate cognitive inequality, marginalization and injustice keep being ignored. Let us show political indignation (Freire, 2006), which needs of resistance, of rebellion and also of hope, which must be an *educated hope* (Giroux, 2013), by (and for the sake of) a critical pedagogy: 'this hope is based on the recognition of pedagogy as part of a wider attempt to revitalize the conditions for individual and social action, by simultaneously addressing critical pedagogy as a project inspired by a democratic political vision, being conscious at the same time of the various ways in which this perspective is influenced in different contexts' (p. 60). An *educated hope* that must be a *critical hope* (Freire, 1993) based on reflection and political analysis in order to undertake actions aimed at cognitive justice, the seed for a liberating social justice. A combination of hopes that need of the dialogue in a framework of negotiation in which borders and abyssal lines are overcome. It is 'the idea of negotiating through dialogue among knowledges so as to create a plural and dynamic world of infinite cognitive possibilities [which] emerges as one of the essential conditions of citizens, emphasizing the interaction / transmission of practices and knowledges, in an active struggle of affirmation against the waste of plural histories' (Meneses, 2011, 32).

There is an action movement against cognitive, social and educational injustices which feeds on that pedagogy of revolution and resistance. 'School institutions are places of struggle, and pedagogy can and must be a form of political-cultural struggle' (Torres Santomé, 1993, 9). This project, political and about *political* issues, needs to be armed with strategies that incorporate a philosophical, sociological and ethical-political perspective of education. This stance is key to oppose uncritical academicism and the exclusionary hegemonic disciplinary curriculum. This is the task of critical pedagogy, to make the impossible possible, for a future governed by an ideology of possibilities open to possible worlds and available realities. This involves making an effort to analyse critical pedagogy in a reflective manner in order to avoid the risk of falling into what is 'politically correct'. Criticism is necessary for pedagogy but not enough.

A counter-pedagogy of power is needed, a *deterritorialized* critical pedagogy which nestles an *itinerant curriculum theory,* that is, a *deterritorialized curriculum* (Paraskeva, 2006, 2016a, 2016b, 2018). A liberating and emancipatory education needs other ways of staying, feeling, telling and being in the world, in those existing *possible worlds*; and for this purpose, an epistemological opening and the privilege of non-exclusive difference (Paraskeva, 2016a) is urgently required in order to make recognition possible: there are no legitimate or illegitimate realities and groups, nor knowledges, or experiences, or stories that fulfil this categorial relation. Breaking this inertia requires a deterritorialized curriculum, which becomes itinerant thanks to the non-conformist commitment of an ethically responsible and politically impelling *pedagogical nomadism*. But this itinerant curriculum and this deterritorialized critical pedagogy do not have a disincarnated character; they have anchorages, even though these do not exclusively belong to the legitimized, the absolute. We are talking about situated curricula and pedagogies which rearticulate themselves to provide shelter to those available realities, which in some way is their way of resistance against the implementation of dominant, authorized and legitimized forms of knowledge. The itinerant curriculum charts a cartography as a project not persisting on knowledge possession but on the dialogue among forms of knowledge, experimentation and narration. This is the way to eradicate the sociopolitical segregation suffered by the 'others', who have been systematically denied 'the right to belong to the political community' (González Arroyo, 2010, 144), being their territories those margins or interstitial spaces defined by being 'outside' and 'inside' at the same time.

To assume forms-others as a pluriverse of knowledges and experiences is to eliminate the borders which delimit the territories in which practices, knowledges and ways of staying and being are crowded together. Without borders the territories come into a relationship in which dialogue is needed; permeability does not eliminate the differences but just abyssal lines in such a way that the curriculum might no longer be anchored in *its* territory, which has been adapted, organized, standardized and technified. It would be that deterritorialized, counter-hegemonic, emancipatory and liberatory curriculum, the one which would make possible cognitive justice – a 'polyglot' curriculum, rich in knowledges, experiences, lands and lives. Its narrative would speak the language of 'diatopic hermeneutics (Santos, 2009, 2010), as it is a movement which links one part with another, one reality with another, one culture with another, one territory with another……. and a movement in which meanings are construed not from universalistic and monolithic attitudes but from a framework of reciprocal transmission among knowledges, relations, behaviours and so on

The deterritorialized curriculum committed to cognitive justice can only go hand in hand with a counter-hegemonic *deterritorialized* critical pedagogy aimed at critical consciousness, which is characterized by emancipatory practices. Emancipation and transformation as an objective for an education dealing with the common good and cognitive justice require a type of pedagogy which reveals against 'frantic disciplinarity', 'headless rhythms of classification and compartmentalization, directed by spurious dynamics and surrendered to segregated results, which comes to be a matter of the curriculum' (Paraskeva, 2016a, 125). Critical pedagogy, in these terms, must be understood as an ethical project and a political and cultural practice that goes beyond methodologies, strategies, contents and, obviously, competences. A critical pedagogy of resistance is needed to achieve a civic education that aims at a democratic public life which guarantees social and common welfare, without hierarchies, without 'ones' and 'others'. This critical pedagogy, understood as a cultural political practice, must seek the common good for the realities available in the possible worlds that coexist.

Note

1 Educational and curricular policies have not incorporated poverty as a social and political question (González Arroyo, 2010, 135).

References

Amaral, M. P., G. Steiner-Khamsi and C. H. Thompson, eds (2019), *Researching the Global Education Industry: Commodification, the Market and Business Involvement*, Palgrave Mcmillan.

Auat, A. (2011), *Hacia una filosofía política situada*, Buenos Aires: Waldhuter Editores.

Bauman, Z. (1998), *Globalization: The Human Consequences*, Oxford: Polity Press.

Benhabib, S. (2008), 'Otro universalismo: sobre la unidad y diversidad de los derechos humanos', *Isegoría. Revista de Filosofía Moral y Política*, 39: 175–203. http://isegoria.revistas.csic.es/index.php/isegoria/article/view/627.

Bilge, S. (2013), 'Intersectionality Undone: Saving Intersectionality from Feminist Intersectionality Studies', *Du Bois Review: Social Science Research on Race*, 10 (2): 405–24. http://doi.org/10.1017/S1742058X13000283.

Cabanas, E. y E. Illouz (2019), *Happycracia: Cómo la ciencia y la industria de la felicidad controlan nuestras vidas*, Barcelona: Paidós.
Cassier, E. (2004), *El mito del Estado*. FCE/Col. Popular.
Césaire, A. (2006), *Discurso sobre el colonialismo*, Madrid: Akal.
Cresswell, T. (1996), *In Place/Out of Place: Geography Ideology and Transgression*, Minneapolis: University of Minnesota Press.
Dussel, E. (2007), *Política de la Liberación. Historia mundial y crítica*, Vol. I, Barcelona: Trotta.
Dussel, E. (2018), 'Siete hipótesis para una estética de la liberación', *Astrágalo*, 24: 13–40.
Ellsworth, E. (1989), 'Why Doesn't This Feel Empowering? Working Through the Repressive Myths of Critical Pedagogy', *Harvard Educational Review*, 59 (3): 297–324.
Escobar, A. (2004), 'Más allá del tercer mundo globalidad imperial, colonialidad global y movimientos sociales anti-globalización', *Nómadas*, 20: 86–100.
Fanon, F. (1999 [1961]), *Los condenados de la tierra*, Tafalla, Navarra: Txalaparta.
Fanon, F. (2009), *Piel negra, máscaras blancas*, Madrid: Akal.
Freire, P. (1970), *Pedagogía del oprimido*, México: Siglo XXI Editores.
Freire, P. (1993), *Pedagogía de la esperanza: un reencuentro con la pedagogía del oprimido*, Buenos Aires: Siglo XXI Editores.
Freire, P. (2006), *Pedagogía de la indignación*, Madrid: Morata.
Giroux, H. A. (1985), 'Teorías de la reproducción y la resistencia en la nueva sociología de la educación: un análisis crítico', *Cuadernos Políticos*, 44: 36–65.
Giroux, H. A. (1992), 'Resisting Difference: Cultural Studies and the Discourse of Critical Pedagogy', in L. Grossberg, G. Nelson and P. Treichler (eds), *Cultural Studies*, 199–212, New York: Routledge.
Giroux, H. A. (2001), *Theory and Resistance in Education: Towards a Pedagogy for the Opposition*, Westport: Bergin & Garvey.
Giroux, H. A. (2005), 'Literacy and the Pedagogy of Voice and Political Empowerment', *Educational Theory*, 38 (1): 61–75. http://doi.org/10.1111/j.1741-5446.1988.00061.x.
Giroux, H. A. (2013), 'Una pedagogía de la resistencia en la edad del capitalismo de casino', *Con-ciencia social*, 17: 55–71.
Giroux, H. A. (2016, 5 de septiembre), 'Escuela y teorías de la resistencia', *Otras voces en educación*. http://otrasvoceseneducacion.org/archivos/158633.
González, N., L. Moll and C. Amanti, eds (2005), *Funds of Knowledge: Theorizing Practices in Households, Communities, and Classrooms*, Mahwah: Lawrence Erlbaum Associates.
González Arroyo, M. (2010), 'Los colectivos depauperados repolitizan los curricula', en J. Gimeno Sacristán (coord.), *Saberes e incertidumbre sobre el currículum*, 128–42, Madrid: Morata.
Han, B. (2012), *La sociedad del cansancio*, Barcelona: Herder.
Han, B. (2014), *Psicopolítica*, Barcelona: Herder.
Haraway, D. (1988), 'Situated Knowledges: The Science Question in Feminism and the Privilege of Partial Perspective', *Feminist Studies*, 14 (3): 575–99.
Haraway, D. (1995), *Ciencia, cyborgs y mujeres: la reinvención de la naturaleza*, Madrid: Cátedra.
Hill-Collins, P. and S. Bilge (2016), *Interseccionalidad*, Madrid: Morata.
Lerena Alesón, C. (1989), *Escuela, ideología y clases sociales en España*, Madrid: Círculo de Lectores/Ciclo Ciencias Humanas.

Liston, D. P. and K. M. Zeichner (1987), 'Critical Teaching anf Liberatory Education', *The Journal of Education*, 169 (3): 117–37.
López Facal, R. (2004), 'El pensamiento crítico debe ser, en primer lugar, autocrítico', *Enseñanza de las ciencias sociales: Revista de investigación*, 3: 95–101.
McLaren, P. (2012), *La pedagogía crítica revolucionaria. El socialismo y los desafíos actuales*, Buenos Aires: Ediciones Herramientas.
Meneses, M. P. G. (2011), 'Epistemologías del Sur: diálogos que crean espacios para un encuentro de las historias', en CIDOB (ed.), *Formas-Otras: Saber, nombrar, narrar, hacer. IV Training Seminar de jóvenes investigadores en Dinámicas Interculturales*, 31–41, Barcelona: CIDOB.
Mignolo, W. D. (2000), *Local Histories/Global Designs*. Princeton: Princeton University Press,
Mignolo, W. D. (2006), 'El giro gnoseológico decolonial: La contribución de Aime Césaire a la geopolítica y la corpo- política del conocimiento', en A. Césaire (ed.), *Discurso sobre el colonialismo*, 197–221, Madrid: Akal.
Mignolo, W. D. (2008), 'La opción de-colonial: Desprendimiento y apertura. Un manifiesto y un caso', *Tabula Rasa*, 8: 243–81.
Mignolo, W. D. (2010), *Desobediencia epistémica: Retórica de la modernidad, lógica de la colonialidad y gramática de la descolonialidad*, Buenos Aires: Del Signo.
Moll, L., C. Amanti, D. Neff and N. González (1992), 'Funds of Knowledge for Teaching: Using a Qualitative Approach to Connect Homes and Classrooms', *Theory into Practice*, 31 (2): 132–41.
Moll, L., J. Tapia and F. Whitmore (2001), 'Conocimiento vivo: la distribución social de los recursos culturales para el pensamiento', en G. Salomón (comp.), *Cogniciones distribuidas. Consideraciones psicológicas y educativas*, 185–213, Buenos Aires: Amorrortu.
Nietzsche, F. (2002), *El crepúsculo de los ídolos*, Madrid: Edaf.
Ordine, N. (2013), *La utilidad de lo inútil*, Barcelona: Acantilado.
Paraskeva, J. M. (2006), 'Desterritorializa o da Teoria Curricular', *Papeles de Trabajo sobre Cultura, Educación y Desarrollo Humano*, 2 (1): 1–34.
Paraskeva, J. M. (2011), *Conflict in Curriculum: Theory Challenging Hegemonic Epistemologies*, New York: Palgrave MacMillan.
Paraskeva, J. M. (2016a), 'Desterritorializar: Hacia a una Teoría Curricular Itinerante', *Revista Interuniversitaria de Formación del Profesorado*, 85 (30.1): 121–34.
Paraskeva, J. M. (2016b), *Curriculum Epistemicide: Toward an Itinerant Theory*, New York: Routledge.
Paraskeva, J. M. (2018), '¿Qué sucede con la teoría crítica (currículum)? La necesidad de sobrellevar la rabia neoliberal sin evitarla', en R. Vázquez Recio (coord.), *Reconocimiento y bien común en educación*, 157–96, Madrid: Morata.
Paraskeva, J. M. (2019), 'O Que Aconteceu Com a Teoria Crítica do Currículo? A Necessidade De Ir Além Da Raiva Neoliberal, Sem Evitá-la', *Linguagens, Educação e Sociedade, Teresina*, 24 (41): 96–134. https://orcid.org/0000-0002-4060-2896.
Pellizzetti, P. (2009), *El fracaso de la indignación. Del malestar al conflicto*, Madrid: Alianza Editorial.
Pucciarelli, A. R. (2005), 'El régimen político de las nuevas democracias excluyentes de América Latina. Argentina 1999–2001', *HAOL*, 8: 105–22.
Quijano, A. (1992), 'Colonialidad y modernidad/racionalidad', *Revista del Instituto Indigenista Peruano*, 13 (29): 11–20.

Ricœur, P. (2004), *La memoria, la historia, el olvido*, Buenos Aires: Fondo de Cultura Económica.
Sánchez Bello, A. (2018), 'Educación y políticas de igualdad en contextos de globalización', en R. Vázquez Recio (coorda.), *Reconocimiento y bien común en educación*, 23–45, Madrid: Morata.
Santos, B. S. (2007), 'Para além do pensamento abissal: das linhas globais a uma ecologia de saberes', *Revista Crítica de Ciências Sociais*, 78: 3–46. https://rccs.revues.org/753.
Santos, B. S. (2009), *Una epistemología del sur: la reinvención del conocimiento y la emancipación social*, Buenos Aires: Siglo XXI Editores.
Santos, B. S. (2010), *Descolonizar el saber, reinventar el poder*, Montevideo: Ediciones Trilce.
Santos, B. S. (2014), *Derechos humanos, democracia y desarrollo*, Bogotá: Centro de Estudios de Derecho, Justicia y Sociedad, Colección Dejusticia,
Segato, R. (2018), *Contra-pedagogías de la crueldad*, Buenos Aires: Prometeo.
Therborn, G. (2015), *La desigualdad mata*, Madrid: Alianza.
Torres Santomé, J. (1993), 'Las culturas negadas y silenciadas en el currículum', *Cuadernos de Pedagogía*, 217: 1–10.
Torres Santomé, J. (1994), *El currículum oculto*, Madrid: Morata.
Torres Santomé, J. (2017), *Políticas educativas y construcción de personalidades neoliberales y neocolonialistas*, Madrid: Morata.
UNICEF (2017), *Children in a Digital World. Summary. The State of the World's Children 2017*, UNICEF. https://www.unicef.org.uk/press-releases/unicef-make-digital-world-safer-children/#:~:text=The%20State%20of%20the%20World%27s,dangers%20as%20well%20as%20opportunities.
Vázquez Recio, R. (2016), 'Aesthesis decolonial y los tiempos relacionales. Entrevista realizada por M. Barrera Contreras a Rolando Vázquez', *Revista Calle 14*, 11 (18): 76–94. https://doi.org/10.14483/udistrital.jour.c14.2016.1.a06.
Vázquez Recio, R. y M. López Gil (2018), 'Interseccionalidad, jóvenes "sin-sistema" y resistencia. Una mirada diferente del fracaso/abandono escolar', *Revista Brasileira de Educação*, 23. http://doi.org/10.1590/s1413-24782018230094.
Vázquez Recio, R. (2018), 'Las paradojas de la cultura de la gestión y del liderazgo en el (des)encuentro de la ciudadanía y la sociedad neoliberal', en R. Vázquez Recio (coorda.), *Reconocimiento y bien común en educación*, 119–56, Madrid: Morata.
Vercellone, C. (2004), 'Las políticas de desarrollo en tiempos del capitalismo cognitivo', en O. Blondeau et al. (ed.), *Capitalismo cognitivo: Propiedad intelectual y creación colectiva*, 66–86, Madrid: Traficantes de Sueños.
Williamson, B. (2019, 1 de febrero), 'Education for the Robot Economy', *Code Acts in Education*. https://codeactsineducation.wordpress.com/2019/02/01/education-for-the-robot-economy/.
Young, I. M. (2000), *La justicia y la política de la diferencia*, Madrid: Cátedra.
Young, I. M. (2011), Responsibility for Justice, Oxford: Oxford University Press.

10

ICT and Curriculum as Everyday Creation

A Doable Possibility of the Emancipation of Curriculum Theory

Inês Barbosa Oliveira

A preamble

Let me start crafting this chapter with a description that insightfully unpacks the importance of the itinerant curriculum theory (ICT) in the current debates of our field.

> The daily emancipation weavings made invisible in the face of eugenic Western macho-patriarchal blindness that causes us to believe in the construction of a possible other world, beyond capital and colonialism, in which we can experience human emancipation. Therefore, it is necessary to create, in research and daily life, rebel and itinerant knowledge and curricula, breaking with conformism and accommodation. (Paraskeva and Süssekind, 2018, 71)

The ICT, formulated by Paraskeva (2011, 2015, 2016a, 2016b, 2022a), takes a theoretical, epistemic and militant approach towards the ecology of knowledge and recognition of the epistemological existence of the Global South (Santos, 2010). It aims to subvert the eugenics of hegemonic social and curriculum models in favour of the creative and mobile possibilities of curriculum *theoriespractices* already existing but made invisible (Santos, 2004, 2010, 2018) by hegemonic thinking, which only admits as existing and valid whatever fits in and that can be understood and formulated. In this sense, we can understand it as a transgressor and anti-canonical theoretical proposal.

Therefore, Paraskeva's approach (2023, 2002a, 2022b, 2021, 2018, 2017a, 2016a, 2016b, 2015, 2011) is a theory that does not freeze curriculum in a scientific, Eurocentric and epistemicidal formulation, as it has been the rule in most dominant and counter-dominant curriculum proposals nowadays. Paraskeva's (2016a, 2016b, 2014, 2011, 2022a) ICT openly challenges what he rightly calls the functionalism of both hegemonic and specific counter-hegemonic Eurocentric platforms. He believes it is necessary to conceive and seek practicing shifts about the established, predicted and hegemonic in a perspective of uninterrupted deterritorialization of such elements.

The roaming idea aims to benefit a recognition of invisible existences, relegated to the abyssal exclusion (Santos, 2010) of knowledge present, seeking to inscribe them in the visible world as co-presence with whatever exists on 'this side' of the abyssal crack. The close relationship between Santos's thinking (2010) and the formulation of his epistemologies in the South inscribes ICT in the search for solid responses to the crisis of modernity identified and denounced by Santos (2000, 2004, 2018), thus avoiding the waste of experiences.

> First, social experience worldwide is much broader and more varied than Western scientific or philosophical tradition knows and considers important. Second, this social wealth is being wasted. [. . .] Thirdly, [. . .] to combat the waste of social experience, more than proposing another type of social science is needed. More than that, it is necessary to propose a different model of rationality. (Santos, 2004, 778)

By moving itinerantly, ICT aims not to repeat the same mistakes committed by others: the canonization of hegemonic values, knowledge and practices (Paraskeva, 2022a, 2022b, 2021).

Thus, being deterritorialized and fluid, ICT joins a struggle that is not so new, but that has been gaining more diffusion and clarity in the last ten years against epistemicides and modern abyssal thinking (Santos, 2010) – a framework based on visible and invisible distinctions. The former would be understood by the latter while making them invisible by establishing a line that divides social reality into two universes: what exists and what is produced as non-existence. Thus, this abyssal thinking disregards the possibility of coexistence and co-presence, assuming specific knowledge as accurate and, consequently, considering other forms of understanding the world as false. Paraskeva's ICT shows that dominant and counter-dominant Eurocentric curriculum movements are implicated in such visibility-invisibility wrangle. He pushes Santos's (2010) notion of the epistemicide but advancing the reversive epistemicide as a praxis that erupts out of the struggle against the epistemicide (Paraskeva, 2023, 2022a, 2022b, 2021, 2018, 2017a, 2016a, 2016b, 2015, 2011). The visibility of the subjects – their knowledge and practices – on one side of the line is based on the denial of the existence of what is sent to the other side. It is in such context that Paraskeva (2023, 2022a, 2022b, 2021, 2018, 2017a, 2016a, 2016b, 2015, 2011) frames curriculum as an abyssal dispositive that legitimizes both the epistemicide and the reversive epistemicide. To break with this modern logic, Santos (2010, 2018) suggests the construction of post-abyssal thinking, which recognizes the existence of two forms of social exclusion, abyssal and non-abyssal, as it occurs through the subordination of the line side of what it exists or as a denial of existence, what happens with whatever is relegated to the other side of the abyssal line. Post-abyssal thinking, he argues, involves

> a radical break with modern Western forms of thought and action. [. . .] It means thinking from the perspective of the other side of the line precisely because the other side is the domain of the unthinkable in Western modernity. [. . .] Post-abyssal thinking can be summarized as learning from the South, using an

epistemology of the South. It confronts the monoculture of modern science with an ecology of knowledge. It is an ecology because it is based on recognizing the plurality of heterogeneous knowledge (one of which is modern science) and on sustainable and dynamic interactions between them without compromising their autonomy. The ecology of knowledge is based on the idea that knowledge is inter-knowledge. (Santos, 2010, 53)

The first condition, therefore, for post-abyssal thinking is the idea of radical co-presence, which seeks to recognize that practices and agents on both sides of the line are contemporary in egalitarian terms, thus implying a conception of simultaneity as contemporary. The recognition of the epistemological diversity of the world and the cognitive injustice represented by the hierarchies between them imposed by abyssal thinking, a characteristic of post-abyssal thinking, implies the abdication of general epistemology and the defence of its impossibility.

However, Paraskeva's ICT complexifies Santos's (2010) approach. In his terms, the struggle for social, cognitive and intergenerational justice should aim not just a post-abyssal momentum but also a non-abyssal metamorphism, which is a-abyssal. ICT is a non-abyssally condition, a non-derivative way of respecting the onto-epistemological diversity of our world. Paraskeva (2023, 2022a, 2022b, 2021, 2018, 2017a, 2016a, 2016b, 2015, 2011) argues that it is the responsibility of the curriculum field to seek creations and recognitions that are configured as alternatives to what was produced by both, hegemonic and counter-hegemonic critical thinking, their fixity and their choice for canons that hinder an understanding of the dynamic flow of life in schools and universities. Unfortunately, as he (2021) insightfully denounces, critical thought, theories and pedagogies have been operating within a reductive hegemonic matrix of knowledge from the North, remaining incomprehensively faithful and stuck to immutable epistemological traditions. Investing in different ways of thinking, respecting and fostering different differences, in the permanent deterritorialization of an onto-epistemological and political itinerancy – also considering the inseparability between both – allows ICT to constitute itself as the best way to overcome the epistemicides that divide social realities and knowledge into two domains: existence and abyss.

> Everything on one side of the line is understood as valid knowledge, and on the other side are knowledge and social practices not recognized as a reality and produced as nonexistent (Paraskeva, 2011, 2022a) proposes that 'the new itinerant curriculum theory' will challenge one of the fundamental characteristics of abyssal thinking: the impossibility of co-presence of the two sides of the line. (Oliveira, 2017, 188)

In this sense, we concur with Süssekind's (2014) take on ICT. ICT operates with and from the South epistemologies as we do with the theoretical development of curriculum as Everyday Creation. They both seek to perceive curriculum and pedagogies beyond the epistemic and eugenic perspectives they assume hegemonic by allowing their formulations and proposals only with European scientific knowledge and cultures, wasting experiences (Santos, 2000) due to the inability to carry out the displacements that could allow them departing from the South and learning from the South as recommended by Santos (2010). To be more precise, both ICT and the perspective of understanding the curriculum as Everyday Creation get involved in the struggle for cognitive and social justice, understanding that it is necessary to commit to curriculum justice. In this struggle, both will conceive solidarity as a value, considering horizontal citizenship as a central notion for the possibilities of subversive, rebellious and transgressor curricular practice. Paraskeva (2023, 2022a, 2022b, 2021, 2018, 2017a, 2016a, 2016b, 2015, 2011) alerts us that there is no social, cognitive and intergenerational justice without a just curriculum.

ICT is political and has attracted several stakeholders' attention in the curriculum and pedagogy field. Today, it occupies a substantial space in the field of curriculum studies, as can be seen in different symposia, sections and roundtables organized in crucial meetings such as the AERA AAACS – where researchers from different countries examine and debate the importance of Paraskeva's ICT. The *Journal of the American Association for Advancement of Curriculum Studies* also has a special issue examining the significance of Paraskeva's work. Bill Pinar (2013), for example, did not fail to mention ICT as one of the great curriculum texts of the present. Antonia Darder (2016), a leading neo-Gramscian feminist, defines ICT as 'an epistemology of liberation that persistently challenges structures of authority, hierarchy, and domination in all aspects of life'. ICT is today treated in curriculum studies as an approach that introduces a new conceptual grammar for the field (Jupp, 2017). Moreira (2017) dissects the importance of ICT and places it as a crucial approach to the challenges of teacher education and supervisors. ICT's footprint is also visible in Brazil. There are critical theoretical studies in Brazil related to ICT. For example, Lopes and her research on Derrida (Lopes and Siscas, 2018); Macedo and her reflections on/with a difference (Tomé and Macedo, 2018); the work of Lopes and Macedo (2011) on Ernesto Laclau's analytical perspective of discourse. Ferraço and Carvalho (2015), labouring within the same Deleuzian references that inspire ICT, look for deterritorialized and powerful analyses and understandings regarding what is happening in our schools and curriculum. Finally, we highlight Süssekind's work (2014, 2017), who has been analysing and dialoguing with Paraskeva (Süssekind, 2017, 2014; Paraskeva and Süssekind, 2018), subverting the order in her own academic and teaching work, producing performance experiments, diving – as (Alves, 2008) would put it – in the unseen knowledge in/from schools and teachers.

In all of these cases, we face deterritorializing theories, which seek to break the theoretical field fixity and the understanding of the curriculum, challenge the canons, aiming to create more powerful theorizations even when they do not reach a dialogue with the epistemologies of the South and with the idea ecology of knowledge, concepts which are so dear to ICT and the notion of Curriculum as Everyday Creation.

As we were able to unpack, several theoretical counter-dominant approaches have been in dialogue with and influenced by ICT in Brazil and other nations. However, we argue that Paraskeva's ICT is closely related to Curriculum and Everyday Creation (Oliveira, 2016). We claim that ICT and Curriculum as Everyday Creation are intertwined.

In what follows, we will examine such confluences and identify the dialogues that both maintain with the work of Santos. Drawing from the onto-epistemological pluridiversity of the South (Paraskeva, 2023, 2022a, 2022b, 2021, 2018, 2017a, 2016a, 2016b, 2015, 2011), we will wrangle within the fabric of North-South dialogue, as advanced by Paraskeva (2021, 2018, 2017a, 2016a, 2016b, 2015, 2011). In doing so, we will unpack the Curriculum as an Everyday Creation concept that strongly relates to ITC.

ICT and Curriculum as Everyday Creation: A dialogue with the epistemologies from the South

One of the principles that rules Southern Epistemologies thinking is the belief that the modern episteme cannot provide satisfactory answers to its crisis and the social system it has erected. Thus, according to Santos (2010), it would be necessary to formulate and recognize other world's understandings to seek the strong responses we need to address the current challenges. In his formulation of ICT, Paraskeva (2023, 2022a, 2022b, 2021, 2018, 2017a, 2016a, 2016b, 2015, 2011) draws on Latour's (2006) approach and warns us about the same problem. As he (2011) argues, 'there is no greater crime than facing current intellectual challenges with the equipment of the past.' This principle also governs the recognition of the need for a deterritorialized curriculum theory to weave and find alternative possibilities of perpetual rupture with curriculum taboos. These taboos imprison us in a modern scientism centrality. ICT moves one permanently and uninterruptedly to endless possibilities, assuming a 'commitment to fighting for a different research platform, one that transpires alternative ways to think and to do curriculum' (Paraskeva, 2023, 2022a, 2022b, 2021, 2018, 2017a, 2016a, 2016b, 2015, 2011). To rely on Santos's (2019) approach, ICT provides the possibility of unending substantial questions and firm answers to the current social demands; it is an exceptional theoretical approach for exceptional times (Santos, 2020).

In the same way, by breaking with the dominant tradition that places curriculum as a pre-packaged device that frames accurately what happens in schools, the notion of Curriculum as Everyday Creation also poses itself as a possibility of a strong response to so many problems faced in our daily lives, no longer from the structured and partial explanation of what supposedly happens in classrooms but from the understanding of how, in our everyday lives, subjects recreate and consolidate curriculum beyond what has been defined as the norm. Curriculum as an Everyday Creation is crucial to curriculum studies as a response to confront and unpack the crisis daily.

Although the struggle for strong responses propelled by ICT and Curriculum as Everyday Creation is relevant, such struggle must be understood as associated with another central point of thought in Southern Epistemologies: the notions of cognitive and social justice, the former the condition to the latter. Paraskeva (2023, 2022a, 2022b, 2021, 2018, 2017a, 2016a, 2016b, 2015, 2011) complexifies the debate advocating for curriculum justice as the imperative for a just society. We will rely on such notion in our examination of ICT. While Connel (2007, 1980) examined the importance of curriculum justice to promote a sustainable democratic social matrix, it was Paraskeva's ICT that placed curriculum justice at the very core of the struggle against the epistemicides.

Along with Ponce and Araújo (2019, 1049), we understand the need to think of curriculum justice as a possibility of assistance 'on the way against discrimination and inequality', leading curriculum to contribute to the fight for social justice.

> Aware that naivety does not fit here, it is stated that the school is both a reproducer of inequalities and a mediator of possibilities for overcoming them. The school curriculum, therefore, can and must be disputed from this contradiction as a space of struggle for dignity, equality and respect for diversity. (Ponce and Araújo, 2019, 1049)

Paraskeva and Süssekind (2019) argue for the need for 'cognitive and social curriculum justice', that is, the possibility of a non-epistemicidal curriculum, which seeks more equal relationships between different knowledges and the knowledge subjects. While emerging from different angles, undeniably, there is a dialogical nexus between Paraskeva (2023, 2022a, 2022b, 2021, 2018, 2017a, 2016a, 2016b, 2015, 2011), Santos (2010, 2018) and Ponce and Araújo (2019) helping us tremendously to shift the focal point of curriculum proposals from modern instrumental rationality to other forms of rationality. Understanding the curriculum not only from the perspective of this rationality but also as a territory of disputes (Arroyo, 2013), we can conceive it as a field of democratizing and emancipating experiments, perpetually itinerant (2023, 2022a, 2022b, 2021, 2018, 2017a, 2016a, 2016b, 2015, 2011) aimed at overcoming cognitive and social injustice, recognizing diversity and individualities within modernity that fosters inequality. As Ponce and Araújo (2019) argues,

> [b]y curricular justice, a curriculum conception that recognizes the cultural plurality of society is taken, raising the knowledge of the least favored beyond the folkloric, stereotyped and fragmented treatment, [. . .] that analyzes content critically; value the diverse cultural knowledge based on the needs and commitment to a fair and democratic world (Santomé, 2013). Curriculum justice is one of the processes seeking social justice through the school curriculum, valuing the character of its collective construction. (Ponce and Araújo, 2019, 1054)

Here, we find the notion of Curriculum as an Everyday Creation and its uncompromising defence of the curriculum as an ephemeral and mutant –itinerant – creation of practitioners (Certeau, 1994) of everyday life. We also found ICT, and not by chance, in its stance of recognizing the need for a curriculum approach that promotes and recognizes 'voluntary and involuntary creations' (Paraskeva, 2011, 177) – and we would add every day.

The close and indispensable relationship between curriculum justice – which allows suppressing the epistemicides committed by modern curriculum matrices, reinforced by some scholars in our field – and the notions of cognitive justice and social justice takes us to two other pillars of Southern Epistemologies: the ecology of knowledge and horizontal citizenship. Let us recapture some of the arguments developed elsewhere (Oliveira, 2017) to dissect the similarities and specificities between ICT and the notion of Curriculum as Everyday Creation. We will explore how they incorporate Santos's rationale in their proposals and formulations.

Paraskeva's work (2023, 2022a, 2022b, 2021, 2018, 2017a, 2016a, 2016b, 2015, 2011) and his struggle against curriculum epistemicides relates to the notion of cognitive justice and addresses the need for an ecology of knowledge to overcome curriculum, cognitive and social injustice. Thus, he recognizes with ICT, like Santos, the epistemological diversity of the world, alerting us about the enormous task that it poses to us:

> The point is to move beyond questions such as 'what/whose knowledge is of the most worth' despite not having figured out a correct answer and to fight for (an)other knowledge outside the Western epistemological harbor. Therefore, we need to engage in the struggle against epistemicides. One needs first to assume consciously that (an) other knowledge is possible and then go beyond the Western epistemological platform, paying attention to other forms of knowledge and respecting local knowledge within and beyond the Western space. (Paraskeva, 2011, 152)

Paraskeva (2023, 2022a, 2022b, 2021, 2018, 2017a, 2016a, 2016b, 2015, 2011) explicitly advocates the knowledge ecology and the struggle against the epistemicides and reversive epistemicides, as we propose with the notion of Curriculum as Everyday Creation (Oliveira, 2016). By understanding curriculum as a collective creation of the practitioners of the schools, in which different knowledge of these different subjects is involved, we are advocating the praxis of school curriculum not necessarily as a hierarchical set of interactions between different knowledge, in addition to the imprisonments and patterns of epistemic curriculum proposals.

> When I refer to practitioners as curriculum creators in everyday life, I assume this creative process, as a result, is always temporary and, therefore, recreated daily from dialogues and entanglements between formal knowledge – arising from different theories with which they came into contact at different times and circumstances of their lives – and other knowledge, learned by *thinkingpractitioners* through other processes. (Oliveira, 2016, 8)

Furthermore, we perceive this notion in the same itinerant perspective that Paraskeva (2023, 2022a, 2022b, 2021, 2018, 2017a, 2016a, 2016b, 2015, 2011) defends since these curricula are mutant, unrepeatable and unapproachable, emerging from particular occasions (Certeau, 1994) in which they are created and weaved as an ecology of knowledge; this notion helps one to understand how, in the daily lives of schools, such weave process is quite towering within the teaching and learning processes. The consciousness that meaningful learning depends on the possibility of meaningful knowledge is growing increasingly among educators, a consciousness that has been solidified through dialogues, as we learned from Paulo Freire.

The struggle against the curriculum epistemicides and reversive epistemicides (Paraskeva, 2023, 2022a, 2022b, 2021, 2018, 2017a, 2016a, 2016b, 2015, 2011) and the recognition and valorization of the interdependence between different knowledge – since all knowledge is co-knowledge (Santos, 2018) – is, therefore, a double struggle; on the one hand, for the recognition of the possible validity of the student's knowledge; on the other hand, for the valorization of these entanglements as a means of consolidating the so-called significant learning – since within the matrix of the ecology of knowledge what matters is to grasp how each knowledge works to solve a particular problem and how such multifarious mosaic of knowledge helps providing comprehensibility.

In his ICT, Paraskeva (2023, 2022a, 2022b, 2021, 2018, 2017a, 2016a, 2016b, 2015, 2011) argues that cognitive justice is a condition for social justice and, therefore, criticizes the curriculum epistemicides committed whenever 'particular hegemonic forms of knowledge' are associated with hegemonic knowledge production in the Northern hemisphere. ICT also understands that these epistemicides work as 'weapons as lethal as genocide in constructing Western supremacy over colonies, their cultures, and knowledge'. For this reason, he defends the need to fight against the hegemonic and counter-hegemonic traditions of the Northern hemisphere in the name of the ecology of knowledge. In other words, Paraskeva's ICT is a laser critique on both hegemonic and counter-hegemonic curriculum studies platforms, situating both right at the core of the colonial field of power and knowledge (Lander, 2000) inscribed in the 'Global North' epistemological and academic tradition (Santos, 2010).

ICT – in its permanent deterritorialization and radical defence of the break with the epistemic curriculum – and the notion of Curriculum as Everyday Creation – and its defence of the fabric in networks of different knowledge in curriculum creation in schools – somehow rub against each other. ICT and Curriculum as an Everyday Creation epitomize the endless plurality of the epistemologies from the South (Santos, 2010). At different levels, they both exemplify the way and the principles that underpin the construction of a social and cognitive justice curriculum framework since they think from and with the South resetting and erasing the abyssal line that separates what exists from what is made non-existent (Santos, 2010). They consider what was previously considered unthinkable, which was excluded and subordinated by the reading of the Western/Northern world.

Through the practice of these epistemologies, both formulations are woven, assuming the co-presence of knowledge, cultures and social behaviours, the mutual recognition that considers the interdependence between the different, overcoming the hegemonic perspective of domination by the ecological perspective, which presupposes relations of authority and legitimacy between them. Using these epistemologies is, therefore, a praxis of the ecology of knowledge in all its dimensions, weaving cognitive and social justice. With this, we reiterate its importance for ICT and the notion of Curriculum as an Everyday Creation of ICT in the making, both in the struggle for these forms of justice, capable of contributing to the democratization of schools, society and social emancipation.

Also, it will be appropriate to bring to our discussion Santo's notion of horizontal citizenship, a pivotal notion to ICT and Curriculum as Everyday Creation – due to their nexus with the ecology of knowledge, which implies associated cooperation and solidarity. The notion of horizontal citizenship recognizes the solidarity relationship between individuals as the superior form of citizenship; it implies a 'pact between them, a commitment to each other in the name of the well-being of the community' (Oliveira, 2013, 192). Such commitment occurs independently or beyond the state and what is formulated vertically as citizens' rights and duties. It is a driven solidarity.

> By the conscience of humanity and otherness. It looks not only at the parties' interests about the whole but also at the interests of the parties among themselves. The awakening of citizenship awareness, besides leading to the demand for *civitas status* on the side of the individual, leads to the discovery of the commitment to collaboration so that everyone can achieve such status. (Silva Neto, 2006, 118)

Therefore, we understand that the exercise of horizontal citizenship is inextricably linked to the possibility of cognitive and social justice. The recognition of the otherness legitimacy, associated with social solidarity practices constitutes a way of building a more egalitarian society; it contributes 'for the reduction of epistemological and social inequalities that characterize our society' (Oliveira, 2018, 4). Solidarity, as a social praxis, implies, among other issues, helping those who need it most and a collective action to solve everyday problems – characteristic of the ecology of knowledge proposed by Santos and required by Paraskeva's ICT.

In the case of the notion of Curriculum as Everyday Creation, we understand that this form of citizenship is present in schools and the curriculum 'practiced-thought' (Oliveira, 2016) by everyday subjects in the way they create alternatives to thinking and challenge hegemonic curriculum proposals. It is crucial to emphasize the collective commitment to solidarity as one of ICT's hallmarks. As we argue elsewhere (Oliveira, 2013), the support provided by those who can towards those who need it differs from charity because it is not characterized by the kindness of someone superior to an inferior person.

From the perspective of equality in difference (Santos, 1999), it is vital to recognize the rights of those needing help. In doing so, such recognition seeks social equality and politicizes aid, making horizontal citizenship itself a citizenship with solid political content contributing to overcoming exclusions, abysmal or not. To paraphrase Santos (1999), it is crucial to recognize the other as an equal against his possible inferiority and as different, against his possible mischaracterization and of everyone as interdependent.

The recognition of the right to equality in difference and vice versa in horizontal citizenship may also be understood using Ubuntu's philosophy, which places the individual's existence only possible within a community context as Paraskeva's ICT so accurately dissects. The Ubuntu philosophy suggests that 'a person is a person through other persons' (Prinsloo, 1998, 43; Maphisa, 1994, cited in Paraskeva, 2011, 164). Such an idea is perfectly compatible with the notion of horizontal citizenship and its recognition of individual responsibility for the construction of social welfare, which we have identified in some school situations through our research in Brazil. Regarding a possible Southern epistemology (Santos, 2010), 'social justice depends not only on cognitive justice but also on the expansion of the concept of citizenship' (Oliveira, 2017, 38).

The same could be argued for the Brazilian indigenous people from the Kambeba ethnic group and their notion of 'Asemuýta', which can be translated as a relative. However, the term 'relative' exemplifies broad meaning and praxis. 'Asemuýta' relates not only with those associated with blood but with all who are 'relatives' of pain and struggle. Thus, solidarity is not just understanding the other's pain or supporting one's struggle. It is to feel the pain of the other, to be in his/her struggle, with him/her, like him/her. In this sense, we can understand the notion as not only similar to horizontal citizenship but beyond it, as a praxis of Southern epistemology in human relations, since to become an 'Asemuýta', it is necessary to understand that 'the other exists', to function from him/her, with him/her and even like him/her, feeling what s/he feels, fighting his/her struggle.

Curriculum as Everyday Creation as a praxis of ICT

Paraskeva's ICT – which announces and denounces the epistemicidal nature of the field – 'signals the birth of post-epistemicidal curriculum studies momentum' (Appelbaum, 2015). It is a theoretical approach that challenges both hegemonic and counter-hegemonic Eurocentric curriculum traditions and introduces in the field a different semiotic, influenced by the work of Santos and so many other non-Eurocentric intellectuals beyond the traditional educational field. He brings to the field of curriculum studies a new vocabulary – curriculum epistemicides, reversive epistemicide, itinerant curriculum theory, itinerantology, indigenestoude, curriculum involution, curriculum disquiet, curriculum occidentosis, curriculum mechanotics, curriculum naparamas, among others (Paraskeva, 2023, 2022a, 2022b, 2021, 2018, 2017a, 2016a, 2016b, 2015, 2011) – and a new language that radically pushed the debate into another level, an approach that has triggered a debate in the curriculum studies field in Brazil as well. ICT expands the field of curriculum studies to new and powerful avenues, reaching new possibilities for approaching contemporary issues and struggles that curriculum theorists must confront, as we have been doing with the notion of Curriculum as Everyday Creation. Through its itinerancy, he refuses sterile, safe ports that can prevent the escape from imprisonment in the modern, Eurocentric, abyssal, hegemonic and counter-hegemonic critical perspectives. Paraskeva's ICT epitomizes Freire's claim (1992, 1974) that as pedagogues we have the duty of not being neutral.

The recognition of the epistemicide character of the field can be perceived as a starting point for the search for the utopian epistemological novelty, inserted in whatever is closest to us as a possibility of formulating new radical needs (Santos, 1995, 106). Its innovations – the openings represented by the new concepts, terms and dialogues – confirm the importance of ICT for the current curriculum inquiry. For us, it announces the endless possibilities of the nexus with the notion of Curriculum as Everyday Creation, rehearsed in this chapter. Both perspectives aim to meet democratic demands with more social-ecological curriculum theories and practices. At a local level, we believe it is necessary to weave emancipatory itinerant curriculum theories and practices, understanding, as Santos (2010) argues, academically produced knowledge needs to be practical and usable by those for whom it is intended to be legitimate.

As I have argued before, Curriculum as an Everyday Creation is ICT in the making, a powerful and just for instance. That is why the notion of Curriculum as Everyday Creation dives into the curriculum 'thought-practiced' created in everyday life, understanding them as generated in circular processes in which knowledge, values, beliefs and convictions are intertwined, inhabiting different social instances and interacting subjects.

Therefore, speaking of the curriculum as a daily creation is in a permanent dialogue between different ways of weaving knowledge, which is the basis of different ways of acting, even if never in a linear way. We also consider that these processes give rise to results as diverse as provisional, unique, unpublished, 'unrepeatable' curricula, constantly changing, perpetually itinerant, forcing researchers, teachers and students to the permanent displacement proposed by the deterritorialization inherent to ICT. Curriculum as Everyday Practice is a powerful 'itinerantology' (Paraskeva, 2021, 2018, 2017a, 2016a, 2016b, 2015, 2014). We confront together, thus, the hegemonic perspectives of understanding school curriculum and curriculum theories, which frame the field as an eternal reproduction of what has been predicted and prescribed, imprisoned by whatever already exists and is already known.

Particularly relevant in the formulation of the notion of Curriculum as Everyday Creation is the work and thought of Michel de Certeau (1994), which helps us to understand the daily ways of creating curriculum alternatives as 'arts of doing' by practitioners who subvert, through of them, their place as consumers of norms, incapable of creation. As we argued in another yet related context (Oliveira, 2016, 75), it is 'by using the spaces, occasions and possibilities found in everyday life, in the gaps left by the strategies of the "powerful," that the "weak," tactically using the "products" of the system, can carry out operations of use such gaps; while registered in the existing networks of power relations, they are not determined by them'. These uses are a knot of circumstances, inseparable from the context, from which it is distinguished abstractly. Inseparable from the 'instant' presence of specific circumstances (Certeau, 1994, 96–7).

In this perspective, we argue that whatever the 'weak' creates is never capitalized; it does not have permanence since it is configured as a tactic, 'movement carried out in the enemy's field', without its own space (Certeau, 1994, 35) – hence the inevitability of the transient character of such creations and their permanent deterritorialization. It is also this fugacity that allows us to perceive a dialogical interplay between Certeau's (1994) gap matrix and Paraskeva's ICT since the permanent reinvention of the curriculum created in daily life and the requirement of itinerancy placed on those who intend to study and understand it implies a creative itinerancy, inhabited by permanent epistemological displacements, through the search for uninterrupted flight lines, as understood by Paraskeva (2023, 2022a, 2022b, 2021, 2018, 2017a, 2016a, 2016b, 2015, 2011). As he argues,

> This itinerant theoretical path affirms a multifaceted curricular approach and 'escapes' from any unfortunate 'canonology'. This itinerant curricular theory is an

anthem against the indignity of speaking for the other. (Paraskeva, 2011, 177; also 2022a)

Another element of great relevance in understanding the proximities between the notion of Curriculum as Everyday Creation and Paraskeva's ICT is the defence of radical co-presence in terms of Santos's notion of post-abyssal thinking (2010) – although Paraskeva (2023, 2022a, 2022b, 2021, 2018, 2017a, 2016a, 2016b, 2015, 2011) moves the debate to another level by advocating ICT not necessarily as a post-abyssal move but precisely as a non-abyssal matrix. Assuming this co-presence of multiple ways of knowing the world and dialoguing with it is essential to overcome the modern idea – quite present in the epistemicidal curriculum – that whatever is situated 'on the other side of the abyssal line' represents barbarism, magic, common sense, beliefs and other pejorative adjectives that characterize the relationship of Northern epistemologies with their others. Eugenically defined as cultures without culture, the social practices typical of these cultures are 'anthropologized' by the metaphorical North (or, as they call themselves, the West), considered simple local curiosities or exoticisms, in addition to the fact that their logics of production and reproduction are seen according to a perspective of the academicism of observation of the other that reaffirms the primacy of the metaphorical North.

Defending the need to carry out the necessary epistemological dislocations and the search for knowledge and cultures that were previously relegated to the other side of the abyssal line and that were produced, therefore, as an absence, the ICT and the notion of Curriculum as Everyday Creation, in different ways, operate towards the recognition of the co-presence and validity of different knowledge and cultures in society and educational *spacestimes*. Both approaches see such recognition as an onto-epistemological educational and curriculum commitment that should frame teacher education programmes. The former argues for the legitimacy of non-Eurocentric perspectives within and beyond the Global North – for instance, indigenous epistemologies and in the 'Ubuntu, Nhada' (Paraskeva, 2016, 2022a) and other cultural matrices – as relevant elements for its itinerancy and affecting the permanent displacements that characterize its very onto-epistemological itinerancy; the latter provides ICT in the making through the valorization of the knowledge woven in everyday life, in co-presence and network with formal knowledge, in schools and their curricula.

Both approaches advocate for the legitimacy of knowledge and cultures created out of dominant modes of production of modern science and thus made invisible by the racial supremacy of the so-called scientific knowledge. Such knowledge and cultures need to be recognized and visible from 'this side of the line,' thus coexisting and interacting with a multiplicity of other knowledge and cultural forms. Undeniably, much of such knowledge and cultural forms are non-existent in the curriculum frameworks and theory – in its dominant and counter-dominant perspectives – which persistently only recognizes particular knowledge formations and specific processes and procedures of what constitutes 'science', thus blocking any attempts to unpack and grasp many transgressions of habitus that permanently happen in everyday life. In doing so, curriculum-dominant and counter-dominant Eurocentric theory is utterly oblivious to the malleability and instability of knowledge itself. Curriculum theory, Paraskeva (2018) argues, is a scandal, a double scandal. Such an oblivious nature is not innocent. By denying the existence of any episteme on the other side of the line, the issue of its legitimacy becomes a non-issue. Paraskeva (2011, 2022a) defends the need to unveil these existences and produce ways of understanding them, arguing that 'curriculum theory needs an encounter with the very practices and the reality that surrounds it' (Paraskeva, 2011, 174, 2022a). Drawing on Deleuze (1990), Roy (2003) and others, Paraskeva challenges curriculum as a simulacrum:

> Curriculum theory should contribute to subverting and reversing the Platonic position, which sees the world as a reproduction of a particular original model and perceives it as a simulacrum or a copy without an original. Rather than approaching 'things' as ideal states, we must find advantages in their variations and dynamics.

In other words, more than a struggle for the recognition of the eugenicism of curriculum modern reason and its abyssal divide, Paraskeva ICT and the notion of Curriculum as Everyday Creation seek to recognize the dynamics of life, schools and curriculum, as well as challenge dominant theoretical yoke that controls the field. The curriculum created daily based on the notion of debate seems fundamental to fostering the struggles against scientific discourses that disqualify schools and their knowledge.

It also allows for demonstrating the fallacy of the idea that the hegemonic curriculum fragmentation is real or that different knowledge circulating in schools can be separated, classified and hierarchized. Many practices and procedures are beyond those which lazy reason has been able to see and study. They are the contents that contribute to the maturing work of curriculum as a daily creation and to the research in/for/with everyday school life. These lines of inquiry seek to unveil those practices and procedures in a permanent learning process to unlearn (Tlostanova and Mignolo, 2012) to better learn about what happens in everyday school life. We argue that unpacking everyday curriculum creations helps to perceive the emancipating elements present in the curriculum, the permanent innovations in which utopias are practiced (Oliveira, 2003). In turn, Paraskeva, in his ICT, greatly contributes to the emancipation of curriculum thinking from the perspective of the ecology of knowledge and cognitive and social justice. As he (2021) argues, it is an epistemological declaration of independence.

Final considerations

The purpose of this chapter was to unveil the similarities between João Paraskeva's ICT and our notion of Curriculum as Everyday Creation, based on a common matrix of Santos's Epistemologies from the South. We need to underline, though, that Paraskeva's ICT and its attack on the curriculum epistemicide and reversive epistemicide provide us with an unprecedented enormous epistemological and political step to our field, challenging us all curriculum scholars who work from and within critical and post-critical perspectives (Tadeu, 1999), with a very uncomfortable truth that we have been unable to avoid: no matter how much we have progressed, we remain 'blind' to curriculum epistemicides and reversive epistemicides, which could render all our reflections and our research meaningless, and naturally appropriated by institutionalized Northern Epistemological coloniality power matrix (Quijano, 1992), which prevent us from offering an effective contribution to the necessary epistemological displacement, from being carried out in order to disclose knowledge and cultures relegated to the other side of the abyssal line. As he (2017b, 2) claims,

> One of my concerns and tough challenges was that both curriculum terrains – hegemonic and counterhegemonic – did not recognize themselves as producers and determinants of such an epistemicide.

Today, we perceive the openness that Paraskeva and his ICT brought us. Through the door of understanding the curriculum epistemicide and reversive epistemicide (Paraskeva, 2023, 2022a, 2022b, 2021, 2018, 2017a, 2016a, 2016b, 2015, 2011), we must enter on the 'other side'; we are right on the other side of the abyssal line, expanding and investing in recognition of knowledge and knowledge's subjects from and in the Global South. Still through such gateway, we can invest in post-abyssality – Paraskeva ICT pushes even further to a non-abyssality – recognizing the existence and the radical co-presence of different subjects and epistemes, and finally think from their perspective and with them; in doing so, one echoes Freire's hope, that one day we will be able to master the act of thinking as they do and that one day we will praxis Kambeba's parental human relations, as a collective and supportive approach of mutual recognition. As we learned from Freire, being hopeful can only be done collectively and in solidarity.

> To be hopeful is to get up, to be hopeful is to go after, to be hopeful is to build, to be hopeful is not to give up! To be hopeful is to move forward; to be hopeful is to join others to do otherwise. (Freire, 1992, 38)

Thus, multiple and plural subjects and epistemes play a crucial role in other ways of existing, creating and knowing the world and interacting with it. Such plurality of subjects and epistemes creates endless possibilities to move from subalternity towards equality, from monocultural homogeneity to heterogeneity recognition that ensures the right to difference when we face non-abyssal exclusion; it builds bridges, crossing the very abyssal line, making visible the production of the invisibilities, towards its recognition and its validity.

This requires us researchers to exercise theoretical, epistemological and political itinerancy, as João Paraskeva and I have done, in our commitment to coherence between what we think and do, as Paulo Freire would put it. Accepting the challenge of being coherent, we argue that one needs to escape the epistemological and pedagogical canons, as Paraskeva (2023, 2022a, 2022b, 2021, 2018, 2017a, 2016a, 2016b, 2015, 2011) so rightly claims. By challenging such racialized canon, we keep hope alive and argue that despite the multiple forms of political and epistemological control of life and social institutions, it is undeniable that different reflections, formulations, social practices and struggles continue to be present, insistently and disobediently, in the world, in the most different spaces, educational or social contexts.

Finally, we appeal to our epigraph to reaffirm that it is the progress of daily emancipating practices, which, in the act of hoping, inscribes us in the fabric of other possible worlds (and curriculum theories) 'beyond capital and colonialism' to 'experiencing human emancipation'. We seek to create 'in research and daily life, rebel and itinerant knowledge and curriculum, breaking with conformism and accommodation' (Paraskeva and Süssekind, 2018, 71). In Paraskeva's (2017b, 30) terms ICT is

> Also, a human rights issue, a challenge to the dichotomy between ethics and chaos, since it is the ethic of the [needed] chaos. ICT praises the consistency of inconsistencies and fosters a reckless philosophy of praxis above and beyond the wrangle of 'being-non-being'; it is a eulogy of 'beyng.' ICT is *a la Marti*, 'an infinite labor of love,' one that perceives that thinking is not just theoretical. ICT works in a never-ending matrix that was determined and continues to be determined by sensations, forces, fluxes, and 'happenings,' all of which are linked and reacting against the capitalist system's modes and conditions of production.

ICT is a curriculum turn. A 'pluri-versal' 'not uni-versal' turn. A decolonial turn. ICT needs to be seen within the cartography of a decolonial being (Paraskeva, 2017b, 30). He (2023, 2022a, 2022b, 2021) argues that it is people's theory.

References

Alves, N. (2008), Decifrando o pergaminho – o cotidiano das escolas nas lógicas das redes cotidianas. In: OLIVEIRA, I. B.; ALVES, N. (Orgs.). Pesquisa nos/dos/com os cotidianos das escolas: sobre redes de saberes. Petrópolis/RJ, DP et Alii.

Appelbaum, P. (2015), 'Endorsement', in J. M. Paraskeva (ed.), *The Curriculum: Whose Internationalization*, New York: Peter Lang.

Arroyo, M. (2013), *Currículo: território em disputa*. Petrópolis: Vozes.

Certeau, M. (1994), *A invenção do cotidiano 1: artes de fazer*, Petrópolis: Vozes.

Connel, R. (1980), *A History of Education in the Twentieth Century World*, Canberra: Curriculum Development Program.

Connell, R. (2007), *Southern Theory. The Global Dynamics of Knowledge in Social Science*, Cambridge: Polity.

Darder, A. (2016), 'Ruthlessness and the Forging of Liberatory Epistemologies: An Arduous Journey', in J. Paraskeva (ed.), *Curriculum Epistemicides*, ix–xvi, New York: Routledge.

Deleuze, G. (1990), *The Logic of Sense*, New York: Columbia University Press.

Ferraço, C. and J. Carvalho (2015), 'Pensando as dimensões éticas, estéticas e políticas da produção e do uso de imagens na pesquisa em educação', *Teias*, 16: 24–36.

Freire, P. (1974), *Education: The Practice of Freedom*, London: Writers Readers Publishing Cooperative.

Freire, P. (1992), *Pedagogy of the Oppressed*, New York: Continuum.
Jupp, J. (2017), 'Decolonizing and De-Canonizing Curriculum Studies', *Journal for the American Association for the Advancement of Curriculum Studies*, 12 (1): 1–22, 1–25.
Lander, E. (Org.) (2000), *La colonialidad del saber: Eurocentrismo y ciencias sociales. Perspectivas latino-americanas*, Buenos Aires: CLACSO.
Latour, B. (2006), *O Poder da Crítica. Discursos. Cadernos de Políticas Educativas e Curriculares*. Mangualde: Pedago.
Lopes, A. and E. Macedo (2011), *Teorias do Currículo*, São Paulo: Cortez.
Lopes, A. and M. Siscar (Org.) (2018), *Pensando a política com Derrida - Responsabilidade, Tradução, Porvir*, 1st edn, São Paulo: Cortez.
Maphisa, S. (1994), 'Man in Constant Search of Ubuntu – A Dramatist's Obsession', Conference Paper Read at Ubuntu Conference (AIDSA) Pietmaritzzburg. University of Natal, Unpublished.
Moreira, M. A. (2017), 'And the Linguistic Minorities Suffer What They Must?': A Review of Conflicts in Curriculum Theory Through the Lenses of Language Teacher Education?' *Journal for the American Association for the Advancement of Curriculum Studies*, 12 (1): 1–17.
Oliveira, I. B. (2018), *Boaventura and Education*, Boston: Brill.
Oliveira, I. B. (2003), *Currículos praticados: entre a regulação e a emancipação*. Rio de Janeiro: DP&A.
Oliveira, I. B. (2013), 'Utopias praticadas: Justiça cognitiva e cidadania horizontal na escola pública', *Instrumento (Juiz de Fora)*, 15: 115–30.
Oliveira, I. B. (2016), *Currículo como criação cotidiana*, Petrópolis: DP et Alii.
Oliveira, I. B. (2017), 'Itinerant Curriculum Theory Against Epistemicides: A Dialogue Between the Thinking of Santos and Paraskeva', *Journal of Curriculum Studies*, 12: 64–86.
Paraskeva, J. M. (2011), *Conflicts in Curriculum Theory: Challenging Hegemonic Epistemologies*, New York: Palgrave.
Paraskeva, J. M. (2014), *Conflicts in Curriculum Theory: Challenging Hegemonic Epistemicides*, New York: Palgrave (Revised, extended paperback Edition, with a new Afterword by Antonia Darder).
Paraskeva, J. M. (2015), 'Opening Up the Curriculum Canon to Democratize Democracy', in J. M. Paraskeva and S. H. Steinberg (eds), *Curriculum: Deconizing the Field*, 3–38, New York: Peter Lang.
Paraskeva, J. M. (2016a), *Curriculum Epistemicides*, New York: Routledge.
Paraskeva, J. M. (2016b), 'The Curriculum: Whose Internationalization?' in J. M. Paraskeva (ed.), *Curriculum: Whose Internationalization?* 1–10, New York: Peter Lang.
Paraskeva, J. M. (2017a), *Towards a Just Curriculum Theory: The Epistemicide*, New York: Routledge.
Paraskeva, J. M. (2017b), 'Itinerant Curriculum Theory Revisited: On a Non-Theoricide Towards the Canonicide: Addressing the Curriculum Involution', *Journal of the American Association for the Advancement of Curriculum Studies*, 12 (10, summer): 1–43.
Paraskeva, J. M. (2018), *The Epistemicide. Towards a Just Curriculum Theory*, New York: Routledge.
Paraskeva, J. M. (2021), *Curriculum and the Generation of the Utopia*, New York: Routledge.
Paraskeva, J. M. (2022a), *Conflicts in Curriculum Theory*, 2nd edn, New York: Palgrave.
Paraskeva, J. M., ed. (2022b), *The Curriculum: A New Comprehensive Reader*, New York: Peter Lang.
Paraskeva, J. M., ed. (2023), *Critical Perspectives on the Denial of Caste in Educational Debate*, New York: Routledge.

Paraskeva, J. M. and M. L. Süssekind (2018), 'Contra a cegueira epistemológica nos rumos da teoria curricular itinerante', *Educação e Cultura Contemporânea*, 15 (39): 54–85.
Pinar, W. (2013), *Curriculum Studies in the United States: Present Circumstances, Intellectual Histories*, New York: Palgrave Macmillan.
Ponce, B. J. and W. Araújo (2019), 'A Justiça curricular em tempos de implementação da BNCC e de desprezo pelo PNE (2014–2024)', *Revista e-Curriculum, São Paulo*, 17 (3): 1045–74.
Prinsloo, E. (1998), 'Ubuntu Culture and Participatory Management', in P. H. Coetzee and A. J. Roux (eds), *The African Philosophy Reader*, 41–51, London: Routledge.
Quijano, A. (1992), 'Colonialidad y Modernidad/Racionalidad', *Perú Indígena*, 29 (1): 11–20.
Roy, K. (2003), *Teachers in Nomadic Spaces*, New York: Peter Lang.
Santomé, J. (2013), *La Justicia Curricular*, Madrid: Morata.
Santos, B. S. (1995), *Pela mão de Alice: o social e o político na transição pós-moderna*, São Paulo: Cortez.
Santos, B. S. (1999), *A construção multicultural da igualdade e da diferença*, Coimbra: Oficina do CES n. 135, Centro de Estudos Sociais.
Santos, B. S. (2000), *A Crítica da razão indolente: contra o desperdício da experiência*, São Paulo: Cortez.
Santos, B. S. (2004), 'Por uma sociologia das Ausências e das emergências', in *Conhecimento prudente para uma vida decente*, 777–823, São Paulo: Cortez.
Santos, B. S. (2010), 'Para além do pensamento abissal: das linhas globais a uma ecologia de saberes', in B. S. Santos and M. P. Menezes (eds), *Epistemologias do sul*, São Paulo: Cortez.
Santos, B. S. (2018), *O fim do império cognitivo*, Coimbra: Almedina.
Santos, B. S. (2019), *O fim do império cognitivo*, Belo Horizonte: Autêntica.
Santos, B. S. (2020), O Vernáculo e o utópico. Coluna Ideias, Jornal de Letras, 26 de agosto a 8 de setembro de 2020, 27.
Silva, N. and J. Leite (2006), Cidadania vertical e horizontal: ensaio para um conceito. Sociedade e direito em revista, 1: 105–121.
Süssekind, M. L. (2014), 'Why a Deterritorialzed Curriculum', *Transnational Curriculum Inquiry*, 11 (2): 67–75.
Süssekind, M. L. (2017), 'Against Epistemological Fascism: A Reading of Paraskeva's Itinerant Curriculum Theory', *Journal for the American Association for the Advancement of Curriculum Studies*, 12 (1): 1–18.
Tadeu, T. (1999), *Documentos de identidade: uma introdução às teorias do currículo*, Belo Horizonte: Autêntica.
Tlostanova, M. and W. Mignolo (2012), *Learning to Unlearn: Decolonial Reflections from Eurasia and the Americas*, Ohio: Ohio State University.
Tomé, C. and E. Macedo (Orgs.) (2001), *Curriculo e Diferenca. Afectacoes em Movimento*, Rio de Janeiro: Editora CRV.

11

Decolonizing International Relations Theory

Towards an Itinerant Curriculum Theory to challenge the Endless (Hi)story of Coloniality

Mekia Nedjar

Dissecting the coloniality veins

Over a decade since the Arab uprising has broken out (2011), the scholarly coverage by academia and international relations reveals serious paradigmatic inquiry deficiencies. The Arab uprising – its causes and effects – continues to be explored theoretically in a substantially deficient, irrelevant (Abozaid, 2020, 2) and inappropriate ways by the field of International Relations theory (hereafter IRt). The dominant inquiries failed to 'admit the real reasons for the setback of emancipatory projects in non-Western societies' (Khouri, 2011).

IRt could not even foresee the emergence of the Arab revolt, much to the fault of its theorists who persistently work in a fundamentally Eurocentric matrix. The 'Arab Spring' has been examined very deficiently by IRt intellectuals. Moreover, there is insufficient solid critical literature on how the Arab uprising impacted international relations in a 'new Middle East' (Valbjørn, 2017b). IRt persists predominantly as a Eurocentric matrix, with complex 'disciplinary divides and silos' (Fawcett, 2020, 178), leading to harsh resistance to moving beyond the area studies controversy (Bilgin, 2008; Teti, 2009; Acharya, 2011; Acharya and Buzan, 2007, 2017; Fawcett, 2016). Furthermore, as we will see, the current dominant educational apparatuses (Althusser, 2001) within the West and the Middle East are quite responsible for such incapacity to provide a 'learning to unlearn' (Tlostanova and Mignolo, 2012) of the current dominant Eurocentric epistemological structures and paving the way to labour an 'alternative' IRt within and beyond the modern Western Eurocentric epistemological yarn. That is, an IRt that emerges out of the epistemologies from the South (Santos, 2014). Relying on Paraskeva's (2022, 2021, 2016) reason, IRt is a web of epistemological despotism that persists in denying the existence of other epistemological formations beyond the West.

Subsequently, one of the challenges studying IRt of the Arab Middle East (or MENA) is the theoretical 'vacuum' related to perspectives beyond modern Western assumptions in academic settings.[1] The dominant reading of this region is patterned by hegemonic mainstreams framed by modern Western Eurocentric epistemologies consolidated by an educational system designed to perpetuate a 'selective social construction of reality' (Williams, 1961; Lockman, 2016, xii). Paraskeva (2022, 2021, 2016, 2011) defines such 'selectivity' as eugenic; echoing Santos (2014), he challenges the educational and curriculum field as an epistemicide. Such hegemony hides and marginalizes the diversity of perspectives in world politics, legitimizing a particular 'scientific' representation based on otherness in knowledge production and favouring a Western reading of world politics (Bilgin, 2008; Acharya and Buzan, 2007). In doing so, it produced as 'non-existent' (Santos, 2014) a vast array of non-Eurocentric epistemological perspectives within and beyond the modern Western epistemological framework. It also dismisses the conditions under which knowledge has been generated as researchers are not clearly positioned within the world they are studying (Bueger and Gadinger, 2015, 458). IRt speaks volumes to an epistemological cleansing, as Paraskeva (2022, 2023) would put it.

This chapter flags the absence and invisibility of Arab Middle East onto epistemes in the dominant narratives of world politics. The exclusion and deliberate epistemic erasure of the periphery from the IRt knowledge production is not innocent; it is a deliberate divisive social construction that legitimizes modern Western Eurocentrism as the totalitarian intellectual foundation and hegemonic thought that frames IRt. Thus, my analysis focuses on succinctly grasping the intellectual backgrounds and imperialist foundations of knowledge – education and curriculum – structural inequalities in the Global South, mainly in AME.[2] Arguably, the chapter examines knowledge as an endless contested site of battles between hegemonic traditions of coloniality historically constructed by the Global North and tough struggles towards emancipation led by movements and groups from the Global South. As critical pedagogues documented (Apple, 1990; Giroux, 1981), knowledge – education and curriculum – is not neutral; it is inherently political. Pedagogy blends politics and ethics to provide knowledge, skills and experience enabling individual freedom and social agency (Giroux, 2011). Conversely, to traditional dominant theories, critical pedagogies shift focus towards places and practices in which social agency has been denied (Freire, 2000 [1971], 1985; 1978; Mayo, 2015).

What constitutes official knowledge (Apple, 2000) is adjudicated by the exclusive narrative issued by the dominant structures – Eurocentrically framed – that monopolize disciplinary boxes embedded in IRt (Paraskeva, 2016; Santos, 2014; Quijano, 2000a, 2000b). The IRt field remains narrow and reductive. It limits itself to focus on the modern Western Eurocentric matrix that has been exacerbated by the emergence of the neoliberal paradigm shaping the doing and reading of politics in the international and national spheres (Acharya and Buzan, 2007, 2017, 2019; Tickner and Wæver, 2009; Fawcett, 2016, 2020; Buzan and Gonzalez-Pelaez, 2009; Tickner and Smith, 2020, 2021). In this regard, the current absence of non-Western, non-Eurocentric perspectives within IR theoretical terrain must be appraised and challenged epistemologically and methodologically to unpack the eugenic nature framing dominant IRt discourses. It will be crucial, though, to provoke a decolonial turning point in the way we have been thinking, theorizing and doing IRt by working within and through the political sociology of IRt (Bueger, 2012; Shilliam, 2011, 2021; Bhambra, 2007; Thomas and Wilkin, 2004) from the epistemologies from the South (Santos, 2014).

Our aim in this chapter is neither to deploy a *methodenstreit* framework nor to reproduce dichotomies of the 'West' versus 'non-West', 'West' versus 'Rest', 'North' versus 'South' or 'us' versus 'them'. Nor do we seek to replace one dominant epistemological formula with another. We claim the need for legitimate recognition of the perspectives from the Global South in the theoretical construction of IRt as a field of study. We claim for a just co-habitus of both epistemological hemispheres – as Paraskeva (2023) argues. And it is at the intersection of this confrontation between the perspectives of the Global North and the Global South that we come across the importance of Paraskeva's itinerant perspective. Paraskeva's itinerant perspective allows us to inaugurate the decolonial turn without dangerous dichotomies; it helps to open the space for a 'decolonizing strategy to unpack complex social and political phenomena' (Sabaratnam, 2011, 783–4). Sentient of the potential of the itinerant curriculum theory (Paraskeva, 2011), this study aims to break down the colonial silences in dominant theories, thus helping to diagnose the AME precarious status in conventional IRt literature and challenging its epistemic and political decay.

The existing AME dominant literature denotes a significant 'non-existence' (Santos, 2014) of autochthonous onto-epistemological frameworks in developing IRt's theoretical map – as if 'middle Easterns' were completely destitute of any valid onto-epistemological vein, which epitomizes a sublime form of eugenicism (Dabashi, 2014). The 'scientific knowledge' canon disseminated in AME studies is derivative of the traditional syllabi, which refer to disciplinary categorization and subfields in Middle East studies (MES)/area studies (AS). This category emerged as governmental geopolitical interests and necessity – especially after the superpower shift from British and French to the United States – to define up-to-down line of AS[3] after the Second World War. The controversial division between economics and politics (according to the needs and interests of the West), on one hand, and the social sciences and humanities, on the other, deepens the gap between the MES/AS and IR, as knowledge on AME was politicized (Kramer, 2001; Said, 1994 [1978]).

In this regard, it is crucial to appreciate the ungirding links between ideology and theory in the field, which are still shaping orientalist conceptions (Nayak and Selbin, 2010). It is crucial to scrutinize the ongoing oppressive condition of coloniality (Mignolo, 2008; Quijano, 1992) – its systemic fragility and authoritative sovereignty – denying agency and eliding any attempt to an emancipatory perspective in AME. The IRt epistemological perspective – despite the Arab uprising – is still theoretically feeble, anchored in reductionism and exceptionalism, and not delinked from the colonial power matrix (Mignolo, 2008; Quijano, 1992). We argue how decolonial approaches grounded on a critical itinerant commitment and engagement (Paraskeva, 2021, 2016, 2011) should be viewed as a road map to strategic knowledge empowerment and emancipation of the region and bringing the world's epistemological diversity to IRt. There is no theoretical emancipation without 'co-habitance' of endless difference and diverse world epistemologies as Paraskeva (2022, 2023) so rightly claims.

In what follows, we examine rather briefly matters related to knowledge production and dissemination and the divisive ethos of the official epistemological paradigm that saturates IRt.

The abyssal divide

That knowledge and science 'are political and social constructions' became a truism (Apple, 2000; Al-Rodhan, 2013d, 2). How knowledge and science have been produced, disseminated and regulated (Johnson, 1986) speaks volumes about the political nature of our social institutions. Knowledge and science play a master role in the coloniality project (Mignolo, 2008; Quijano, 1992; Shilliam, 2011; Dabashi, 2019; Venn, 2000; Paraskeva, 2022). The inherently oppressive nature of what is constructed, protected and disseminated as 'official knowledge' in schools (Apple, 2000) paves the way for the very coloniality nature of what is defined as science – or the monumentality of Eurocentric science (Santos, 2018). For example, under the modern Western Eurocentric reign, the advancements in science and technology were always driven to secure and reinforce the power of certain dominant groups than to reduce or eliminate poverty, inequality or hunger that rages across the world (Alvares, 1988, 33). The truth is that the IRt – as it has been conceptualized and developed – has not even managed to invert this equation based on greed. It thus became part of the problem.

Analysing the connection between knowledge, science and oppression is one of the subsets of a much wider range of growing global structural oppression. Our educational institutions are not detached from such structural oppressive dynamics. As I have argued before, that IRt coloniality's malaise is not dissociated from the epistemological frame that structures our educational institutions. Through our classrooms, curriculum and evaluation forms, such dynamics have been consolidated in classed, raced and gender terms. Classroom activities constitute the lab for class, race and gender supremacy of particular epistemological forms (Paraskeva, 2016, 2022, 2023). Dominant power formations are constructed daily in the classrooms, embraced by an ill-prepared and deskilled teaching force (Paraskeva, 2011; Apple, 2000). Thus, structural social and economic inequalities constitute a pillar of the current dominant power formations (Collyer ., 2019). The dominant traditions framing world politics and social policies reflect an ever-increasing monopoly of particular Eurocentric epistemological typologies only possible due to the exclusive cognitive capacity held by 'Westerners'. Modern Western Eurocentric institutions have been historically presented as the sole owner of 'legitimate knowledge'.

Inayatullah (2014) considers that such 'exclusive knowledge', advocated by 'modern Western imperialism as the most dangerous impulsive element', constitutes the missing epistemological piece in the 'Other'; in fact, concomitantly, such imperialistic vein defines the 'Other' as someone deprived of such important epistemological legacy. This is how the 'Other' emerges (Paraskeva, 2022). The 'Other' ceases to be what it really 'is'; it can no longer function as a social being in its autochthonous epistemological plateau. IRt – as it has been conceptualized – helps in the social construction of such 'Other'; It refuses to speak of the subject of the Global South from the point of view of the epistemology that makes the existence of this same subject of the Global South.

Also, this impulse element constitutes the eugenic evidence of a Eurocentric creed that claims to know what is good for the 'Other' and what constitutes the 'Other'. There is indeed a self-satisfaction in promoting the 'incredible projection of exclusivity'[4] through what Freire (2000 [1971]) would call as a pedagogy of the oppressed – or the epistemology of the oppressed as Paraskeva (2022) would put it – which epitomizes the narcissism and so-called modern Western Eurocentric exceptionalisms (Hamati-Ataya, 2014, 13; Paraskeva, 2016; Shilliam, 2011; Inayatullah, 2014; Bhambra, 2007). This is the racialized rational core of Eurocentrism still present in IRt literature and inquiry. As Paraskeva (2022, 2023) adamantly argues, Eurocentrism is also about the cult of the identical grounded on the presumption of epistemological uniqueness.

I argue that if there is a field of studies in which one can overtly notice the footprint of the hegemonic modern Western epistemological matrix and the consequences of such coloniality power, such field is the IRt – a field overwhelmingly strangled by a eugenic Eurocentric exclusiveness of theory. While considered 'deficient in research, it only engages international relations practices and structures indirectly via existing theories' (Hellmann, 2020, 20), thus revealing a glaring inability to move beyond the Global North Eurocentric epistemological impulses and dialogue with the Global South.[5]

Crafting on Paraskeva's perspective (2021, 2016, 2011), I would argue that IRt needs to decolonize – to deterritorialize from its theoretical architecture. Despite the growing attempts to decolonize and decentre IRt to incorporate non-Western, non-Eurocentric approaches, the 'discipline' resists change. The lack of resilience of IRt is understandable through its bonds to a historical account of its origins and foundation (Blaney and Tickner, 2017). Also, it continues, bizarrely, to reproduce (neo)imperialist features that exclude non-Western, non-Eurocentric critical anti-colonial and decolonial avenues – or even to consider them as irrational and non-cognitive producers.[6] Such non-Western, non-Eurocentric platforms have been considered as non-reality and non-existent. IRt is a vivid example of a field echoing a modern Western Eurocentric thinking, which 'is an abyssal thinking' (Santos, 2007, 45).

> It consists of a system of visible and invisible distinctions, the invisible ones being the foundation of the visible ones. The invisible distinctions are established through radical lines that divide social reality into two realms, the realm of 'this side of the line' and the realm of 'the other side of the line'. The division is such that 'the other side of the line' vanishes as reality, becomes nonexistent, and is indeed produced as nonexistent. Nonexistent means not existing in any relevant or comprehensible way of being. Whatever is produced as nonexistent is radically excluded because it lies beyond the realm of what the accepted conception of inclusion considers to be its other. What most fundamentally characterizes abyssal thinking is thus the impossibility of the co-presence of the two sides of the line. To the extent that it prevails, this side of the line only prevails by exhausting the field of relevant reality. Beyond it, there is only nonexistence, invisibility, non-dialectical absence.

Such cognitive divide, so insightful dissected by Santos (2007), frames the IRt – a divide that is intimately connected with the epistemicidal nature of schools and curriculum (Paraskeva, 2021, 2016, 2011) – and it is one of the sources of the social and economic challenges facing the AME region and communities. These challenges – that become exacerbated under the current Covid-19 pandemic[7] and the current war in

Ukraine – have a direct impact to the obstacles encountered in the consolidation of a truly social democratic platform. To rely on Paraskeva (2022, 2021, 2016) approach, the AME educational and curriculum systems epitomize the epistemicide – or at least they have been unable to interrupt the epistemicide that frames institutionalized forms of knowledge and science, such as IRt.

Naturally with a crippled educational system and a *quasi*-endless sociopolitical turbulence, the discourse that the West has developed in talking about the 'rest' emerges, and it is a consequence of its power structures. As we noted, science – what constitutes science and whose science are we talking about – is not ideologically innocuous; it is tainted politically and crossed by racial, gendered and class dynamics (Harding, 2008; Paraskeva, 2021; 2016; 2011; Santos, 2005). Sourabh Singh states:

> The taken-for-granted reality of the world is a product of the long history of the political dominant elite's interested practices. Thus, social objects that appear natural (e.g., class hierarchy or race relations) area product of politically dominant social groups' point of view. (2019, 3)

Epistemic oppression and epistemic injustice refer to the persistent epistemic exclusion that hinders one's contribution to knowledge production. It relates to the killing of knowledge (Santos, 2014). It is understood as an unwarranted infringement on the epistemic agency of knowers (Dotson, 2014, 115–16). As we have mentioned before, the official knowledge (Apple, 2000) and science (Santos, 2005) – perpetuated through the Eurocentric educational, curriculum and research systems – is related to the very nature of the structure of a classed, racialized and genderized state, with an impact on IRt as a field of studies. Anna Wojciuk in her book *Empires of Knowledge in IR* offers a systematic account of how education and science came to affect the position of state in IRt as well as the mechanisms that contribute to the power of the state within IR. State building relies also on the mechanisms, interactions and typologies between agency and structure (Wojciuk, 2018). Hence, it is important to unpack and contextualize the Middle East – as a fluctuating and unstable region – within the international system order and why it is still politically dependent to regional and international arrangements.

To begin with it would be prudent to take into consideration IRt's historical trends to shed light on this particular path. It is impossible to examine or even to describe the real world without being historical given the reality that is constantly changing and evolving (Wallerstein et al., 2011). As a social science, IRt morphology, as a way of creating a preliminary coherent intellectual order and structure, requires 'to examine carefully and repeatedly its philosophical, epistemological premises and debate them' (Wallerstein, 2004, 279). IRt needs to be committed to the world's epistemological diversity and difference (Paraskeva, 2021; 2016), it needs to challenge the dominant knowledge trend within academia and it needs to break from selective institutionalized forms of knowing (Bhambra, 2014; Paraskeva, 2021, 2016; Santos, 2014; Darder et al., 2016).

Understanding the IRt dynamics and grasping the challenges facing AME also implies opening the veins of the history of the world order (Mignolo, 2011). The concept of 'order' that frames IRt is abyssal and derivative (Santos, 2014); that is, the West is the orderly wealthy, industrialized and the primarily space of knowledge and science production. The disorderly space – so-called Third World and Global South – is the opposite and subjugated to the first one (Tickner and Smith, 2020). Such abyssal nature (Santos, 2014) elucidates a logic of 'coercion-exclusion as a crucial factor to maintain the international political order' (Buzan and Schouenborg, 2018, 17–37). Bertrand Badie exteriorizes lucidly the core of the international agenda 'as an item of "humiliation" which has become a standard parameter of international relations and a display of still colonial powers' (2017, 5). 'Struggling for status' in a disputed international arena implies symbolic (and physical) battles. That is:

> someone acts so to force a partner to accept a lowering of status, in complete contradiction to the norms and values upon which international life is based (p. 5). An international system, that is, the arrangement of a set of international norms and practices, identifiable at a moment in history, can generate humiliation and thus provoke the emergence of reactive diplomacies of various and disordered kinds. The disorders that today affect power relations are giving rise to new forms of humiliations, more varied and more frequent. (p. 7)

The logic of the international system is built on power hierarchical positionality. The most powerful on the top then comes lesser and lesser powerful. 'This pathology of power' (Nayak and Selbin, 2010, 20; Bueger, 2014) – so well dissected by Quijano (1992) as *el padron colonial de poder* – emanates from imperial narcissism emerged from the colonial expansion and expeditions, made possible thanks to the Enlightenment discoveries of knowledge (Hamati-Ataya, 2014). After all, knowledge and science define 'who man is, and reveal his nature to us' (Todorov, 1995, XII). The explicit reference of man here, according to Todorov, applies only to the enlightened and dominant. Consequently, 'people who are ontologically inferior human beings are also designed as epistemologically deficient' (Dabashi, 2014, 40–1).

It is crucial to reconceptualize IR's theorization enterprise (Shami and Miller-Idriss, 2016) from the epistemologies of the South. The South – and its subjects – cannot be reduced to 'raw empirical data that can then be analyzed by scholars in the North, much the same as raw materials are exported from the global South to be turned into manufactured goods elsewhere, only to be sold back' (Tickner and Smith, 2020, 5). Unfortunately, what counts as knowledge relies on setting parameters that pronounce eugenic common sense naturalized as truth and usually idyllic to give privilege to a dominant group (Vaditya, 2018, 1–2). The epistemic privilege of the West is built on the 'sustainability of epistemic inferiority' over the rest. As Santos (2007) adamantly explores, the visibility of 'this side of the line' is produced by the 'invisibility of the other side of the line'. Consequently, this supremacist positionality involves endless epistemic subordination and subjugation to the hegemonic knowledge system regardless of the geo-social location.

The first step towards a decolonial move is to attain a satisfactory understanding of emancipatory trends regarding the obvious condition of coloniality and its groundings in AME region, theoretically and practically. The fact that the Global South onto-epistemological veins have been sidelined, non-existent, invisible, within the grand 'agora' of IRt begs the following questions: Whose real epistemological colours framing IRt? Who benefits? It is thus crucial to critically unpack how IRt is regulated. Who gets the authority to represent whom (Dabashi, 2009)? Who and what gets included and excluded (Bhambra et al., 2018)? What is central? What is marginal in studying IRt? What belongs intellectually elsewhere? Why? Under which criteria (Puchala, 2003)? Who speaks for whom (Alejandro, 2017)? Who produce, diffuse and dictate the global research agendas (Collyer et al., 2019; Bueger, 2014) linked to nations preferences and world affairs? Who frames the 'official' debate?

The core-periphery structure of the international system is a vivid example of the abyssal divide, a sublime characteristic of the hierarchy or privilege differentiation that designates the core as dominant and the periphery as subordinate. Such abyssal matrix produces a very specific epistemological logic of coloniality, a segregated logic that maintains that 'on the other side of the line' (Santos, 2007) the barbarians and tribal societies had to be ruled by (this) civilized (side of the line)[8] (Davis et al., 2020, 57–8; Santos, 2007). That is, IRt segregated nature helps to establish an empire organized around racial differences and not in world peace (Thakur et al., 2017, 19). The dehumanization of non-Western communities was set in the academic research agenda as irrational and unorthodox (Tuhiwai Smith, 2012). Thus, IRt research agenda puts boundaries and silences endless narratives, sites and histories of struggle. One of such sites of struggle is the linguistic domains. IRt is also about an 'official' narrative, a linguistic narrative which is a 'co-constitutive foundational myth', that relies on Anglosphere-centrism (Acharya and Buzan, 2019). Such a myth is quite connected with the current global neoliberal academia dynamics. Inanna Hamati-Ataya (2018) sheds light on the problems of transmission of IRt:

> Academics rely heavily on, and sometimes exclusively, on the textual medium to communicate their knowledges to others. This reflects that most of what we know academically we know because we are told by others. this 'knowledge by description,' as opposed to 'knowledge by acquaintance,' is our predominant, language-mediated epistemology. (p. 24)

Let's take an illustrative example of a recurrent phenomenon in the Global South, especially in AME region, known for the endless conflicts and unfruitful resolution attempts. Related strategies to conflict resolution mediation have been applied – however, all of them fundamentally designed in Eurocentric epistemological terms; as a result, they have been 'constantly contested, questioned and criticized for ignoring the relevant knowledge', as Pinar Bilgin (2019) pointed out. Such expertise ignorance (Bueger, 2014) – which is never innocent – illustrates the epistemic fascism (Paraskeva, 2021) towards the marginalized and so-called underdeveloped societies. The systemic excess of credibility of so-called international experts prevents experts from the Global South from sponsoring and leading in interpreting their own societies 'realities' (Vaditya, 2020; Behera, 2016; Anderl and Witt, 2019; Dotson, 2014)[9]. The abyssal reality between authoritative knowledge structured on unexamined areas of local knowledge constitutes manufactured ignorance protecting particular political agendas (Leander and Wæver, 2019, 215). IRt has been incapable of interrupting stereotyping representations of the Global South (Fuller, 2018, 141).

IRt has been framed within Western cultural traditions and systems of social control (Wallerstein, 2004) which raises serious questions about its political implications. The well-known and dominant theoretical tradition derives from the imperial science where the metropole became the main site of theoretical labour in knowledge production. In it, the periphery continues to be a rich source of raw materials for knowledge. These disciplinary institutions block the epistemological possibilities for 'diversity and alternatives due to the growing authority of the Northern-centered knowledge formation' (Collyer et al., 2019, 15). The systematic denial of other forms of knowledge (Nanda, 1998) is a symptom of the epistemicide (Paraskeva, 2016; Santos, 2005). By denying other forms of knowledge, IRt dominant research blocks a dialogue between existing forms of intersubjectivity within and beyond the Eurocentric territories and in doing so produces what Robbie Shilliam calls *monologue* in social scientific tradition – 'the worthy interlocutor must be implicitly authentic modern' (Shilliam, 2011, 2021), *à la Européenne.*

The way epistemic invisibility is strategically managed in IRt indicates a high degree of epistemic violence. It is based on the denigration of knowledge systems that were dissimilar and judged to be inferior to that of modern Western science (Tickner and Smith, 2020, 7), a science that was granted 'epistemological privilege' (Santos, 2007, 2018). The essence of Eurocentrism is defined as fantasy that captures the imagination. The relationships of Europe to its outside are based on a sense that Europe constructs its *empathy* and outreach overflowing to define all others/the abject by a *lack*.[10]

The silence of IRt on coloniality explains the ongoing prominence of the 'segregated gaze' that occupies such field of studies. This translates a kind of systematization of absences of the 'Other' in terms of agency and theorization which decipher how the epistemic invisibility is strategically managed and universalized in the so-called field of international relations and its theory – or theories. Its (meditative) amnesia, or forgetfulness of coloniality – as Maldonado-Torres (2004) would put it – vis-à-vis the colonial inflictions and horrors perpetuated to the Global South, illustrates well the irrelevance and rebuff of the coloniality fact from its agenda. Thus, relying on Paraskeva's (2021, 2016, 2011) approach I would argue the need to deterritorialize IRt, to delink out of the dangerous racialized myth Eurocentric universalism and the exceptionalism of the Western Eurocentric epistemological matrix. IRt needs to be decolonized to understand the coloniality fact and effect in the field (Goody, 2015; Todorov, 1995, 2000).

The need for a decolonial turn through an itinerant education and curriculum theory

Needless to mention that such abyssal thinking and exceptionalism has been facing a lot of resistance from some post approaches. For example, postcolonial approaches constitute a strong paradigm within AME. Scrutinizing IRt under postcolonial lenses allows to contextualize the Arab Middle East in the world system in their evolution, forms (state-nation/sovereignty) and political and cultural articulations (knowledge/power/agency). The postcolonial impulse 'widens the focus of enquiry beyond IR's traditionally Western mindset' (MacGlinche et al., 2017, 8) and its Eurocentric culture that was able to manage and produce epistemically the *Orient* (Said, 1994 [1978], 3).

Also, post-structuralist perspectives, at the first stage, are an attempt to enable the peripheral and subaltern to be subject and agent of intellectual expression and critique. Adopting the postcolonial approach as a recurrent paradigm in IR turns the 'object' into 'subject' as a contestation of 'global hierarchy and its persistence' (Fawcett, 2020, 179). Post-structural postcolonial impulses place the 'local' at the core of IR and highlights bottom-up orientation recovering subjecthood (adopting Shilliam's term). The critical postcolonialist and post-structuralist perspectives challenge the reductive web of IR's Western Eurocentric platform and its concomitant racialized modes of abyssal reasoning. One of the major targets of post-structural approaches was the coloniality of English language (Paraskeva, 2021, 2016). IR mainstream approaches erroneously neglected 'whose' English has become worldly hegemonic, not just as a norm to marginalize other ways and *languages* of writing from other geographies (Bigo et al., 2020, 16) but also to 'serve as an enduring structure of coloniality' (Hsu, 2015, 125). In terms of education, it means a pedagogy for invisibilizing the other. Global neoliberalism has been able to impose and consolidate its hegemonic position by conquering the common sense an important agora in which cultural battles are fought. Language is undeniably one of the key components of such battles.[11]

Despite the developments and accomplishments done by the post-structural armada, it is undeniable that such developments – although laudable – have been short of smashing the dominant traditions colonizing IRt as a field of studies. As Paraskeva (2021) helps us understand, part of that is related to the fact that most post-structural approaches work only within the Eurocentric epistemological platform. Most of them, in their struggle against the epistemicidal nature of the social apparatuses of the empire, ended up producing a 'reversive epistemicide' (Paraskeva, 2021). IRt needs to assume a decolonial commitment – an itinerant one (Paraskeva, 2022)

Such decolonial path must proceed in acknowledging the current eugenic nature of IRt. Moreover, the reflexive epistemology of IRt might be able to question the 'erasure of what makes possible and credible a theoretical thought from its memory' (Hamati-Ataya, 2018, 22). In fact, an interesting debate has started among IRt scholars around the world. One of the globalization effects is the globalized scholarship for research discussions from the Global North and the Global South. Also, in a globalized world and along its history, we can find clear examples which elucidate 'how mimicry may emerge as the way of doing world politics in seemingly similar yet truly different way' (Bilgin, 2008, 5). According to Pinar Bilgin, leaving out the non-Western challenges, interventions and contributions from IR scholarship often sterilizes the history of the West. She considers that we need to ponder the geo-epistemological absences/erasures (Santos, 2005; Mignolo, 2000, 2005) of non-Western ways of thinking about and doing world politics (Bilgin, 2008). This 'decentring' of the intellectual enterprise entails exploring different ways of thinking about the 'international' based on the local conceptions and modes of seeing/doing world affairs. Along with Paraskeva (2022), I argue that such 'decentre' is only just if it assumes an itinerant commitment.

Decentring (Nayak and Selbin, 2010; Shilliam, 2011; Mignolo, 2011, XVI) from a 'common sense' (thinking) of the Western theory and history, according to Kimberly Hutchings (2016), must avoid the judgement deliver status. Nora Fisher Onar calls for the 'double decentering' as a foregrounding position on Middle East in IRt, which implies examining how the questions and answers may (or may not) reproduce orientalist binaries. Then eliciting these questions culminates the will of naming what shapes Orientalism and Occidentalism (Fisher Oner, 2015). The Arab uprising and the continuing sociopolitical *malaises* are still challenging the traditional academia starting to hear the *unheard agecement* (Braun et al., 2018, 796) of Arab people. Herein, the political and scholar situations are addressing huge structural challenges. The precariousness of the AME is due to the legacy of coloniality and its new faces. The endless political instability of the Arab Middle East, utterly counterproductive, moved to the enduring proxy wars in benefit of profiteers who are certainly not Arab societies (Kovalik, 2018, 2020). The way to challenge the 'binaries' is through an 'itinerantology', an itinerant logic (Paraskeva, 2022).

The current so-called post-Western world system has not changed the hierarchical dynamic networks whose beneficiary is the Global North. Coloniality is not ending despite the apparent failure of the capitalist model and the general unrest of the West. Arguably, the struggle is crucial and might fit the pedagogy enterprise as epistemic topology of coloniality (Paraskeva, 2016, 2014). IRt needs to commit to processes of 'intercultural translation' (Santos, 2015) beyond the system of domination and oppression. IRt needs to engage in 'interpolitical translation processes promoting political dynamics that are counterhegemonic to globalization' (Santos, 2015, 213) IRt and its scholars and intellectuals need to be sentient of the world's endless onto-epistemological diversity, championing 'an ecology of knowledges' (Santos, 2007); they need to be committed to delink from the modern Western Eurocentric epistemological matrix – what Quijano (1992) calls *el padron colonial del poder*. IRt needs to deterritorialize and open up the canon of Eurocentrism, which has provided a misleading dream (Harding, 2008). A just way to do such decolonial turn is to engage in what Paraskeva (2021, 2016, 2011) calls itinerant theory.

IRt and its scholars and intellectuals need to champion a non-derivative non-abyssal intradisciplinary commitment within and beyond the modern Western Eurocentric epistemological terrains. They need to deterritorialize, to exist out of the coloniality matrix, and assume a perpetual itinerant path as advanced by Paraskeva (2021, 2016, 2011), one that provides the possibility of a radical co-presence of Western Eurocentric and non-Western, non-Eurocentric epistemes (Santos, 2014). In doing so, IRt epitomizes a just way to think and to do theory from and with the epistemologies from the South (Santos, 2014). Paraskeva's (2011) itinerant educational and curriculum approach deserves to be quoted in length:

> Itinerant curriculum theory (ICT) confronts and throws the subject to a permanent unstable question of 'what is to think?' Moreover, ICT pushes one to think in the

light of the future as well as to question how can 'we' actually claim to really know the things that 'we' claim to know, if 'we' are not ready specifically to think the unthinkable, but to go beyond the unthinkable and mastering its infinitude. ICT is to be (or not to be) radically unthinkable. ICT is a metamorphosis between what is thought and nonthought and unthought, but fundamentally about the temerity of the colonization of the non/un/ thought within the thought. ICT attempts to understand to domesticate how big is infinite, the infinite of thought and action. If one challenges infinity, 'than it is chaos because one is in chaos'; that means that the question or questions (whatever they are) are inaccurately deterritorialized and fundamentally sedentary. The focus is to grasp that ICT implies an understanding of chaos as domestic, as public, as a *punctum* within the pure luxury of immanence. In such multitude of turfs, ICT needs to be understood as *poesis*. It plays in the plane of immanence. Being immanence 'a life,' ICT is 'a life.' A life paced by a *poesis* or a revolution? 'Yes please,' in a full Žižekian way. ICT is a *poesis* that itinerantly throws the subject against the infinite of representation to grasp the omnitude of the real(ity) and the rational(ity), thus mastering the transcendent. Being more *poesis* than just theory (and not because it is less theory), its itinerant position *epitomizes* a transcendent nomadography that is not transcendental.

IRt decolonial turn implies a radical different IR*theorist* – one that understands that 'the master's tools will never dismantle the master's house, they may allow us temporarily to beat him at his own game, but they will never enable us to bring about genuine change' (Lorde, 2007, 112); the decolonial turn implies an IR*theorist* that understands IRt as a commitment to onto-epistemological justice – an IR*theorist* that is perpetually engaged within a critical itinerantology (Paraskeva, 2021) that voices the silences of the Global South from an epistemology for the Global South.

Notes

1 The literature diffused on the region perceived as productive and sophisticated is considered as highly descriptive analyses output of Middle Eastern studies (Area Studies) and comparative political scholarships.
2 Exceptions are made for the Gulf countries where the education policy systems – dependent to the Western regimes – are well funded and tracing path to effective knowledge economy in the world.
3 For further details see Martin Kramer (2001), *Ivory Towers of Sand: The Failure of Middle Eastern Studies in America,* Washington: The Washington Institute for Near East Policy.
4 See also this interview 'The Politics of Pedagogy with Naeem Inayatullah', *This Rhetorical Life,* 15 Nov 2013, episode 15, pp. 7–8.
5 It is important to clarify the Global South as a new term – for an old division – which emerged in the 2000s as an output of new geopolitical arrangement after the Cold War and which eventually is not simply synonymous of the Third World. As Alina Sajed points out, there are several layers of the term Global South new geography of neoliberalism with its global capillaries of exploitation and dehumanization,

integrating corrupted political elites and institutional arrangements in South/Third World which benefit primarily the North. In addition to referred spaces of Third World, the Global South incorporates also spaces from the North that undergo similar characteristics of exploitation, oppression and neocolonial conditions, like indigenous, Black communities and immigrants (non-Western others) in Western societies. Thus, the Global South intellectual and struggles premises interconnect the North and the South as the West and its neoliberal capitalism deprecate the 'other' in both. See Alina Sajed (2020, 27 July), 'From the Third World to the Global South', *E-IR,* retrieved from https://www.e-ir.info/2020/07/27/from-the-third-world-to-the-global-south/. accessed 30 July 2020.

6 As a contestation to the (in)ability of non-Westerners in thinking and producing knowledge, some imminent philosophers and scholars highlight historical and socio-cognitive accounts as answers to *Can the Subaltern Speak?* (Spivak, 1988); *Can Asians Think?* (Mahbubani, 2004); *Can non-European Think?* (Dabashi, 2014).

7 For further details see: Arab Knowledge Report 2014 at https://www.knowledge4all.com/uploads/files/AKR2014Gen/en/AKR2014_Full_En.pdf; Arab Knowledge Index at https://knowledge4all.com/admin/uploads/files/AKI2016/En/ArabKnowledgeIndex2016.pdf; see also United Nations Arab Human Development Report which denounced dire conditions of Knowledge in 2003 at http://www.arab-hdr.org/reports/2003/english/ahdr2003e.pdf.

8 Emphasis mine.

9 It is important to highlight that the epistemic injustice and the systematic credibility deficit practiced in the aid-related and international cooperation and political mediation at different levels assert the continuous discriminatory imaginary as a criterion of the socio-epistemic order to classify marginalized and unintelligible groups.

10 According to Shilliam the Eurocentrist imaginary foundations see Europe to be an eternal myth more than historical expansion and exercise of material colonial power.

11 We should notice that there is an intensive production of research in Arab Middle East in Arabic language; however, its dissemination is barely exposed locally and hardly reach the core. In this case, the English language turns to be an impediment – among of others – to any promotion and scientific progress in the region especially in social sciences and humanities.

References

Abozaid, A. (2020), 'Critical International Relations Theories and the Study of Arab Uprisings: A Critique', *Athens Journal of Social Sciences*, 8 (2): 111–50.

Acharya, A. (2011), 'Dialogue and Discovery: In Search of International Relations Theory Beyond the West', *Millennium Journal of International Studies*, 93 (3): 619–37.

Acharya, A. and B. Buzan (2007), 'Why There Is No Non-Western International Relations Theory? An Introduction', *International Relations of the Asia-Pacific*, 7: 287–312.

Acharya, A. and B. Buzan (2017), 'Why There Is No Non-Western Theory in International Relations Theory? Ten Years On', revisited forum, *International Relations of The Asia-Pacific*, 17 (3): 341–70.

Acharya, A. and B. Buzan (2019), *The Making of Global International Relations: Origins and Evolution of IR at its Centenary*, New York: Cambridge University Press.

Alejandro, A. (2017),*Western Dominance in International Relations? The Internationalisation of IR in Brazil and India*, London: Routledge.
Al-Rodhan, N. (2013d), 'Knowledge and Global Order', *BBVA Open Mind*. https://www.bbvaopenmind.com/wp-content/uploads/2013/08/Knowledge-and-Global-Order_Nayef-Al-Rodhan.pdf (accessed December 10, 2020).
Althusser, L. (2001), *Lenin and Philosophy Another Essays*, New York: Monthly Review Press.
Alvares, C. (1988), 'Science, Colonialism and Violence: A Luddite View', in A. Nandy (ed.), *Science, Hegemony and Violence: A Requiem for Modernity*, The United Nations University: P.K. Gosh.
Anderl, F. and A. Witt (2019), 'Problematising the Global in Global IR', *Millennium Journal of International Studies*, 49 (1): 32–57.
Apple, M. (1986), *Teachers and Texts: A Political Economy of Class and Gender Relations in Education*, New York: Routledge.
Apple, M. (1990), *Ideology and Curriculum*, New York: Routledge.
Apple, M. (2000), *Official Knowledge: Democratic Education in a Conservative Age*, New York: Routledge.
Badie, B. (2017), *Humiliation in International Relations: A Pathology of Contemporary International Systems*, Oxford: Hart Publishing.
Behera, N. (2016), 'Knowledge Production', *International Studies Review*, 18 (1): 153–55. https://doi.org/10.1093/isr/viv024.
Bhambra, G. (2007), *Rethinking Modernity: Postcolonialism and the Sociological Imagination*, New York: Palgrave Macmillan.
Bhambra, G. (2014), 'A Sociological Dilemma: Race, Segregation and US Sociology', *Current Sociology*, 62 (4): 472–92. https://doi.org/10.1177/0011392114524506.
Bhambra, G. et al. (2018), *Decolonising the University*, London: Pluto Press.
Bigo, D. et al. (2020), 'The Art of Writing Social Sciences: Disrupting the Current Politics of Style', *Political Anthropological Research on International Social Sciences (PARISS)*, 1 (1): 9–38. https://doi.org/10.1163/25903276-bja10008.
Bilgin, P. (2008), 'Thinking Past, Western IR', *Third World Quarterly*, 29 (1): 5–23. https://doi.org/10.1080/01436590701726392.
Bilgin, P. (2019), 'Worlding Conflict Resolution and Mediation Expertise in the Global South', in A. Leader and O. Waever (eds), *Assembling Exclusive Expertise: Knowledge, Ignorance and Conflict Resolution in the Global South*, 77–92, London & New York: Routledge.
Blaney, D. and A. Tickner (2017), 'Worlding, Ontological Politics and the Possibility of a Decolonial IR', *Millennium Journal of International Studies*, 45 (3) : 1–19.
Braun, B. et al. (2018), 'Rethinking Agency in International Relations: Performativity, Performances and Actor-Networks', *Journal of International Relations and Development*, 17 (1): 30–60.
Bueger, C. (2012), 'From Epistemology to Practice: A Sociology of Science for International Relations', *Journal of International Relations and Development*, 15 (1): 97–109.
Bueger, C. (2014), 'From Expert Communities to Epistemic Arrangements: Situating Expertise in International Relations', in M. Mayer, M. Carpes and R. Knoblich (eds), *International Relations and Global Politics of Science and Technology*, Berlin: Springer.
Bueger, C. and F. Gadinger (2015), 'The Play of International Practice', *International Studies Quarterly*, 59 (3): 449–60. https://doi.org/10.1111/isqu.12202.
Buzan, B. and A. Gonzalez-Pelaez (2009), *International Society and the Middle East: English School Theory and the Regional Level*, Basingstoke: Palgrave Macmillan.

Buzan, B. and L. Schouenborg (2018), *Global International Society: A New Framework for Analysis*, Cambridge: Cambridge University Press.
Collyer, F. et al. (2019), *Knowledge and Global Power: Making New Sciences in the South*, Johannesburg: University of the Wittswatersrand.
Darder, A. et al. (2016), *Critical Pedagogy Reader*, New York: Routledge.
Dabashi, H. (2009), *Post-Orientalism: Knowledge and Power in Time of Terror*, London: Transaction Publishers.
Dabashi, H. (2014), *Can Non-Europeans Think?* London: Zed Books.
Dabashi, H. (2019), *Europe and Its Shadows: Coloniality After Empire*, London: Pluto Press.
Davis, A. et al. (2020), *The Imperial Discipline: Race and the Founding of IR*, London: Pluto Press.
Dotson, K. (2014), 'Conceptualizing Epistemic Oppression', *Social Epistemology*, 28 (2): 115–38. https://doi.org/10.1080/02691728.2013.782585.
Fawcett, L. (2016), *International Relations of the Middle East*, Cambridge: Oxford University Press.
Fawcett, L. (2020), 'International Relations and the Middle East: Bringing Area Studies (Back) In', *St Antony's International Review*, 16 (1): 177–83.
Freire, P. (1978), *Pedagogy in Process: The Letters to Guinea-Bissau*, New York: The Seabury Press.
Freire, P. (1985), *The Politics of Education: Culture, Power and Liberation*, Westport: Bergin and Garvey.
Freire, P. (2000 [1971]), *Pedagogy of the Oppressed*, New York: Bloomsbury.
Fuller, S. (2018), *Post-Truth: Knowledge as a Power Game*, London: Anthem Press.
Giroux, H. (1981), *Ideology, Culture and the Process of Schooling*, Philadelphia: Temple University Press.
Giroux, H. (2011), *On Critical Pedagogy*, New York: Continuum.
Goody, J. (2015), *Le Vol de l'Histoire, Comment L'Europe a imposé le récit de son passé au reste du monde*, trans. F. Durand-Bogaert, Paris: Gallimard.
Hamati-Ataya, I. (2014), 'Outline for a Reflexive Epistemology', *Epistemology and Philosophy of Science*, 42 (4): 46–66.
Hamati-Ataya, I. (2018), 'The Sociology of Knowledge as Postphilosophical Epistemology: Out of IR's "Socially constructed" Idealism', *International Studies Review*, 20: 3–29.
Harding, S. (2008), *Sciences from Bellow: Feminisms, Postcolonialities and Modernities*, Durham: Duke University Press.
Hellmann, G. (2020), 'International Relations Theory', in B. Badie, D. Berg-Schlosser and L. Morlino (eds), *The Sage Handbook of Political Science*, 1–33, Thousand Oakes: Sage Publications.
Hsu, F. (2015), 'The Coloniality of Neoliberal English: The Enduring Structures of American Colonial English Instruction in the Philippines and Puerto Rico', *L2 Journal*, 7 (3): 123–45.
Hutchings, K. (2016), 'Quiet as a Research Strategy, the Essence of Critique, and the Narcissism of Minor Differences', *Theory Talks*. http://www.theory-talks.org/2016/10/theory-talk-73-kimberly-hutchings.html (accessed October 10, 2018).
Inayatullah, N. (2014), 'Why Do Some Know What's Good for Others?' in J. Edkins and M. Zehfuss (eds), *Global Politics: A New Introduction*, New York: Routledge.
Johnson, R. (1986), 'What Is Cultural Studies Anyway', *Social Text*, 16: 38–80.
Khouri, R. (2011), 'Drop the Orientalist Term "Arab Spring"', *The Daily Star*. https://bit.ly/30VmZ6H (accessed July 5, 2020).

Kovalik, D. (2018), *The Plot to Attack Iran: How the CIA and the Deep State Have Conspired to Vilify Iran*, New York: Skyhorse.
Kovalik, D. (2020), *How the West Violates International Law by Using 'Humanitarian' Intervention to Advance Economic and Strategic Interests*, New York: Hot Books.
Kramer, M. (2001), *Ivory Towers of Sand: The Failure of Middle Eastern Studies in America*, Washington, DC: The Washington Institute for Near East Policy.
Leander, A. and O. Wæver (2019), *Assembling Exclusive Expertise: Knowledge, Ignorance and Conflict Resolution in the Global South*, London: Routledge.
Lockman, Z. (2016), *Field Notes: The Making of Middle East Studies in the United States*, Stanford: Stanford University Press.
Lorde, A. (2007), *Sister Outsider*, Berkeley: Crossing Press.
MacGlinchey, S. et al. (2017), *International Relations Theory*, Bristol: E-IR Publishing.
Mahbubani, K. (2004), *Can Asians Think?* Singapore: Marshal Cavendish International.
Maldonado-Torres, N. (2004), 'The Topology of Being and the Geopolitics of Knowledge: Modernity, Empire, Coloniality', *City*, 8 (1): 29–56. https://doi.org/10.1080/1360481042000199787.
Mayo, P. (2015), *Hegemony and Education Under Neoliberalism: Insights from Gramsci*, New York: Routledge.
Mignolo, W. (2000), 'The Many Faces of Cosmo-Polis: Border Thinking and Critical Cosmopolitanism', *Public Culture*, 12 (3): 721–48.
Mignolo, W. (2005), 'On Subalterns and other Agencies', *Postcolonial Studies*, 8 (4): 381–407.
Mignolo, W. (2008), 'El pensamiento des-colonial, desprendimiento y apertura: Un manifiesto', *Telar*, 6: 7–38.
Mignolo, W. (2011), *The Darker Side of Western Modernity: Global Futures, Decolonial Options*, Durham: Duke University Press.
Nanda, M. (1998), 'The Epistemic Charity of the Social Constructivist Critics of Science and Why the Third World Should Refuse the Offer', in N. Koertge (ed.), *A House Built on Sand: Exposing Postmodernist Myths About Science*, New York: Oxford University Press.
Nayak, M. and E. Selbin (2010), *Decentering International Relations*, New York: Zed Books.
Oner, N. F. (2015), 'IR and Middle East Studies: Speaking Truth to Power in a Multipolar World', *International Relations Theory and a Changing Middle East*, September 17, Aarhus: Aarhus University.
Paraskeva, J. M. (2011), *Conflicts in Curriculum Theory: Challenging Hegemonic Epistemologies*, New York: Palgrave.
Paraskeva, J. M. (2016), *Curriculum Epistemicides: Towards an Itinerant Curriculum Theory*, New York: Routledge.
Paraskeva, J. M. (2014) *Conflicts in Curriculum Theory: Challenging Hegemonic Epistemologies*, New York: Palgrave.
Paraskeva, J. M. (2021), *Curriculum and the Generation of Utopia*, New York: Routledge.
Paraskeva, J. M. (2022), *Conflicts in Curriculum Theory: Challenging Hegemonic Epistemologies*, New York: Palgrave.
Paraskeva, J. M. (2023), *Critical Perspectives on the Denial of Caste in the Educational Debate*, New York: Routledge.
Puchala, D. (2003), *Theory and History in International Relations*, New York: Routledge.
Quijano, A. (1992), 'Colonialidad y modernidad/racionalidad', *Perú Indígena*, 13 (29): 11–20.

Quijano, A. (2000a), 'Colonialidad del Poder, Eurocentrismo y América Latina', in E. Lander (ed.), *La Colonialidad del Saber: Eurocentrismo y Ciencias Sociales. Perspectivas latinoamericanas*, 201–46, Buenos Aires: CLACSO.
Quijano, A. (2000b), 'Modernidad y democracia: intereses y conflictos', *Anuario Mariateguiano*, XII (12): 777–832.
Sabaratnam, M. (2011), 'IR in Dialogue…But Can We Change the Subjects? A Typology of Decolonising Strategies for the Study of World Politics', *Millennium Journal of International Studies*, 39 (3): 703–81. http://doi.org/10.1177/0305829811404270.
Said, E. (1994 [1978]), *Orientalism: Western Conceptions of the Orient*, New York: Vintage Books.
Sajed, A. (2020, July 27), 'From the Third World to the Global South', *E-IR*. https://www.e-ir.info/2020/07/27/from-the-third-world-to-the-global-south/ (accessed July 30, 2020).
Santos, B. de S. (2005), *Foro Social Mundial. Manual de Uso*, Barcelona: Icaria.
Santos, B. de S. (2007), 'Beyond Abyssal Thinking: From Global Lines to Ecologies of Knowledges', *Review*, 30 (1): 45–89.
Santos, B. de S. (2014), *Epistemologies of the South: Justice against Epistemicide*, Boulder: Paradigm Publishers.
Santos, B. de S. (2018), *The End of Cognitive Empire: The Coming of Age of Epistemologies of the South*, Duke University Press.
Shami, S. and C. Miller-Idriss, eds (2016), *Middle East Studies for the New Millennium: Infrastructure of Knowledge*, New York: New York University Press.
Shilliam, R., ed. (2011), *International Relations and Non-Western Thought: Imperialism, Colonialism and Investigations of Global Modernity*, London: Routledge.
Shilliam, R. (2021), *Decolonising Politics: An Introduction*, Cambridge: Polity Press.
Singh, S. (2019), 'Science, Common Sense and Sociological Analysis: A Critical Appreciation of the Epistemological Foundation of Field Theory', *Philosophy of Social Sciences*, 49 (2): 87–107. https://doi.org/10.1177/0048393118819823.
Smith, L. T. (2012), *Decolonizing Methodologies: Research and Indigenous Peoples*, 2nd edn, London: Zed Books.
Spivak, G. (1988), 'Can the Subaltern Speak?' in C. Nelson and L. Grossberg (eds), *Marxism and the Interpretation of Culture*, 271–316, Urbana, IL: University of Illinois Press.
Teti, A. (2009), 'The ME and the Production of Knowledge', in B. Firat, S. De Mul, S. van Wichelen et al. (eds), *Commitment and Complicity in Cultural Theory and Practice*, 81–101, London: Palgrave Macmillan.
Thakur, V. et al. (2017), 'Imperial Mission, "Scientific" Method: An Alternative Account of Origins of IR', *Millennium Journal of International Studies*: 1–20. http://doi.org/10.1177/0305829817711911.
Tickner, A. and O. Wæver, eds (2009), *International Relations Scholarships around the World, Worlding Beyond the West*, London: Routledge.
Tickner, A. and K. Smith (2020), *International Relations from the Global South: Worlds of Difference*, London: Routledge.
Thomas, C. and P. Wilkin (2004), 'Still Waiting After All These Years: The Third World on the Periphery of International Relations', *Political Studies Association BJPIR*, 6 (2): 241–58. http://doi.org/10.1111/j.1467-856X.2004.00138.x.
Tlostanova, M. and W. Mignolo (2012), *Learning to Unlearn: Decolonial Reflec- tions from Euroasia and the Americas*, Ohio: Ohio State University.
Todorov, T. (1995), *The Morals of History*, Minneapolis: University of Minnesota Press.

Todorov, T. (2000), *Imperfect Garden: The Legacy of Humanism*, Princeton: Princeton University Press.
Vaditya, V. (2018), 'Social Domination and Epistemic Marginalisation: Towards Methodology of the Oppressed', *Social Epistemology*, 31 (4): 272–85. https://doi.org/10.1080/02691728.2018.1444111.
Vaditya, V. (2020), 'Social Imaginary and Epistemic Discrimination: From Global Justice to Epistemic Injustice', *Social Epistemology*, 9 (10): 1–7. https://wp.me/p1Bfg0-5nU.
Valbjørn, M. (2017b), 'Strategies for Reviving the International Relations/Middle East Nexus after the Arab Uprisings', *PS: Political Science & Politics*, 50 (3): 647–51. https://doi.org/10.1017/S1049096517000312.
Venn, C. (2000), *Occidentalism: Modernity and Subjectivities*, London: Sage Publications.
Wallerstein, I. (2004), *The Uncertainties of Knowledge*, Philadelphia: Temple University Press.
Wallerstein, I., D. Aerts, B. D'Hooghe and H. Pinxten, eds (2011), *Worldviews, Science and Us: Interdisciplinary Perspectives on Worlds, Cultures and Society*, Singapore: World Scientific.
Williams, R. (1961), *The Long Revolution*, New York: Columbia University Press.
Wojciuk, A. (2018), *Empires of Knowledge in International Relations: Education and Science as Sources of Power for the State*, New York: Routledge.

12

Moving the Abyssal Lines

Contemporary Disputes within Brazilian Curriculum Field

Maria Luiza Süssekind

Displace, dislocate, decolonize.[1] Moving throughout this curriculum river, taking advantage of its itinerancy, we approach the field following some movements towards epistemological South, aware that we are running into curriculum fascism and decentring the canons of the theory. Questioning Professor João M. Paraskeva's thinking we defold and revisit some tensions of the field that seem to be appropriate, especially in times of internationalization, pandemic, economic, sanitarian and humanitarian crises.

We start this chapter with the belief that the modern way of built, create or produce knowledge also breeds ignorance and, thus, produces injustices, as we point out according to Boaventura de Sousa Santos theories (1987, 2001, 2007, 2010, 2013, 2019), that curriculum documents, Eurocentric theories and, *lato sensu*, the scientific hegemonic thinking is an abyssal thinking characterized by being arrogant, indolent and malevolent. Such ignorance produces injustices, invisibilities and inexistences.

That is a major issue also in dialogue with Santos theoretical framework, as Paraskeva offers a theoretical image to confront the abyssal map: a river (2011). Picture a river, turbulent waters flowing in an hegemonic direction, that goes flooding and drowning, throwing everything into the abyss of the epistemicide.

> While critical theorists come from a number of traditions, the river metaphor helps show how these traditions flow, both together and individually, in the history of the field. Although this group of scholars has never occupied a dominant position in the field, it is undeniable how much they have contributed to the struggle for a more just curriculum. (Paraskeva, 2011, 2)

Paraskeva argues, it is a river flooded by non-monolithically radical and critical perspectives, whose legacy needs to be preserved. That is the space-time dominated for a 'careless reason that does not feel the need to exercise for imagining itself unconditionally free' (Santos, 2001, 42) and therefore abyssal. However, such task implies to move the theoretical debate to a different path, one that is fully deterritorialized and allows the natural emergence of an itinerant theoretical path – an itinerant curriculum theory (ICT) – a clear challenge to the Western abyssal curriculum thinking. That's movement one out of three: displacing the theory.

> [W]e must ask if this international conversation is challenging what Sousa Santos (2007) denounced as epistemicides. Is it engaged in opening up the canon of knowledge? Or, as we fear – and we hope we are wrong – is it an attempt to edify a new canon? If so, it would be a disaster. (Paraskeva, 2016, 145)

Towards the epistemological South, fighting against the murder of knowledge, experiences, life and events, Paraskeva stipulates (2011, 2016) that the curriculum knowledge desired to be democratic is displacement and conversation. It is permanent resistance to the unique, homogeneous, univocal, unison, thus it is not common, it is difference and it is dissent. A liquid curriculum field that flows and penetrates; moreover, existing and infiltrating the walls and barriers erected by the abyssal canons. Are those banks rotting and falling down?

We have been drawing attention about this lazy way of thinking, creating and practicing knowledge and curriculum policies (Süssekind, 2014). Careless and lazy because, as we understand from the work of Santos (2001, 2007, 2010, 2013, 2019), the way of producing knowledge is monocultural; therefore, it is based on an indolent reason, which is also too lazy to recognize different modes and experiences of knowledge, nullifying the plurality of the world and the ontological difference that make humanity human. Thus, dominated by the laziness of recognizing the 'other', its own existence, the knowledge that was configured as Western, Eurocentric, capitalist, colonial, white and heteropatriarchal and became hegemonic has an indolent reason. In a careless and arrogant manner it boasts such superiority recognizing itself as unique, better, total and even neutral. As a malefic consequence, the epistemicides, this knowledge becomes not only hegemonic but also unique. And even the world forgot how to be plural.

The curriculum field's DNA is labelled by theoretical disputes, as we learn from Paraskeva, historicized and problematized in the book *Conflicts in Curriculum Theory: Challenging Hegemonic Epistemologies* (2011) presenting the field of disputes, as 'a critical curriculum river' (p. 1). The author presents his investigation, moving back and forth in history, towards an ICT that flows in the 'critical curriculum river', as the book assigns a vast significance to the concept of curriculum and retells the history of the field with a particular inspiration: the idea of crisis. ICT, Paraskeva claims, is 'a' future for the field of curriculum studies. As Paraskeva says, he prefers 'the crisis. It is the crises that allow inclusively the debates silences, however it cannot allow silencing the conversation. That is a tragedy' (p. 143). Here we are. A humanitarian crisis that none of the contemporary canons could imagine: silence, tragedy, mass death, governmental fascisms collide with the idea of development, democracy and First World. The coronavirus ripped open the chasms of the abyss.

The indolent reason is powerful, although powerless and, in its monoculture form, produces invisibilities, inexistences, being epistemicidal in its condemnation of the other to the abyss. Any *other* than Eurocentric patriarchal capitalism. It needs to be seen in its contradictory impotent face, since, by failing to perceive or solve the complex problems of a plural world, it has become so arrogant, as it is also metonymic and proletatic. Also, could be the time to take some advantage of 'Western scientific hegemonic dominance [that] is facing a profound crisis of epistemological confidence' (Paraskeva, 2011, 181).

This mode of knowledge production is monoculture, based on oppression and monolithic imprisonment in different ways by which it is possible to weave other 'knowledges'. It is abyssal, Eurocentric, colonial, slavery, heteropatriarchal and so on. Thus, the arrogance ends up being inherent to the indolent reason as well as impotence, proletatic and metonymy that accompany it.

This abyssal reason is metonymic because is perceived as the only possible form of rationality. Therefore, it is obsessed with the primacy of the whole over the parts, implied in the very idea of totality, which leads to the conviction that there is only one logic that governs the behaviours of both the whole and each of its parts and the homogenization of all 'others' parts. As if one classroom could represent the whole school or one school the whole system. Dislocating this idea from the centre of understanding curriculum, ICT, as Paraskeva's curriculum proposal, decolonizes the theoretical and methodological frameworks (2011, 182) and also explains that

> [t]aking the example of teacher education, deterritorialized curriculum theory is exploring new ways of thinking and feeling and finding ways to produce new and different purposes of mind . . . giv[ing] voice to an engineering of differences by deterritorializing itself and looking for new ways of thinking and feeling about education. (p. 174)

Paraskeva's theory is a dialogue with Southern epistemologies – he cites specifically 'some interesting and powerful curriculum research platforms emerging in Brazil' (2011, 150) – as a fruitful initiative to grow the efforts to realize that the knowledge of the world and curricula are things that go much further than Western/Northern understandings of them (Santos, 2013, 25). Paraskeva's 'call for the democratization of knowledges that is a commitment to an emancipatory, non-relativistic, cosmopolitan ecology of knowledges' (2011, 154) also displaces the field.

Without admitting that, given the complexity of the social, the whole is not the sum of the parts as it does not represent the sum of all of them, even without admitting that the whole is also a part, the indolent reason makes metonymic operations and creates mirrors that arrogantly obscure the wealth and events in the world of life, plural, local and unprecedented. In another abyssal movement that colonized the possibility of co-presence, modern European rational thinking (or the Global North) swallows the plurality and present possibilities and funnels them into a single possibility (and linearity) for the future. Mirroring a world of sameness where we are all European, male, white, bourgeois, thus annihilating all otherness. Pointing too much towards the future, it erases the present and its possibilities of knowledge, democracy and emancipation. Teleological, prolific, abyssal thinking wastes, along with the present, innumerous possibilities for existence, creation and resistance. Must be decentred.

Being indolent, abyssal reason becomes more and more arrogant and impotent, as well as metonymic, because by taking the part for the whole it contracts, diminishes, subtracts the present and its actions, not allowing us to have a broad view of it. Therefore, when exercised over social practices, it creates the notion that everything and everyone is configured in only one totality, as if we were a homogenized humanity and, therefore, we had symmetrical and linear characteristics. In a way, it kills materiality, historicity and humanity of the everyday life ongoing fluxes, creations and plural knowledges. Modern Western thinking is an abyssal way of mapping and representing the world and, as Santos defines it, consists of a system of visible and invisible distinctions, the invisible being the basis of the visible (2007). In the field of curriculum, the abyssality of this hegemonic thinking is responsible for multiple violence against teachers, students, cultures, histories, gender and ethnicities.

Therefore, the hegemony of the North, sustained by the unquestionable mastery of reason and by the disrespect of Western thought to experience (Santos, 2001), affects curriculum policies and practices within schools. According to Santos, Western reason is lazy and makes knowledge of experience invisible, which wastes human knowledge. This translates into a perpetual movement to make school knowledge invisible, treating it as inexistent, reproduction or application, but always inferior to scientific. So, we can say with Santos (2001) that the North-Western, global culture and the hegemonic tradition of science (as well as Modern Law) are offering outdated and insufficient explanations to our current challenges (Santos, 2010). Besides its laziness or inadequacy, it is fascist (Paraskeva, 2011, 2016) and epistemicidal.

> It would be difficult not to recognize that the crisis of coloniality and Eurocentrism they are intimately related to the profound and irreversible crisis of the scientific rationality model. (Santos, 2001, 68)

We also understand with Santos's abyssal theory (2007, 2010, 2013) that this dichotomous and hierarchical image, in which the North is the centre of scientific knowledge, culture, industry and technology, does not accurately represent the reality because the world is learning more and more from the South. Without a doubt, we need to recognize it in a counter-hegemonic epistemological approach, which is defined by the political commitment to social emancipation and also by the astute criticism and inversion of modern science principles.

That is why with a wide criticism of the scientific model and announcing his way of seeing and understanding the world (1987), Santos maintained that the hegemonic model of modern science comes from a model of rationality that was constituted from the Scientific Revolution. It is a model of knowledge that is based on the formulation of general laws and whose field of action seemed to be restricted to the scope of natural sciences, by colonizing other scientific possibilities causing erasures and murders of other non-/pre-scientific knowledge – the epistemicides. At the same time, it provoked epistemicides and strengthened itself as a unique model of create and recognize knowledge, being indolent and arrogant, the hegemonic tradition of science was questioned from within by the ideas of relativity, chaos and complexity, which visit school curricula very rarely. It is a matter of going beyond the view that science makes of itself as something that is objective, factual and rigorous, that has hijacked experience, human feelings from understanding and knowledge.

Paraskeva's work displaces this abyssal thinking in the same direction, asking often about curriculum fascism presenting ICT, that is, if the field could move towards the creation of not asymmetrical but more *ecological and prudent* (Santos, 2010) and plural knowledges. So, knowledge is movement, dissensus, displacement and reinvention of the world, knowledge, theories, in a permanent complicated dialogical conversation with the past and the future, although school curricula still being conceived massively as a space-time of control, reproduction of already established knowledge. And, acknowledge social, cultural and personal experiences because, as we understand from Santos (2001), all knowledge is self-knowledge.

Paraskeva (2011) illustrates Karl Marx's historic materialism while confronting the idea that school curriculum is absent of conflict. In the author's analysis, the conflict was undertaken by theories and history of the field, like something not formative that should be repressed. Conflict, also understood as a method, is a contend. Those absences aim

> [t]o divorce the educator's educational existence from his political existence is to forget that education, as an act of influence, is inherently a political act, as has been insightfully argued by some of the major exponents of the critical curriculum river. (p. 13)

Here, we point out how much modern science thinking has contributed to the production of ignorance and invisibility, with school knowledge being an important victim of these epistemicides. Theoretically explained (Paraskeva, 2011) because of the domination of positivism, that framed the field and stuffed it with the idea of non-critical curricula, those processes influenced all disciplines and contends by abducting historicity and context from them. Adding to this, Paraskeva quotes Henry Giroux about understanding schools as 'a social construct that serves to mystify rather than illuminate reality' (2011, 22).

From time to time, since the nineteenth century, the river banks are captured by a political-social project, based on controlling curricula in order to achieve uniformity, standardization. And as we can see in currently global reformism tendencies, based on common core and standardized tests. Paraskeva reinforces this idea by declaring, 'The lack of consensus about what should be taught in the schools highlights the need for a serious debate about school content' (2011, 149). In order to recognize 'the powerful relation of conflict that is established between the hidden curriculum and the knowledge relayed in schools' (p. 14) in its dialogism and tensions (p. 19), it is important not only to understand the role of criticism as a theory but also to take *critique* as a tool to fight against reproduction and domination.

Hustling abyssal lines towards South, Paraskeva argues that there is a claim by critical progressive curriculum scholars for social justice and equality embedded in this debate. He points out to today's main goals for critical progressive educators as being social justice and real democracy, which are not possible without cognitive justice (2011, 21). This is a towering issue in Paraskeva's ICT rationale. As he claims, the struggle for curriculum justice which is a struggle for social justice implies a struggle for cognitive justice. This is one of the pillars of Paraskeva's deterritorialized ICT (2011, 2016) and for Santos's post-abyssal thinking (2010, 2019). Wisely, Paraskeva engages politically in arguments to show how curriculum is a field of conflicts in all its aspects. For him (2011),

> [t]he need to fight for an education system that would challenge savage social inequalities (Kozol, 1992), that would provide the proper political tools to 'read the word and the world' (Freire, 1998), that would challenge the pedagogy of the big lies and the positivist trap that has been dominating the educational apparatus (Macedo, 2006) was inevitable. (p. 14)

The dominant idea is that curricula are fixed documents or even an area in which general techniques can be developed to improve practice (as something inferior to theory) or a space where controlled experiments can be carried out. We witness a dangerous obsession with the elaboration of textbooks and other curriculum materials produced by 'illuminated academics' and their super-scientific ideas, which a priori are so good that they 'serve' any classroom from anywhere at any time. Such policies are also abyssal when called upon to defend revolutionary and dispiriting content.

Indolent, current curriculum reforms refuse to recognize the multiple and profound adversities of the national education system. Differences are thrown into the abyss, shortening democratic possibilities in schools. Some scholars, understanding that education could be an effective tool to 'shape civilization' (Paraskeva, 2011, 53) and also improve equality, became dominant but were not in unison, so this dominance was built over all kinds of conflicts about the role of culture and the primacy of science, among others. Those multiple understandings of the relationship between education and society not only guided the debates on curriculum field for many years, but as Paraskeva (2011) clearly demonstrates all other notions of curriculum are relegated to a less important role.

When it comes to thinking about current policies on curriculum and belief in the 'reinvent[ion] [of] a democratized democracy' (Paraskeva, 2011, 172) and co-presence, the contemporariness of Professor Paraskeva thinking gains new strength by the potential power of the critical theory world view against the epistemicide of positivism, both historical and in its current manifestation, a new tsunami internationalizing standardized assessments, national curricula and the not acknowledgement of teachers' work.

> In a spaceless world (Bauman, 2004) profoundly segregated by neoliberal globalization doctrine, critical pedagogy in its different windows (Kincheloe, 1991), more than ever before, needs to win the battle to democratize democracy. The schools and the curriculum have a key role in such a struggle (cf. Counts, 1932) – in fact, the reinvigoration of the Left, as Aronowitz (2001) argues, depends on this. (p. 21)

It is in this sense that Western thinking is abyssal, curricula policies are fascist and especially the current reforms are malevolent. They feed on impossible solutions, preach intangible results, using falsehood as an alternative truth (Santos, 2019). Maleficent, maker of Fake News as ideological harassment and the privileges of the class of teachers, nourishing themselves with fixed images which erase life and creation from school's everyday life curriculum creation. Maleficent, the neoliberal globalized curriculum reforms sell the solution to problems they manufactured. The indolent and abyssal mode of production of knowledge, that is, the fascist curricula, does not exist in isolation from arrogance and, moreover, both combine to produce ignorance, invisibility and non-existence effectively. When we consider that everything that is created in everyday life does not exist in numbers, in indexes, in many research methodologies and even as curriculum knowledge, that is, if we consider that what happens in a classroom (Süssekind, 2017), it is not recognized as curricula by those policies that value abyssallity, because they value, recognize or bring to existence only the knowledge prescribed outside schools in tests, textbooks and by specialists who are not on school floors. Who are not living and experiencing the curriculum as an everyday life creation or as a complicated conversation (Süssekind, 2014, 2017). In the ground of the debate Paraskeva seems to conclude that, despite all the efforts to develop curricula, methods, objectives and evaluation forms and reformulate the relationship between education and society oriented by audacious ideals (Paraskeva, 2011, 69), education was taken as a simplistic tool and totally inadequate to answer what the industrialism, 'a lethal phenomenon', demanded.

Malevolent ignorance deprives democracy (society in general and public officials) of facts, perceptions and opinions. Expanding indolence and arrogance to the maximum, the abyssal thinking forgets the intellectual function of teaching, undermines the intelligence and intellectual autonomy of students and subjugates education to the place of social machinery. Thus, malevolent arrogance becomes possible in a society saturated by faith in the monopoly of scientific truth and the reification of knowledge, therefore being vulnerable to any falsehood that presents itself as an alternative truth, using the mechanisms of faith, for example, in relation to the nasty invention of the idea of 'gender ideology' or the refusal of wearing masks against coronavirus.

In conclusion, based on the affirmation of the right to difference, which we consider an important contribution by Boaventura Santos (2013) to think about the relationships between curricula, knowledge and school life, we shifted the debate on reforms, seeking to argue contrary to the unification and homogenization of curricula, engineered by capitalistic managerial rationality in a malevolent way. Against the idea of curriculum control and intentionality of knowledge for learning-teaching, we have also seen some movements towards contesting linearity, neutrality and totality, against unique thinking, deconstructing the single story, fighting against the unison. Advocating for the deconstruction of the hegemony of theory and the fallacy of harmony in the curricula, we have evoked ecological relations between knowledge that demand appreciation for dissensus and, at times, archaeological movements of absences, to be produced as existing again, through criticism of indolent reason. There's the motivation for dislocate the centre, to deterritorialize and ram the margins of the river because

> we need a curriculum theory and practice that re-escalate their very own territorialities, which reflects an awareness that the new order and counter-order must be seen within the framework of power relations. (Paraskeva, 2011, 176)

The decentralization is caused by this criticism of critique and, where it is a production of invisibilities and how it affects, daily, our lives, writings and identities, possibilities and curricula, based on how we deal with difference. To recognize the abyssality is to understand that difference is an ontological compass, culturally and socially constructed, often dictated and abysmally printed as a binary 'map of life' by the North, hierarchizing and distancing, in a perspective of normalization, in which we teachers are, in curricula creation, victims and executioners.

Another João, also from the South, the famous Brazilian writer Guimaraes Rosa (1908–67), brings many times the image of the river. A *third bank* is the mote of a book and, as he tells in the tale 'The margins of joy', the inexistent river is an epitenon of the experience that interferes in the learning, in the languages. The margin is the story. A story of joy. And, while telling, we see that dislocation is knowledge and it is experiencing while inventing the world and the words, confronting even the language of the colonizer.

> This is the story. A boy was going, with the Uncles, to spend days in the place where the great city was being built. It was a journey invented in the happy, for him, it took place in the event of a dream. They left home early in the dark still, the thin air of unknown smells. Mother and Father came to bring him to the airport. Auntie and Uncle took care of him, justly together. One smiled, greeted one another, all heard and spoke. The plane belonged to the Company, special, four-seats. They answered all his questions, even the pilot talked to him. The flight was going to be just over two hours. The boy, shaken happy to laugh at himself, very comfortable, with a leaf-like way to fall. Life could sometimes dawn on an extraordinary truth. Even if his seat belt was fastened, felt like a strong caress, of protection and, therefore, a new sense of hope: to the unknown, to the most. So a growth and disconcert – certain as the act of breathing – the escaping to the blank space. A boy.
>
> [. . .] Did those birds drink cachaça*?
>
> [. . .] The boy repeated the name of each thing intimately. The dust, inviting. The hollyhock, the lentisks. The plush white canopy. The green snake crossing the road. The arnica: and pale chandeliers. The angelic appearance of parrots. *Pitangas* and their dripping. The peasant deer: the tail. The purplish purple flowers of cinnamon-rhea. What Uncle said: that there was 'filth of partridges'. The *seriema* troop, fleeing beyond, in line, Indian-to-Indian. (Rosa, 2001, 45–9)

The navigation in this deterritorialized river enforces us to a shift. Pushing the lines of abyssality, on this river, in a movement to flood the world and schools with postcolonial thoughts that value experiences local, native, traditional, gender, ethnic knowledge as plural; and more, that emerge in facing the indolent reason. Yet, like Rosa says, 'Life could sometimes dawn on an extraordinary truth.' Fascist curricula generalize students, make the teachers knowledge invisible, taxing them as breeders, exacerbating the role of science and technique in terms of understanding and practicing curricula in schools. Against the unique and dehumanizing thinking, which destroys the difference, the *joy*, the dreams and the *sense of hope of a boy*, we respond, with displacement, sailing towards the epistemologies of the South.

The task is to fight for cognitive diversity as the best way for schools to fight for a just and equal society – especially when facing the impact of neo-radical centrist policies and strategies. (Paraskeva, 2011, 152, 153)

Note

1 Research granted by CNPq and FAPERJ, Brazil.

References

Aronowitz, S. (2001), *The Last Good Job in America. Work and Education in the New Global Technoculture*, Lanham: Rowman & Littlefield Publishers.
Bauman, Z. (2004), *Globalization. The Human Consequences*, London: Blackwell Publishers.
Counts, G. (1932), *Dare Schools Build a New Social Order?* Carbondale, IL: Southern Illinois University Press.
Freire, P. 1998), *Teachers as Cultural Workers. Letters to Those Who Dare Teach*, Boulder: Westview Press.
Kincheloe, J. (1991), *Teachers as Researchers. Qualitative Inquiry as a Path to Empowerment*. London: Falmer.
Kozol, J. (1992), *Savage Inequalities*, New York: Harper Collins.
Macedo, D. (2006), *Literacies of Power*, Boulder: Westview Press.
Paraskeva, J. M. (2011), *Conflicts in Curriculum Theory: Challenging Hegemonic Epistemologies*, New York: Palgrave MacMillan.
Paraskeva, J. M. (2016), *Curriculum Epistemicides*, New York: Routledge.
Rosa, J. G. (2001), 'As Margens da Alegria [The Margins of Joy]', in J. G. Rosa (ed.), *Primeiras Historias [First Stories]*, 45–9, Rio de Janeiro: Editora Nova Fronteira.
Santos, B. S. (1987), *Um discurso sobre as ciências [A Discourse About the Sciences]*. Porto: Afrontamento.
Santos, B. S. (2001), *Crítica da razão indolente: Contra o desperdício da experiência [A Critique of Lazy Reason: Counter to the Waste of Experience]*, São Paulo: Cortez.
Santos, B. S. (2007), 'Para além do Pensamento Abissal: Das linhas globais a uma ecologia de saberes [Beyond Abyssal Thinking: From Global Lines to Ecologies of Knowledges]', *Revista Crítica de Ciências Sociais*, 78(1), 3–46. https://doi.org/10.4000/rccs.753.
Santos, B. S. (2010), 'Pr'além do pensamento abissal [Beyond Abyssal Thinking]', in B. S. Santos and M. P. Meneses (eds), *Epistemologias do Sul [Epistemologies of the South]*, 31–83, São Paulo: Cortez.
Santos, B. S. (2013), *Se Deus fosse um activista dos direitos humanos [If God Were a Human Rights Activist]*, ed. P. T. Coimbra, Almedina.
Santos, B. S. (2019), 'As três ignorâncias: Arrogante, indolente e malévola [The Three Ignorances: Arrogant, Indolent and Malevolent]', *Jornal de Letras*. Lisboa: Caderno Ideias.
Süssekind, M. L. (2014), 'Taking Advantage of the Paradigmatic Crisis: Brazilian Everyday Life Studies as a New Epistemological Approach to the Understanding of Teachers' Work', *Citizenship, Social and Economics Education*, 13 (3): 199–210. https://doi.org/10.2304/csee.2014.13.3.199.

Süssekind, M. L. (2017), 'O que Aconteceu na Aula? Políticas, currículos e escritas nos cotidianos da formação de professores numa universidade pública [What Happened in the Class? Policies, Curriculum and Writing in Everyday Teacher Education at a Public University]', *Revista Teias*, 18 (51): 134–48. https://doi.org/10.12957/teias.2017.30506.

13

Itinerant Curriculum Theory and Decolonization

Alternate Planes of Projection for the Global South, Africa, South Africa and Beyond

Shervani K. Pillay

Curriculum theory and its concomitant canon is under curation (Pillay, 2014). It is curated for the role it played in the brutality of colonialism. The curriculum struggle in Africa, South Africa, the Global South and beyond is a thus struggle for both epistemological and ontological recognition. Decolonization is ultimately a recoup of our sequestered humanity from the colonial grip in general and the curriculum specifically. The metaphor of the curriculum as a battlefront thus depicts this zonal engagement:

> Within the course of the twentieth century and within the context of broader complex social – local and global – issues, curriculum became a open political and ideological battlefield, in which dominant and counterdominant groups re-escalate the animosity with sides basically assuming a 'taking no prisoners commitment'. (Paraskeva, 2020b, 31)

Colonization is a savage opponent whose secret weapon is subterfuge. Decolonization requires stealth and inviolability. The solidarity of the Global South and our commitment to collective epistemological vigilance and struggle (Pillay, 2014) is critical as we try and reimagine a fully inclusive sociopolitical/economic world and our legitimate place in it as beings-in-this-world.

Despite the seriousness of the task, decolonization is an arduous battle. Uncertainty is a challenge of note. There are many factors that invoke this uncertainty.

Among the various factors that contribute to this uncertainty is the myth that the hegemonic epistemological and ontological frameworks as we currently know and enact them are irrefutable and indispensable. The very idea of the overwhelming enormity of displacing colonial ways of knowing, being and acting is what immobilizes us as we try and engage with decolonizing imperatives. Waziyatawin (2012, 76) talks about an 'illusion of permanency and inevitability' of the colonial image. It is this image that feeds and reinforces the myths of our 'colonial dependency' (Mudimbe, 1985, 150) and which invariably immobilizes us as we try to engage in counter-dominant decolonizing practices. How do we imagine a world that is not imbedded in a singularly Euro-Western logic, let alone how do we even begin to engage in reconstructing such a world? Is what we know completely of Euro-Western origin, if so, how do we start from point zero? Decolonization is a very traumatic struggle that defies everything that we have come to know and understand:

> (re)claiming Indigenous knowledge as a necessary exercise in decolonization is a messy, violent, contradictory and painful undertaking. (Sefa Dei, 2011, 16)

Suddenly we are faced with deep epistemological and ontological existential dilemmas, which disrupt our colonial sensitivities of certainty, regulation and control. Instead of motivating us to move forward with courage, these dilemmas often render us immobile and or disinterested. These should not be used as deterrents to overcome this uncertainty, messiness and complexity with courage and commitment and resilience (Sefa Dei, 2011; Sium et al., 2012).

In his analysis of the African Renaissance Ngũgĩ (Wa Thiong'o, 2009, 108) decries the brutality of colonization and the use of education as one of the means to enable this violence:

> Colonialism tried to control the memory of the colonized . . . the colonizing presence sought to induce a historical amnesia on the colonized by mutilating the memory of the colonized; and where that failed, it dismembered it, and then tried to re-member it to the colonizer's memory – to his way of defining the world, including his take on the nature of the relations between colonizer and colonized.
>
> This relation was primarily economic. The colonized as worker, as peasant, produces for another. His land and his labor benefit another. This arrangement was, of course, effected through power, political power, but it was also accomplished through cultural subjugation – for instance, through control of the education system.

While we are able to recognize the aggressive and convoluted mechanisms of colonization, to disassemble this nexus is a challenge of note. However, despite the complexity of the challenge it is not an insurmountable challenge. We should therefore pull ourselves out of the quagmire of performative paralysis as we face the decolonization imperative of uncertainty and struggle. The role of the curriculum, in particular, but not exclusively so, in the development, reinforcement and sustenance of the subaltern in Africa, South Africa and the Global South in general has to be foregrounded. The criminality of the field of curriculum is well described by Sussekind as (2017, 1)

> the leading ideological locomotive of epistemicide.

The hegemony of the innocence of the curriculum as a neutral and thus emancipatory mechanism must be abandoned.

Scholarship on decolonization has surged in the education context both locally and globally (Shahjahan et al., 2022, 74). The need for this engagement and process is becoming increasingly clear:

> Why is this important? Curriculum and pedagogy are deeply implicated in grounding, validating, and/or marginalizing systems of knowledge production. (Shahjahan et al., 2022, 74)

The curriculum thus becomes a critical space for the decolonization of education (Shajahan et al., 2022, 77). Decolonizing imperatives have thus featured more in the education contexts than in any other parastatals.

The South African (SA) higher education (HE) arena has been decried for dragging its feet in the face of decolonization and indigenization imperatives (Ndlovu-Gatsheni and Zondi, 2016, 39).

Sium, Desai and Ritkes (2012, viii) caution us about this *time sensitivity of decolonization*.

In 2016, SA universities were brought to a standstill by the #FeesMustFull (FMF) revolt by students, who called for decolonization:

> South African students have taken the torch of epistemic decolonization and successfully put decolonization squarely on the public agenda. In the process, they have forced universities to revive their mission to be torch-bearers of equality, democracy, justice and human rights. (Ndlovu-Gatsheni, 2018, 189)

They mooted for the transformation from a state of imminence to a state of immediate humanitarian urgency. Students questioned the idea of the university and its identity in the SA HE context. They challenged the sociopolitical commitment of SA universities as social institutions which are constitutionally proscribed to be bearers of social justice and transformation:

> The transformation enterprise at institutions of higher learning in South Africa was either forgotten or lulled until the students protests 'brought about an awakening' and revived this important agenda. (Masenya, 2021, 3)

The FMF protests were part of a longer and wider struggle for decolonization:

> The South African students who spearhead the Rhodes Must Fall and the Fees Must Fall movements must be understood broadly as heirs to the long-standing struggles for an African university and the wider decolonization of Africa. (Ndlovu-Gatsheni, 2018, 189)

Students revolted against the reinforcement of their subaltern position and identity at universities. They fought for the decolonization of the funding model and curricula in SA higher education (Mpofu and Ndlovu-Gatsheni, 2020, 4), which regulated their identities as human beings whose very being and experiences are rendered invisible and othered. In so doing the 2016 FMF protests invoke Hoppers's (2009, 4) message to the late Nyerere:

> rest easy Papa **you have not died in vain**. We are **right there on the spot . . .** But only that **this time... this time**, we are not developing **sterile critiques of colonialism and the subsystems it left to eternally paralyse this continent.**

The student protests highlighted the nexus between epistemology and ontology colonization. Decolonizing the curriculum is critically influenced by how the curriculum shapes not only what we know and what we do not know, how we know and what we cannot know but also how the field constructed our ontological statuses. It would be a vicious crime to dismiss the role that the curriculum plays in normalizing the brutal dehumanization of, inter alia, its recipients and its protectors. Hoppers speaks to this hegemonic dehumanizing through education very poignantly:

> To many critical readers, education has stood by . . . unable to find the words and strategies deep enough to deal with epistemological disenfranchisement and cognitive justice with untold consequences for the development of the 'whole person' in Africa. (Hoppers, 2017, 2)

We must recognize this brutality and seek alternatives to reimagine different ways of knowing and being in this world.

The itinerant curriculum theory (ICT) (Paraskeva, 2011; 2022b) has significant potential in enabling us to reimagine ourselves otherwise in our decolonizing education warfare:

> The itinerant curriculum is a radical means of changing the archaic curriculum used in African higher education developed by their colonial masters. (Fomunyam, 2022, 146)

What then is ICT and how can it enable us to reimagine different ways of being and knowing or, as Hoppers describes it, 'plane of projection from which a wide variety of issues are viewed, reviewed, judged, or propositions for new visions or directions are made' (Hoppers, 2017, 3)?

Itinerant curriculum theory

ICT invokes a military metaphor to repurpose curriculum:

> What we need is to engage in a battle against the modern Western Eurocentric 'monoculture of scientific knowledge [and fight for an] ecology of knowledges' (Santos, 2004, xx), which is an invitation 'to the promotion of non-relativistic

dialogues among knowledges, granting equality of opportunities to the different kinds of knowledge engaged in ever-broader epistemological disputes aimed both at maximizing their respective contributions to build a more democratic and just society and at decolonizing knowledge and power'. (Paraskeva, 2021, 6)

It is within this context that ICT is critical of the limitations of focusing on social justice only and calls on us, 'to redefine the struggle for social justice as a struggle for cognitive justice' (Janson and Silva, 2017, 3).

The critical significance of ICT is how it rejects epistemicide in the field of curriculum specifically. In so doing ICT disrupts the oppressive mechanisms of knowledge that underpin the curriculum field and explains how the field has been deployed to be a surreptitious conduit of both epistemic and ontological epistemicide within exclusionary discourses that constrain counter-hegemonic forces and approaches:

> It is perhaps needless to mention how the educational system, in general, and curriculum/Bildung, in particular, are both profoundly implicated in such epistemicide. In fact, by identifying particular forms of knowledge as 'official,' schooling participates in a blunt epistemicide (Paraskeva, 2011; Santos, 1997) – It is perhaps needless to mention how the educational system, in general, and curriculum/ Bildung, in particular, are both profoundly implicated in such epistemicide. In fact, by identifying particular forms of knowledge as 'official,' schooling participates in a blunt epistemicide (Paraskeva, 2011; Santos, 1997) – a lethal tool that feeds the dynamics of white supremacy and a eugenic empire (hooks, 1994). (Paraskeva, 2021, 6)

I teach a curriculum module to second-year education students and have been focusing on social justice in the curriculum, because I mistakenly assumed that students would struggle to understand such an abstract concept.

I found that the furthest that students could come in critiquing curriculum and designing an alternate curriculum for the SA contexts has been to identify the structural challenges that are so endemic to SA schools. They were unable to bring epistemicide into their understandings and application for the SA context. This year, in the middle of a lecture, I spontaneously decided to introduce them to cognitive justice. And that was it! They understood it immediately! They were then able to critique the curriculum and its implications in the SA context fluidly. They were able to do this because as marginalized *Others* they struggled with being taught in a language that was not their mother tongue. They felt isolated in a curriculum discourse and pedagogical experiences that ignored their presence in the class at a multiplicity of levels, inter alia, language, cultural knowledge, ways of knowing, the plurality of their identities and so on. Suddenly the students who were once very quiet became very lively as they found expression for their isolation, and more importantly they found the tools to express their isolation and alienation that was deliberately constructed to exclude them. This is a typical example of what Paraskeva refers to as 'curriculum epistemicide' (2020a; 2020b, 2) which silences and constrains students who have been historically othered:

> This epistemicide 'suppresses the epistemic agency of some members of the group while elevating that of others, thus producing privileged'. (Patin et al., 2021, 1307)

Curriculum epistemicide obstructs agency in fundamental ways and constrains the ability to move beyond this conceptual cage. Decolonizing the curriculum should therefore also be about:

> nurturing capacities to imagine alternatives. (Shahjahan et al., 2022, 83)

Curriculum epistemicide also fragments society in differential ways under the auspices of universalism. In this way some students are able to flourish within classrooms and others are forever stunted and isolated. ICT decries this impetus and supports an alternate curriculum and paradigm that cultivates and nurtures solidarity and the recognition of citizenship and place of previously silenced learners/students:

> It attempts to bring to the fore voices/discourses that have been systematically produced as nonexistent. (Paraskeva, 2017, 309)

ICT (Paraskeva, 2020a, 8; 2020b) provides the impetus to reimagine alternatives within curriculum space through deterritorializing these alternate spaces. The 'deterritorializing of curriculum theory' is a space for the disruption of Eurocentric constructed axiologies, epistemes and ontologies (Paraskeva, 2020a, 8; 2020b). In so doing this space is one of affirmation of different epistemologies and ontologies and one which is based on justice for all. This possibility of inclusion is thus located in its very impossibility of modernist certainty.

Deterritorialization is a plane of projection that enables the impossibility of colonial exclusions. It is much like the 'trans-modernity' that Dussel refers to, which he argues is not a mere disavowal of the tyranny of Modernism (cited in Escobar, 2007, 187). It is what Mignolo refers to in his 'un paradigma otro' (cited in Escobar, 2007, 179):

> to make a decisive intervention into the very discursivity of the modern sciences in order to craft another space for the production of knowledge – an other way of thinking, un paradigma otro, the very possibility of talking about 'worlds and knowledges otherwise'.

It is not just about speaking within another paradigm, such as jumping from the perch to the feeding cup in a bird cage; this different way of thinking and being is a deliberate opening of the conceptual cage and a conscious decision *to be* and *to know* in ways that are not determined by an exclusionary Eurocentric episteme and its concomitant logic.

ICT was first mooted by Paraskeva in 2006 (Paraskeva, 2017a, 1–2). Since then, it has been a game changer for curriculum theory and has thus provided the conceptual tools for understanding and disclosing the proverbial 'tain in the curriculum mirror' (Pillay, 2016, 528).

Paraskeva creates the possibilities for the 'plane of projection' (Hopper, 2017, 3) by his central proposition which is, to de-link from the matrix of coloniality – the eugenic logic underlying Western civilization – and to assume a posture that slides constantly among pluriversal epistemological frameworks, an itinerant position, thus giving one a better tool to interpret and interrupt schools as social formations of domination. (Paraskeva, 2022a, 8)

ICT is scandalized by the criminal nature and intent of the Western episteme and the way it normalizes its brutality (Paraskeva, 2018, 129).

It is constructed upon the recognition and rejection of epistemicide, a concept first mooted by Santos (2014, 149) which exemplifies the criminal nature of Western epistemology and its hegemonic imposition. ICT is an aggressive and assertive rejection of this brutality (Paraskeva, 2018, 129).

In their extension of the understanding of epistemicide, Patin, Sebastian, Yeon, Bertrolini and Grimm (2021) break down epistemicide into four kinds of injustices which constitute epistemicide. These injustices are testimonial, hermeneutical, participatory and curricular injustice (Patin et al., 2021, 1309). They decompose epistemicide to demonstrate its complicity in *dismembering* the humanity of the historically marginalized *Other*.

Hermeneutical injustice is inflicted by the inability to understand and empathize with the experiences of the *Other* (Patin et al., 2021, 1309). The experience of the marginalized is othered and in so doing is dismissed as inconsequential. The experiences and the concomitant accounts of the *privileged* as subject and the *violated* as object are mutually exclusive. The hegemonic and regulatory nature of the privileged subject's epistemological and ontological status validates this dismissal.

Participatory injustice occurs in contexts in which there are distinct roles linked to differential allocations of power such as in a classroom (Patin et al., 2021, 1311). In such instances the power of the privileged educator provides a legitimate tool for the dismal of the learner (Patin et al., 2021, 1311). The latter is not just a dismissal of what the learner-as-object is saying but also a dismissal of who is saying it and the objects' imposed invisibility (Patin et al., 2021, 1311). The learner's ontological expulsion as a being-in-the-classroom is a predicate of the learner's collective ontological expulsion as a human being-in-the-world. A caveat must be inserted at this point, to clarify that teachers as marginalized *Others* are also objects. As South African and Africans teachers we are also excluded as marginalized *Others*; we can thus only hold a pseudo privilege to enable us to be complicit in epistemicide.

Patin et al.'s distinction between participatory and testimonial injustice is a shortcoming in what is actually a very valuable explication of epistemicide:

This experience diverges from testimonial injustice as it does not question one's testimony, but rather one's existence in a particular space. Participatory injustice is a matter of who belongs. (Patin et al., 2021, 1311)

Participatory injustice is inflicted when the testimonies of historically marginalized *Others* are dismissed as incredulous (Patin et al., 2021, 1308). For me the credulity of the testimony is imbricated in the ontological-being-of-the-testifier and the extent to which that being is considered being-in-the-word or excluded from it. A testimony cannot and does not stand alone and disengaged from the testifier.

Testimonial, hermeneutic and participatory injustices are enabled by the recognition that the colonized *Other* is not human:

> A uniform rationale for European settlements in Kenya, Zimbabwe, and South Africa was that the land was empty of human beings. (Wa Thiong'o, 2009, 22)

Curricular injustice (Patin et al., 2021, 1311) is the extent to which the curriculum neutralizes its ideological and dehumanizing intentions of *othering*:

> By not acknowledging the form a curriculum takes, it may come across to students and others in academia that a curriculum developed as the result of 'natural' progression of knowledge building over time – knowledge building that, in Western societies, has to fall within certain parameters to 'count'.

Critically implicit in these epistemicides are the politics of inclusion and exclusion which permeates the curriculum, so much so that even children who are marked present in these classrooms are absent in that classroom/school. Black learners and teachers in South Africa were and continue to be historically excluded from such classrooms in the myriad and fundamental ways that the curriculum excludes.

Curriculum epistemicide inflicts hermeneutic, participatory and testimonial injustices through- and -in- learning spaces.

Ngugi's (Wa Thiong'o, 2009, 27) metaphor of education as a factory denotes the subterfuge of curriculum epistemicide in Africa and beyond:

> products of colonial educational factories may come to see the illusionary promises of the Europhone memory as the beginning of their history – a process that of course means the loss of their own history.

Epistemicide has been inflicted through a racist legacy which is validated through the objectivity of science (Hountondji, 2000, 5). Hountondji explains how scholars such as Levy Bruhl were able to generate theories that justified this racism:

> an accumulation of real facts can be arranged, organised and interpreted in such a way that they serve as a means to reinforce sheer prejudice. (Hountondji, 2000, 5)

Deficit conceptions of African epistemes and ontologies made by early twentieth-century European scholars such as Levy Bruhl were based on their subjective prejudices and biases (Masolo, 1994, 138–9).

Such epistemicides form the foundations of the disciples, which curricula and curriculum theories disseminate and reinforce.

In so doing the curriculum is instrumental in normalizing what is otherwise unjust and brutal and in so doing enables the anesthetization of being *othered* not just as not-being-in this world but also *not-being at all*. It is this colonial imposed *identity-of-and-in-absence and worthlessness* that ICT rages against and which it urges us to dismember and disrupt (Paraskeva, 2018, 129).

According to Paraskeva (2021, 9), 'ICT is thus a way to challenge curriculum epistemicides.' To see epistemicide as distinctly epistemological would be criminal. Knowing and ways of knowing are in an inextricable nexus of being-in-this-world or not-being-in-this-world. To kill one is to kill the *Other*. Epistemicide and ontology are so inextricable that epistemicide is nothing less than a 'colonial technology of dismemberment' (Ndlovu-Gatsheni, 2018, 18).

Epistemology is imbricated in ontology which is why Santos (2014, 149) qualifies his definition of epistemicide to include the effacement of the marginalized *Other* as a being-in-this-world:

death of the knowledge of the subordinated culture, hence the death of the social groups that possessed it.

Through a colonial hegemony the Eurocentric nature of the curriculum canon has become normalized and indisputable.

So much so, that even when attempts are made to disrupt this hegemony, this disruption is ineffectual because the change imperatives are conceptualized and orchestrated within a limiting colonial paradigm.

Paraskeva reflects on such attempts at counter-hegemonic disruptions in curricula:

For example, among other issues, I actually was able to identify the same laudable ideological frustrations that I was facing, related with the same theoretical distress and agonies within specific counter-dominant positions and battles. I was disturbed, not only with their incapability of – at least – interrupting a eugenic epistemological platform, but also with the so-called 'sepoys of coloniality'. (Paraskeva, 2017a, 1–2)

Such counter-hegemonic attempts that Paraskeva laments are circumscribed by a paradigm whose discursive underpinnings have been deliberately constructed to exclude the *Other*. It is within such a discursive framework that the very epistemological and ontological injustices that counter-hegemonic forces are trying to rupture are deliberately imbricated.

In his rejection of the epistemological and ontological *othering* implicit in the curriculum canon, Paraskeva outrightly rejects not only the curriculum canon but also any form of canonization (2020a; 2020b, 40). ICT enables a 'plane(s) of projection' (Hoppers, 2017, 3) to both, inter alia, recognize and reject the historical brutalizing, invisibility and silencing of the Global South (Paraskeva, 2020, 40). In doing ICT is thus premised upon three critical imperatives: the *ontological recognition of the Global South*; *recognition and enactment of the relational impetus of the Global South*; and the *recognition of and engagement with epistemologies from the South* (Paraskeva, 2020, 40). However, none of these can be enacted if the Global South is not allowed to reappropriate our identities and to thus reject historically constructed, disparate identities that have been imposed on us (Paraskeva, 2020, 40).

It is this ontological-epistemological nexus (Pillay, 2016, 534), its preservation and reinforcement and its concomitant rejection and dissolution, that lies at the heart of ICT's critiques of current counter-hegemonic attempts to engage in curriculum change. Unless we reject these historically constructed identities as *othered* non-beings and redefine ourselves, our change efforts will continue to be immutable. The *desire* to revolt and reject is not enough; we need to *become curriculum vigilantes*.

It is because of the implicit and explicit prejudices and false constructions of the African identity that is imbricated in Western epistemes that Hountondji (2000, 8) argues for alternative ways of understanding. Colonial epistemic and ontological constructions have enabled the violent oppression, repression and *othering* of, inter alia, the African identity and experiences.

Referring to the African gnosis Mudimbe foregrounds this proposition when he argues that African epistemologies have been analysed within a Western epistemological structure (Mudimbe, 1985, 150). He refers to this default disposition as a silent dependence on a Western episteme (Mudimbe, 1985, 150). His description of the exclusive structure of this epistemic blockade is what counter-hegemonic movements need to consider when considering the decolonization of the curriculum. Any attempt at change within such Eurocentric epistemic blockades will be counterproductive in the African context, if we rely on

> theories and methods whose constraints, rules, and systems of operation suppose a non – African epistemological locus. (Mudimbe, 1985, 150)

These exclusive epistemological and ontological blockades and injustices pervade and diffuse the curriculum canon as we know it. Colonial epistemes are logically structured on an exclusive European epistemology and ontology in which *othered* identities and ways of knowing are denied access and are rendered invisible.

Counter-dominant positions and agencies thus find themselves floundering in a void because alternate epistemologies and ontologies cannot be accommodated in a paradigm that has been constructed to exclude and deny access to these participants. The *Other* cannot find recognition and place within this conceptual cage.

Santos describes this conceptual cage as 'abyssal thinking':

> It consists of a system of visible and invisible distinctions, the invisible ones being the foundation of the visible ones. The invisible distinctions are established through radical lines that divide social reality into two realms, the realm of 'this side of the line' and the realm of 'the other side of the line'. The division is such that 'the other side of the line' vanishes as reality, becomes nonexistent, and is indeed produced as nonexistent. Nonexistent means not existing in any relevant or comprehensible way of being.

> Whatever is produced as nonexistent is radically excluded because it lies beyond the realm of what the accepted conception of inclusion considers to be its other. What most fundamentally characterizes abyssal thinking is thus the impossibility

of the co-presence of the two sides of the line. To the extent that it prevails, this side of the line only prevails by exhausting the field of relevant reality. Beyond it, there is only nonexistence, invisibility, non-dialectical absence. (Cited in Paraskeva, 2017b, 11; 2007, 45–6)

ICT rejects abyssal thinking and is premised on non-abyssal thinking, but non-abyssal thinking is only possible in a different zone (Paraskeva, 2017b, 27, 11). In so doing ICT invokes Mignolo's *'un paradigma otro'* (Paraskeva, 2017b, 27). *Un paradigma otro* is not just an alternate paradigm working within the confines of coloniality (Escobar, 2007, 179); it runs on a completely different plane of projection and in so doing enables possibilities-of-being and impossibilities-of-not being within alternate logics. ICT is thus at the very forefront a contradiction; it revels in **contradiction** as a being-I-want-to-be. In this way it is a Loaf Theory, in that it forces us to 'think the unthinkable' (Paraskeva, 2020b, 36) and in so doing forces us to dismantle colonial epistemologies, ontologies and axiologies. ICT advocates for Mignolo's rejection of the 'totalitarian notion of Totality' which, Mignolo argues, 'negates, exclude, occlude the difference and the possibilities of other totalities' (Mignolo, 2007, 451). As an alternate space and way of knowing and being ICT is out of necessity always in a state of disequilibrium, it cannot be closed because then it would simply be a replacement of a rigid canon. It is predicated on disequilibrium yet promises solace (Paraskeva, 2020, 42). As a Theory of Disquiet (Paraskeva, 2020, 35) ICT recognizes and validates the anxiety-provoking nature of curriculum epistemicide and decolonization. This state of instability is a requisite provocation for dismantling rigidly imposed ways of being and non-being in the curriculum. ICT is a people's theory (Paraskeva, 2021, 10; Paraskeva, 2020, 43); it rehumanizes the curriculum struggle and the reappropriate of the humanity of the *othered*. ICT is a Theory of Solidarity and Citizenship which declares the death of the colonial citizen. The reappropriation of the colonial object into a subjective-being-in-the-world is premised on the destruction of the *other-as-object-who-is-not-in-this-world* (Paraskeva, 2021, 10). ICT invokes conflict as a necessary way of being in a world that is ordered by colonial brutality (Paraskeva, 2021, 10). As a Theory of Change ICT invokes conflict but also advocates co-presence (Paraskeva, 2021, 49). In advocating co-presence ICT destabilizes the Master-Slave dialectic of Modernity. It traverses boundaries and forces us to think the unthinkable (Paraskeva, 2021, 9).

Through contradiction ICT invites and enables other thought structures, languages, ways of being and thinking which are premised on non-binary, self-identifying laws of colonial logic and structure.

It enables planes projections for a myriad of possibilities and impossibilities as it engages around an ecology of epistemologies (Paraskeva, 2020, 42). In so doing it enables the silenced to speak and frozen and effaced knowledges to be re-energized. It does this by dismantling the epistemological and ontological tools of coloniality because such reawakenings and reappropriations are systemically impossible within the colonial logic of automatic expulsion of the *Other*.

The ICT provides a fuzzification of the rigidity of colonial logic as it is enabled through the curriculum and its many iterations. Its fuzzy logic disarms the Modernist logic of binary exclusions and certainty and enables new way of being-in-the-world-with-*others*-who-are-human-like-me.

ICT as a plane of new projections of being-in-this-world is an 'ethical lake' (Paraskeva, 2020, 38). In doing it brings together the ontological, epistemological and the ethical dimensions of being-in this-world with people who recognize and value each other. ICT provides new planes of possibilities for decolonization in the curriculum. It prepares us for new ways of being and thus new ways of doing.

ICT's most significant contribution to the curriculum war in general and decolonization specifically is that 'it is above all, the language for/of doing' (Paraskeva, 2020b, 37).

References

Adora Hoppers, C. (2009), 'Engaging Critically with Tradition, Culture, and Patriarchy Through Lifelong Learning: What Would Julius Nyerere Say? 6th Julius Nyerere Annual Lecture on Lifelong Learning', University of the Western Cape. https://repository.uwc.ac.za/xmlui/bitstream/handle/10566/1569/NYERERELECTURE2009%206th%20lecture%20Odora%20Hopper's%20Paper.pdf;sequence=1 (accessed August 25, 2022).

Escobar, A. (2007), 'Worlds and Knowledges Otherwise', *Cultural Studies*, 21 (2–3): 179–210. http://doi.org/10.1080/09502380601162506 https://www.tandfonline.com/doi/abs/10.1080/09502380601162506 (accessed June 23, 2022).

Fomunyam, K. G. (2022), 'The Itinerant Curriculum as an Alternative Pathway for Responsiveness in African Higher Education in the Era of the Fourth Industrial Revolution', *African Journal of Inter Multidisciplinary Studies*, 4: 141–54. https://www.researchgate.net/publication/362304267_The_Itinerant_Curriculum_as_an_Alternative_Pathway_for_Responsiveness_in_African_Higher_Education_in_the_Era_of_the_Fourth_Industrial_Revolution (accessed October 7, 2022).

hooks, b. (1994), *Teaching to Transgress: Education as the Practice of Freedom*, New York: Routledge.

Hountondji, P. (2000), 'Traditions, Hindrance or Inspiration?' *Quest*, XIV (1–2): 5–11. https://www.quest-journal.net/Quest_2000_PDF_articles/Quest_14_hountondji.pdf (accessed August 3, 2022).

J., G. (2011), 'Introduction to Sections Source', *Counterpoints*, 379: 15. https://www.jstor.org/stable/42980881

Janson, E. and C. M. Silva (2017), 'Itinerant Curriculum Theory: Navigating the Waters of Power, Identity, and Praxis', *Journal of the American Association for the Advancement of Curriculum Studies*, 12 (1 Summer). https://www.google.co.za/url?esrc=s&q=&rct=j&sa=U&url=https://www.semanticscholar.org/paper/Itinerant-Curriculum-Theory%253A-Navigating-the-Waters-Janson-Silva/8efc5e34871c774c144fd8c28ff8a792fba5e946&ved=2ahUKEwjxuM2wg4z4AhXam5UCHWf5DD0QFnoECAgQAg&usg=AOvVaw2-RCHfVYjfaat1fZwAT0fb (accessed November 16, 2021).

Masenya, M. J. (2021), 'Toward a Relevant De-colonized Curriculum in South Africa: Suggestions for a Way Forward', *SAGE Open*, 11 (4). https://doi.org/10.1177/21582440211052559 (accessed September 28, 2022).

Masolo, D. A. (1994), *African Philosophy in Search of Identity*, Bloomington: Indiana University Press.
Mignolo, W. G. (2007), 'Delinking the Rhetoric of Modernity, the Logic of Coloniality and the Grammar of Decoloniality', *Cultural Studies*, 21 (2–3): 449–514. https://doi.org/10.1080/09502380601162647 (accessed July 20, 2022).
Mpofu, B. and S. Ndlovu-Gatsheni (2020), 'Introduction: The Dynamics of Changing Higher Education in the Global South', in B. Mpofu and S. Ndlovu-Gatsheni (eds), *The Dynamics of Changing Higher Education in the Global South*, 1–12, Cambridge Scholars. https://www.cambridgescholars.com/resources/pdfs/978-1-5275-5514-3-sample.pdf (accessed August 1, 2022).
Mudimbe, V. (1985), 'African Gnosis Philosophy and the Order of Knowledge: An Introduction', *African Studies Review*, 28 (2/3): 149–233. Cambridge University Press Stable. http://www.newtunings.com/miriam/docs/Ethnophilosphy/AfricanGnosis_Ethnophilosphy_524605.pdf (accessed August 1, 2022).
Ndlovu-Gatsheni, S. J. (2018), *Epistemic Freedom in Africa: Deprovincialization and Decolonization*, London: Routledge. https://openresearchlibrary.org/ext/api/media/1a2e5e3f-ca25-44df-a48c-9f69c13fc10e/assets/external_content.pdf (accessed Ocober 3, 2022).
Ndlovu-Gatsheni, S. J. and Zondi, S. (2016), *Decolonizing the University, Knowledge Systems and Disciplines in Africa*, Durham: Carolina Academic Press.
Odora Hoppers, C. (2017), 'Transformation and Change in Knowledge Generation Paradigms in the African and Global Contexts: Implications for Education Research in the 21st Century', *Educational Research for Social Change*, 6 (1): 1–11. http://doi.org/10.17159/2221-4070/2017/v6i1a1 (accessed September 8, 2022).
Paraskeva, J. M. (2011), *Conflicts in Curriculum Theory: Challenging Hegemonic Epistemologies*, New York: Palgrave. (1st edition).
Paraskeva, J. M. (2017a), 'Against the Epistemicide: Itinerant Curriculum Theory and the Reiteration of an Epistemology of Liberation in Uljens', in M. Ylimaki (eds), *Bridging Educational Leadership, Curriculum Theory and Didaktik: Non-Affirmative Theory of Education*, Vol. 5, Spinger Open. https://link.springer.com/content/pdf/10.1007/978-3-319-58650-2.pdf (accessed August 1, 2022).
Paraskeva, J. M. (2017b), 'Itinerant Curriculum Theory Revisited on a Non-Theoricide Towards the Canonicide: Addressing the "Curriculum Involution"', *Journal for the American Association for the Advancement of Curriculum Studies*, 12: 1–43. https://www.researchgate.net/publication/319325459_ITINERANT_CURRICULUM_THEORY_REVISITED_ON_A_NONTHEORICIDE_TOWARDS_THE_CANONICIDE_ADDRESSING_THE_%27CURRICULUM_INVOLUTION%27 (accessed June 8, 2022).
Paraskeva, J. M. (2018), 'Against the Scandal: Itinerant Curriculum Theory as Subaltern Momentum', *Qualitative Research Journal*, 18 (2): 128–43. https://www.google.co.za/url?esrc=s&q=&rct=j&sa=U&url=https://www.academia.edu/36194194/Against_the_Scandal_Itinerant_Curriculum_Theory_as_Subaltern&ved=2ahUKEwjAmofqmIz4AhVwupUCHXz-A6EQFnoECAgQAg&usg=AOvVaw0hz9x7Ci5uIgAIAbIP8N-E (accessed February 1, 2022).
Paraskeva, J. M. (2020a), 'Justice Against the Epistemicide. Itinerant Curriculum Theory and the Struggle to Decanonize Curriculum Studies', https://www.researchgate.net/publication/345182034_Justice_Against_the_Epistemicide_Itinerant_Curriculum_Theory_and_the_Struggle_to_Decanonize_Curriculum_Studies (accessed November 22, 2021).

Paraskeva, J. M. (2020b), 'Itinerant Curriculum Theory: An Epistemological Declaration of Independence', *Revista Qurriculum*, 33: 31–47. https://riull.ull.es/xmlui/bitstream/handle/915/19618/Q_33_%282020%29_03.pdf?sequence=1&isAllowed=y (accessed November 22, 2021).

Paraskeva, J. M. (2021), 'Challenging Epistemicides: Toward an Itinerant Curriculum Theory', https://www.researchgate.net/publication/355612131_Challenging_Epistemicides_Toward_an_Itinerant_Curriculum_Theory (accessed October 1, 2022).

Paraskeva, J. M. (2022a), 'The Generation of the Utopia: Itinerant Curriculum Theory Towards a "Futurable Future"', *Discourse: Studies In The Cultural Politics of Education*: 1–20. https://doi.org/10.1080/01596306.2022.2030594.

Paraskeva, J. M. (2022b), *Conflitcs in Curriculum Theory*. New York: Palgrave (2nd edition).

Patin, B., M. Sebastian, J. Yeon, D. Bertolini and A. Grimm (2021), 'Interrupting Epistemicide: A Practical Framework for Naming, Identifying, and Ending Epistemic Injustice in the Information Professions', *Journal for the Association for Information Science and Technology*, 72: 1306–18. http://wileyonlinelibrary.com/journal/asi (accessed July 1, 2022).

Pillay, S. K. (2014), 'Analysing Policy Contexts as a Political Strategy', *Policy Futures in Education*, 12 (5): 707–17.

Pillay, S. K. (2016), 'Curriculum as Discourse: From Africa to South Africa and Back', in J. M. Paraskeva and S. R. Steinberg (eds), *Curriculum: Decanonizing the Field*, 527–45, New York: Peter Lang.

Santos, B. S. (2004), A Critique of Lazy Reason: Against the Waste of Experience. In *The Modern World-System in the Longue Durée*, Boulder: Paradigm Publishers: 157–197.

Santos, B. S. (2014), *Epistemologies of the South Justice against Epistemicide*, Paradigm Publishers. USA.

Süssekind, M. L. (2017), 'Against Epistemological Fascism: The (Self) Critique of the Criticals - A Reading of Paraskeva's Itinerant Curriculum Theory', *Journal of the American Association for the Advancement of Curriculum Studies*, 12 (1): 1–18. https://ojs.library.ubc.ca/index.php/jaaacs/article/view/189707 (accessed June 1, 2022).

Shahjahan, R. A., A. L. Estera, K. Surla and K. T. Edwards (2022), 'Decolonizing Curriculum and Pedagogy: A Comparative Review Across Disciplines and Global Higher Education Contexts', *Review of Educational Research*, 92 (1): 73–113. https://www.google.co.za/url?esrc=s&q=&rct=j&sa=U&url=https://journals.sagepub.com/doi/abs/10.3102/00346543211042423&ved=2ahUKEwi3vtblxc34AhVIg5UCHa2PAo0QFnoECAAQAg&usg=AOvVaw0NgDOuJ8_sLm_gOAgFKGKE (accessed June 20, 2022).

Wa Thiong'o, N. (2009), *Something Torn and New: An African Renaissance*, New York: Basic Civitas Books.

Waziyatawain. (2012), 'The Paradox of Indigenous Resurgence at the End of Empire', *Decolonization: Indigeneity, Education & Society*, 1 (1): 68–85 https://jps.library.utoronto.ca/index.php/des/article/download/18629/15553/43257 (accessed July 1, 2022).

Decolonizing Thai-Centric Curriculum Is Yet Enough?

Transgressing Beyond 'Currere' to Itinerant Curriculum Theory

Omsin Jatuporn

A just beginning of a Thai curriculum river

Based on the analysis of epistemological and methodological frameworks for educational inquiry, in general, and curriculum studies, particularly, those frameworks used in educational research have various features which resemble to the field of education in other countries, especially North America, Western Europe and Australia and other countries in the Global North (Jatuporn, 2018). However, I found that most of research works emphasize on instructional research as a main framework. This remark appears in the search by information queries system of Thai digital library regarding curriculum and instructional research during 1990 – 2015 of universities that offer programme and instruction in the field of curriculum and instruction (hereafter C&I) in graduate levels. In other words, by analysing MA thesis's topic in C&I in depth back to before 1997 or studying contemporary trends during around not over ten years ago, the results indicate that research works in C&I principally conducted by graduate students are development of lesson plans, and secondary are development of drill practices and instructional materials, learning activities, learning management skills and other 'learnification of education' skills (Biesta, 2005), which are emphasized in national curriculum, comparison of effective learning results from varied instructional methods and curriculum development, respectively. Based on these recent observations, almost all research works in the field of education, broadly defined, in Thailand can be categorized under the academic field of C&I.

While thesis's topic that PhD students in C&I from large public research universities principally conduct is the development of instructional models and curriculum development models. It can be seen that research in C&I has various features, but most conventional research works are still regarding how to develop curriculum or instructional and learning management efficiently in order to apply the so-called 'curriculum innovation' and 'instructional and learning innovation' to develop students appropriately according to varied context of educational provision by employing research method called research and development (R&D).

Under this condition, many aspects of curriculum studies have been left under theorizing in C&I such as curriculum theory and history, sociocultural and philosophical foundations of curriculum and multicultural and progressive legacies in curriculum and education. In other words, the educational discourses that go far beyond the ideology of neutrality will be left under theorizing and for the most parts of them will be depoliticized and neutralized by curriculum specialists and policy elites for (re)production of these recontextualized knowledge into school and teacher education institutions (Hung, 2016). In addition, one of the explicit goals in the establishment of C&I programme is to construct curriculum specialists, educational supervisors and instructional experts who have expertise in developing, implementing, instructing and evaluating curriculum. Underlying this tradition, I argue that the dominant educational discourse in Thailand is still under the virus of 'despotic epistemology' implicated in various forms of positivist-functionalist approach and technical-instrumental rationality especially in curriculum studies (Paraskeva, 2017). I am to place it under the proposal of critical decolonial education scholar João M. Paraskeva (2018). The essence of Paraskeva's broad perspectives requires us as curriculum scholar, teacher educator and educationalist to have a radical thought of our field in the age of neoliberal surveillance and governmentality. I also employ the notion of the critical curriculum river to sensing, positioning and conceptualizing the historic, present and future moments towards those scenarios that illustrate both challenges facing the contemporary status of curriculum studies and teacher education, in particular, and education, in general, and the competing epistemological and methodological frameworks implicit in the responses to these challenges (Miles and Nayak, 2020).

I question the contemporary status of curriculum studies in Thailand since the feeling of unknowing and alienation in a DuBoisian 'peculiar sensation' has been the impetus for this inquiry (Brown and Au, 2014). Why R&D approach becomes the dominant epistemological and methodological framework in curriculum studies? Who or what group of people are instrumental in constructing R&D integrated with traditional curriculum development until they become hegemonic authorities in the field? And why do Thai curricularists internalize traditional curriculum development embedded in *Thai-centric epistemology* situated only in Thailand and not actively resist, challenge and criticize against this hegemonic epistemicide embedded in the field in order to decolonizing curriculum in light of *non-Thai-centric epistemology* and diverse epistemologies that exist in many parts of the world (Lin, 2012)?

Overall, the traditional curriculum development discourse has been systematically transformed into the dominant discourse, as it arises from the systems and reproduction processes constructing unique identity and specific signified meaning, reproducing the existence of legitimate discourse and becoming institutionalized in the field. The dominant discourse has gained its absolute power meanwhile marginalizes other possible narratives from arising (Foucault, 1973). Thus, the historicity of Thai curriculum history is traditional curriculum development and this hegemonic epistemicide has become the foundation of Thai curriculum studies as well as for epistemological and methodological inquiry in education for at least five decades. In other words, this tradition had been systematically and institutionally constructed since its initial establishment of the field.

Hegemonic epistemicide in Thai curriculum studies and teacher education

During the late twentieth century, there were varied curriculum and education scholars defining the word 'curriculum' based on a variety of orientations. There were more than 1,100 English-language textbooks written about curriculum, and each book defined the meaning of the word 'curriculum' differently according to the philosophical, ideological, political and historical standpoints they belonged to (Cuban, 1992). All these texts provided the meaning of curriculum from the English which had derived from the Latin as 'currere' which means running course. Later on, this word has become curriculum metaphor in education as 'learning experience' (Pinar, 1975).

In the late 1980s and onwards, textbooks on curriculum that had been used in core teaching and teacher preparation curriculum in most large public teacher education institutions in Thailand were a translation of seminal texts on the traditional curriculum development by prominent American curriculum scholars and educators who had influential impacts for the field of the US curriculum studies. Curriculum textbooks had been translated and rearticulated into Thai language and, interestingly, all these textbooks had the same title as 'curriculum development' or *Karn-Pad-Ta-Na-Lak-Sood* in Thai. In the 1990s, many teacher education institutions could produce their own texts. This scenario emerged from the process of recontextualizing curriculum development theories from the major US textbooks on curriculum development models (Thongthew, 2008). Thus, this became the impetus for curriculum studies for both teacher preparation and MA and PhD in C&I as well as another specialized fields in education such as educational evaluation and measurement, educational administration and educational technology.

However, the period of time since 2000 onwards, I found that textbooks and documents including articles published in Thai about C&I, as those documents described the definition of curriculum not only as education plans or educative experiences learners receiving through curriculum. Underlying this scenario, another conceptions of curriculum appear to have significant spaces in the scholarly texts on curriculum. This is because emerging curriculum scholars and educators have translated some parts of English textbooks written by the US scholars into Thai and have articulated their ideas for designing innovative curriculum and instructional research.

The conceptions of curriculum include the followings: curriculum as personal, sociocultural and political narratives, curriculum as cultural politics, curriculum as social practices, curriculum as deliberation, curriculum as gendered and sexuality texts, curriculum as lived experiences (Jatuporn, 2018). The aforementioned conceptions of curriculum are significant to curriculum studies in Thailand as the US and Western curriculum discourse has shifted from curriculum development to curriculum understanding. The essence of curriculum understanding implicated in various texts such as philosophical, historical, political, aesthetical, phenomenon and autobiography (Pinar et al., 1995). This is consistent with the reconceptualist curriculum studies proposed by Pinar in order to reconceptualize the field of curriculum studies and education generally.

Seen this way, traditional curriculum development resides under a positivist and functionalist approach which focuses on seeking objective scientific knowledge and the highest truth by applying scientifically based principles as an important instrument in the process of seeking true knowledge without any discrepancies. Curriculum development is therefore comparable to manufacturing process in the industrial sector, which is a step-by-step process that begins with determining curriculum objectives, then defining content structure, and methods of transmitting content to methods of evaluating learning outcomes expected to conform to the determined objectives. Moreover, curriculum can be considered fragmentedly segregated as main steps including process of planning and design, implementation and evaluation, respectively. Because this view expected the learning outcomes to be achieved as determined objectives (Ornstein and Hunkins, 2008), curriculum discourse that is consistent with this framework is the traditional curriculum development such as the Tyler's rationale. The curriculum development begins with setting the objectives and assessing how many the outcomes of the curriculum achieves the determined objectives in the last. The traditional curriculum development thus is a linear process with logical sequence of steps and has strengths which enable curriculum specialists to implement curriculum systematically.

It is likely that the state of Thai curriculum studies and the dominant curriculum discourse is significantly related to the contemporary character of the mainstream educational reform discourse (Jatuporn, 2022). Curriculum as a part of Thai educational reform has been a playing field for social actors who were instrumental for educational changes in the age of educational reform in B.E. 1999. The social actors, particularly curriculum specialists and policy elites, had been taken curriculum and educational reform issues into the complicated conversation both in public and private spheres of educators. This scenario was assembled as a result of the announcement of basic education curriculum B.E. 2001 as standard-based national core curriculum which composed of learning standards as a direction for determining content, skill, process, learning activity and evaluation in order to develop students to be knowledgeable and able to reach specified standards.

Under the context of educational reform fuelled by both the forces of globalization and Thailand's socio-economic, industrial and technological growth pushing tremendous demands for competent knowledge workers and skilled labourers, this scenario has significantly demonstrated how a neoliberal and neoconservative rationality that focuses on economic impacts could germinate curriculum and substantially internalized and finally established. This has resulted in neoliberal and neoconservative platforms for 'curriculum involution' (Paraskeva, 2017) such as standard-based curriculum in 2000s and competency-based curriculum as impetus for educational reform in B.E. 2020.

The process by which a neoliberal and neoconservative curriculum discourse has been justified and became the dominant narrative in curriculum studies, teacher education and educational studies as well as a broad arena of Thai higher education could be investigated from Thailand's Education Act 1999 (revised edition 2002) and contemporary educational policies and reform discourses that constitute principles and approaches for educational provision to uplift Thailand to be a knowledge-based industrialized society (Poupansawat, 2006; Boossabong, 2018). So that all Thais will have equal opportunities in access to educational provision and in developing oneself as lifelong learners which is a condition for achieving desired goals of the country as driven by knowledge-based economy. This dominant discourse is congruent with socio-economic neoliberal reform policies pushed forward by neoconservative public-private think-tanks and educational technocrats through Thailand's national development plan as well as institutionalized reforms for both public and private sectors in general (Nozaki, Openshaw and Luke, 2005). This is demonstrated in curriculum and educational reform discourse that includes, for example, Thailand's Qualifications Framework (TQF) and curriculum and instructional innovations such as competency-based and outcome-based curriculum, backward design and flipped classroom.

In light of the provision of basic education, the Office of Basic Education Commission (OBEC) is a principal organization responsible for standard-based educational administration through education policies and curriculum standards. As such, the national curriculum framework which currently appears as the Basic Education Core Curriculum B.E. 2008 was institutionally framed by OBEC and officially approved by curriculum specialists and policy elites appointed by the Ministry of Education. Thus, OBEC has produced academic documents, curriculum manuals and teachers' guidelines that explain the importance of backward design approach by focusing on technical curriculum development and teaching units which start from summative evaluation to initial learning activities, including principles of curriculum design and teaching units starting with determination of learning objectives, organizing learning experiences in accordance with the objectives and, then, specifying methods of measurement and evaluation. The dominant characteristic of backward design, as supported by curriculum specialists, is to provide the opportunity for teachers to conceptualize their role as curriculum designer rather than just viewing themselves as teacher-technician and using evaluation as a main framework for curriculum development and classroom instruction.

In terms of schooling curriculum, traditional curriculum development has been championed by technocratic curriculum specialists. Not only this happens in school curriculum discourse but also unfolds its normative discourse at the level of university-based higher education institutions. Major public teacher education institutions throughout Thailand have been formally reproduced the traditional curriculum development discourse through academic research, pre-service preparations, in-service and continuous professional training for teachers to have knowledge, skill and disposition in curriculum development and instructional design. All these teacher education institutions, juxtaposed with technocratic curriculum specialists and policy elites from the OBEC and its governmentality, have systematically instrumentalized both school curriculum discourse and university-based curriculum studies as an academic field under the traditional curriculum development.

Given this context, the status of Thai curriculum studies is consistent with neoliberal and neoconservative curriculum and educational reform discourse. The dominant curriculum discourse is institutionally constituted and dominated by traditional curriculum development and has not yet deliberated from varied platforms of technical/functionalist/positivist embedded curriculum thinking as implicated in the neo-Tylerian's curriculum approach. However, those documents provided by OBEC never explicitly have any references to historical, political, philosophical and sociocultural foundations of technical-scientific approach and traditional curriculum development. In essence, the traditional curriculum development discourse is both material and epistemological construction of curriculum studies as a scholarly field in education and an ongoing curriculum and educational reform project in the present.

While the US curriculum studies had institutionally established as a field since the early twentieth century – arguably even less so since the late nineteenth century – Thai curriculum studies had secured its own positionality in teacher education since 1980s or even less for few years. While the construction project in our field is yet incomplete, Thai curriculum studies had continuously encountered with the global and international discourse in education at the turn of the twenty-first century. As such, Thai academics and policy elites have warmly welcomed, rather than resisted, the Western modern Eurocentric epistemicide as a new era of the twenty-first-century reform discourse in curriculum, teacher education, educational policies as well as pedagogical approaches (Lao, 2019).

As a result of push and pull by the global/international educational reform discourse and socio-economic advancement in Thailand after recovering from the Asian economic crisis in the dawn of the twentieth century, Thailand has systematically mobilized the twenty-first-century reform rhetoric to revitalize public awareness in terms of education as a mechanism for transforming socio-economic, political, scientific and technological advancement of the nation, from the status of developing to developed nation in South East Asia and the Pacific region. Given this context, data collected from documents launched by the government suggest that the twenty-first-century reform rhetoric has formally appeared in Thai curriculum and educational reform discourse since 2005 or even less so for few years – wherewith the Thai government stipulated a subsequent phase of educational reform or known as educational reform in the second decade (2008–17). The dominant feature of the recent reform discourse was to revise previous official curriculum to be a new official Basic Education Core Curriculum B.E. 2008 to comply with the direction of educational reform discourse of the Global North and established industrialized nations in Asia-Pacific regions such as South Korea, Hong Kong, Japan and Singapore. As a result of this new multiplicity of languages and rhetoric of educational reform in curriculum studies, teacher education and pedagogical practices had been assimilated into Thai curriculum and educational reform discourse such as standard-based learning unit, backward design, active learning, teach less learn more, professional learning community (PLC), school as learning community, flipped classroom, coaching and mentoring, lesson study and so on. The aforementioned terms implicit in both a neoliberal and neoconservative discourse in education that Thai government had played fewer roles and emphasized devolution of power and decentralization to all involved segments for educational provision (Rivera, 2003). Thus, neo-Tylerian's curriculum approach emphasizing the development of learners with knowledge, skills and abilities recognized as necessary and effective enough to create innovative and effective productivity under the rationality of neoliberalism and neoconservative in the twenty-first century becomes a new form of 'curriculum involution' embedded in Thai-centric epistemology.

However, it can be argued that if Thai curriculum discourse has recently expressed the recognition of multiple conceptions of curriculum rather than curriculum as educational plan, subject matter, product and expected learning outcomes; why the status of knowledge and the dominant epistemological and methodological inquiries in curriculum studies are still being dominated by the 'despotic epistemology' implicated in various forms of positivist-functionalist approach and technical-instrumental rationality (Paraskeva, 2017)? This impetus has become my own struggling to find thoughtful explanation ever since the beginning of doctoral journey in curriculum studies in Thailand. I begin my inquiry by extensively reading MA and PhD theses' topics and search for digital databases using keywords such as curriculum, instruction, pedagogy, teaching and learning; data collected suggest that there were research works beginning with the titles 'curriculum development', 'development of teaching model' and 'development of teaching and learning model' in relatively affluent numbers. Based on these notices, I have been reinvoked to problematize why MA and PhD theses focusing on curriculum posit merely the R&D as a conceptual framework based on neo-Tylerian's curriculum approach? What are the relationships between the political economy of knowledge production within curriculum studies of the Global North such as the United States and Canada and the global-local mediated and recontextualized process influencing knowledge production as well as a result of de-cold war geo-politics and global cultural imperialism in Thailand? Who are the dominant actors exercising hegemonic governmentality to establish the traditional curriculum development in historic, present and future moments? Why are they not struggling to transcend beyond the hegemonic discourse to the pluralities of epistemological knowledge?

I begin to realize that reconceptualizing curriculum discourse which I have discussed so far is not something I personally assume without academic evidence. In the field of the US curriculum studies, there have been movements and efforts of scholars both within and outside the field trying to transform the traditional curriculum development discourse to the real meaning of curriculum. In light of this, Pinar (1975) suggested that the word 'curriculum' has a derivation from Latin version of '*currere*' which should be translated into verb – the running of the race. Therefore, curriculum means a journey of individual to find authentic own's self by interpreting and crafting new meanings in one's life, by the process of creating and reflecting ideas from lived history and autobiography. The ultimate goal of a curriculum is to cultivate students to deeply understand themselves and deliberating themselves from limitations caused by ideologies, cultures, beliefs and world views and helping them to see another opportunities and possibilities for themselves, others and the world.

In this case and other international curriculum studies scholarship suggest that the curriculum studies and their curriculum discourses in varied nation states throughout the world is still under the traditional curriculum development, corresponding with Tyler's rationale and technical-scientific management in education as principal framework for approaching curriculum in all levels of education (Zhao, Popkewitz and Autio, 2022). The traditional curriculum development has been formally institutionalized and finally becomes the most powerful hegemonic epistemicide in curriculum studies, particularly, and, generally, in the field of education, since its initial establishment to the present. Paraskeva (2011) argued that Tyler's rationale for curriculum development and continuing legacies had tremendous influences upon the contemporary field and his approach became the dominant discourse and has its lethal hegemonic consequences in curriculum studies. Paraskeva suggested that Tyler was championed over other curriculum discourses proposed by curriculum scholars during the twentieth century by integration of theories and practices in curriculum studies together, both the dominant and other less accepted and well-established approaches. It was at this juncture of the reproduction of the curriculum studies that finally became the traditional curriculum development as the virus of a despotic epistemology. However, the educational process and its results from Tyler's rationale have been severely criticized for decades. Paraskeva argued that Tyler's curriculum approach reduced the real meaning of human beings and humanity, suppressing the voices of the oppressed, the subalterns and the others. For curricularists working to discover the nexus between knowledge, culture and power in educational spheres, these are significant premise in which they can demonstrate the cultural politics in education to transform sociocultural, political and ideological of their society. This is a real essence of curriculum and educational reform discourse that Tyler did not emphasize, including neglecting the analysis of the important roles of dominant hegemonic groups that have influential impacts on the political decision-making process in educational policies and curriculum development.

As the earlier current status of curriculum studies illustrate, I come up with the recurring question of the subject: how to decolonize my own subjectivity entrapped by the traditional curriculum development as a result of hegemonic epistemicide and how to reposition the Thai curriculum studies as a field out of the dominant discourse which has been strongly legitimized in all areas of personal and public discourses on curriculum and education. Given this context, the Thai curriculum studies remains stable and unchanged which is inconsistent with the international curriculum studies that has been shifted from curriculum development to curriculum understanding in reconceptualist turns. It is likely that the state of the field is related to similar characteristic of other university-based academic fields in Thailand which are still lagging behind when compared to the same fields of the global academia (Winichakul, 2014). Thus, reconceptualizing the Thai curriculum studies through itinerant curriculum theory (hereafter ICT) that has been pushed forward by Paraskeva (2016) must be taken into accounts. In this light I would like to reinvoke that our field is currently still circulating under the abyssal thoughts on critical curriculum traditions and some forms of postmodern/structural theorizing and dissolve at becoming 'an anti-Eurocentric/Western critique from a Eurocentric/Western fundamentalist position' (p. 76). Thus solidarity efforts to deterritorrialize the binaries between positivist-functionalist dominant and critical/radical progressive counter-dominant narratives and move beyond a dichotomous knowing and epistemological construction must be articulated.

'Currere' for decolonization is not enough: Struggling toward itinerant curriculum theory

During my PhD journey, I had been struggling to find some answers for the recurring questions. Are there any Thai curriculum scholars whose lived experiences, backgrounds and positionalities can be conceptualized as an influential approach for later generations of scholars to further study and continue their legacies as well as to enrich their approaches? Who are those scholars and how significant their contributions have been in curriculum studies? And whether curriculum studies as an academic field has shifted from the traditional curriculum development to reconceptualist curriculum or not?

One of the major influential academic essays written in Thai by Thongthew (2008), twenty-five pages in length, which appeared in the *Journal of Education Naresuan University* describing the evolution of curriculum theory and alternative conceptual frameworks for theorizing curriculum and development, is an important contribution to curriculum studies and must be considered as a foregrounding framework for conceptualizing curriculum as complicated conversation. I will discuss about the essence of this essay later.

By positioning the Thai curriculum studies within these questions, even though they are based on my own personal inquiry and subjectivity, I strongly believe in the notion of *'currere'* which provides an individual with freedom and imagination to pursue his/her own educational pathway with deliberative transformation – that is, subjectivity can be both personal and political. Therefore, I have committed myself with two important academic missions. One is to reposition the current status of the field beyond the canon of dominant curriculum river in Thailand direct this complicated discourse in a non-existent direction arguing that curriculum scholars, teacher educators and educationalists need to imagine another possible alternatives to the taken-for-granted dichotomies such as between technical curriculum development and reconceptualist understanding curriculum and normative curriculum and critical progressive curriculum approaches. Another is to reimagine and readdress the inter disciplinary/transdisciplinary/transnational/international/translocal curriculum discourse by embracing a complex 'ecology of knowledges' which provides another possible discourse for reconceptualizing our world views about curriculum, teacher education and pedagogical approaches (Santos, 2007). These also include the contemporary social movements of educators, youths and students and their politics of hope, imagination and solidarity which have continuously been built up in Thailand for a while.

In this light, Jatuporn's (2018) study finds that traditional curriculum development discourse is not rigid but having dynamic, fluid and contentious movements. There are counter-hegemonic and oppositional movements to traditional curriculum development within the specific educational contexts in which the educational praxis has been articulated. In other words, the curriculum development does not have an absolute power to govern the mentality and all codes of conducts practiced by curricularists. They are still able to resist the hegemonic discourse by constructing specific counter-dominant movements under the hegemonic regime. Although Thongthew (2008) did not clearly discuss reconceptualist curriculum discourse, she instead emphasized a variety of alternative forms for rethinking about curriculum development implicit in the conception of another knowledge is possible. This remark is very important because one of Thongthew's implications is that the most widely utilized curriculum development approach by schools and teacher education institutions is still embedded in traditional curriculum development despite the existence of many other approaches to curriculum. With the technical/functionalist approach to curriculum development in this manner, this obstructs new educational goals to efficiently occurr in more complexified unknowing contexts. In addition, educators under that curriculum epistemicide cannot produce meaningful educational outcomes since they cannot overcome the functionalist limitation of traditional curriculum development – no matter how they try to use progressive pedagogical approaches to teach students.

As aforementioned, the contemporary status of the Thai curriculum studies has been brutalizing by the Thai-centric curriculum epistemicide; that is, traditional curriculum development that itinerated through Thai curriculum policies had been systematically constructed from the legacy of Western modern Euro/American-centric epistemology and transgressed it through the process of rearticulation and recontextualization into Thai academia. Through selective appropriation for the Thais, technocratic curriculum specialists and policy elites then established the field of curriculum studies out of traditional curriculum development. Since then, the curriculum development has been reproduced through institutionalized epistemological structures under the Thai-centric curriculum epistemicide. This epistemic political project was thus determined by the nation state to administrate the directions of educational reform and development. In this light, conceptualizing the curriculum studies historicity in the global-national-local nexus and specific contextualization provides a critical perspective that is in contrast with the traditional curriculum development (Lim and Apple, 2018). In Paraskeva's standpoint, this demonstrates the Western modern Eurocentric epistemicide and this particular process has been recontextualized in the so-called Thai-centric curriculum epistemicide which Thai curriculum specialists and policy elites perform their positionality in such the same manner as Western colonizers.

However, the reproduction of knowledge, power and culture is not only evil or just the means of marginalizing people but also has productive quality as well such as the construction of body of knowledge and the creation of curricularists and teacher education institutions. In such cases, it is formally accepted that curriculum development should at least begin firstly with the determination of objectives and assessing the outcomes to achieve the determined objectives in the last, including viewing school as formal institution for educating children and young citizens and national curriculum as standardized knowledge that all learners must receive. This curriculum development process is considered acceptable as foundational principles in curriculum studies, since all Thai textbooks and documents would describe the principle of curriculum development in accordance with this dominant narrative (Thongthew, 2008).

For MA and PhD students conducting research in curriculum studies and teacher education, they usually conceptualize their research frameworks under the tradition of R&D. The research processes consist of the steps as follows: first, assessing the sociocultural, political and ideological contexts for curriculum development; second, designing and developing curriculum; third, implementing curriculum; and last, evaluating and assessing curriculum. Embedded in this tradition, the curriculum which is a product of research and development approach should demonstrate both productive and innovative characteristics of curriculum. In other words, the managerial languages of curriculum must be clearly articulated and must be empirically quantified by numbers and showcases a series of numerals on test scores (Pinar, 2014; Zhao, Popkewitz and Autio, 2022).

In terms of structural and institutional supports, a large amounts of research funds have been allocated and distributed for the development of curriculum design and instructional approaches. The significant part of this project can be seen in the identity construction of the network of curriculum specialists who have been responsive for the broader academic areas of C&I. This should be noted that, from Pinar's standpoint, they are rather technocratic curriculum specialists than curriculum scholars. These actors play an important role in both constructing the dominant discourse for school and teacher education institutions and, more importantly, reorienting the Thai curriculum studies as manifested in its aforementioned abyssal status. The epistemicide mechanism for traditional curriculum development proceeded seamlessly according to the art of governmentality which internalizes biopower by supervising, coaching and mentoring the curriculum development process to be efficient and effective in accordance with the predefined objectives. Thus, the majority of educational research works can be categorized under the traditional curriculum development and this becomes the Thai-centric curriculum epistemicide which has been the dominant curriculum discourse in Thailand.

However, in the past decade, various groups of interdisciplinary social sciences and humanities scholars as well as broadly defined educators have been enquired through curriculum discourse and praxis by utilizing the same unit of analysis regarding ethnicity, race, class, gender, sexuality, language and culture. This implies that they have been significantly influenced by one another. As clearly indicated in the production of university-based academic research, the research works in the field of social sciences, humanities and fine arts funded by the Thailand Research Fund (TRF) demonstrate the objectives and outcomes aiming at developing learners in different educational contexts to have knowledge, skills and disposition as well as enhancing learners' world view to be active global citizens under the democratic regime (Jatuporn, 2018). As shown in the examples of research works as follows: 'The factors and problems in English competencies of Thai people: Strategies and innovations for solving the problems', 'The Computer-Assisted Instruction (CAI) lessons for developing the use of Thai literacy skills of early primary school students of Karen and Mon ethnic' and 'The teaching and learning of English literary works for developing students' environmental awareness and intercultural learning'. These works have been conducted by social sciences and humanities scholars in order to improve educational equity and equality for Thai citizens. At the same time, curriculum scholars have employed social theories, alternative epistemological approaches and methodologies such as the concept of linguistic, critical, postmodern, post-structural, postcolonial and cultural turn in broad disciplinary social sciences and humanities into curriculum studies and teacher education (Jatuporn, 2018). Within this nexus, the interdisciplinary approaches influenced by the social sciences and humanities to the curriculum inquiry and teacher education begin to expand beyond the established conventional traditions of epistemological and methodological inquiry.

Even though the traditional curriculum development has been formally institutionalized and has gained its legitimacy in the Thai curriculum studies, its status does not exist without contestations and challenges. In this vein, influenced by the cultural politics and resistance in education I would like to stress the importance of philosophy of praxis as a tool for reimagining and repositioning the field of curriculum studies by theorizing my own lived experiences and subjectivity as itinerant curriculum. Constructing this curriculum metaphor provides me a multiplicity of language for critiques and possibilities for understanding the intersection between knowledge, power and culture and viewing culture as a space for everyday life struggles of human actors. In addition, the potentiality of philosophy of praxis and its strong commitment to understanding the lived world of educators through critical reflexive self-understanding needs to be addressed.

What is significant in the critical/radical progressive counter-dominant narratives is that this tradition is not warmly welcomed by the dominant discourse in education because of its perceived feature as dangerous, intolerant and disloyal for the three pillars of religion (Buddhism), monarchy and nation (Thais). Given this context, as a PhD student, I, in some manners, have to conform to the traditional curriculum development discourse. But I am not saying that I must comply wholeheartedly with the dominant discourse since we all humans have lived stories, experiences and histories and, more importantly, define our own identity based on these social constructs. Even considered as personal narrative, in this sense, they are imbued with sociocultural, ideological, historical and political implication. The personal is always political. The construction of narratives can be considered as a process for creating the discourse of knowledge, power, culture, being and knowing. The narrative is often followed by specific discursive praxis and constructing a legitimated hegemonic power for praxis.

Seen this way, a form of struggle that I can appropriately articulate is through writing academic articles and discussing its essence in public venues, mostly organized by domestic academic institutions and universities in Thailand. This kind of cultural practice provides me a possibility to know comrades who have ideological and political orientations in common. This, in turn, leads to one of the most important cultural practices. As such, we have demonstrated them through the politics of resistance and contestation in creating the identity of new generation of curriculum studies and teacher education scholars. Such practice has resulted in our newly established group to practice together reading the seminal texts in curriculum studies by using reading back and contrapuntal method as implicated in postcolonial/decolonial education including the process of reading, writing, critique, deconstruct and theorizing concepts from academic articles and texts related to curriculum studies, generally, and, more particularly, reconceptualist curriculum discourses (Merryfield, 2001; Subedi and Daza, 2008). In addition, the emergence of educational network alliances to create democratic citizenship, young liberal progressive activists and students' coalition and the multicultural education programme as a scholarly field that is closely related to curriculum studies may be considered as new imagination for curriculum and education reform in Thailand.

As aforementioned, the contemporary social movements of educators, youths and students and their politics of hope, imagination and solidarity for curriculum and educational reform must be critically anchored in this complicated conversation because of its embedded abyssal forms of thinking to decolonize education in Thailand. However, I am not saying that the liberal/critical/progressive education movements are not meaningful and significant but rather that both dominant and specific counter-dominant movements had principally presumed a form of abyssal thinking and reproduced curriculum epistemicide and homogeneity of epistemological knowledge in such the same way as it had been established in the traditional curriculum development and the counter-dominant efforts to destabilize it (Zhao, 2020).

Our condition needs a multitude of new language(s) and an alternative vocabulary to conceptualize curriculum. I have been informed by my sensibility that *currere* for deconstruction, reconstruction and decolonization is not enough and this must be situated in the present moment to move from *currere* towards ICT as implicated in Deleuze's notion of politics of desire which places an emphasis upon an individual's desire to make something happen not only for his or her own's sake but also for the transformation of the society. I employ ICT as an epistemological platform for reframing the changing aspirations of, broadly defined, the liberal progressive curriculum scholars and educators who wish to push other non-dominant epistemologies and methodologies into the curriculum studies. In this light, it is interesting to note that since the last decade, liberal progressive-oriented educators have explicitly demonstrated continuing desires by signifying a warm welcome of other alternative discourses circulating in the humanities and social sciences which have been traditionally established as a sociocultural foundation of education.

By employing the notion of politics of desire, it provides me with a language and linguistic device to problematize, conceptualize and challenge normativity (Masny, 2013). It is clearly indicated in the dimensions of interdisciplinary studies and methodological reconceptualization by using curriculum as a unit of analysis and point of reference. The politics of desire expressed by myself and those committed scholars is not only for the field itself but also for a real transformation of education by reconceptualizing curriculum in new linguistic and epistemological terrains.

The reconceptualization of curriculum and educational discourses, however, does not occur within the graduate programme of C&I, in particular, and the field of curriculum studies, generally. This kind of linguistic shifts has been vigorously demonstrated in the field of sociocultural foundations of education which has a strongly related academic orientation with the curriculum studies. Based on my own investigation, the courses provided by sociocultural foundations department under the schools of education have significantly expressed the articulation of alternative epistemological and methodological discourses in curriculum and education. For example, the graduate programme of development education (DE) in Chiang Mai University has offered topics related to curriculum and the intersection among discourse of knowledge, culture and power under the requisite courses such as philosophy of critical education and qualitative inquiries in education. The courses also emphasize the application of conceptual frameworks derived from post-ism orientations such as postmodernism, post-structuralism, postcolonialism and currently posthumanism to be used for understanding and conceptualizing educational phenomena in the sociocultural, economic, political and historical contexts of the globalization, transnationalism and multiculturalism. In addition, the critical traditions of epistemological inquiry and methodology in cultural studies, neo-Marxism, critical feminism and radical decolonial studies have been employed in conceptualizing and conducting educational research by emerging scholars and graduate students.

This phenomenon has currently occurred about one and a half decade in the field of sociocultural foundations of education, development education and multicultural education. This might provide an impetus that the linguistic shifts from positivist-functionalist and means-ends instrumental rationality to alternative epistemologies have gained its momentum as implicated in reconceptualist curriculum discourse. By searching a new epistemological genre for being and reasoning for curriculum studies is correspondent with Dwayne Huebner's (1966, 1974) notion of curricular language and the nature of curriculum studies since the 1960s (Zhao, 2020). This scenario has yielded the potential possibility for curriculum scholars, teacher educators and educationalists to reinvoke not just an alternative thought but rather an alternative thought of alternatives on curriculum (Santos, 2007) and advance curriculum studies further in order to critically decolonial itself from both traditional positivist-functionalist curriculum discourse and reconceptualist discourse to ICT and – through shared solidarity – nourish once again (Price, 2017; Zhao, 2020).

Beginning again from the final?

At this point, I still do not have empirical evidences to prove the numbers of curriculum scholars, teacher educators and educationalists who are interested or oriented themselves towards reconceptualist curriculum studies which has far more implications than traditional curriculum development as well as approaching for a non-Thai-centric epistemology implicated in such the same metaphor with moving beyond the Western modernity-coloniality episteme in ICT. Only by using my sensibilities, I recognize the existence of emerging Thai curriculum scholars, teacher educators and educationalists who are struggling to non-theorizing towards the canon knowledge and are articulating for the curriculum involution (Paraskeva, 2017). In terms of academic movements, trends and changes in educational inquiries both epistemological and methodological frameworks occurring in the fields of sociocultural foundations of education, development education and multicultural education may be a phenomenon that reflects solidarity efforts to construct new imagination in the Thai curriculum studies and educational reform that needs to push beyond territorial divides between traditional positivist-functionalist discourse and contemporary reconceptualist discourse by proposing that these dichotomous binds limit rather than reinvoke new meanings, contextualizing and historicizing identities (Jupp, 2013).

By employing Paraskeva's ICT for curriculum theorizing in Thailand, this contribution is to recognize the diverse ecology of knowledges and epistemes that, by including epistemological and methodological traditions from Kuan-Hsing Chen's (2010) notions of *Asia as method* and the method for deimperialized/colonized the knowledge construction and the Asian Global South initiative by *Aruna Global South* group that aim to expand the knowledge about the social, political, cultural and educational landscapes in the Asian Global South through an alternative innovative research culture and foster and propagate research collaboration and solidarity between researchers working on Asia with shared histories of underrepresentation and marginalization within mainstream academia. These solidarity efforts are taking our field beyond the Western modernity-coloniality episteme and the various forms of its legacy that has colonized it such as Thai-centric epistemology and embracing a non-Thai-centric epistemology in different international, transnational, regional and national-local contexts (Moreira, 2017). In this light, the efforts towards decolonial and post-abyssal rethinking and struggling towards global cognitive justice must be established. Paraskeva's contribution opens 'for the building of a new language in which we think of education as a critical source for edifying a more just society and leading to the transformation of the world; a world fuelled by a cultural and economic justice' (Paraskeva, 2016, 194).

References

Biesta, G. (2005), 'Against Learning: Reclaiming a Language for Education in an Age of Learning', *Nordik Pedagogik*, 25: 54–66.

Boossabong, P. (2018), 'Neoliberalizing Higher Education in the Global South: Lessons Learned from Policy Impacts on Educational Commercialization in Thailand', *Critical Policy Studies*, 12 (1), 110–115.

Brown, A. L. and W. Au (2014), 'Race, Memory, and Master Narratives: A Critical Essay on U.S. Curriculum History', *Curriculum Inquiry*, 44 (3): 358–89.

Chen, K.-H. (2010), *Asia as Method: Toward Deimperialization*, Durham: Duke University Press.

Cuban, L. (1992), 'Curriculum Stability and Change', in P. W. Jackson (ed.), *Handbook of Research on Curriculum*, 216–47, New York: Macmillan.

Foucault, M. (1973), *The Order of Things: An Archaeology of the Human Sciences*, New York: Vintage Books.

Huebner, D. (1966), 'Curricular Language and Classroom Meanings', in J. Macdonald and R. Leeper (eds), *Language and Meaning*, 8–26, Washington: ASCD.

Huebner, D. (1974), 'The Remaking of Curriculum Language', in W. Pinar (ed.), *Heightened Consciousness, Cultural Revolution and Curriculum Theory*, 36–53. Berkeley: McCutchan Publishing Corporation.

Hung, C.-Y. (2016), 'Ambiguity as Deliberate Strategy: The "De-Politicized" Discourse of National Identity in the Taiwanese Citizenship Curriculum', *Critical Studies in Education*, 57 (3): 394–410.

Jatuporn, O. (2018), *Another Epistemological & Methodological Inquiry in Curriculum Studies: On Negotiated Ideological Praxis in the Field of Teacher Education in Thailand*. Paper presented at the 12th annual humanities research forum in Thailand. Nakhon Pathom: Faculty of Arts, Silpakorn University.

Jatuporn, O. (2022), 'Deliberating Complicated Conversation in Curriculum Discourse for Social Justice', *Journal of International Social Studies*, 12 (1): 22–37.

Jupp, J. (2013), 'Undoing Double Binds in Curriculum: On Cosmopolitan Sensibilities in US Curriculum Studies', *Journal of the American Association for the Advancement of Curriculum Studies*, 9 (1): 1–19.

Lao, R. (2019), 'The Politics, Economics and Cultural Borrowing of Thai Higher Education Reforms', in P. Chachavalpongpun (ed.), *The Routledge Handbook of Contemporary Thailand*, 318–29, New York: Routledge.

Lim, L. and M. W. Apple (2018), 'The Politics of Curriculum Reforms in Asia: Inter-Referencing Discourses of Power, Culture and Knowledge', *Curriculum Inquiry*, 48 (2): 139–48.

Lin, A. M. Y. (2012), 'Towards Transformation of Knowledge and Subjectivity in Curriculum Inquiry: Insights from Chen Kuan-Hsing's "Asia as Method"', *Curriculum Inquiry*, 42 (1): 153–78.

Masny, D. (2013), *Cartographies of Becoming in Education: A Deleuze-Guattari Perspective*, Rotterdam: Sense Publishers.

Merryfield, M. M. (2001), 'Moving the Center of Global Education: From Imperial World Views That Divide the World to Double Consciousness, Contrapuntal Pedagogy, Hybridity, and Crosscultural Competence', in W. B. Stanley (ed.), *Critical Issues in Social Studies Research for the 21st Century*, 179–208, Greenwich: Information Age.

Miles, J. and P. Nayak (2020), 'Curriculum Co-Presences and an Ecology of Knowledges', *Curriculum Inquiry*, 50 (2): 99–104.

Moreira, M. A. (2017), '"And the Linguistic Minorities Suffer What They Must?": A Review of Conflicts in Curriculum Theory Through the Lens of Language Teacher Education', *Journal of the American Association for the Advancement of Curriculum Studies*, 12 (1): 1–17.

Nozaki, Y., R. Openshaw and A. Luke (2005), *Struggles Over Difference: Curriculum, Texts, and Pedagogy in the Asia-Pacific*, New York: SUNY Press.

Ornstein, A. C. and F. P. Hunkins (2008), *Curriculum: Foundations, Principles and Issues*, Boston; Allyn & Bacon.

Paraskeva, J. M. (2011), *Conflicts in Curriculum Theory: Challenging Hegemonic Epistemologies*, New York: Palgrave Macmillan.

Paraskeva, J. M. (2016), *Curriculum Epistemicide: Toward an Itinerant Curriculum Theory*, New York: Routledge.

Paraskeva, J. M. (2017), 'Itinerant Curriculum Theory Revisited on a Non-Theoricide Towards the Canonicide: Addressing the "Curriculum Involution"', *Journal of the American Association for the Advancement of Curriculum Studies*, 12 (1): 1–43.

Paraskeva, J. M. (2018), 'The Struggle Towards a Nonfunctionalist Critical River: Towards a Curriculum of Hope Without Optimism', in J. M. Paraskeva (ed.), *Towards a Just Curriculum Theory*, 1–49, New York: Routledge.

Pinar, W. F. (1975), *Curriculum Theorizing: The Reconceptualists*, Berkeley: McCutchan.

Pinar, W. F., ed. (2014), *International Handbook of Curriculum Research*, New York: Routledge.

Pinar, W. F., W. Reynolds, P. Slattery and P. Taubman (1995), *Understanding Curriculum: An Introduction to the Study of Historical and Contemporary Curriculum Discourses*, New York: Peter Lang.

Poupansawat, W. (2006), 'The Role of the World Economy in the Evolution of Education Policy in Thailand', *Journal of Political Science*, 27 (3): 183–206.

Price, T. A. (2017), 'Welcome to the New Taylorism! Teacher Education Meets Itinerant Curriculum Theory', *Journal of the American Association for the Advancement of Curriculum Studies*, 12 (1): 1–12.

Rivera, F. D. (2003), 'In Southeast Asia: Philippines, Malaysia and Thailand: Conjunctions and Collisions in the Global Cultural Economy', in W. F. Pinar (ed.), *Handbook of Research on Curriculum*, 553–74, Mahwah: Lawrence Erlbaum Associates.

Santos, B. S. (2007), 'Beyond Abyssal Thinking: From Global Lines to Ecologies of Knowledges', *Review (Fernand Braudel Center)*, 30 (1): 45–89.

Subedi, B. and L. Daza (2008), 'The Possibilities of Postcolonial Praxis in Education', *Race Ethnicity and Education*, 11 (1): 1–10.

Thongthew, S. (2008), 'The Evolution of Curriculum Theory and Alternative Frameworks for Curriculum Development', *Journal of Education*, 10 (3): 91–124.

Winichakul, T. (2014), 'Asian Studies Across Academics', *The Journal of Asian Studies*, 73 (4): 879–97.

Zhao, W. (2020), 'Problematizing "Epistemicide" in Transnational Curriculum Knowledge Production: China's *suyang* Curriculum Reform as an Example', *Curriculum Inquiry*, 50 (2): 105–25.

Zhao, W., T. Popkewitz and T. Autio (2022), 'Historicizing Curriculum Knowledge Translation and Onto-Epistemic Coloniality', in W. Zhao, T. Popkewitz and T. Autio (eds), *Epistemic Colonialism and the Transfer of Curriculum Knowledge Across Borders: Applying a Historical Lens to Contest Unilateral Logics*, 3–18, New York: Routledge.

Curriculum in the Viral Age

Itinerant Curriculum Theory as a Just Path

Todd Alan Price

The field of curriculum studies should pay more attention to *virality*. Endemic to everything as cause and effect, to centre virality instead of the other social constructs would reveal far more now of the current human condition.

There are biological and technical tendencies to virality, and they intersect. As a launching point for exploration, consider

> The *tendency* of an image, video, or piece of information to be circulated rapidly and widely from one internet user to another: the quality or fact of being viral. (*Oxford English Dictionary*, 2023)

Drawing inspiration from itinerant curriculum theory (ICT) (Paraskeva, 2011, 2016, 2021, 2022a, 2022b, 2023) and recognizing the nature of epistemicide in the curriculum field (pioneered by Paraskeva), I argue now that *virality is curriculum*. How so? Virality shares the ICT position of travelling nomadism and idea(s) spread. However, virality also presents several problems for curricularists. How does one deterritorialize virality? What constitutes a territory in the first place? Given boundless virtual space (provided by the internet) and continuous technological replication (malware, for example), how do we make sense of the 'real world'?

I pondered these questions for some time, well before the faddism of virtual reality, searching for clues in evolving viral conditions with no satisfying answer. Studying the educational programming, the 'information superhighway' legislation, the proliferation of 'mobile' technology and the subsequent fog of 'the cloud', I now argue that with artificial intelligence, a 'different difference' is setting upon us: *virality has gone viral*.

To my contention, however, this seismic change is largely undertheorized in curriculum studies scholarship, conversation and literature. Curricularists are perseverating on identity politics; they would do better to include the impression left on identity and the social by virality. Provided are suggestions in this chapter, not answers, on how we might (re)reconceptualize curriculum in this *viral era*. Fever, flow and fluidity are generative viral metaphors to start with.

As an example, amidst various electronic communications technology tools, Jeremy Rifkin decades ago had already shared this critical observation:

> The computer works in a time frame in which the nanosecond is the primary temporal measurement. The nanosecond is a billionth of a second. Though it is possible to conceive theoretically of a nanosecond and even to manipulate time at that speed of duration, *it is impossible to experience it.* (Rifkin, 1987, 15)

While we live in reality, we operate in virtual reality and metaphor. Using fever, flow and fluidity, virality becomes centred in curriculum inquiry. Let us begin with a brief survey of fiction to see how virality is exposed and how exploration might be engaged.

Love, post-apocalypse and 'bots'

Fiction depicts viral eras with fever, flow and fluidity. Dual, multiple realities coexist, like 'the river' in ICT (Paraskeva, 2011, 2022a) – currently a very influential discourse (Pinar, 2013) that inaugurates the current turn in our field – a post-abyssal non-derivative turn. Reconceptualizing reality, fictional characters serve as Jungian archetypes and are generative of viral themes. Positioned, but not fixed, in dialogue, they reimagine the future while reconciling memory for a present hermeneutic. Put simply, fictional literature is pregnant with virality from beginning to end. Several examples of curriculum study follow.

The first is the epic *Love in the Time of Cholera*. With elegant, sweeping brush strokes, Marquez (1989) paints a feudal past, a slower, more plodding life woven with occasional flash, revolution and desire. *Florentino* performs an archetype, the quintessential romantic. He loves *Fermina*, but she is already married to another. Irrationally, he enchains himself to her, spending the rest of his life creating art, writing letters and dwelling in rumination. Finally, decades later, with the death of her husband, Florentino has his chance to be with Fermina.

In this novella romántica, life flows down like a boat on the river, lush, exuding sound, smell and warmth. The condition of Florentino to Fermina is a contagion, a form of virality: 'Marquez's title is based on this systematic ambiguity – cholera as both disease and passion. Love is a sickness comparable to cholera and creates physical symptoms and effects as lovesickness' (Peters, 2021, 758).

In stark contrast, the second novel opens on a snowy evening in Toronto's Elgin theatre. While performing King Lear, the lead actor, Arthur Leander, collapses on stage, signalling the collapse of society and the spread of the deadly *Georgia Flu*. The world, like Arthur, shuts down, the grid goes dark, machines stall, digital phones fail and cars run out of gas. *Station Eleven* differs from the typical post-apocalyptic fare; there are no laser beams, space aliens or zombies, simply a lull at the end of civilization, almost an afterthought, and endless walking: 'The Traveling Symphony moved among the settlements of the changed world and had been doing so since five years after the collapse' (Mandel, 2015, 37).

In this dystopia, the past is recounted in present daydreams. Kirsten is the nostalgic archetype, cast as the young girl on stage that fateful evening when mighty Arthur fell (also an archetype of the aged, past-his-prime, celebrity patriarch). Left behind to face the music (as it were), she and a handful of brave souls band together to make life meaningful. 'Survival is insufficient' (Mandel, 2015) becomes her/their song. To invoke ICT, this 'different difference', this metaphysical life is reassembled with

> No more Internet. No more social media, no more scrolling through litanies of dreams and nervous hopes and photographs of lunches, cries for help and expressions of contentment and relationship-status updates with heart icons whole or broken, plans to meet up later, pleas, complaints, desires, pictures of babies dressed as bears or peppers for Halloween. No more reading and commenting on the lives of others, and in so doing, feeling slightly less alone in the room. No more avatars. (Mandel, 2015, 32)

The virus brings an end to one refrain but also an unlikely lyrical rebirth to another.

The third novel, *Super Sad True Love Story*, is a ludicrous, infuriating and wildly entertaining satire, a clever idiocracy of the not-too-distant future (Shteyngart, 2011). The main protagonist is the archetype of a gloomy, middle-aged, sad sack named Lenny. An employee of the dystopic Post-Human Services, Lenny falls in love with Eunice, another archetype – the twenty-first-century version of the valley girl who – like all youth depicted here – is glued to her GlobalTeen account, making her TV show on a 'bot'. Eunice is Korean, and Lenny is Eastern European. Both are held out as hapless characters, flawed yet deserving of sympathy, bumping along amidst a soulless world. Lenny is well-meaning and pitiful and has pangs for Eunice. Eunice struggles with what she should be, feels remorse for not living up to the expectation of her traditional mother and thinks Lenny dim but perhaps sweet. He extols his moribund feelings in this grim, automated world; she trivializes and then gets serious in this mess of a society where life is reduced to media, credit and retail.

Surreal as it is, *Super Sad True Love Story* foreshadows virality in our real world: credit scores popping up on billboard signs, routine invasive scans and invasive facial recognition technology. People are television programmes, the rich pursue shallow immortality through technocracy, while the lower classes grovel, ultimately to protest war, while the US standing dips further into economic abyss. Making no apologies here, Shteyngart characterizes Chinese bankers as waiting in the wings, ready to pounce on any sign of American default.

Each novel and, admittedly, every imperfectly cast or stereotyped character in these plays portray an oddly centred universe. In each fictional world, virality spins, either in an abundance or a dearth of technology. These peculiar technocultures exude utopian and dystopian storylines. Moreover, fiction or not, they hover like drones in our present reality.

A final example is set in the 1930s when newspaper headlines captured the imagination and radio broadcasting blared. In the grim, folksy fiction *It Can't Happen*

Here by Sinclair Lewis (1935), journalist Doremus Jessup recounts the contagion of fascism. Doremus (artfully meaning 'doormouse') feels he has not done enough to as President 'Buzz' Windrip and his sadistic Minute Men torment and dispose of their opposition in this satire. The novel mirrors the proliferation of Depression-era figures, like Father Charles Coughlin, who spread the propaganda of demagoguery, fear and othering like a virus.

Fascism failed to take hold in the United States in the 1930s; however, in the twenty-first century, it *did* happen here. President Trump and his Proud Boys mirrored the Lewis caricatures. Perhaps it was only by good fortune (massive mobilization of voters by citizen activists) that this modern-day autocrat/kleptocrat/fascist was exposed, that his Oath Keeper/Proud Boy/MAGA mob overreached on 6 January with their quixotic, destructive insurrection. Trump was shown the door in 2020, and in the 2022 midterms, his waning influence was revealed as several of his endorsements fell. An exploration of virality reveals much concerning the demagogue archetype, in fact, as well as fiction.

Television and flow

To restate, fiction hovers like a drone over our present reality. During the Pax Americana, the audience aimed for was predominantly white, middle-class households. A large box with moving pictures was placed in the centre of the living room, with parents and children sitting around. In her startling (for its clarity) expose, *The Perfect Machine,* Joyce Nelson argues that this scene recalls the 'Golden Age of Television', an idyllic respite from a world at war. However, this scene, much like the Cold War, is packaged as a TV show. According to Nelson, (tele)vision grew from the same technological garden as the bomb. Nelson theorized that TV for the 'nuclear family' offered

> what's called 'the sweetening machine' – the apparatus that generates prerecorded laff-tracks and applause-tracks to augment, or 'sweeten' the sound-track of television productions . . . invented at the time the Hollywood studios and production companies were gearing up to take over from the networks the making of most product for the airwaves. (Nelson, 1987, 61)

Prominently featured in the 1950s were sitcoms – often about the same idealized nuclear family presumed to be watching. Additionally, live broadcasts brought entertainment and news from around the world into the home. The 'sweetening machine', with children perched around, was thought by another theorist, Marshal McLuhan, to have another effect: to replace the classroom and overwhelm the teacher. As a result, television would outcompete textbooks when it came to capturing children's attention:

> There is a world of difference between a modern home environment of integrated electrical information and the classroom. Today's television child is attuned to up-to-the-minute adult news – inflation, rioting, war, taxes, crime and is

bewildered when he enters the 19th-century environment that still characterizes the educational establishment. (McLuhan and Fiore, 1967, 18)

McLuhan celebrated this change when, in the 1960s, he coined the familiar trope 'the medium is the message'. Equally evocative is the screed 'the medium is the massage' . . . an electronic salve to soothe the anxiety of living in modern society.

Essentially, TV both created and reflected what cultural studies theorist Stuart Hall aptly described as 'flow':

> two diametrically opposed images of the television experience: that of being swept away by an external force, and that of coolly and calmly regarding a river at a distance, possibly now and again distracted by what goes on in the immediate surroundings. (Gripsrud, 1998, 29)

Like the biological virus, the electronic virus flows. Undoubtedly, the experience of being 'swept away' or 'distracted by' is familiar to the experience of not only Hall but all of us. Nor is the idea of television as educational – 'edutainment' to early educational television theorist Kenneth Komoski – revolutionary. While television has been likened to electronic junk food or 'wasteland' (FCC chairman Kenneth Minnow), the most generative idea is of 'electronic flow'. Moving pictures at a distance have been transmitted by a singular cathode ray tube through a few commercial channels, to hundreds on fibre optics cable and satellite, and thousands due to the World Wide Web, the internet.

Digitally mediated identity

Theorists who reconceptualize curriculum perseverate on culture. This is demonstrated in the numerous publications which draw upon culture and centre race, class and gender. Culturally relevant, responsive and sustainable pedagogy is particularly germane to complicated conversations on culture. Additionally, the current educational discourse focuses entirely on the cultural values of diversity, inclusion and equity.

Indeed, a focus on culture in teaching and learning and curriculum studies is familiar. The first wave started with the scholarship of William Jameson and Stuart Hall, the Birmingham Centre for Cultural Studies. Former British colonies, including Canada, Australia and the United States, embraced the idea of studying culture. British cultural studies was the dominant form that spread like a virus through American curriculum studies, English departments and the humanities. For example, positing the existence of 'subcultures of youth', Mike Brake (1985) and Leslie Roman, Christian-Smith and Ellsworth (1988) established the idea of *textually mediated culture* or cultures within cultures formed as resistance. This work foreshadows today's *digitally mediated culture*.

Emphasizing further retrenchment into predetermined categories instead of more undetermined or open-ended ones, subject to (re)interpretation, identity politics often benefits a few at the expense of the many. One does not have to search far for anti-establishmentarian, reactionary or virtue-signalling revolutionaries who 'call out' others and use a 'cancel culture' as a cudgel:

> modern online public sphere, a place of rapid conclusions, rigid ideological prisms, and arguments of 280 characters, favors neither nuance nor ambiguity. Yet the values of that online sphere have come to dominate many American cultural institutions: universities, newspapers, foundations, and museums. (Applebaum, 2021, 62)

Controversial and complicated conversations in popular critical academic discourse prove that 'culture' as presently engaged in is intellectually thin but not just of a paucity of characters. Instead, curriculum scholars' contributions seem forgotten, which once called for incredulity towards fixed categories and metanarratives. Nothing is fixed or absolute in a viral world, so why do we insist on centring race? Or gender, class, ethnicity and ability? Indeed, race, class and gender (and other, no less critical, social constructs) are essential for understanding power and oppression. However, essentializing a particular social construct misleads. The article 'Contradictions of Identity: Education and the Problem of Racial Absolutism' issues a warning to this problem and

> offers a critique of tendencies toward dogmatism and essentialism in current educational theories of racial inequality. I argue that, paradoxically, you cannot understand race by looking at race alone. Different gender, class, and ethnic interests intersect with racial coordination and affiliation. Programmatic reforms that underestimate the decisive role of nuance, contradiction, and heterogeneity within and between racial groups in education are not likely to succeed either in reducing racial antagonism or ameliorating educational inequities. (McCarthy, 1988, 297)

Rereading the prophetic prose of Cameron McCarthy, culturally responsive pedagogy appears lacking in 'nuance, contradiction, and heterogeneity' because

> The problem of racial origins and racial authenticity is a problem all around. The elusiveness of racial identity not only affects blacks; it also affects whites. Racial identities can never be gathered up in one place as a final cultural property. Moreover, as we approach the end of the twentieth century, what seemed like stable white ethnicities and heritages in an earlier era are now entering a zone of recoding and redefinition. (McCarthy, 1995, 297)

To paraphrase: You cannot understand identity by looking at identity alone. Looking more closely at identity calls for 'recoding and redefinition' . . . and reviewing the effects of virality.

Similitude *and* difference

What would this pivot towards studying virality as a culture reveal? Digitally mediated identities, representative of technoculture, require a change in the focus of curriculum inquiry. The lore of William Pinar (1975) and Pinarian Reconceptualization of Curriculum Theory (2004) drew extensively from the following movements: Paulo Freire (1969) and social justice orientations and critical pedagogy; Jacques Derrida (1967) and *difference*; Stuart Hall and the (Birmingham School) Center for Contemporary Cultural Studies (1964); Judith Butler (1990), Donna Haraway (1991) and colleagues and postmodern feminism; and various iterations of Derrick A. Bell (1973) and critical race theory. Each movement and pedagogical moment from my reading fully embraces culture as a centre for curriculum inquiry. An exhaustive review of these voluminous movements and moments is not possible here, but suffice it to say that a (re)reconceptualization of culture as technoculture, especially now that digital identities are being formed over social media, *should be the primary focus* for curriculum inquiry in this viral era.

ICT suggests a focus with multiple tones, diverse approaches and different lenses. ICT should nonetheless centre virality (and virtuality) as essential for curriculum study. Given contemporary societies' utter fixation and, to several psychologists' diagnosis, literal addiction to mobile devices, *both* of the following observations of virality become essential to the foreground:

1. The *similitude of experience* in a technologically mediated environment.
2. The *difference of experience* in access and power within the same domain.

Exploration of *similitude of experience* and correspondingly (not contradictorily) *difference in experience* starts with technoculture culture(s). I observe that omnipresent, rhizomatic technology infusion and dissemination (virality) into and out of individual and social group consumptive and productive communication patterns confirm and disrupt identity formation. Social media stated another way, changes being and knowing (ontology and epistemology) in similar and radically different ways, likely more diverse than previously imagined or considered possible.

Donna Haraway (1991) reconceptualizes what it means to be a human and machine-like identity, drawing upon technical and science-fiction literature with the *Cyborg Manifesto*. Though helpful, a more grounded, relevant and less abstract text for pragmatic educators focuses on educational media and outlines a fundamental problem critical scholars may have missed. A 'significant gap [exists] in the otherwise growing literature on hidden curriculums' – that of visual representation and the construction of knowledge using educational media. Elizabeth Ellsworth dismisses the idea that 'conventions of film, video, and photographic representation are mere neutral carriers devoid of content implications' (Ellsworth and Whatley, 1990, 3). Along with Henry Giroux and Dick Hebdige, Ellsworth describes visual and auditory text as gendered, and gendered identity formation follows. Educational media works like mass media, entertainment media and social media do for the consumer; it positions the viewer to face an imagined centre. If not positioned there, the consumer/student is relegated to the margins and experiences, not surprisingly, marginalization.

Students, nonetheless, are not passive consumers. They are steady producers of digitized material for social media streaming. Through corporate, oligopoly-owned dissemination channels, all communication and information are now reduced to digitized, optimized and monetized flow. Communication is packaged by and through corporations, sold as useful information, but whose purpose is mainly to identify the target audience and deliver advertising through 'clickbait'.

As a result, what is created is the 'like economy'. Media is packaged, transforming flow into clickbait: surfing, swiping, immersion. As Benjamin Herm-Morris warns, 'By digitally capturing our relationships, the Like economy monetizes affiliation' (2021). We might recall the Nielsen TV Ratings, determinative of who was watching and where advertisers should advertise. Currently, with video streaming social media, a 'dislike' society is also manufactured, clicks are tallied (anger is a good incentive) and advertisers can use algorithms to create 'filter bubbles', siphoning information and steering dollars to grease the digital wheels. Moreover, this dislike society is coming to the schools:

> Within the Dislike Society, hate becomes the primary mode of communication between communities who increasingly view each other as existential threats. Now, this phenomenon built into the systems we use to communicate is poised to take over exchanges within educational institutions. (Herm-Morris, 2021, 502)

It is all programming of one sort or another. Curricularists might reconceptualize education in the viral age with the following caution:

> The human mind needs 'deprogramming' while computers catch devastating 'viruses.' We live, then, in a Technopoly – a self-justifying, self-perpetuating system wherein technology of every kind is cheerfully granted sovereignty over social institutions and national life. (Postman, 1992, back cover)

Undoubtedly, education that disrupts technological flow will counter Technopoly's 'cheerfully' accepted rule. We love our phones; hence, it will be jarring for the viral student (or teacher) to turn them off or put them down. But necessary.

With the iPhone, endless channels or streams are made possible for flow. Flow becomes a quintessential experience in the viral age. As empirically documented in *IGen* (Twenge, 2017) and *Generation* (Twenge, 2023), every child/teenager has the means to cast a digital identity virally, adults too. Studies indicate that these same children and young people are *more* tolerant but *less* happy than their parents. Additionally, according to Catherine Steiner-Adair in *The Big Disconnect* (2013), childhood is 'going, going, gone', shortened as the tweens navigate their identity online with their posts, tweets and likes, sometimes with humourous and sometimes dangerous implications. Like *Super Sad True Love Story*, IGen has its own 'bot' where everyone becomes a television channel. Everyone flows.

Technoculture

In their book *Technoculture,* Constance Penley and Andrew Ross were among the first curricularists to connect the viral contagion of biology and technology. In one compelling chapter, Paula Treichler describes how the Centers for Disease Control (CDC) was protested for seeming inaction and refusal to move fast enough in the face of the deadly HIV/AIDS spread. The flow of information was glacial, and treatment, it was argued, was barely forthcoming. Healthcare workers and activists, in alliance with gay rights organizations and the community, rallied and built a counterculture. Medical patients and their friends aimed to speed up the flow of information concerning herbal remedies, alternative medicines and experimental drugs through direct action (consider, for example, ACT UP). Their efforts to bypass a staid bureaucracy and serve the afflicted through informal, grassroots networks went viral after television captured a protester for the cause being dragged down Wall Street.

Treichler believed it was crucial to organize communities to challenge the government, in this instance, the CDC and the Food and Drug Administration (FDA), which were at the time perceived as too slow to act in the face of biological virality. The spread of the human immunodeficiency virus (HIV) called for the reconceptualization of the medical culture and the gay liberation movement. Why? Treichler believed that culture is dynamic with

> significant renegotiations of the geography of cultural struggle – of sources of biomedical expertise, relationships between doctor and patient, relationships of the general citizenry to science and to government bureaucracies, and debate about the role and ownership of the body. (Penley and Ross, 1991, 97)

The vigorous and sometimes caustic debate was needed in the early treatment of AIDS to affirm new rights and a newly enfranchised culture. Much was needed in this struggle, and activism and direct action went viral, likely raising as much critical change as reasoned instrumental discourse. Treichler argued that passion and virality changed the debate's terms and culture itself.

Decades later, with the novel coronavirus, it seems passion returned in the opposite direction. This time, a proactive CDC immediately called for social distancing, masking and vaccination. While many citizens heeded the call and complied with what became local, state and federal mandates, a counter-reaction went viral, coalescing against immunization. Passionately opposed were these anti-vaxxers, fighting the restrictions, launching disruptions at school board meetings and rejecting science while spreading conspiracy on social media, seeking to undermine the CDC, casting dispersion on its credibility and spreading quackery, bogus remedies and dangerous misinformation.

How will this passion benefit the 'renegotiations of the geography of cultural struggle' (Treichler, 1991, 97)? This remains to be seen, but perhaps the challenge for bureaucratic structures (local, state and federal governing bodies) must be more open and flexible and provide more nimble approaches to conflict resolution. One can dream, of course.

In another chapter of *Technoculture*, Ross reflects upon the wedding of the biological and the technological, how drawing similarities between the two phenomena links in the public mind the concerns with both a biological threat and terrorism of 'hackers':

> Ever since the viral attack engineered in November of 1988 ... the ramifications of the Internet virus have helped to generate a moral panic ... a controversial editorial titled 'A Hygiene Lesson', drew comparisons not only with sexually transmitted diseases but also with a cholera epidemic. (Penley and Ross, 1991, 107)

It is instructive to think of the recent and ongoing novel coronavirus spread and its response as reminiscent of HIV/AIDS. Viral biological conditions were infused with an increase in meaning through technologically radical communication forms that, in turn, went viral. This phenomenon continues. In the viral age, biological contagion spreads, and rhizomatically spreading electronic memes create imitation and paradoxically an excess of and reduction in meaning.

Virality stoking fear and unrest

Tony D. Sampson argues that virality is

> evident in corporate and political efforts to organize populations by way of the contagions of fear as represented through, for example, the *War on Terror*. However, the potential for the spreading of social power epidemics is also evident in a tendency to be automatically drawn toward and contaminated by mesmeric fascinations, passionate interests, and joyful encounters. As Tarde argued, we tend to follow (and imitate) those we love, those in whom we put faith and hope, and those whom we idolize and take glory in their fame as much as those whom we fear. (Sampson, 2012, 14)

Drawing from Sampson's passage, I echo concerns that our viral time informs and misinforms our (mis)understandings of the pandemic, war in Europe, and insurrection in the United States. Let us consider the following two excerpts and the implications of virality on education (and society) in the first few decades of the twenty-first century, beginning of a viral age.

Education is in an existential crisis. The turn from neoliberal audit (2001–15) to outright illiberal assault (2016–23+) continues unabated. With underfunding from state and federal budgets coordinated attacks on school boards, teacher unions and public officials, seeds of doubt are sewn into education as a public good. Ideological frames (distrust of authority) and illiberal themes (anti-science) are fuelled by the viral conditions. Or stated another way:

> What Republicans learned as they refined their strategies . . . is that issues, whether economic or social, are much less potent than identities . . . it is identities – perceptions of shared allegiance and shared threat – that mobilize . . . This fateful turn toward tribalism, with its reliance on racial animus and continual ratcheting up fear, greatly expanded the opportunities to serve the plutocrats. (Benjamin Herm-Morris, 2021, review of *Let Them Eat Tweets*, 109–17)

The virality of identity politics (not intended to be pejorative) is well documented, and the spread of (dis)information on social media is well established. These forms of virality go hand in hand and, although comprehensively exposed and discussed in public and civic discourse, *go largely unexamined in academia*. Social unrest and democratic meltdown, chaos and confusion evolved because viral information, *sometimes factual but more often patently false*, leads to rumour, fear and unrest, laying the groundwork for influencers and also, as mentioned previously, for a demagogue, a 'strongman' autocrat/kleptocrat, to swoop in and take control:

> Trump's election was the first social media candidacy it's fully adopted meme wars is a campaign messaging strategy. With a strategy came red pills and rabbit holes, the pathway towards insurgency. (Donovan, Dreyfuss and Friedberg, 2022, 21)

> Creating unwavering support for President Trump, they built a powerful conspiratorial faction of believers across the nation. This community, connected by memes and outrage, became an echo chamber of disappointment and paranoid hate. (Donovan, Dreyfuss and Friedberg, 2022, 243)

In China, virality exploded in reverse in the form of social protest against state control and government-inspired disinformation:

> Subtle online protest is fairly common on Chinese social media, but some of that has bled into real life, including at colleges like Tsinghua University, where protesters [in clever defiance] held up blank pieces of paper in a silent, practically un-censorable protest. (Ioanes, 2022)

Viral moments work in remarkably diverse ways, we learn. The instances just described involve populist support and communication through *memes*. The idea is to spread information rapidly in all directions but to code it in particular ways to include and exclude. Social movement facilitation is amplified, but often enough, what is amplified is simply ignorance. Virality corresponds with emotion-filled communication, which may or may not offer solutions to real problems.

Meme matters; bits and bytes

While illiberal autocracy was denied, it was not eliminated, and reactionary politicians continue to pave the way for future tyranny. This involves stoking anti-establishmentarian, populist support for xenophobia and the viral spread of ignorance, fear, distrust, hatred and a call for cultural upheaval.

Lewis's fictional novel struck a chord and warned against American fascism. So does *Meme Wars* by Donovan, Dreyfuss and Friedberg (2022). In this non-fiction documentation of gaming culture, virality is exposed as dragging the many in the country rightward and essentially into an alternative right-wing version of pseudo-reality. *Memes* became the standard bearer for the cult movement; the more toxic the meme, the more xenophobic the politics that followed. Memes, in violation of transparent social and cultural mores of decency, corresponded with secrecy, lit the fire for and justified an emotion-filled, rage-like attack on 'the other': BIPOC, 'illegal' immigrants, the LGBTQIA+ community, government workers, educators and anyone whose values stood in conflict with 'Make America Great Again'. Nativism and outright bigotry were reignited.

To regress somewhat, the 'shock and awe' (2001–15) culminated in the rolling back of 'big government' and deregulation; it began under Reagan and continued through Clinton. However, following the trauma of 11 September 2001, an audit culture was placed on society; education experienced this audit culture most profoundly with the infamous *No Child Left Behind* slogan. The ultimate debacle of the US wars in the Middle East and the collapse of FIRE (financial, investment, real estate), which began with Bush II, meant throwing out the audit and returning to the government bailout of the corporate state. So much for reducing government.

A tepid response to financial speculation for middle-class families (2008–12), on the other hand, was a sore point. The Obama administration did inherit an economy said to be going over a fiscal cliff and acted to bail out the corporations and banks. For Barney Smith (this is a literal person who spoke of also needing to be helped much as the Smith & Barney corporation was), the devastation and slow-moving recovery – for several small business owners and workers like himself – was trauma-inducing, like having one's basement fill up with flood water. To stretch the alliteration, the dam finally burst during the last few years of the Trump administration. The pandemic, a summer of social unrest and pent-up trauma spilled over. Outrage among working people went viral, precipitating attacks on school boards.

It is not difficult to draw a direct line between domestic stress, upheaval and attacks on education. Economic collapse, government bailouts of corporations and growing white resentment of immigrants were exacerbated through social media. Virality stoked the smouldering rage concerning the twin pandemic(s) (the novel coronavirus and socio-economic precarity) . . . a sizeable number of working- and middle-class families had had enough, regardless of who was to blame. Perversely, the echo chamber of 'fake news' blamed schools and substituted crackpot remedies for essential vaccinations to mitigate pandemic-induced sickness. Virality carried equal parts unease and disease, with the increasingly impossible demands on beleaguered people, mostly healthcare workers and school personnel.

Criticality and what became characterized as 'wokeness' created a certain weariness in public; families, unlike curricularists and academics, concern their selves less with lofty problems of Eurocentrism and bias and more with frustration about not knowing how to get their child the education he/she needs, let alone how to put food on the table. To the frightened parent, the question is, how are my student's grades? How do I get my child into a good school? These sentiments far outweigh the academy's fixation on race, class and gender, let alone decolonization.

The right wing picked up on this disconnect, the idea that education was failing, focused on 'equity' instead of academics and ran with the frame. What followed were attacks on 'critical race theory', gender expression and has resulted in literal book bans. Speaking generously here, the left has been late to respond to this carnage or, less than generously, has been cowed into silence lest they offend someone or get fired.

On the other hand and indicative of the problem of virality is that the entire form of knowledge in the academy as well as outside the academy, mostly in big business, is changing and needs to be acknowledged as a general reduction of knowledge into bits and bytes as a function of technology and digitization. A particularly interesting kind of epistemic or epistemological blindness (Andreotti, 2011; 2013) is how knowledge is undergoing metamorphosis. The form follows function, and in higher education today, that function is for knowledge to simply be put into producing evidence, massaging data and crafting algorithmic systems for speedy data recovery, supposedly for robust analysis. Simply put, virality as speedy production, consumption and data dissemination matters far more than parsing identity into socially constructed categories (although universities would have you think otherwise). In a word, matters of virality should be of more significant concern to curriculum theory.

Education and curriculum in the viral era

Now, the viral era is one in which constant distraction reigns. Memes, doxing and swatting are resplendent through social media. Electronic, viral plagues are making their way into the K-12 school operations, with frequent barrages of spam, scams, hacks and systems held hostage to ransomware. My own school district had its network broken into with employee social security numbers compromised, followed by random e-mails threatening to shoot up schools. Technology-enhanced communication is often breeding mayhem. Digital information grows exponentially, spreads rhizomatically and, with further digitization, leads to *optimization*, to the joy of accountants and no one else. What counts, then, is what can be measured. Words, symbols, codes and communications systems; what survives in this devolution is that which can be weighed, parsed, broken up into discrete parts, the parts edited, (re)mixed and further transmitted over seamless tubes, wires and airwaves, then (re)assembled into still more digital bits and bytes. That is what communication and education in the hypermodern look like – production for consumption.

The implications of such a process for education are painfully obvious – when once copied, mechanically reproduced (Benjamin, 1935), codified and remixed in image and symbol, the original referent is lost. The remaining is simulacra (Baudrillard and Glaser, 1994). Knowledge becomes an endless cacophony of sounds, a kaleidoscope of mirrors, each echo and image merely hearing and echoing each other.

Pre-packaged curricula were ushered during the 1990s to align with the high-stakes, world-class standards movement. Technology integration into schools proceeded apace through educational reforms dreamt of by others (Pinar, 2004). With the 'information superhighway' (1989–99), such pre-packaged curricula were readily converted to our current modules. Digitalization proliferates. As a result, particular curricula packages went viral, transmissible through computer disks, video distance learning programs (Price, 2000) and ultimately the internet. Only a few critics questioned the idea of putting education online and going viral during this first-wave frenzy. Scant dissidents were listened to. Indeed, progressive educators almost entirely jumped on board the technology-as-reform bandwagon.

Let us name a few, however. David Noble in *America by Design* (1988) warned that engineers are inclined towards social engineering and are hardly the best people for fixing social problems. Robert McChesney (1993) argued that telecommunications deregulation, littered with promises of helping schools, was a lot of smoke and mirrors, largely just commercialization. In *Failure to Connect* (1998), Jane Healy dismissed the value of computers for young children. Todd Oppenheimer lambasted the profiteering of school districts in *The Flickering Mind* (2007).

Noble's criticism still powerfully resonates, that online education would result in 'digital diploma mills' (1999), students reduced to customers and the degradation of teaching and learning would surely follow. I argued that teaching and knowledge would be reduced to a 'fast-food curriculum' (Price, 2000). Noble went so far as to say that one day, faculty would wake up to a university in ruins – no buildings, just protruding fibre optic cable(s). As if waking from a bad dream, they would ask: Where did the university go? I have extended the image and argument, and, as one who still ventures to walk the often-empty halls of the university, I find the real question to be: Where did the faculty go?

The reluctance of faculty (and students) to fully return to the face-to-face classroom is particularly pronounced in higher education, reflecting similar concerns in the corporate workplace. Many faculty opt not to attend college meetings face-to-face anymore and prefer meetings from home, teaching from home and staying mainly behind a computer with a camera. As a further digression, this is troubling and instructive because (1) some physical relationality is needed for some types of educational work, and (2) educators in this precarious viral world (from my anecdotes) find viral work less than rewarding.

Education newspapers of record are now questioning whether the university's mission *has been lost*. Academic freedom, freedom of inquiry and the idea of sifting and winnowing for the truth have become suspect . . . who is to blame? How long will 'we' as faculty be viable and relevant if we are not attending to these significant issues, let alone whether online courses are equivalent to the face-to-face variety? I subscribe, as did Noble and a scant few others, that a correlation exists between the increase in educational virality and the decrease in embodied faculty along with the strength of the university mission. The physical disappearance of faculty, administration and students corresponds with the acceleration of all mentioned behind screens. Why? This is a question that must soon be addressed.

Virality is global

With numerous channels, sources of information, disinformation or noise, multi-various iterations of what is newsworthy or worthless constantly falling like streams from a waterfall, tumbling around quickly, so quickly indeed that there is no time to peer in at, reflect upon their meaning or be able to make any of. Media spin from mainstream to a computer terminal in one's basement concerns the 'twin pandemics' of biological spread and social unrest, an insurrection in the United States, the latest war in Europe and the surprising viral protest lockdowns in China. Virality, in these instances, means volatility, toxicity and irrationality spinning out of control in a digital 'dislike society' (Herm-Morris, 2021), stoking anxiety, fear, hatred and sometimes violence. Or, as Paraskeva notes:

> Under the current social phenomena, we will examine later on; fascism became viral. The fear of the 'Other' saturated the commonsense, fertilized the typology of the identic(al) (Han, 2018), and gave carte blanche to embark on the neo-crusade against the 'new Other.' These were a must for stabilizing what I would best call the 'fourth hegemonic' phase of capitalism, neoliberal tribal populism. (Paraskeva, 2022b, 163)

Despite this warning, some of the worst instances of reactionary anti-establishmentarianism appear to have been contained; the fever seems to be receding. At the time of this writing, for example, the virally induced phenomenon of 'election denial', spread by misinformation on the internet, was partially deflated. A hearing on insurrection documenting meme-induced madness concludes with damning testimony to the fruits of unthinking, viral rage, serving (hopefully) as a warning to would-be followers of rumour-mongering tyrants. The virulent nature of spin machines that fostered these rumours has primarily been exposed – some even collapsed. On the other hand, election deniers still retain a hold on Congress.

Failing to realize any eternal meaning or greater truth, the cacophony of data leaves it up to venerable institutions such as higher education and universities, which used to serve as truth-tellers, 'sifting and winnowing' to come up with and make meaning. However, universities are already cautious, given the culture wars, and are just playing catch up:

> Like Yameel, technological innovation has been running so fast that society – the soul of civilization – has struggled to keep pace . . . e-mail has eliminated the wait time and expense associated with snail mail: In a mere 40 years, it has displaced how civilization has handled written communication for the past 4,000 years. (Leon and Price, 2016, 97)

Viral thoughts for a viral world

ICT and its implications for understanding the viral age rest upon various premises. The viral age is the condition wherein information is always spread rapidly and in all directions, then identified and lastly translated, often before the meaning of the condition can be fully appreciated or deeply understood. Imagine information packed into a tube of toothpaste; once pushed out, the information cannot be placed back into the tube. Then, imagine the flight of disinformation. It is an oft-told tale that lies travel the world seven times before the truth starts. Perhaps the 'gap' in the arrival of truth to offset lies is further still in times of war. Realistically, it is undeniable that bits and bytes of data speed across the internet and the cloud in a manner where the human mind cannot process or truly comprehend weigh their veracity before confirming information lands. What to do?

One answer is to consider the analogy with biological contagion; to slow the spread of the virus, use measures such as social distancing and sometimes quarantine, or even vaccination. However, avoid lockdowns for endless weeks and months, depriving people of food and care, as happened in China. The same answer might be imagined for the viral spread of disinformation: to slow the toxicity (that breeds hatred and leads to violence), a modest, virtual cooling-off room is needed. To quell dangerous confusion, for example, quarantining sites may be necessary, at least for those that are charged with spreading violence, calling for the violent overthrow of an elected leader(s), undermining the representative government or selling contraband and weapons; these could be shut down or inoculated until such time the threat assessment has been duly processed. Of course, this would be ideal if it were subject to democratic deliberation to sustain freedom of speech and association, virtual or otherwise.

ICT can and must play a role here. ICT situates curriculum theory as always and already being in motion, not a staid theory, but in action (Darder, 2016, 2021). *Viral theorizing in motion and action* might detoxify and slow toxicity by demonstrating proactive hindsight and non-reactionary foresight (already in motion, rather than leaping to a conclusion from a resting position, i.e., confirmation bias). Using the 'reptilian' brain, which nervously hovers between fight and flight, leaves few choices. Employing a 'different difference', ICT could be incredibly flexible, nimble and able to pivot. Drawing on the mammalian brain, warm heart, and seeking understanding and resolution, not just tired ideological talking points, ICT could be a theory/theorizing for all time, not cryptically as a prelude to the end time.

References

Andreotti, V. O. (2013), 'Actional Curriculum Theory', *Journal of the American Association for the Advancement of Curriculum Studies*, 10: 1–10.

Applebaum, A. (2021), 'The New Puritans, a Growing Illiberalism Fueled by Social Media, Is Trampling Democratic Discourse: The Result Is a Chilling Atmosphere in Which Mob Justice Has Replaced Due Process and Forgiveness Is Impossible', *Atlantic Monthly*: 60–71.

Baudrillard, J. and S. F. Glaser (1994), *Simulacra and Simulation*, Michigan: University of Michigan Press.

Benjamin, W. (1935), *The Work of Art in the Age of Mechanical Reproduction*, New York: Penguin.

Brake, M. (1985), *Comparative Youth Culture: The Sociology of Youth Cultures and Youth Subcultures in America, Britain, and Canada*. Routledge. https://doi.org/10.4324/9780203408940.

Darder, A. (2016), 'Foreword. Ruthlessness and the Forging of Liberatory Epistemologies: An Arduous Journey', in J. M. Paraskeva (ed.), *Curriculum Epistemicide*, ix–xvi, New York: Routledge.

Darder, A. (2021), 'The Generation of the Utopia: Foreword', in J. M. Paraskeva (ed.), *The Generation of Utopia: Interrogating the Current State of Critical Curriculum Theory*, xiv–xviii, New York: Routledge.

Donovan, J., E. Dreyfuss and B. Friedberg (2022), *Meme Wars: The Untold Story of the Online Battles Upending Democracy in America*, New York: Bloomsbury Publishing.

Ellsworth, E. A. and M. H. Whatley (1990), *The Ideology of Images in Educational Media: Hidden Curriculums in the Classroom*, New York: Teachers College Press Teachers College Columbia University.

Gripsrud, J. (1998), 'Television, Broadcasting, Flow: Key Metaphors in TV Theory', in C. Geraghty and D. Lusted (eds), *The Television Studies Book*, London: Arnold; Distributed Exclusively in the USA by St. Martin's Press.

Guattari, F. (2015), *Lines of Flight: For Another World of Possibilities*, Bloomsbury Academic. https://search.ebscohost.com/login.aspx?direct=true&scope=site&db=nlebk&db=nlabk&AN=1717467 (accessed December 9, 2022).

Han, B.-C. (2018), *The Expulsion of the Other*, London: Polity.

Haraway, D. (1991), 'A Cyborg Manifesto: Science, Technology, and Socialist-Feminism in the Late Twentieth Century', in D. Haraway (ed.), *Simians, Cyborgs and Women: The Reinvention of Nature*, 149–81, New York: Routledge.

Healy, J. M. (1998), *Failure to Connect: How Computers Affect Our Children's Minds-For Better and Worse*, New York: Simon & Schuster.

Herm-Morris, B. (2021), 'Education and the Dislike Society: The Impossibility of Learning in Filter Bubbles', *Educational Philosophy and Theory*, 54 (5): 502–11. https://doi.org/10.1080/00131857.2021.1935233.

Ioanes, E. (2022, November 27), 'The Wave of Protests Testing China's Zero-Covid Policy, Explained', *Vox*. https://www.vox.com/2022/11/27/23480144/urumqi-xinjiang-apartment-fire-china-zero-covid-uyghur-xi-jinping-protest (accessed September 19, 2023).

Kirmayer, L. J., E. Raikhel and S. Rahimi (2013), 'Cultures of the Internet: Identity, Community, and Mental Health', *Transcultural Psychiatry*, 50 (2): 165–91. https://doi.org/10.1177/1363461513490626 tps.sagepub.com.

Leon, M. R. and T. A. Price (2016), 'On the Cutting Edge: Movements and Institutional Examples of Technological Disruption', *New Directions for Higher Education*: 97–107. https://doi.org/10.1002/he.20183.

Lewis, S. (1935), *It Can't Happen Here*, New York: Penguin Classics Penguin Random House.

Mandel, E. S. J. (2015), *Station Eleven: A Novel*, 1st edn, New York: Alfred A. Knopf.

Marquez, G. G. and E. Grossman (1989), *Love in the Time of Cholera*, Penguin Books.

McCarthy, C. (1988), 'Marxist Theories of Education and the Challenge of a Cultural Politics of Non-Synchrony', in L. G. Roman, L. K. Christian-Smith and E. A. Ellsworth (eds), *Becoming Feminine: The Politics of Popular Culture*, London: Falmer Press.

McChesney, R. W. (1993), *Telecommunications Mass Media and Democracy: The Battle for the Control of U.S. Broadcasting 1928–1935*, Cambridge: Oxford University Press.

McLuhan, M. and Q. Fiore (1989 [1967]), *The Medium Is the Massage*, New York: Touchstone.

Moreira, M. A. (2017), 'AERA 2017 Symposium: Decolonizing and De-Canonizing Curriculum Futurity: An Engaged Discussion on João Paraskeva's Conflicts in Curriculum Theory', On Linguistic Epistemicides and Colonization: Looking at Subtractive Education for Bilingual/ Bicultural Children. Research Centre in Education, University of Minho, Portugal.

Mumford, L. (1934), *Technics and Civilization*, New York: Harcourt, Brace and Company.
Nelson, J. (1987), *The Perfect Machine: TV in the Nuclear Age*, Toronto: Between-the-Lines.
Oliveira, V. O. (2011), *Actionable Postcolonial Theory in Education*, 1st edn, Palgrave Macmillan. https://doi.org/10.1057/9780230337794.
Oppenheimer, T. (2007), *Flickering Mind: Saving Education from the False Promise of Technology*, Random House. http://www.myilibrary.com?id=431591 (accessed December 20, 2022).
Paraskeva, J. M. (2011), *Conflicts in Curriculum Theory: Challenging hegemonic Epistemologies*, New York: Palgrave Macmillan.
Paraskeva, J. M. (2016), *Curriculum Epistemicide*, New York: Routledge.
Paraskeva, J. M. (2021), *Curriculum and the Generation of Utopia*, New York: Routledge.
Paraskeva, J. M. (2022a), *Conflicts in Curriculum Theory*, 2nd edn, New York: Palgrave.
Paraskeva, J. M. (2022b), '"Did COVID-19 Exist Before the Scientists?" Towards Curriculum Theory Now', *Educational Philosophy and Theory*, 54 (2): 158–69. https://doi.org/10.1080/00131857.2021.1888288.
Paraskeva, J. M. (2023), *Critical Perspectives on the Denial of Caste in Educational Debate*, New York: Routledge.
Penley, C. and A. Ross (1991), *Technoculture*, Minneapolis: University of Minnesota Press.
Peters, M. A. (2021), 'Love and Social Distancing in the Time of Covid-19: The Philosophy and Literature of Pandemics', *Educational Philosophy and Theory*, 53 (8): 755–59. https://doi.org/10.1080/00131857.2020.1750091.
Pinar, W. F. (1975), *Curriculum Theorizing: The Reconceptualists*, New York: McCutchan Pub. Corp.
Pinar W. F. (2004), *What Is Curriculum Theory?* Lawrence Erlbaum.
Pinar, W. F. (2013), *Curriculum Studies in the United States: Present Circumstances, Intellectual Histories*, New York: Palgrave Macmillan.
Postman, N. (1992), *Technopoly: The Surrender of Culture to Technology*, 1st edn, New York: Knopf.
Price, T. A. (2000), 'Wiring the World', in G. D. White and F. C. Hauck (eds), *Campus Inc.: Corporate Power in the Ivory Tower*, Amherst, NY: Prometheus Books.
Price, T. A. (2014), 'Complexity and Complicity: Quality(s) and/or Effectiveness in Teacher Education', *European Journal of Curriculum Studies*, 1 (2). http://pages.ie.uminho.pt/ejcs/index.php/ejcs/article/view/168/97.
Price, T. A. (2018), 'Itinerant Curriculum Theory Meets Teacher Education: Educational Foundations, Knowledge Production, and the Teaching and Learning Context', *Revista Educacao e Cultura Contemporanea*, 15 (39): 31–53. http://periodicos.estacio.br/index.php/reeduc/article/view/5284/47966076.
Price, T. A. and D. Caster (2020), 'After Currere: The Meaning of Education in North American Curriculum Studies', *European Journal of Curriculum Studies*, 6: 4–20.
Rifkin, J. (1987), *Time Wars: The Primary Conflict in Human History*, New York: Simon & Schuster.
Roman, L. G., L. K. Christian-Smith and E. A. Ellsworth (1988), *Becoming Feminine: The Politics of Popular Culture*, New York: Falmer Press.
Ross, A. (1990), 'Hacking Away at the Counterculture', *Postmodern Culture*, 1 (1). https://doi.org/10.1353/pmc.1990.0011.
Sampson, T. D. (2012), Virality: Contagion Theory in the Age of Networks, University of Minnesota Press. http://site.ebrary.com/id/10613531 (accessed September 19, 2023).

Shteyngart, G. (2011), *Super Sad True Love Story: A Novel*, New York: Random House Trade Paperbacks.
Steiner-Adair, C. and T. Barker (2013), *The Big Disconnect: Protecting Childhood and Family Relationships in the Digital Age*, New York: Harper.
Treichler, P. A. (1991), 'How to Have Theory in an Epidemic: The Evolution of AIDS Treatment Activism', in C. Penley and A. Ross (eds), *Technoculture*, 57–106, New York: University of Minnesota Press.
Twenge, J. M. (2017), *IGen: Why Today's Super-Connected Kids Are Growing Up Less Rebellious, More Tolerant, Less Happy-And Completely Unprepared for Adulthood and What This Means For the Rest of Us*, Atria Books.
Twenge, J. M. (2023), *Generations: The Real Differences between Gen Z Millennials Gen X Boomers and Silents-And What They Mean for America's Future (First Atria Books Hardcover)*, New York: Atria Books.

16

Itinerant Curriculum Theory

Contributions to the Study of 'Education *in* Rights' in the Context of the Brazilian Public Defender's Office

Arion Godoy and Maria Cecilia L. Leite

Initial considerations

The Legal sphere, whether understood as a set of norms or rules or understood as an institutionality, has historically played the role of both instituting and legitimizing privileges and oppressions.

Although this is not the entire history of the legal system, it is also a depository of emancipatory and progressive expectations, consolidating or projecting practical social advances, as indicated by intellectuals such as Boaventura de Sousa Santos (2019) or Raúl Zaffaroni (2019); the product obtained until now is not to make jurists committed to social emancipation proud.

In the context of the new Latin American constitutionalism (Bello, 2013), the public defenders appear both as spokespersons for vulnerable people as well as serving as gateways to official justice systems that, historically, had only admitted them to punish them through criminal proceedings that would make medieval inquisitors proud. Access to rights or claiming social benefits had never occurred on a reasonable scale.

With this, there is a purely legal procedural dimension that is of interest, above all, to jurists. Still, a vast field is also inaugurated that allows for a series of other approaches that demand the intervention of sociologists, political scientists and educators. Therefore, the form of production and circulation of legal knowledge ceases to be the 'private property' of lawyers, prosecutors, public defenders and judges and becomes democratized somehow.

This chapter attempts to analyse how the learning of the legal sphere is structured by people who seek the services of the Brazilian Public Defender's Office, which is built based on an investigation produced in the scope of the Graduate Program in Education at the *Universidade Federal de Pelotas*.

At the time, research was carried out on how the elaboration and enactment of curricula designed by public defenders who assisted women in the area of family rights in the cities of Santa Vitória do Palmar, in Southern Brazil, and in Manaus, in the Northern region, took place. The research is found within the epistemologies of the South and adopts, in the curricular aspect, the itinerant curriculum theory (ICT) elaborated by João Menelau Paraskeva as a theoretical framework.

Itinerant curriculum theory and its political and social assumptions: Some notes

The ICTory, authored by the pedagogue and public intellectual João Menelau Paraskeva, can be situated within the framework of decolonial curricular theories, given the emphasis on political, historical, social and subjective processes linked to the domination and reproduction of oppression from educational systems.

Paraskeva (2007, 2008, 2011a, 2016b, 2021, 2022a, 2022b, 2023) pushed Boaventura de Sousa Santos's (2019) theorizing to another level – recognized as the pioneer of the non-derivative and post-abyssal turn/momentum in the field.

He (2008) argues that what is currently experienced in the field of education needs to be perceived as the unfolding of a process that started with the economic, political, ideological and cultural capitalist revolution that occurred during the 1970s and 1980s, which can be demarcated, in Anglophone countries, as from the governments of Ronald Reagan and Margaret Thatcher.

The first premise emphasized by the Mozambican pedagogue and social theorist concerns the effects on language and, more precisely, on a specific process of reframing concepts and expressions. Specifically, according to Paraskeva (2004, 2011a, 2016b, 2021, 2022a, 2022b, 2023), in essence, we are facing a reconfiguration process, within common sense, of the true meaning of certain words, with the aim of operating, therefore, a reconfiguration within common sense, a process that meets the desideracies of the new right and which implies careful and intricate processes of articulation and rearticulation (2004, 102).

For example, a shift affects the notion of state or public. Effectively, there is a transition, especially starting in Europe, of a welfare state, which exists or at least is seen as a goal, to a logic of 'state phobia', in which a process of hypertrophy of the private sector and the privatizing logic is inaugurated.

In parallel, democracies, conceptually or about social expectations, have also developed a downward path in the last half century, moving towards 'low intensity' (Santos, 2019). Precisely, the horizon of expectations and discourses of integration and equality of rights were weakened, gaining ground in narratives that contemplate differentiations among citizens and even the defence of non-republican privileges, converting democracies into true 'plutocracies' (Paraskeva, 2007, 2008).

These processes of resignification also reached the field of language through the appropriation of expressions historically identified with movements of a solidary character. Notions such as 'social justice', for example, are disconnected from their origin of community perspective and start to be submitted to an individual logic, related to the particular success, to the success of each one, and not as a socially constructed objective (Paraskeva, 2008).

The second aspect concerns the economic system: capitalism in its neoliberal stage. It is a 'sophistically predatory' capitalism (Paraskeva, 2009) that focuses on subjectivities (Dardot and Laval, 2016) and reaches segments, such as education or justice, far from the economic game until then.

According to Paraskeva (2011a, 2011b, 2016b, 2021, 2022a, 2022b, 2022c, 2023), we are before an erudite pilgrim of reinvention between the nation state and the citizen, in short, before a thorny process of reimagining and rebuilding the welfare state based on a dangerous ideological mess that manages to combine anti-welfarist perspectives (which understand the welfare state as economically non-productive) and anti-statists (who understand the market as a normative mechanism for resources, goods and services) (2011a, 220).

On a broader spectrum, about education, there are two immediate consequences: the gradual withdrawal of the state through a deliberate policy of disinvestment, which aims to create spaces and promote the educational 'business'; the abandonment of a project, even at the discursive level, of social transformation grounded on equal access and opportunities based on quality educational training.

In this context, ICT reveals itself as a theorization that dialogues with a broader political and social framework to provide tools that enable not only the simple opposition to the elements identified in mainstream theories but that, above all, allow the rearrangement of strategies and policies, perspectives and even values that are subject to constant dispute.

The path to this collective construction passes through the contraposition to epistemicides, the fight against the pedagogy of 'the big lies' through deterritorialization and cognitive justice[1] (Paraskeva, 2008, 2018a). According to Paraskeva (2019), critical theories and pedagogies need a new logic for the utopia of a fair world. To do this, critical theories need to radically detach themselves from their own oppressive Western Eurocentric epistemological matrix without denying it and engaging in what Paraskeva (2011b, 2016b, 2021, 2022a, 2022b, 2022c, 2023) coined as the ICT, the one that pushes to non-abyssal momentum. As stated by Paraskeva (2019), ICT is a new conceptual grammar that moves itinerantly within and beyond: (1) the coloniality of power, knowledge and being; (2) epistemicides, linguicide, abyssality and ecology of knowledge; and (3) post-structuralist hermeneutic itinerancy that produces a new non-abyssal alphabet of knowledge (p. 123). According to him (Paraskeva, 2011b, 2016b, 2019, 2021, 2022a, 2022b, 2022c, 2023), ICT is, therefore, a way to challenge curricular epistemicides (Paraskeva, 2016a; Santos, 2014) and implies deterritorializing both the curriculum and the fields of teacher training that cannot be done without neutralizing linguistics or commit epistemological euthanasia carried out by colonial powers in the past (but still happening in the present) (p. 123). In doing so, according to Paraskeva (2019), it floods the ground with a language beyond Western Eurocentric linguistic formations in the hope of an alternative philosophy of praxis. ICT aims at 'a general epistemology of the impossibility of a general epistemology' (Santos, 2016, 302).

As it can be noted, it is a theorization that is not presented in a merely instrumental way but proposes a review of the premises on which educational activity is developed and its insertion in the historical and current dynamics of power.

The curricula, perceived in a not merely utilitarian view, must embrace the world's diversity and need to recognize that knowledge sprouts and circulates everywhere – not exclusively from 'metropolises' – with no privileged holders of knowledge. As Paraskeva (2015) points out:

> Understanding curriculum in such a way shows how we are caught in a non-stable terrain determined by the myriad experiences of students, teachers, and the community. These experiences reveal a relevant pedagogic environment through dialogue and negotiation, knowing – as I claim elsewhere (Paraskeva, 2011a, 2011b) – that there is no social justice without cognitive justice. Such a curriculum posture also encourages what I have called the curriculum indigenous (students and teachers) to engage in a nonstop confrontation with real problems, thus establishing a connection within daily life, which, one must say, is non-deterministic. (p. 280)

This theoretical basis leads to the following reflections on curriculum, education *in* rights and the Brazilian Public Defender's Office.

Education *in* rights: Characteristics and spaces

The curriculum field constitutes one of the leading research segments in educational research, and its origin dates back to the beginning of the twentieth century. More recently, however, is the promotion of investigations that promote the interface of curriculum studies in non-school environments. The legal sphere and the Brazilian scenario is a process structured at the end of the last century (Leite, 2003) and has expanded since then. Regarding the conceptual dimension, it is worth paying attention to what is understood by education in rights, distinguishing it from legal and human rights education.

At first, under legal education, studies have been developed involving teaching legal science, especially in the university environment or, more specifically, in university law courses. In this scenario, digressions not limited to human rights education and may involve any of the fields of the teaching of legal science are included, such as civil law, criminal law or any other field.

Human rights education involves a wide range of studies, university students or not, state-owned or not, aimed at a vast and very heterogeneous population whose standard reference is teaching from the cultural and legal tradition that stems from the Universal Declaration of Human Rights. In these terms, the first category is mainly characterized by being inserted in the university context. At the same time, the second is identified from the theoretical matrix – linked to the Universal Declaration of Human Rights and the studies that follow – being the space where teaching and learning takes place irrelevant.

In turn, what is labelled as education *in* rights (Costa and Godoy, 2014) claims decolonial premises and, therefore, is treated by other theorists, such as Pereira and Pinheiro (2016), as education *in* rights in a decolonial perspective, and that its basic structure is the presence of two fundamental elements: the non-limitation to the rationality expressed in the Universal Declaration and the recognition of multiple pedagogical spaces. Conceptually, it has been defined, according to Godoy (2020), as an instrument of conscious insertion of the citizen in the language of law and the power circuits created and regulated by the legal system so that the subject can understand the possibilities – and the limits – inherent to any legal order or system for solving conflicts or claims of rights, being responsible, even if partially or in terms, for the results of its initiative (p. 137).

Thus, on the pedagogical level, it derives from the idea that formal places of education – schools and universities – do not represent the totality of educational spaces and that, therefore, pedagogical practices go beyond these places (Andrade and Costa, 2017). These contributions derive from several studies that have come to light since the end of the last century, having intellectual protagonists such as Elisabeth Ellsworth (2005) and Henry Giroux (2004), who explored the educational potentialities, for example, from museums and architecture, in the first case, or cinematographic productions, in the second case.

The interest in studying education *in* rights from the lens of the ICT derives from its proposal of displacements and decentring characteristics of decolonial theses, its plasticity and the claim for spaces other than the officially dedicated establishments to teaching.

Specific approaches, themes or focuses will have greater or lesser relevance or may even be incompatible. This, however, includes the usefulness of promoting the intended dialogue. It is similar to what happens when Paraskeva (2009, 5824) points out that homeschooling is not simply 'school at home' but another kind of teaching, which does not prevent the sharing of assumptions and specific analyses.

In these terms, the conclusion is that the curricular discussions, even if tempered, can be articulated, either in legal education itself or in less explored territories, such as education *in* rights governed by different matrices, in various spaces in which it can be developed – and not in purely school or university environments. Using Santos's vocabulary, it would be a regrettable 'waste of experience' (Santos, 2019) to abdicate a century-old curriculum tradition to tackle themes that, in the end, are common to the official or non-official spheres of education.

Education *in* rights and Public Defender's Office: Premises and construction

This section intends to articulate education *in* rights and the Public Defender's Office, placing it in the Brazilian context. The first step is to clarify what the institution is and what it is for.

The Public Defender's Office, at the normative level, in a brief overview, was created nationally by the 1988 Brazilian Federal Constitution to provide legal assistance to people with insufficient financial resources to resort to the judiciary.

Currently, however, after constitutional changes occurred, especially in the last decade, the institution has assumed a broader purpose of access to justice – which involves other mechanisms for resolving conflicts or claiming rights – starting to assist not only people without sufficient income to complain to the judiciary but also other groups in vulnerable situations (LGBTQ+, Black people, women victims of domestic violence, etc.). It is assumed, then, that access to justice is not restricted to access to the institutionality of the Legal System – institutions, buildings, processes, subjects, rituals – but, above all, to a system of power that is mediated by the language of law (Costa and Godoy, 2014).

In addition to the language, clothing and buildings, it is found that the citizen, the one who seeks, in the Public Defender's Office, access to specific power circuits that are regulated by the legal system and by language that mirrors, constitutes, produces or reproduces this individual, reflecting on values, privileges or hierarchies. Finally, besides claiming access to a jurisdictional body, it is also a claim for cognitive justice. Therefore, it is argued that the interaction between the citizen and the actors that make up that institution is as important or, at times, more important than the process, the verdict or any other strictly legal or procedural category. Hence, in part, the relevance of education *in* rights.

Hence, education *in* rights is the locus of reflection on the approaches, purposes, mechanisms and instruments that will make the interaction between subjects viable and the instrument itself operated through projects or initiatives that honour it. In this way, it is both an incidental and ancillary activity in an ordinary legal service, as it can be the primary objective of the interaction, as in the case of a lecture, training or workshop.

According to Freire (2013), raising awareness about the subject is central to ordinary legal assistance activities or events such as courses or workshops. In this approach, awareness does not assume a tendency towards fullness, as some critical theorists wanted. However, it stems from the contours and complexity of the concrete case brought by the person interested in the matter – which functions as 'generating themes'[2] – in order to enable a reasonable understanding of what could be done by the institutions, what could not be achieved, what would be up to the citizen to do, what would be up to the Defender's Office to ensure, all based on a specific situation of interest. In short, it is not a question of assuming the rational individual, not even the average individual, that the moderns tell us about but rather understanding that the citizens must have a certain level of comprehension about the process (in a broad sense) of solving their conflict or claim to their rights.

It is not convenient for the citizens to be *aliens* in their case; they must have actual conditions to choose among the possible solutions, a notion of which ones are impossible and which routes are available, with the respective bonus and bonuses. This turns out to be a harmony that is tried to be established in a very complex way, and that is always casuistry, as it is derived from concrete situations and, therefore, specific to the experience. This is so because, at the same time that it recognizes the citizen as a subject and intends to admit (and even encourage) him to become a protagonist, the limits arising from all institutionality are communicated. Thus, besides announcing a space of power where the subject can circulate, the Public Defender's Office is also aware of the existing borders. This is why the ICT is so relevant to the proposed analysis.

It is understood that law is not limited to mere abstraction, being constructed interactively, arising from social relations and meanings attributed by the subjects involved (Araújo, 2016); it is that a lens – just like the one of the ICT, which has for premise the myriad above of experiences, the unstable terrain on which it is based as well as the horizontality and the dialogue as structuring elements – proves to be so pertinent.

Because it is, above all, an epistemological posture – of respect and consideration for the knowledge that is born and circulates independently of socially constructed hierarchies and that precisely intends to 'broaden the legal canon by expanding the range of known legal experiences' (Araújo, 2016, 91) – is that the ICT can be thought of based on merely individual or procedural institutional action as well as on a collective and purely educational action. At this point, it is convenient to deepen this differentiation.

As examined in Godoy (2020), education *in* rights within the scope of the Public Defender's Office emerges with a focus on building a theoretical basis that supports activities of a collective nature – lectures, courses and workshops, among others. Thus, in education, mechanisms and assumptions were sought for structuring courses aimed at the community or professionals who maintained some interface with the legal sphere – social workers, tutelary counsellors, agents or community leaders. Even today, this aspect is the one that generates the most debates and interest.

However, just a decade ago, texts such as the ones of Costa and Godoy (2014) or J. V. dos Santos (2017) emphasized that the institution's entire performance, including what is the most ordinary of its work, such as providing legal guidance or clarifying the progress of a court case, is loaded with effective legal content and that this content can be developed in an educational perspective.

Illustratively, when providing legal guidance on divorce or custody of a child, in addition to dealing with the specific case, communication is promoted of what the legislation or the justice system considers to be due, at the same time as the abstract content of this message is resignified based on the circumstances or nuances that are presented by the person involved.

It is precisely in this type of interaction that it is possible to see a significant potential for the development of education *in* rights. The reasons are varied. Firstly, as already mentioned, the concrete case serves as a generating theme, enabling a genuine interest of the citizen in what is being dealt with and debated. Secondly, the construction of knowledge will take place dialogically, with Legal Science being effectively produced from the peculiarities of the concrete case in comparison with the entire institutional legal framework.

Thirdly, a trending horizontal relationship between subjects is made possible, avoiding reproducing what Freire (2013) calls 'banking education', which is one that assumes that there is a teacher who knows everything and who will deposit his knowledge in the one who knows nothing, the student. In this way, legality will be born in the interstice of what is brought by the citizen with what is added by the jurist.

Fourthly, there are quantitative reasons – which are always considerable regarding public policies. Although the number of lectures, workshops and activities of the same type is increasing, the work of the Public Defender's Office, in its daily life, is primarily developed in individualized care.

So that the reader can estimate the scale of what is being discussed, it is mentioned that in Rio Grande do Sul alone, one of the twenty-seven federative units in Brazil, the institution carried out more than one million individual consultations in 2020, according to the Annual Report of the Rio Grande do Sul's Public Defender's Office (2020).

Briefly, these are the reasons that lead to the conclusion that education *in* rights, considered in the daily work of the Public Defender's Office, has significant potential for the construction of Brazilian citizenship and the promotion of cognitive justice.

The Public Defender's Office and everyday life: Building knowledge and curricula

Between 2017 and 2020, empirical research was conducted to support the elaboration of a doctoral dissertation in education, in which conversations were held with women who sought the Public Defender's Office to deal with family cases in Santa Vitória do Palmar in the far South of Brazil, and Manaus, the far North of the country (Godoy, 2020).

It should be noted that although the notions of North/South in Santos (2019) are metaphorical, it was understood that it would be opportune to play with duality in the Brazilian context, promoting dialogues in regions that, in the national imagination, are considered quite distinct, for cultural and socio-economic reasons that are not of interest to explore at this time.

It should also be pointed out that the conversation is a 'methodological process' (Alves, 2013) that has differences in the interview, especially regarding the researcher's premises and posture. As Süssekind (2012) clarifies, this can be done by listening to the stories that the teachers tell us, talking with teachers and students instead of questioning them, asking school teachers or pedagogy students, teachers in training to make oral or written narratives, such as those created from the application of the free writing technique, being alert to what small talk and gossip say – whether it is flattering or slanderous (p. 8). Above all, as Süssekind (2012) points out, following the plots and people in schools and creating and recreating their rich and disobedient daily lives (p. 8–9). The author asks: Is the conversation the means to an end of the research? Above all, research, in its broadest or narrowest interpretation, according to Süssekind (2012), is always part of a long conversation (p. 9). Drawing on Doll and Trueit (2012), she affirms that conversation is, in turn, a practice of exchange and sharing in research, curriculum construction or in personal life; it is something that does not require a method or protocol, even when there is provision for the latter. So, there is no better or worse way to search, but there are tips, such as following the people, the plots and the allegories as we learn from postmodern ethnography (Süssekind, 2012, 9).

Although the scope and volume of matters dealt with in the doctoral dissertation are broader than those discussed later in the chapter, two topics were selected that demonstrate some critical conclusions of the investigation and its connection with ICT.

About 'what' is taught

It was argued, in this text, that education *in* rights can be defined as the teaching and learning processes that lead the citizen to understand the possibilities and limits of the legal system for resolving their conflicts or claiming their rights.

A very relevant analysis is to investigate how education *in* rights is developed in the daily service of the Public Defender's Office, that is, not only as a conceptual issue but also how it is produced or enacted. It is a bit of sociology of emergencies (Santos, 2002) since it intends to assess what is already being built in the present and which can broaden imagination about the future about the possibilities of access to justice.

The first aspect on which reflection is proposed is to evaluate *what* is taught. From the analysis of the conversations held in general after the consultations had been carried out, it was noticed that those women had adequate knowledge, about their own rights[3] and procedural law, always taking into account the existing contexts and their respective focuses of interest.

In the dialogue held with Delia,[4] who had sought the service to deal with child support for her daughter, she spontaneously reported the amounts owed accurately, dealt with the fact of receiving different amounts for her children naturally, demonstrating some level of understanding about the legal system.[5]

Soraya, who dealt with a similar topic, made an interesting report that, considering the amount to which her child would be entitled – as reported to her in the care provided – she would need to find ways to insert herself professionally, as she could foresee that the alimony would be insufficient to cover her daughter's expenses. Thus, the simple concrete parameter of the alimony that will be arbitrated allows the citizen to organize in terms of housing and paid work, which results, as stated earlier, not from the legal provision itself but, above all, from the elaborated knowledge.

It is also important, in addition to the aspects linked to having or not a certain right or its respective quantification, to clarify basic procedural rules. When asked, Natacha, Anastacia, Emilie and Soraya adequately reported the next steps of the processes they had promoted – discussing expected deadlines, necessary actions and so on. Effectively, the satisfactory understanding of the respective scripts to be followed is noticeable concerning their pretensions.

It is noteworthy that these notions are pretty important because not only do they make it possible for processes to have agile progress, but they also contribute to people being able to project consequences that are not adequately procedural, occurring in the social or family plan, such as the need to employ or foresee possible discomfort with other litigants/family members.

Moreover, in addition to procedural rules in the strict sense, measures of an instrumental nature are also considered, which are essential for exercising rights. Illustratively, Yasmine narrated that she had a troubled relationship with her son's father and that she faced difficulties in receiving the amounts owed because with each payment – usually made in cash, in person – a series of discussions disturbed her.

During assistance, Yasmine was instructed to provide a bank account to avoid unnecessary contact. Hence, considering the person's actual context of experience made it possible to provide a recommendation that is not correctly legal but which serves to enforce the child's rights and for the mother's preservation.

Furthermore, it is essential to understand how education *in* rights enhances other forms of conflict resolution that need to be appropriately judicial and, above all, that are not adversarial.[6] It is specifically about the relationship between education *in* rights and the auto-compositive solution of conflicts,[7] in which it is noted that an adequate expectation about the limits and possibilities of law allows greater security for the formulation of agreements – which enhances the protagonism of the people interested – in the same way that consensus contributes to a better understanding of the solutions in each case.

For example, it is possible to note that the citizens interviewed demonstrated more specific knowledge about the visitation regime set in an agreement mediated by the Public Defender's Office than when there is a simple arbitration by the judge, reported through mere notification.

Similarly, it is also noted that there is greater clarity about the amounts and forms of payment when adjusted directly by those involved, as well as a greater propensity for a collaborative posture and subjective recognition of the justice of what was agreed, as already argued with greater detail in another opportunity (Costa and Godoy, 2014).

Education *in* rights designed, reflected and acted upon through a public institution that values the treatment of legal knowledge in the way it is argued also contributes to the undoing of certain misunderstandings that often in the eagerness to inform are provoked by the means of communication and reflected by citizens in general, notably through social networks.

In the Brazilian scenario, this involves issues related to the need for consent to divorce or the legal forms of custody of minor children. It is not interesting to develop these matters in a text with this approach. However, it is interesting to point out the importance of this perspective for the reliability of information at a time of such fluidity in communications.

Finally, education *in* rights reveals itself, in this context, as an instrument of dealienation of subjects about conflicts or processes, as it allows referrals not to be purely delegated (or alienated) to the legal professionals, enabling a growing protagonism of the citizens in resolving their own issues or conflicts.

About 'how' is taught

After analysing how education *in* rights effectively develops in the context of the Brazilian Public Defender's Office, it is appropriate to investigate how the institution and its agents organize the activity in what way the curriculum has been understood, thought, organized and enacted contextually. In terms of the broader organization of the Public Defender's Office, whether in Rio Grande do Sul or in Amazonas, no parameters affirm the existence of a curriculum in a formal sense.

However, based on the ICT and other critical and post-critical theorizations, the curriculum is not only what is documented; it is not just a sheet of paper. Therefore, it should be reflected if it is possible to think about the existence of 'itinerant curricula', places which are produced and acted in the studied units. In this perspective, it is understood that the answer is affirmative. It is a little more sociology of emergencies. It is another attempt to extend the possibilities of 'futures' from the present experiences.

It should be recalled at this point that Paraskeva (2018b) states that the ICT undergoes the overcoming of the Eurocentric matrix, denying the colonial grammar and valuing other hermeneutics, languages and knowledge. It is central, as already mentioned, the idea of deterritorialization that precisely opposes a pasteurized, uniformed notion about knowledge and their ways. It presupposes a utopian vision for not considering that the logics of progress or single thought definitely subjugate the alternatives of the future.

In the investigation, the public defender Gustavo de Oliveira da Luz reported that many of the people seeking care, more than a judicial process in itself – a divorce, for example – intend to understand which would be, from the legal regulation, the practical consequences for their lives, if they refer a particular process. Thus, more than a specific legal request, there is an expectation of understanding the possibilities that would exist if a specific provision was made, which is decisive for analysing whether it is convenient.

Gustavo also highlighted the relation he perceives between education *in* rights and auto-compositive solutions, allowing the imagination of a less vertical, less dogmatic law. He narrates that when people can understand the functioning of the legal system, they are more willing to negotiate with the other interested parties and build solutions compatible with their respective realities. Because of this, law ceases to be something that *focuses* on the concrete case or the lives of people and becomes something built by the interested parties, exercising the system of justice a less mandatory function, especially the protection of what was adjusted and supported to vulnerabilities.

However, Gustavo claims that the path of dialogue, negotiation of solutions and recognition of the interested parties as subjects require an active posture of direction for these paths, which the Public Defender's Office structure must carry out.

The traditional or historical posture of jurists that can be synthesized in the Brocard signals that it is up to the citizen only to give the facts, since legality will be given by the judge[8] and can only be reversed from some craftsmanship of practices[9] (Santos, 2019). That is, education *in* rights and its interface with other non-adversary instruments is something dependent on initiative approach rather than occurring spontaneously.

It is precisely in this organization of themes, approaches, practices that one sees the existence of curricula, although not formalized and with some flexibility. Its concrete realization is also noticed not only from what Gustavo enunciates or what can be observed in Santa Vitória do Palmar or Manaus but also from the dialogues in the research, in which approaches consistent with the referred assumptions are seen.

In this sense, it is considered reasonable to affirm that there are, in each studied city, from the perceptions, inclinations and sensibilities of each public defender, attentive to the peculiarities of each context, curricula that are constructed from guidelines such as strengthening of auto-compositive solutions, the attempt of the functionalization[10] of law (Nunn, 1997), clarification of procedures that will follow, among other characteristics or guidelines.

These attributes are even to identify an affinity with the decolonial theories insofar as it presupposes the legal sphere not as something given but built. It also allows that law to be appropriated by people, thus avoiding processes of disidentification or strangeness, which are essential characters in the construction of autonomies and social emancipation, understood in Boaventura de Sousa Santos's terms.

It is a breakup, although perhaps equivalent to a small crack in the Brazilian legal building, with the logic that historically based and structured relations between citizenship and Law, especially in the Global South.

Final considerations

This study signals that education *in* rights is an essential mechanism for promoting cognitive justice and that citizens seeking the Brazilian Public Defender's Office may be effectively protagonists in resolving their conflicts or claiming their rights.

It should be noted that it is identifiable, either by the narrative of public defenders or by listening to people who have been assisted, as well as by existing flows, that certain understandings, practices and postures can be read as curricular. That is, there are signs of the existence of curricula constituted and enacted according to concrete scenarios and particularities.

About that, the ICT is adequate, in particular for the sharing of premises and understandings on the respective roles of education and law in contemporary societies, so that the deepening of ICT studies denotes the ability to contribute to the qualification of the service of an educational nature provided by the Public Defender's Office.

In the investigation carried out, the studies led by Paraskeva enabled the mapping and allocation of meanings to practices and flows – understood as being of a curricular nature – which was carried out without this recognition and that, from the disclosure of the results, they may influence the improvement of the initiatives themselves, as well as the expansion of a less colonial justice model.

In these terms, the improvement and propagation of existing itinerant curricula are a possible and relevant institutional strategy based on the definition of epistemological postures and the establishment of assumptions that can contribute to the deepening of emancipatory projects of education *in* rights that are already ongoing and for the invention of other possibilities that are still in time to be produced.

Notes

1 Cognitive justice, according to Santos (2014), consists of 'equity between different ways of knowing and different forms of knowledge' (p. 237).
2 In summary, the generative themes constitute an alternative to curriculum models that promote the definition of contents to be taught beforehand. Therefore, the

generating themes are produced by educators and students dialogically rather than in advance by policymakers.
3   In a rather superficial way, material right is right in itself; procedural law concerns the rules and rites that regulate the processes in which material proper claims are made.
4   The names referred to are taken from literary works so as not to allow the identification of the people with whom the researcher spoke.
5   In Brazilian law, there are no fixed amounts for alimony, depending on the analysis of the child's needs and the concrete possibilities of each parent. Therefore, eventually children who have the same mother but different fathers will require different amounts.
6   Adversarials are processes of a non-collaborative nature in which the people who litigate are in open opposition, and it is up to the judge to define what is proper or due, with no effective participation of citizens in terms of the solution.
7   Auto-compositive solutions of conflicts constitute a genre that includes several kinds of collaborative procedures, such as mediation, conciliation or restorative justice, among others, in which the people interested actively participate in the solutions constructed.
8   'Da mihi factum, dabo tibi ius'.
9   According to B. de S. Santos (2019), given that knowledge is produced in the struggles or for the struggles, always considering the articulations between the forms of oppression, which end up being, therefore, always contextual, there is no room for standardization. Processes, tools and materials impose some conditions but leave room for a significant margin of freedom (p. 988).
10 Even though it is not a merely practical perspective, the idea of functionalization recognizes that the legal system has a social and political role that should be considered, opposing self-referenced literacy of law.

References

Alves, N. (2013), 'Possibilidades de "uso" de fotografias nas pesquisas de "espaçostempos" de escolas', *Revista Brasileira de Educação em Geografia*, 3 (6): 158–76.
Andrade, P. D. and Costa, M. V. (2017), 'Nos rastros do conceito de *pedagogias culturais*: invenção, disseminação e usos', *EDUR – Educação em Revista*, 13 (1): 1–23.
Araújo, S. (2016), 'Para lá dos códigos. O papel do Estado e a heterogeneidade do pluralismo jurídico em Moçambique', *Politéia*, 2 (1): 19–38.
Bello, E. (2013), *A cidadania na luta política dos movimentos sociais urbanos*, Caxias do Sul (Brasil): EDUCS.
Costa, D. B. da and A. E. de Godoy. (2014), *Educação em Direitos e Defensoria Pública: Cidadania, Democracia e atuação nos processos de transformação política, social e subjetiva*. Curitiba (Brasil): Juruá.
Dardot, P. and C. Laval (2016), *A nova razão do mundo: ensaio sobre a sociedade neoliberal*, (Brasil): Boitempo.
Doll, Jr. W. and D. Trueit (2012), *Pragmatism, Post-Modernism, and Complexity Theory*. New York: Routledge.
Ellsworth, E. (2005), *Places of Learning: Media, Architecture, and Pedagogy*. New York: Routledge.
Freire, P. (2013), *Pedagogia da autonomia: saberes necessários à prática educativa*. Curitiba (Brasil): Paz e Terra.

Giroux, H. A. (2004), 'Cultural Studies, Public Pedagogy, and the Responsibility of Intellectuals', *Communication and Critical/Cultural Studies*, 1 (1): 59–79.

Godoy, A. E. de. (2020), *Educação em Direitos e Defensoria Pública: ausências e emergências no cotidiano de atendimento dos casos de família prestado às mulheres nas cidades de Santa Vitória do Palmar/RS e Manaus/AM* (Unpublished Doctoral dissertation, Faculdade de Educação, Universidade Federal de Pelotas, Pelotas, Rio Grande do Sul, Brazil).

Leite, M. C. L. (2003), *Decisões pedagógicas e inovações no ensino jurídico* (Doctoral dissertation, Faculdade de Educação, Universidade Federal do Rio Grande do Sul Porto Alegre, Brasil). Lume Database. https://lume.ufrgs.br/handle/10183/175323.

Nunn, K. B. (1997), 'Law as a Eurocentric Enterprise', *Law & Inequality: A Journal of Theory and Practice*, 15 (2): 323–71.

Paraskeva, J. M. (2004), 'O nome, a coisa… e o currículo. Perversos motes da perigosa glosa neo-centrista radical', *Psicologia e Sociedade*, 16 (2): 101–13.

Paraskeva, J. M. (2007), *Ideologia, Cultura e Curriculo*, Lisboa. Didatica Editora.

Paraskeva, J. M. (2008a), 'Racismo com racistas. O colonialismo [colonial-mente] colonizado português. Um Caliban Próspero ou um Próspero Calibanizado', *Revista Angolana de Sociologia*, 1 (1): 35–59.

Paraskeva, J. M. (2009), *O colonialismo da tecnologia educativa*. Paper presentation. 10th Internacional Galego-Português de Psicopedagogia da Universidade do Minho, Braga, Portugal. https://umassd.academia.edu/JParaskeva.

Paraskeva, J. M. (2011a), 'Capitalismo acadêmico em Portugal "Tandem Abvetere Patientia Nostra?"', *Cadernos de Educação – UFPel*, 40 (1): 215–57.

Paraskeva, J. M. (2011b), *Conflicts in Curriculum Theory*, 1st edn, New York: Palgrave.

Paraskeva, J. M. (2011c), *Nova Teoria Curricular*, Lisboa: Pedago.

Paraskeva, J. M. (2015), 'Epistemicides: Toward an Itinerant Curriculum Theory', in J. M. Paraskeva and S. R. Steinberg (eds), *Curriculum: Decanonizing the Field*, Vol. 491, 261–289. New York: Peter Lang.

Paraskeva, J. M. (2016a), 'Desterritorializar: Hacia a una teoria curricular itinerante', *Revista Interuniversitaria de Formación del Profesorado*, 30 (1): 121–34.

Paraskeva, J. M. (2016b), *Curriculum Epistemicides*, New York: Routledge.

Paraskeva, J. M. (2018a), 'Against the scandal: itinerant curriculum theory as subaltern momentum', *Qualitative Research Journal*, 18 (2): 128–43.

Paraskeva, J. M. (2018b), What Happened to Critical Theory?' in J. M. Paraskeva, J. Menelau and E. Janson (eds), *Voicing the Silences of Social and Cognitive Justice*, Vol. 2, 1–61. Rotterdam, Zuid-Holland: Sense Publishers.

Paraskeva, J. M., ed. (2018c), *The Epistemicide: Towards a Just Curriculum Theory*, New York: Routledge.

Paraskeva, J. M. (2019), 'O que aconteceu com a teoria crítica do currículo? A necessidade de ir além da raiva neoliberal, sem evitá-la', *Linguagens, Educação e Sociedade*, 41 (1): 96–134.

Paraskeva, J. M. (2021), *Curriculum and the Generation of Utopia*, New York: Routledge.

Paraskeva, J. M. (2022a), *Conflicts in Curriculum Theory*, 2nd edn, New York: Palgrave.

Paraskeva, J. M., ed. (2022b), *The Curriculum: A New Comprehensive Reader*, New York: Peter Lang.

Paraskeva, J. M. (2022c), 'The Generation of the Utopia: Itinerant Curriculum Theory Towards a 'Futurable Future'', *Discourses: Studies in the Cultural Politics of Education*, 43 (3): 347–66.

Paraskeva, J. M. (2023), *Critical Perspectives on the Denial of Caste in Educational Debate*, New York: Routledge.
Pereira, I. B. L. and D. A. R. Pinheiro (2016), 'Direitos humanos em perspectiva decolonial: por um direito inclusivo da sexualidade', *Revista de Movimentos Sociais e Conflitos*, 2 (1): 166–87. http://doi.org/10.26668/IndexLawJournals/2525-9830/2016.v2i1.362.
Santos, B. de S. (2002), 'Para uma sociologia das ausências e uma sociologia das emergências', *Revista Crítica de Ciências Sociais*, 63 (1): 237–80.
Santos, B. de S. (2014), *Science, Emancipation, and the Variety of Forms of Knowledge*, Paradigm Publishers.
Santos, B. de S. (2016), *Epistemologies of the South: Justice Against Epistemicide*, Routledge.
Santos, B. de S. (2019), *O fim do império cognitivo: a afirmação das epistemologias do Sul*, Autêntica.
Santos, J. V. dos. (2017), *O diálogo na educação em direitos* (Master's thesis, Faculdade de Educação, Universidade de Caxias do Sul. UCS Repository). https://repositorio.ucs.br/xmlui/bitstream/handle/11338/3333/Dissertacao%20Juliano%20Viali%20dos%20Santos.pdf?sequence=1&isAllowed=y.
Süssekind, M. L. (2012), 'O ineditismo dos estudos *nosdoscom os* cotidianos: currículos e formação de professores, relatos e conversas em uma escola pública no Rio de Janeiro, Brasil', *Revista e-Curriculum*, 9 (2): 1–21.
Zaffaroni, E. R. (2019, October 2), *Acesso à justiça na América Latina* [Video]. YouTube. https://www.youtube.com/watch?v=s5ec_tq9XoA&list=WL&index=229.

Index

absence 12, 13, 17, 18, 22, 26, 59, 64, 78, 86, 101, 107, 110, 154, 162, 166, 169, 170, 183, 185, 187, 199
Abya-Yala 55, 57, 63, 65
abyssal 22, 27, 152, 167, 179, 184, 213, 215
   canons 180
   crack 144
   discourse 92
   divide 25, 155, 164, 168
   line 29, 39, 56, 64, 130, 138, 150, 154, 156, 179
   non- 14, 17, 23, 24, 28, 145, 171, 243
   reason 12, 170, 181, 182
   status 213
   theory 182
   thinking 20, 29, 86, 103, 154, 165, 168, 169, 179, 180, 183–5, 198, 199, 210, 215
abyssality 14, 22, 23, 29, 182, 186, 243
Agamben, Giorgio 14, 24, 76
Ahmad, Aijaz 22
Alba, Alicia 11
Al-l-Ahmad, Jalal 15
Althusser, Louis 161
Amdedkar, Bhimrao Ramji 26
Amin, Samir 24
Angulo Rasco, José Félix 28, 81–3, 85
annihilation 48, 66, 181
anti-colonial 12, 29, 40, 97, 104, 108, 109, 166
anti-dialectical 17
Anyon, Jean 12
Anzaldua, Gloria 20
Appadurai, Arjun 20
Apple, Michael 3, 4, 12, 70, 102, 108, 109, 120, 162, 164, 166, 212, 226
Aristoteles 100

Badiou, Alain 18
Baker, Bernadette 12

Baum, Graciela 16, 28, 55, 64
Bauman, Zygmunt 20, 92, 131, 133, 184
Benhabib, Seyla 21, 131
Benjamin, Walter 233
Berardi, Franco 'Bifo' 14
border
   counter-pedagogies 64
   epistemologies 132
   lines 138
   thinking 44, 103
   voices 55, 128
Bourdieu, Pierre 85
bunker
   praxis 14
   theory 14
Burns, Richard 25

Cabral, Amilcar 21
Caliban reason 15
canon 3, 4, 14, 16, 24, 28, 29, 58, 62, 65, 85, 87, 88, 99, 100, 145, 146, 156, 163, 171, 179, 180, 189, 197–9, 211, 216, 218, 247
canonology 17, 153
capital xvi, 58, 60, 134, 143, 144, 157
   accumulation xv
   symbolic 58, 60
capitalism 131, 235, 243
   consumer 39, 40
   financial 131, 134
   global 52
   industrial 66
   neoliberal 173
   patriarchal 181
caste 26
Cesaire, Aimé 131
Chamboredon, Jean Claude 85
chaos 19, 21, 22, 157, 172, 231
class xvi, 4, 16, 26, 31, 38, 50, 56, 60, 65, 89, 102, 109, 131, 136, 164, 166, 193, 213, 225, 226, 233

lower   223
middle   102, 224, 232
ruling   89
social   4, 131, 136
of teachers   185
working   38
clinamen   22
cognitive
  capitalism   134
  diversity   78, 116, 178, 187
  divide   165
  Empire   15
  injustice   103, 130, 136, 138, 145
  justice   13, 21, 24, 29, 30, 58, 72, 77, 87, 97, 98, 110, 116, 129, 133, 134, 139, 146–9, 151, 152, 155, 183, 184, 192, 193, 217, 243, 244, 246, 248, 252
  matrix   25, 73, 74
  and social justice   13, 21, 24, 29, 155, 164
co-habitus   13, 15, 20, 23, 27, 163, 183, 231
colonialism   3, 22, 30, 56, 57, 71, 97, 103, 131, 143, 157, 189, 190, 192
  of being   14
  coloniality   17, 25, 28, 29, 37–40, 45, 46, 49, 55–8, 61, 62, 71, 74, 75, 161–4, 167–71, 182, 199, 216
  English curriculum   58
  episteme   75, 216, 217
  of gender   115, 232
  of knowledge   14, 22
  matrix   51, 195
  post   72, 117, 216
  of power   14, 20, 22, 24, 57, 63, 156, 165, 243
  present day   37, 38, 45, 56
  racialized   52
  sepoys of   197
  Spanish crioulx   46
  Western Modernity   57, 72, 73, 217
coloniality power matrix   156, 163
commonsense   14, 235
communal   xvi, 13, 50–2, 57
conscientization   40, 49, 50, 137
contemporarysm   18
corazonar   16, 17, 87
counter
  culture   229
  current   28, 37
  dominant   11, 13, 17, 18, 24, 25, 27, 28, 72, 143, 144, 146, 154, 189, 190, 197, 198, 211, 212, 214, 215
  hegemonic   11, 12, 19, 23, 26, 27, 130, 139, 143, 145, 146, 150, 152, 182, 183, 193, 197, 198, 212
  narrative   47
  pedagogy   64, 138
  publics   20
  reform   43
  sense   15
  technopolys   228
Couto, Mia   15, 25
critical
  Caste Curriculum Theory (CCCT)   26
  curriculum river   180, 204
  theory   15, 184
curriculum
  capitis diminutiu   12
  complicated conversation   12, 16, 17, 26, 183, 185, 206, 211, 215, 225, 226
  deterritorialized   13, 87, 147, 181, 185, 194
  epistemicide   3, 11, 16, 27, 70, 71, 136, 149, 150, 152, 154–6, 193, 194, 196, 199, 212, 213, 215
  everyday creation   146–8, 150–5, 170
  fascism   179, 183
  hegemonic   71, 130, 133, 138, 143, 151, 152, 155
  hypertrophia theoricae   12
  imparity   24
  involution   11–13, 20, 21, 137, 152, 206, 209, 216
  modern   148
  mythomaniac   39
  non-epistemicidal   148
  occidentosis   21, 152
  reason   16
  reform   28, 69–72, 74–6, 78, 85, 89, 102, 120, 121, 184, 185, 207, 208, 210, 215
  scandal   155, 195
  simulacra   125, 233
  standardization   28, 81, 83, 91, 137, 183

Thai-centric 30, 206, 208–12, 214, 217
theory 3, 11, 13, 15, 20, 26–30, 55, 81, 83, 85, 87, 89, 95, 98, 110, 116, 118, 123, 129, 145, 149, 155, 169, 181, 185, 189, 194, 204, 211, 236
theorycide 11–13
translation 117

Dabashi, Hamid 20, 163, 164, 167, 168, 173
Dalit
  chetna 26
  reason 26
Darder, Antonia 13, 17, 20–2, 24–7, 146, 166, 236
De Certeau, Michel 148, 149, 153
decolonial 12, 21, 25, 27, 40, 48, 50, 51, 56, 58, 70–2, 75, 78, 86, 165, 170, 217, 245
  curriculum 242
  education 56, 204, 215, 216
  hispanophone 17, 28, 37, 40, 42, 43, 45–50, 52
  intellectual 46, 52
  Itinerant 29, 61
  language 74, 75
  literature 12
  method 55, 57
  praxis 44
  theory 252
  thinking/thought 20, 38, 47–9, 52, 59, 78
  turn 30, 87, 157, 162, 163, 169, 171, 172
decolonizing 28, 56, 75, 78, 115, 163, 189–92, 194
  curriculum 115–17, 192, 194, 204
  English curriculum 55–7, 61, 62
  international relations theory 29, 161
  knowledge and power 107, 193
  Korean curriculum 116, 117
  native narratives 20
  Thai-centric curriculum 30, 203–5
de-linking 17, 26, 40, 44, 51, 64, 72, 76, 103, 108
derivative 21, 28, 71, 163, 167
deterritorialization 27, 86, 129, 143, 145, 150, 153, 194, 243, 251

Dewey, John 1, 3
Diop, Cheikh Anta 21
Dussel, Enrique 21, 41, 104, 105, 131, 132, 194

Eagleton, Terry 11, 12, 18, 19, 22, 23, 27
ecology of knowledge 14, 22, 59, 86, 98, 143, 145, 146, 148–51, 155, 171, 181, 192, 199, 211, 212, 217, 218, 243
economic/economy xvi, 3, 25, 38, 39, 41, 44, 45, 48, 50, 51, 60, 65, 70, 89, 102, 103, 105, 109, 130, 133, 134, 137, 163, 165, 179, 189, 190, 206, 208, 216, 230, 242, 243, 248
  abyss 223
  Chile 89
  collapse 232
  despair 2
  development 73, 134
  inequality 131, 164
  justice 217
  neoliberal reform 207
  theory 110
education/al xv, 1–6, 15–17, 23, 25, 26, 28–30, 37, 39, 42, 44, 49, 51, 55, 56, 58–61, 63, 66, 69, 70, 74–8, 81–4, 86, 87, 89, 91, 92, 97–108, 110, 116–19, 121, 122, 124, 125, 129–31, 133–6, 138, 139, 146, 152, 154, 157, 161, 162, 164, 166, 169–72, 181, 183–5, 190–3, 196, 203–17, 225–8, 230, 232–5, 241–5, 247, 248, 250
  Korean 120, 121, 123, 124, 126
  policy 4
  praxis 212
  rights 109
  in rights 241, 244–52
  Super 123
el padron colonial del poder 167, 171
Ellsworth, Elizabeth 12, 136, 137, 225, 227, 245
Empire 1, 3–5, 15, 26, 57, 98, 100–2, 124, 125, 166, 168, 170, 193
enslavement 3, 17
epistemic
  decolonization 191
  detachment 132
  disobedience 64

diversity   71
fascism   59, 168
inferiority   167
injustice   20, 166, 173
invisibility   169
market   62
'minga'   15
monoculture   59
oppression   20, 166
privilege   167
violence   136, 169
epistemicidal   12, 14, 26, 72, 143, 148, 152, 154, 165, 170, 180, 182
epistemicide   3, 5, 11, 14, 16–18, 20, 26, 27, 30, 43, 44, 62, 65, 70–5, 86, 98, 115, 124–5, 135, 136, 144, 145, 148–50, 152, 155, 156, 162, 166, 169, 170, 177, 179, 180, 182–4, 190, 193–5, 197, 199, 204, 205, 208, 210, 212, 213, 215, 221, 243
  cultural   72
  curriculum   11, 16, 70, 136, 152, 193, 194, 199, 212, 213, 215
  hegemonic   30, 204, 205, 210
  linguistic   71, 72
  reversive   11, 17, 26, 144, 145, 149, 150, 152, 155, 156, 170
  western modern Eurocentric   18, 208, 212
epistemological
  'alphabet of thought'   18
  blindness   20, 26, 233
  cleansing   162
  displacements   153, 156
  diverse/sity   92, 109, 145, 149, 171
  euthanasia   24, 243
  fog   109
  freedom   17, 23
  Freudian-hysterical   26
  hegemony   30
  independence   11, 21, 23, 29, 155
  justice   172
  liberation   6, 21, 23, 28
  macho-patriarchal   143
  matrix   20, 243
  pariah   15
  'plateau'   164
  South   179, 180
  subjugations   88
  theory   100
  turn   86
epistemologies   18, 20, 25, 27–30, 50, 57, 59, 71, 85–8, 98, 99, 103, 106, 115, 116, 119, 123–5, 132, 144–8, 150, 154, 155, 161–3, 167, 171, 180, 181, 186, 194, 197–9, 204, 215, 216, 242
  African   198
  beyond the global north   25
  colonial   199
  Eurocentric   119
  indigenous   154
  in/of/from the South   144, 146, 150, 155, 161, 167, 171, 186, 197, 242
  Latin American   50
  Non-Western   125
  of the North   59
  Northern   154
  from *nuestros locales*   28
  Ottoman-centric   99
  Pre-islamic   99
  Southern   147, 148, 181
  Thai-centric   216
  Western   27, 116, 123, 162
ethnic   xvi, 4, 106, 131, 133, 135, 152, 186, 213, 226
ethnicity   4, 131, 136, 182, 213, 226
eugenic   16, 17, 21, 23, 26, 27, 39, 71, 73, 143, 145, 146, 154, 155, 162–5, 167, 170, 193, 195, 197
Eurocentric   11–13, 15, 17–21, 24–7, 29, 39, 70, 71, 78, 85, 92, 115, 119, 123, 143, 161, 162, 164, 166, 168–70, 180, 181, 194, 197, 198
  abyssal thinking   20, 152, 165
  canon   29, 99
  curriculum   98, 144, 152
  disciplinary knowledge   20
  epistemes/epistemic   17, 105, 171, 198
  epistemicide   208, 212
  exceptionalism   165
  logic   26
  matrix   12, 15, 161, 169, 171, 243, 251
  post-modern   15
  river   25
  science   164
  theory   154, 179

Eurocentrism   16, 85, 86, 115, 119, 162, 165, 169, 171, 182, 232
exploitation   38, 48, 172, 173

Fanon, Frantz   3, 17, 46, 116, 118, 123, 130, 131
fascism   130, 180, 224, 231, 235
Foucault, Michele   15, 17, 69, 75, 118, 204
Fraser, Nancy   20
Freire, Paulo   xvi, 4, 46, 49, 50, 104, 118, 137, 149, 152, 156, 162, 165, 184, 227, 246, 247
Freud, Sigmund   104
freudian hysterical blindness   26
fronteirización   58
functionalist   13, 26, 30, 204, 206, 208-10, 214, 216, 217

Galeano, Eduardo   12
Gandhi, Mahatma   112
gender   4, 5, 16, 28, 38, 55, 109, 110, 115, 131, 136, 164, 166, 182, 185, 186, 205, 213, 225-7, 232
Generation of Utopia   25
genocide   17, 38, 42, 60, 72, 150
Gil, José   11-19, 21, 22, 137
Giroux, Henry   xv, 4, 7, 12, 102, 104, 108, 109, 136, 137, 162, 163, 227, 245
Global
   North   5, 15, 23, 25, 39, 47, 49, 154, 162, 163, 165, 170, 171, 181, 203, 208, 209
   South   2, 3, 5, 6, 15, 29, 44, 56, 58, 98, 143, 156, 162-4, 167-70, 172, 173, 187, 189, 190, 217, 252
globalization   62, 65, 108, 170, 171, 184, 206, 216
Godoy, Arion   30, 242, 244-8, 250
Goody, Jack   87, 169
Gramsci, Antonio   146
Grosfoguel, Ramon   38, 51

Han, Byung Chul   20, 21, 26, 77
Harding, Sandra   24, 168, 171
Hardt, Michael and Negri, Toni   20
Harvey, David   20
hegemonic   11, 17, 19, 23, 24, 26, 27, 29, 39, 41, 43, 44, 46, 47, 49, 54, 56, 57, 59, 61-3, 73, 78, 85, 98, 130, 131, 133, 136, 144, 145, 152, 153, 156, 162, 165, 167, 170, 179-82, 189, 195, 204, 209, 212, 214
   anti   51
   dehumanizing   192
   epistemicide   30, 205, 210
   epistemology   135
   forms of knowledges   72, 150
   Western discourses   72
hegemony   16, 30, 39, 71, 97, 133, 135, 162, 182, 185, 191, 197
   of the English language   20
Heidegger, Martin   69, 70, 75, 77
Henry, Paget   26
heterotopia   135
hooks, bell   27, 193
Huebner, Dwayne   4, 12, 14, 16, 23-7, 86, 88, 216
   syndrome   12

IC*theorist*   18, 25, 27
identical   20, 21, 26, 126, 165
ideology   xvii, 16, 107, 108, 110, 131, 135, 138, 163, 204
   gender   185
   hongikingan   118
   neoliberal   130
   Ottoman-Islamic   99, 100
   Turkishness   105
   Turk-Islam   107
imperialism   3, 5, 38, 45, 56, 57, 70-2, 99, 118, 164, 184, 209
indigenous   3, 16, 17, 20, 28, 37-48, 52, 59, 60, 66, 71, 115, 118-20, 122-4, 152, 154, 173, 190, 244
indigenoustude   20
inequality   27, 29, 38, 57, 88, 89, 129, 132, 136, 137, 148, 164, 226
International Relations Theory   29, 161
Islam/Islamic   97-102, 105-8
Itinerant curriculum theory (ICT)   xvii, 1, 2, 5, 6, 11, 13-30, 55, 56, 58, 59, 61, 62, 69-72, 75, 77, 78, 81, 83, 85, 87, 89, 91, 93, 95, 97, 101, 110, 116, 129, 138, 143-50, 152-7, 160, 161, 163, 168, 171, 172, 180, 183, 184, 189, 192-5, 197, 199, 200, 203, 211, 215-17, 221, 222, 227, 235, 236, 241-3, 245-7, 250, 252

within Confucianism   28
curriculum   75, 76, 81, 85, 92, 137, 180, 214
decolonial   61, 71
intellectual   23
itinerantology   20, 152, 153, 171, 172
knowledge   143, 157
posture   20, 72
theoretical path   17, 25, 29
theorist   15–19

Jal, Murzban   26
Jameson, William   225
Jatuporn, Omsin   17, 30, 203, 205, 206, 211, 213, 214
Johnson, Richard   25, 164
Jung, Jung Hoon   28, 29, 115, 120, 122–4
Jupp, James   13–15, 17, 21, 28, 37, 51, 146, 217
justice
   cognitive   13, 21, 29, 30, 58, 71, 72, 77, 87, 98, 110, 124, 136, 148–50, 152, 183, 192, 193, 217, 243, 244, 246, 248
   social   4, 21, 27, 28, 40, 46, 49, 97, 98, 108, 110, 125, 129, 133, 134, 136, 137, 139, 146–8, 150, 151, 155, 183, 184, 193, 227, 242, 244

Karatani, Kojin   13
Kellner, Douglas   25
Kim, Young Chun   29, 115, 117, 119
Kliebard, Herbert   12, 102
knowledge/s   2–4, 13–17, 20–2, 24, 28, 29, 39–42, 44, 48, 51, 57–9, 61–5, 68, 70, 71, 74–80, 85, 86, 88, 98–101, 104–10, 115, 116, 118–20, 122–6, 129, 132, 134–9, 143–6, 148–51, 153–7, 162–4, 166–71, 179–86, 190–4, 196, 197, 199, 204, 206, 207, 209–17, 227, 233, 234, 240, 241, 243, 244, 247, 248, 250–3

Lacan, Jacques   116
Laclau Ernesto   146
Leite, Maria Cecilia Lorea   30, 241, 244
LGBT community   134, 232, 246
liberty   2
Liston, Daniel   136
Lorde, Audre   116, 125, 172

Macdonald, James   4, 23
McCarthy, Cameron   4, 226
McLaren, Peter   12, 133
madness   24, 235
Maldonado-Torres, Nelson   71, 73, 169
Mallon, F.   20
Marcos, Sub Comandante   41, 46, 48, 51
Marx, Karl   20, 25, 183
Marxism   20
Mbembe, Achille   16
mechanotics   10, 152
Memmi, Albert   17, 29, 97, 100, 106, 108, 109
meritocratic   55, 63
Merlau-Ponty, Maurice   14
mestizx   38–47, 49, 50, 52
Mignolo, Walter   12, 18, 19, 23, 44, 51, 55, 57, 59, 64, 65, 108, 131, 132, 155, 161, 163, 164, 166, 170, 171, 177, 194, 199
Mizikaci, Fatma   17, 28, 97, 100, 106, 108, 109
modern   38, 39, 56, 57, 59, 62, 64, 65, 69, 72, 73, 75, 76, 78, 100–2, 106, 109, 147, 152, 154, 169, 179, 191, 224–6, 246
   abyssal thinking   144
   Chinese language   74
   colonial   55, 58, 59, 63
   education   97, 104, 108, 121
   episteme   147
   humanity   22
   instrumental rationality   148
   reason   155
   science   145, 182, 183, 194
   scientific knowledge   132
   sub-humanity   22
   trans   41
   un   40
   Western Eurocentric   11, 12, 18, 20, 22, 23, 25, 71, 73, 85, 86, 161, 162, 164, 165, 169, 171, 182, 192, 208, 212
modernity   11, 19, 24, 25, 28, 55–7, 59, 61, 63, 64, 71, 102–6, 132, 144, 148, 199
   coloniality   25, 55, 57, 72–5, 216, 217
   Eurocentric   13, 20
   rhetoric of   28

trans   194
Turkish   104
Western   20, 22, 72, 105, 207, 217
momentism   18
monumentality   16, 164
Moreia, Maria Alfredo   13, 146, 217

Nedjar, Mekia   20, 29, 161
neo-Gramscian   146
neoliberalism   4, 81, 82, 89, 97, 132, 133, 170, 172, 209
neo-Marxism   216
Nietzsche, Friedrich   133
Nkrumah, Kwame   21
nomad/ic   13, 55
nomadism   134, 221
nomadography   19, 87, 172
non dialectical absence   165, 199
non-derivative   13, 27, 29, 145, 171, 242
  conciencism   21
  critical caste curriculum theory (CCCT)   26
  defibrillator   13
  praxis   15
  theoretical/theory   17, 23, 27, 28
  theory of translation   14, 23
  thinking   25

Occidentalism   86, 171
occidentosis   21, 152
Oliveira, Ines Barbosa   13, 29, 98, 143, 145, 146, 149, 151-3, 155, 233
oppressed   xvi, 5, 46, 51, 132, 165, 210
oppressor   46, 48, 51, 64, 135
otherness   20, 59, 64, 151, 162, 181
Ottoman
  centric epistemology   99
  Empire   98, 102, 110
  historical context   97
  Islamic ideology   100
  Millets   101
  State   106
Ottomanism   97, 99

Pachamama   59, 63
palavrar   15, 28
Paraskeva, João M.   xvii, 1-6, 11-14, 16, 18, 20-7, 30, 39, 43, 51, 55, 56, 62, 70-7, 85-7, 92, 98, 99, 102, 103, 107, 109, 110, 115, 116, 124, 135-9, 143-57, 161-6, 168-72, 179-85, 187, 189, 193-5, 197-200, 204, 206, 209, 210, 212, 216, 217, 221, 222, 235, 242-5, 251, 252
Passeron, Jean Claude   85
patriarchal/ism   50, 63, 130, 131, 143, 180-1
  hetero   180
physical brain   15
Pillay, Shervani   18, 21, 29, 189, 194, 198
Pinar, William   4, 5, 12, 16, 18, 26, 35, 37, 115-18, 120-2, 146, 205, 206, 209, 213, 222, 227, 233
Plato   100
poesis   19, 20, 87, 172
political   xv, xvii, 2, 4, 5, 14-17, 22, 24-7, 29, 38, 39, 45, 46, 48, 50, 51, 55, 56, 58-60, 64, 65, 81, 82, 87, 90, 91, 100, 102, 105-7, 109, 110, 131-9, 146, 151, 155, 156, 162-4, 166-73, 182-4, 189-91, 205, 206, 208, 210-14, 216, 217, 230, 241-3, 253
  bio   27
  decay   163
  economy   209
  geo   28, 55, 62
  Islam   98, 108, 109
  itinerancy   145, 156
  left   89
  theory   26
Popkewitz, Thomas   20, 69, 210, 213
post
  colonial/ism   4, 5, 57, 115-19, 122-4, 126, 169, 170, 186, 214-16
  modern   4, 15, 17, 71, 72, 210, 214, 216, 227, 248
post-abyssal
  epistemology   86
  momentum   22, 87, 242
  terrain   24
  thinking   78, 86, 144, 145, 154, 184, 217
  turn   222
poverty   27, 129-31, 134, 139, 164
Price Todd Alan   15, 30, 216, 221, 233-6
proletarian   41, 45
Prosperous reason   15, 26

punctum   19, 23, 172
purity   23

Quijano, Anibal   12, 55, 57, 119, 122, 131, 156, 162–4, 167, 171

race   16, 26, 38, 50, 64, 65, 109, 164, 166, 209, 213, 225–7, 232
racism   25, 65, 121, 196
radical
   co-habitus   13, 15, 22
   co-presence   13, 26, 144, 145, 150, 154, 156, 171
Revolution   3, 19, 42, 44–7, 89, 97, 99, 104, 108, 109, 119, 133, 136–8, 172, 182, 184, 195, 222, 225, 226, 242
rights
   civil   1, 3
   democratic   97
   education   109, 241, 246–52
   human   30, 130, 131, 157, 191, 244
   indigenous peoples   60
   linguistic   63
   non-human   137

Said, E.   3, 13, 98, 103, 118, 119, 163, 170
Santos, Boaventura de Sousa   3, 12, 14–18, 20–8, 39, 44, 51, 52, 55, 56, 59, 62, 64, 70, 71, 77, 98, 102–5, 107, 110, 115, 116, 130, 135, 137, 139, 143–55, 161–71, 179, 180, 182–5, 192, 193, 195, 197, 198, 211, 216, 241–3, 245, 248, 249, 251–2
Saramago, José   13, 21
Schubert, William, H.   1–6, 12, 16, 20
segregation   103, 132, 136, 138
sexuality   38, 205, 213
slavery   181
Snaza, Nathan   27
socialism   51, 106
South-south dialogue   37, 40, 41, 47, 48, 50–2
state   xv, 1–5, 51, 60, 78, 82, 83, 90, 98–103, 105, 107, 108, 110, 130, 151, 155, 170, 210, 212, 229–31, 242–4

Stenhouse, Lawrence   25
Süssekind, Maria Luiza   13, 20, 29, 143, 145, 146, 148, 157, 179, 180, 185, 248
synopticality   16

Teltumbde, Anand   26
theorycide   11–13
theorycity   13
translation   3, 14, 42, 48, 72–5, 100, 106, 205
   cross-cultural   74
   curriculum of   171
   intercultural   171
   semantic   73
   theory of   14, 26, 27
   translingual   78
tribal/ism   26, 168, 230, 235

utopianism   21, 42
utopia/utopian   3, 13, 15, 18, 19, 21, 25, 29, 42, 48, 129, 137, 152, 155, 223, 243, 251
utopists   25

Vázquez-Recio, Rosa   13, 14, 29, 129, 130, 132–4

Walsh, Catherine   17, 23, 55, 58, 64
wa'Thiongo, Ngũgĩ   20
Watkins, William   4, 12
white
   canon   3
   ethnicities   226
   privilege   39
   supremacy   42, 46, 193
whiteness   4
Williams, Raymond   15, 18, 19, 162
Wright Mills, C.   2

Zeichner, Kenneth   136
Zhao, Weili   xviii, 16, 20, 28, 69, 70, 73–6, 210, 213, 215, 216
Žižek, Slavoj   24, 27
Žižekean   19, 172

www.ingramcontent.com/pod-product-compliance
Lightning Source LLC
Chambersburg PA
CBHW071811300426
44116CB00009B/1281